T H E
HOME REMEDIES
BIBLE

pil

Publications International, Ltd.

This book is for informational purposes and is not intended to provide medical advice. Neither the Editors of Consumer Guide® and Publications International, Ltd., nor the authors, consultant, or publisher take responsibility for any possible consequences from any treatment, procedure, exercise, dietary modification, action, or application of medication or preparation by any person reading or following the information in this book. The publication of this book does not constitute the practice of medicine, and this book does not attempt to replace your physician or other health-care provider. Before undertaking any course of treatment, the authors, consultant, editors, and publisher advise the reader to check with a physician or other health-care provider.

The brand-name products mentioned in this publication are trademarks or service marks of their respective companies. The mention of any product in this publication does not constitute an endorsement by the respective proprietors of Publications International, Ltd., nor does it constitute an endorsement by any of these companies that their products should be used in the manner represented in this publication.

Contributing Writers:

Timothy Gower is a freelance writer and editor whose work has appeared in many publications, including *Reader's Digest, Prevention, Men's Health, Better Homes and Gardens, The New York Times,* and *The Los Angeles Times.* The author of four books, Gower is also a contributing editor of *Health* magazine.

Alice Lesch Kelly is a health writer based in Boston. Her work has been published in magazines such as *Shape, Fit Pregnancy, Woman's Day, Reader's Digest, Eating Well,* and *Health.* She is the coauthor of three books on women's health.

Consultant:

Ivan Oransky, M.D., is the deputy editor of *The Scientist.* He is author or coauthor of four books, including *The Common Symptom Answer Guide* (McGraw-Hill, 2004), and has written for publications including the *Boston Globe, The Lancet,* and *USA Today.* He holds appointments as a clinical assistant professor of medicine and as adjunct professor of journalism at New York University.

Photo credits:

Front and back covers: **PhotoDisc Collection.**

Artville Collection: 141; **Corbis Collection:** 28, 86, 108 (top), 126, 133, 171 (bottom), 202 (bottom), 218, 298; **Creatas Collection:** 52, 114, 127, 282, 284; **Digital Vision Collection:** 10, 27, 178 (left), 208; **PhotoDisc Collection:** 5, 9, 11, 12, 14, 18, 19, 20, 22, 27, 30, 31, 33, 34, 35, 36, 37, 42, 43, 44, 45, 46, 48, 49, 51, 53, 56, 59, 61, 63, 65, 67, 70, 71, 73, 74, 75, 76, 78, 82, 83, 85 (top), 87, 89, 91, 93, 94, 96, 98, 99, 100, 102, 111, 112, 116, 119, 121, 122, 123, 125, 128, 129, 131, 132, 135, 137, 138, 139, 140, 143, 145, 147, 148, 150, 151, 153, 156, 158, 159, 160, 161, 163, 165, 170, 171 (top), 173, 175, 176, 177, 178 (right), 179, 180, 181, 182, 183, 184, 185, 190, 191, 192, 193, 194, 195, 196, 197, 199, 201, 202 (top), 204, 206, 207, 210, 211, 212, 213, 214, 216, 217, 220, 221, 222, 223, 224, 227, 228, 232, 233, 234, 236, 238, 240, 242, 245, 246, 247, 248, 250, 252, 253, 254, 255, 256, 257, 258, 259, 261, 263, 264, 265, 267, 268, 272, 274, 276, 277, 278, 283, 285, 286, 287, 289, 290, 291, 292, 294, 295, 296, 297, 298, 301, 304, 307, 308, 311, 312; **PIL Cookbook Collection:** 50, 77, 85 (bottom), 117, 154, 187, 215, 231, 302; **Stockbyte Collection:** 40, 41, 66, 104, 219, 260; **ThinkStock Collection:** 107, 108 (bottom), 109, 194.

Louis Weber, CEO
Publications International, Ltd.
7373 North Cicero Avenue
Lincolnwood, Illinois 60712

Permission is never granted for commercial purposes.

ISBN-13: 978-1-4127-1261-3
ISBN-10: 1-4127-1261-0

Library of Congress Control Number: 2006901043

Manufactured in China.

8 7 6 5 4 3 2 1

Contents

Introduction

Very few of us these days can afford to see a doctor for every ache, sniffle, or itch. But that doesn't mean you have to suffer through life's common maladies without comfort or cure. Indeed, most doctors would tell you (if they had the time) there are many things patients can and should do to remedy, ease, and prevent many health problems themselves.

First, however, you need a basic understanding of which conditions you can safely attempt to deal with at home and which require professional medical attention. Then you need trustworthy, concrete, and understandable suggestions for tackling the problems that do lend themselves to self-care.

The Home Remedies Bible provides both. This valuable guide includes profiles of more than 75 common medical symptoms, illnesses, and diseases. In addition to providing clear information to help you identify and understand the condition, each profile explains when it's safe to self-treat and alerts you to signs or circumstances that signal the need for professional care (you'll often find this information called out in boxes titled "Hello, Doctor?" so pay special attention to these). Each profile also provides a collection of easy-to-follow steps, or *remedies,* from the professionals to help you cure, ease, and/or prevent the problem that is being discussed.

The Home Remedies Bible is designed to give you the expert advice you need to help yourself. Yet we also encourage you to share this guide with your health-care team, so they can advise you about any special situations or concerns you'll need to take into account as you follow the guide's suggestions. After all, you and your team know your individual medical history, your current health status, and the medications you use.

Indeed, *The Home Remedies Bible* is meant to complement the care you receive from your doctor, dentist, and other health-care providers by giving you handy, reliable, self-care guidance and advice. Use it to spark more and better communication with your health-care team to ensure you get the best possible care. Use it—with our best wishes—to improve and protect your good health.

Acne

13 Skin-Clearing Solutions

Acne. If you're a teenager, you can't wait to get rid of it. If you're an adult, you can't believe it's back. Fortunately, improvements in acne treatments over the years mean you don't have to put up with it anymore.

In general, genetics determines who gets acne—if your skin is breaking out, you may have inherited a skin characteristic that makes you more likely to develop acne.

You have thousands of oil glands in the skin on your face, chest, and back.

In fact, there are as many as 2,000 oil glands per square inch in the middle part of your face. These oil glands serve to lubricate the skin by producing oil, or sebum. The oil from the glands flows through tiny ducts, or follicles, to the skin surface.

Sometimes, these oil ducts become plugged with sebum, bacteria, and dead skin cells that are shed from the lining of the duct. That's acne. The condition often appears during adolescence because of changing hormone levels, which enlarge the oil glands and encourage them to produce more oil. Although the process is not well understood, the increase in oil appears to fuel acne, perhaps by stimulating the production of "sticky" skin cells that, when shed, tend to plug the duct. The situation usually settles down by the end of the teen years or during the early 20s.

So why do some adults develop acne? There are a variety of reasons, among them:

- **Hormones.** Pregnancy, changes during the menstrual cycle, menopause, and birth control pills can cause fluctuations in

Hello, Doctor?

When should you see a dermatologist for your acne? When it seems serious, is causing scarring, or just won't go away, because prescription drugs can treat it successfully. Children should be treated fairly young if they start showing signs of acne, especially if either parent had severe, or cystic, acne, marked by nodules, or cysts ("Acne Glossary," page 9, explains types of blemishes).

See a dermatologist if you:

- Use benzoyl peroxide products for six to eight weeks and still have problems.
- Have pustules larger than a match head or nodules the size of the end of your little finger.
- Have any scarring from your acne.

Today's arsenal of treatments includes topical and oral antibiotics and a class of medications called retinoids. Tretinoin (Retin-A) is applied to the skin, while isotretinoin (Accutane) is taken orally. Pregnant women should not take isotretinoin; it has been shown to cause birth defects. It's considered a last-ditch treatment, but it's especially effective for cystic acne.

hormone levels and subsequent outbreaks of acne in women. In some women, low-dose oral contraceptives improve acne; in others, they make acne worse. If you have acne along with menstrual irregularities, you may want to see a physician to find out if abnormal hormone levels are to blame for both.

- **Stress.** Dermatologists agree that high levels of stress can affect hormone levels, which can in turn trigger acne breakouts.
- **Cosmetics.** Wearing heavy, oily makeup may clog pores and cause acne.
- **Occupational exposure.** If you're a mechanic or you're standing over the deep-fat fryer at the local fast-food joint, your face may be getting assaulted by oils, some of which may cause acne. Numerous chemicals in the workplace can also cause acne.
- **Certain medications.** Some drugs, such as Dilantin (used to treat epilepsy) and lithium (used to treat bipolar disorder), can cause acne.

No matter what's causing your acne, there are steps you can take to help clear up your skin and keep it blemish-free.

Do no harm. Don't pick, squeeze, rub, or otherwise manipulate those

Who Gets Acne?

Nearly every teenage boy and around 80 percent of teenage girls will suffer from acne. (Blame those male hormones.) Boys are also more likely than girls to have severe acne during adolescence.

In contrast, women are much more likely than men to report acne in their 20s, 30s, and 40s. Some doctors say it's because of cosmetic use and birth control pills. But at least some of the apparent gender difference may actually be due to the fact that women are more likely than men to visit a dermatologist. In other words, they may not experience acne that much more frequently than men, they may simply be more likely to "report" it by seeking professional treatment.

pimples, because doing so can spread bacteria and raise the risk of scarring. The plug at the top of the pore is like a balloon. You can pop it, but below the surface, the sebum, bacteria, and skin cells may be forced into the surrounding tissue, causing inflammation.

Use benzoyl peroxide. A number of over-the-counter (OTC) products contain this ingredient, which helps break up the plug of dead skin cells, bacteria, and oil in pores and cuts down on the bacteria as well. Start with the lowest concentration—a 2.5 percent or 5 percent lotion or gel once a day. After a week, if it doesn't irritate your skin, increase to twice a day, morning and night. If your acne doesn't improve within four to six weeks, use a 10 percent lotion or gel once a day and, if needed, twice a day. Work your way up gradually, especially if you have sensitive skin, because the higher the concentration, the more irritating it may

Acne Rosacea

If you're over 40 and suddenly develop severe acne, you could be suffering from acne rosacea, which is a different disease from acne vulgaris, the medical name for your garden variety of acne.

How can you tell the difference? Acne rosacea is characterized by redness, inflammation (swelling), and dilated blood vessels. Further clues: You don't have any blackheads, the acne is located mainly on the central part of your face (your nose and cheeks), and you have a lot of pustules (pus-containing pimples). You're more likely to suffer from this type of acne if you're light-skinned.

Acne rosacea can be treated with a medicated cream prescribed by a dermatologist. You should also avoid the sun, since sun exposure can worsen the condition. Certain foods, such as those that are spicy or hot in temperature, can also make rosacea worse.

be. If it dries your skin too much, apply a mild moisturizer as well (either at a different time of day or after applying the benzoyl peroxide).

Give one of the other OTC products a shot. Other acne products contain sulfur or resorcinol, both of which help unplug oil glands by irritating the skin. Most dermatologists, however, believe benzoyl peroxide is the most effective anti-acne ingredient available without a prescription.

Apply that OTC product for prevention, too. Use acne medication not only on pimples that have already formed but also on acne-free areas that are prone to breakouts. That can include your entire face (avoiding the lips and eyes, however), back, and chest.

Go easy on your face. You can't wash away acne with hot water and a rough washcloth. Washing only removes oils from the skin's surface, not from within the plugged ducts. Adults can suffer from both acne and dry skin. In fact, if you're too aggressive in your quest for cleanliness, you may very well end up drying out or irritating the sensitive skin on your face.

Wash properly. Wash only once or twice a day. For the delicate facial skin, use a soap or nonsoap cleanser labeled "mild" or "for sensitive skin" (Dove Unscented, Tone, Basis, and Neutrogena are some options). Rub lightly with your fingertips and warm water; do not use a washcloth. If your skin is oily, try using a soap that contains benzoyl peroxide for its drying properties.

Don't exfoliate your face. Exfoliating refers to removing the top layer of dead skin cells using a rough washcloth, loofah, or specially designed product. But skin with acne is already irritated, and scrubbing can make things worse. Don't use brushes, rough sponges or cloths, cleansers with granules or walnut hulls, or anything else of that nature on the delicate facial skin. For the back and chest, where skin is less sensitive, you can try one of the acne scrub pads along with soap that contains benzoyl peroxide.

Watch out for oily products. That goes for oily pomades on your hair, heavy oil-based moisturizers, and even oily cleansers such as cold cream.

Use water-based makeup. Check the label to find out if makeup is water- or oil-based. If the label is unclear, use this guideline: If it separates into water and powder when left to sit undisturbed for a while, it's water-based, and if it stays mixed, it contains oil. Better yet, use powder blushes and loose powders instead of liquids and creams. Eye makeup and lipstick are okay, because you don't generally get acne in those areas.

Forgo the facial. Facials—particularly those given by over-enthusiastic aestheticians who haven't been taught how to handle acne-prone skin—can do more harm than good.

Don't rest your chin on your hands. Try not to touch your face. It causes trauma to acne, just like picking pimples does. Tight sweatbands on baseball caps and chinstraps on protective headgear can have the same effect.

Screen out the sun. Too much sun can lead to skin cancer and premature aging. Protect your skin without promoting more acne by using an oil-free sunscreen that has a sun protection factor (SPF) of 15 or higher. Unfortunately, many waterproof sunscreens are too likely to clog oil glands to use on the face; so if you'll be sweating heavily or plan on swimming, you'll have to stick to the oil-free variety but be diligent about reapplying it often (as recommended on the label).

Don't worry about diet. Chocolate, greasy foods, nuts, and other foods have not been proven to have anything at all to do with causing teenage acne. Of course, if you notice a correlation between something you eat and your face breaking out, you could try avoiding the offending food.

Acne Glossary

Most of us think of pimples when we think of acne. We don't bother dividing up the different annoying spots we see on our face. But dermatologists have broken pimples down into the following categories:

Comedo (pl. comedones). An oil duct plugged up with oil, dead skin cells, and bacteria.

Whitehead. A closed comedo, or a comedo with skin covering the top. It looks like a tiny, white bump.

Blackhead. An open comedo, or a comedo that does not have skin covering it. It appears black not because it contains dirt, as is commonly believed, but because the material has been exposed to oxygen.

Papule. A ruptured comedo in which there is inflammation and secondary infection. It looks like a small, hard, red bump.

Pustule. A ruptured comedo in which there is inflammation and secondary infection. In contrast to the papule, the pustule has more pus near the surface, giving it a yellowish center.

Nodule (sometimes called a cyst). A ruptured comedo that is generally larger, deeper, and more painful than a pustule and is more likely to result in scarring. This type of lesion marks the most severe form of acne.

Allergies

29 Ways to Feel Better

Spring's pollens. Summer's smog. Autumn's falling leaves. Winter's house dust. For millions of Americans, each change of season brings its own brand of allergy triggers and irritants. For people with common hay fever and allergies, these pollutants can bring on symptoms ranging from a continuous, annoying postnasal drip to a full-scale, coughing, sneezing, itchy-eyed allergy attack. For other allergy sufferers, such as those with allergic asthma or an allergy to bee stings, attacks can be fatal.

In many cases, allergy symptoms are difficult to differentiate from the symptoms of other disorders and illnesses,

such as a cold, deformity of the nose, or food intolerance. For this reason, many doctors suggest that allergies be properly diagnosed by a board-certified allergist (a medical doctor specially trained to treat allergies) to avoid the self-administration of inappropriate medications or other remedies. Also, many allergy sufferers can benefit from today's wide range of available treatments, such as new antihistamines that don't cause drowsiness (including both prescription and over-the-counter drugs), nasal corticosteroids, and allergy injections that can provide immunity to a specific allergen. (An allergen is any substance, such as pollen, that causes an allergic reaction.) If you don't go to the doctor, you may be missing out on a beneficial treatment.

Still, many mild allergies, such as seasonal hay fever or an allergy to cats, can be eased with a combination of properly used, over-the-counter antihistamines and strategies to reduce or eliminate exposure to particularly annoying allergens.

The following tips are designed to help reduce the discomfort caused by the most common allergies. They may be used in combination with an allergist's treatment or, if your allergies are mild, by themselves.

Avoid the culprit. Sometimes, the best way to reduce the discomfort of an allergy is to avoid exposure to the allergen as much as possible. If you are allergic to cats, for example, avoid visiting the homes of friends who own them. If you must be around a cat, make the visit as short as possible, avoid touching or picking up the animal, and wash your hands when you leave.

Rinse your eyes. If your eyes are itchy and irritated and you have no access to allergy medicine, rinsing your eyes with cool, clean water may help soothe them. Although not as effective as an antihistamine, this remedy certainly can't do any harm.

Try a warm washcloth. If sinus passages feel congested and painful, a washcloth soaked in warm water may help get things flowing. Place it over the nose and upper-cheek area and relax for a few minutes.

Use saline solution. Irrigating the nose with saline solution (salt water) may help soothe upper respiratory allergies by removing irritants that become lodged in the nose and cause inflammation. In fact, saline solution may even wash away some of the inflammatory cells themselves. You can buy ready-made saline solution at your local drugstore, or you can make your own fresh solution daily by mixing a teaspoon of salt in a pint of warm distilled water and adding a pinch of baking soda. Bend over a sink and sniff a bit of solution into one nostril at a time, allowing it to drain back out through the nose or mouth; do this once or twice a day. (If you also have asthma, however, check with your doctor before trying this remedy.)

Wash your hair. If you've spent long hours outdoors during the pollen season, wash your hair to remove pollen after you come inside. The sticky yellow stuff tends to collect on the hair, making it more likely to fall into your eyes.

Take a shower. If you wake up in the middle of the night with a coughing, sneezing allergy attack, a hot shower may wash off any pollen residue you've collected on your body throughout the day. (You might want to change your pillowcase, too.) It may also help open up your sinuses, at least for a while, making breathing a little easier. The warm water may even help you relax and go back to sleep.

Wear glasses. On a windy day in pollen season, a pair of sunglasses (or your regular prescription eyeglasses, if you wear them) may help shield your eyes from airborne allergens. For extra protection, try a pair of sunglasses with side shields or even a pair of goggles.

Beware of the air. Breathing polluted air can worsen symptoms. In fact, airborne toxins

Bust the Dust

The following tips can help you make your bedroom less hospitable to dust mites—microscopic insects that feed on your dead skin cells. The feces and corpses of these little buggers trigger allergies in millions of people. Since the bedroom is the dust mite's favorite hangout, and we spend at least a third of our lives there, you may get considerable relief by focusing your greatest allergy-proofing efforts there.

Encase pillows and mattresses. Pillows and mattresses contain fibrous material that is an ideal environment for dust-mite growth, so invest in airtight, plastic or vinyl cases or special covers that are impermeable to allergens for your pillows and mattresses (waterbeds don't need these covers). These cases are usually available at your local department store, through mail-order companies, and over the Internet.

Wash your bedding. Down, kapok, and feather comforters and pillows are out for people with allergies. The feathers have a tendency to escape and can wreak havoc with your respiratory tract. Comforters and sheets should be washed every seven to ten days in the hottest water they'll tolerate. Wash your mattress pads and synthetic blankets every two weeks.

Clean once a week. Putting off cleaning for longer than this may allow an excessive amount of dust to collect. However, since cleaning raises dust, it's best not to clean more than once a week. If necessary, you can spot-dust with a damp cloth more often.

Avoid fabric-covered furniture. Wood and vinyl furniture are better choices.

Choose washable curtains. If possible, invest in curtains that can be washed, since dust mites often hide in the fabric.

Vacuum the venetians. The slats of venetian blinds are notorious dust collectors. If you can't replace your venetian blinds with washable curtains, at least run the vacuum over them lightly or dust them well during your thorough weekly cleaning.

Don't use the bedroom as storage space. Stored items and knickknacks tend to collect dust and have no place in an allergy-proof bedroom. If the bedroom is the only storage space you have, seal items in plastic bags and display tchotchkes in a closed glass-front cabinet.

Clean out your air conditioner and heating ducts. Every month or so, clean out the vents on your heating and air-conditioning units, or have someone clean them for you. These ducts are breeding grounds for mold, dust mites, and bacteria. If you let such nasties collect, they'll be blown into the room each time the unit kicks on.

can actually cause allergies in some people. If you suspect that air pollution triggers your attacks, spend as little time outdoors as possible on smoggy days. When you must go outside, wear a surgical mask, especially while exercising. Don't expect miracles—the mask won't screen out all allergens—but it may help you breathe a little easier.

Make your house or apartment a no-smoking zone. Tobacco smoke is a notorious irritant, either causing or aggravating respiratory allergies. Don't let your friends and family foul the air with cigarettes, cigars, or pipes. And, of course, if you still light up, stop it!

Keep the windows shut. A fresh breeze blowing through an open window on a spring day may sound inviting, but it's bad news for an allergy sufferer, since it can fill the house with pollen. So keep windows closed at all times. Air purifiers, especially those with HEPA filters, may help eliminate pollen that's entered your home, but they also tend to stir up dust, which might worsen some allergies.

Go bare. Carpets are notorious for harboring dust mites (microscopic bugs that feed on the dead skin cells we constantly shed and whose droppings spur allergies in millions of people). Bare floors, vacuumed and damp-mopped frequently, will help keep your home's dust-mite population down (you can't get rid of them all). If you can't remove all the carpeting in your home, at least opt for bare floors (if necessary, use small, frequently laundered throw rugs) in your bedroom; studies show the bedroom has more dust mites than any other room in the home, and you probably spend about a third of your time there every day.

Filter your vacuum. When carpets can't be removed, keeping them as clean as possible will help you breathe a bit easier. But beware: Many vacuums blast small particles of dust back into the air, leaving behind plenty of allergens to keep you sneezing and wheezing. Use a vacuum that has a built-in HEPA filter, or attach a filter to the exhaust port of your canister vac (uprights usually don't have an exhaust port). If dust really bothers you and you've got the money, consider investing in an industrial-strength vacuuming system. Some allergists recommend a brand called Nilfisk, which has an excellent filtering system and retails for about $500. To find out whether such products are appropriate for you and where you can purchase filters or special vacuums, talk to your allergist.

Dust with a damp cloth. Dusting at least once a week is important, but if done improperly, it may aggravate respiratory allergies. Avoid using feather dusters, which tend to spread dust around; instead, control dust with a damp cloth. Dusting sprays may give off odors that can worsen allergies.

Or don't dust at all. If dusting aggravates your allergies, don't do it. Instead, ask a spouse or family member to do the dirty work, or hire a housekeeper, if possible.

Dehumidify. Dust mites love a humid environment, which allows them to reproduce like crazy. Invest in a dehumidifier or use an air conditioner, which works equally well. A dehumidifier can also help prevent mold, another allergen, from growing (just be sure to follow the manufacturer's maintenance instructions). When cooking or showering, take advantage of the exhaust fan—another way to help keep humidity to a minimum.

Think before you burn. Although in some areas it is common to burn household and construction refuse, this may not be such a wise idea. The smoke from burning wood that has been treated with heavy metals or other chemical-laden materials can make anyone gag, but people with allergies or asthma have ultra-

Is It a Food Allergy?

Do you feel congested after you eat dairy products? Does red meat make you feel sluggish? Does sugar give you a headache? If you answered "yes" to any of these questions, you probably *don't* have a food allergy.

Many people confuse food allergies with food intolerances. While the latter can trigger unpleasant symptoms such as those described above, true food allergies can be extremely serious—even deadly.

If you are truly allergic to a food, the reaction will be almost immediate, occurring from within a few minutes to two hours after you eat it. The most common symptoms are hives, diffuse swelling around the eyes and mouth, or abdominal cramps. A less common symptom is difficulty breathing. In severe cases, extremely low blood pressure, dizziness, or loss of consciousness may result. In these instances, emergency medical attention is required.

Hello, Doctor?

If your allergies are causing you to cough, wheeze, and have trouble breathing, you should see an allergist. You may have allergic asthma, which should be monitored by a doctor. People with allergic asthma, which is sometimes mistaken for bronchitis, must often be prescribed inhalers and other medications. Trying to self-treat allergic asthma may endanger your health.

sensitive respiratory systems, making them even more vulnerable. Also, think twice about any material you burn in the fireplace. Of course, your best bet is to stay away from a fireplace or woodstove altogether when it's in use.

Cut through the smoke. Many people with respiratory allergies find that wood smoke poses a particular problem. With woodstoves, the biggest problem is "choking down" the stove, or decreasing the amount of oxygen in order to cool down the fire. Choking down throws irritating toxins into the air, which you and your neighbors will breathe in.

Leave the mowing to someone else. During pollen season, a grass-allergic person is better off letting someone else—anyone else—mow the lawn. Call your local county extension service and find out when the pollination season occurs in your area, then arrange for a lawn-care company, friend, or relative to cut your grass during that time. (As a rule, in many parts of the country, people who are allergic to grass should avoid mowing between May and the Fourth of July.)

Wash your pet. A little-known trick for the dog or cat owner who is allergic to Fido or Felix: Bathe your pet frequently. Dogs and cats constantly shed dead skin cells called dander, which is a common allergen. Fortunately, this allergen dissolves in water, so regular warm baths can help rinse away some of the problem. If you can't imagine bathing your beloved feline for fear of being mauled, take heart: Some cats learn to tolerate baths. If you start bathing your feline regularly during kittenhood, chances are higher that bath time will be a harmonious experience in later years. Wash your pet in warm water, without soap, once every other week.

In addition to bathing your pet, try to wash your hands soon after you've had direct contact with your furry friend.

Make sure your final rinse really rinses. Chemicals in detergents and other laundry products can cause skin irritation in many people. That may hold true even for detergents advertised as "mild." Be sure that your washer removes all of the detergent from your clothes after the final rinse cycle. Try adding yet another rinse cycle to see if skin irritation decreases.

Call ahead. When planning a trip, call ahead to find a room that will be easier on your allergies. Ask for a nonsmoking room that's not on the lower level, since a ground-floor room may have been flooded in the past and may still be a haven for mold. Choose a hotel or motel that doesn't allow pets, so you won't be subject to the leftover dander of the last traveler's dog or cat. If possible, bring your own vinyl- or plastic-encased pillow.

Choosing and Using OTC Oral Antihistamines

Over-the-counter oral antihistamines may be an economical way for you to relieve your allergy misery, although you'll need to check with your doctor first, since certain individuals—described below—should not use them. These drugs work by halting production of chemicals in the body that cause itchy eyes, runny nose, and coughing. Pollen, dust, and other allergens wreak havoc by entering the body, usually through the nose, and triggering the immune system to produce substances called antibodies. These antibodies attach themselves to cells in the nose, eyes, lungs, and skin. Allergens interact with antibodies and cause the release of a variety of substances that produce allergic symptoms. Histamine is one of the most potent of these volatile chemicals.

Scientists have known for decades that certain drugs can reduce allergy symptoms by blocking histamines from doing their work. A variety of over-the-counter medications—including diphenhydramine (the best known brand is Benadryl), chlorpheniramine (Chlor-Trimeton, for example), and clemastine (Tavist)—may do the trick. But these antihistamines can also cause drowsiness and slow your reaction time.

Fortunately, scientists eventually figured out a way to produce equally effective antihistamines that don't make your eyelids droop. Several so-called second-generation oral antihistamines have been sold by prescription since the 1980s, and one of these medications—loratadine, better known by its brand name, Claritin—is now available over the counter. Unfortunately, it costs much more than older antihistamines, even if you purchase generic loratadine.

Which medication should you use? Talk it over with your doctor. Although older antihistamines can cause daytime drowsiness, it may be possible to minimize this problem by gradually building up your tolerance. For example, if you try chlorpheniramine, start with one-fourth of the dose recommended on the package, and then slowly build up to the full daily dose (take half of the full dose in the morning and the other half in the evening), providing you can maintain that dosage without feeling sleepy. Since drowsiness tends to go away in a week or two, start out taking only an evening dose each day, and then add a morning dose as you begin to tolerate the medication. At an adequate dose, these medications help about three-quarters of patients ease the symptoms of pollen allergies.

Some people should never use older-generation antihistamines, however, including airplane pilots and people who drive a lot or operate heavy machinery. What's more, these drugs should not be used by anyone with an enlarged prostate or other bladder problems, intellectual impairment, or elevated intraocular pressure (which occurs in glaucoma). Children and the elderly should avoid older antihistamines, too.

Whichever medication you choose, use it properly. Most antihistamines will not unclog a stuffed-up nose; so if that's one of your symptoms, look for a combination product that includes a decongestant. As a rule, antihistamines are not effective for spot-treating symptoms; they work better as preventive therapy, so try to anticipate the onset of hay fever season and begin taking medication a week or so in advance.

Antihistamines can be used to prevent other types of allergic reactions. For example, people with pet-dander allergies who know they will be exposed to someone else's cat or dog should try taking antihistamines beginning 10 to 14 days in advance.

Arthritis

46 COPING STRATEGIES

An estimated 43 million Americans are caught in the grip of some form of arthritis or other joint problem. And few of us will make it to a ripe old age without joining the fold. If one of these conditions has a hold on you, be sure to keep reading. While there are no cures for arthritis (short of replacing a seriously affected joint, which isn't an option in all situations), there are steps you can take to ease discomfort and get back more control over your life.

There are more than 100 different forms of arthritis, with a host of causes, according to the Arthritis Foundation in Atlanta. Among the more widely known forms of the disease are osteoarthritis, rheumatoid arthritis, gout, and lupus. Osteoarthritis is by far the most common form.

Osteoarthritis is primarily marked by a breakdown and loss of joint cartilage. Cartilage is the tough tissue that separates and cushions the bones in a joint. As cartilage is worn away and the bones begin to rub against each other, the joint becomes irritated and painful. This breakdown of cartilage is accompanied by minimal inflammation, hardening of the bone beneath the cartilage, and bone spurs (growths) around the joints. Most people develop some osteoarthritis as they age.

Rheumatoid arthritis, on the other hand, is not an inevitable aspect of the aging process. For reasons unknown, the synovial membrane, or lining, of a joint becomes inflamed, resulting in pain, swelling, heat, and redness.

In the case of gout, needle-shaped uric acid crystals collect in the joints, due to a fault in the body's ability to metabolize, or process, purines. Purines are naturally occurring chemicals found in certain foods, such as liver, kidney, and anchovies. The disease primarily targets overweight, fairly inactive men over the age of 35.

Lupus, on the other hand, affects many more women than men. It is a condition in which the body's own immune system attacks healthy cells. The symptoms are wide ranging, from joint pain to mouth sores to persistent fatigue.

There is no cure for arthritis, but you can adopt a variety of coping techniques that will leave you more active and in control of your life.

Easing Stiffness and Discomfort

Here are some tips to help relieve discomfort and get you back into the swing of things.

Keep moving. Maintain movement in your joints as best you can. This can help keep your joints functioning better for a longer amount of time and, at the same time, brighten your outlook on life. Walking, gardening, and even housecleaning can help your joints.

Exercise, exercise, exercise. There are different types of exercises that are used to help arthritis sufferers. The simplest, easiest exercises that can and should be done every day by almost any arthritis sufferer are called range-of-motion exercises. These flexibility exercises help maintain good movement by putting the joints through their full range of motion. They can help reduce the risk of joint injury, and they provide a great warm-up for more vigorous exercise. You'll find several sample range-of-motion exercises in the box titled "Range-of-Motion Exercises" on page 23.

Aerobic exercise (an activity in which you continuously move the large muscles to increase heart rate and breathing), such as walking or swimming, increases the endurance of the muscles that support joints; improves the health of the heart, blood vessels, and lungs; and aids weight loss. *Weight-bearing* aerobic exercises, such as walking or playing tennis (as

Heat or Cold: Which Is Best?

There are no hard and fast rules when it comes to deciding which—heat, cold, or a combination of the two—will provide the most relief from arthritis pain and stiffness, so you should experiment to see what helps you most.

Heat relieves pain primarily by relaxing muscles and joints and decreasing stiffness. In some instances, however, heat may aggravate a joint that's already "hot" from inflammation, as is sometimes the case with rheumatoid arthritis. On the other hand, osteoarthritis causes minimal inflammation and may respond well to heat application. If you find that your hot compress cools down quickly, you may want to try methods that offer more consistent heating. An electric blanket or heating pad can provide sustained dry heat. A warm shower, bath, or whirlpool can keep the wet heat coming. You can also purchase, at many drugstores and variety stores, a product consisting of a sealed cloth pouch (often cylindrical in shape) filled with a natural grain that, when heated in the microwave and placed on the sore area, supplies more portable moist heat (one such product is named Bed Buddy). Using warmth to loosen up the muscles before exercise can help them perform better.

Cold is ordinarily used to reduce pain in specific joints and can be helpful if you have gout. Cold therapy should not be used if you have vasculitis (inflammation of the blood vessels) or Raynaud's phenomenon (a condition, characterized by spasms of the arteries in the fingers and toes, that may occur in conjunction with rheumatoid arthritis) without a doctor's approval, however. There are many ways to make a cold pack: You can use a plastic bag filled with crushed ice, a package of frozen peas, or a pack of blue ice, for example. Apply the cold pack to only one or two joints at a time, so you don't get a chill, and be sure to keep a thin cloth between the ice pack and the skin to prevent frostbite.

You may find that alternating heat and cold gives you the most relief. For the best results, the Arthritis Foundation recommends the contrast bath: Soak your hands and feet in warm water (no more than 110 degrees Fahrenheit) for about three minutes, then soak them in cold water (about 65 degrees Fahrenheit) for about a minute. Repeat this process three times, and finish with a warm-water soak.

opposed to swimming, in which the water holds you up), also strengthen the bones. You should try to gradually work up to doing at least 30 minutes of aerobic exercise on most days.

Finally, resistance exercises should be included two or three times a week to strengthen the muscles that support and help protect the joints. Isometric exercises, in which you create resistance by tightening a muscle without moving the joint, can be especially good for people with arthritis. Certain isotonic exercises, in which you strengthen the muscles while moving the joints (leg lifts and arm curls using light weights are examples of this type of resistance exercise), may also be okay. To determine which strengthening exercises are best for you and to learn how to do them safely and effectively, consult your doctor or a physical therapist.

Give your hands a water workout. Try doing your hand exercises in a sink full of warm water for added ease and comfort.

Don't overdo it. If exercise makes your pain worse, cut back on the frequency and/or amount of exercise until you find a level and routine that keeps you mobile without adding to your discomfort.

Play in a pool. If you find even simple movements difficult, a heated pool or whirlpool may be the perfect environment for exercise (unless you are pregnant, in which case you should avoid heated whirlpools and hot tubs, or have other chronic health problems, in which case you should get your doctor's approval first). Try a few of your simpler exercises while you are in the water. The buoyancy will help reduce the strain on your joints. Warm water helps loosen joints and makes muscles more pliable. In a pinch, a hot shower may do: Running the stream of water down your back, for instance, may help relieve back stiffness and discomfort.

Don't overuse over-the-counter (OTC) creams. These arthritis rubs may provide temporary relief by heating up the joints. However, using them too often may activate enzymes that can break down the cartilage in the joints.

Use OTC pain relievers with care. Over-the-counter medications that ease pain—such as the analgesic acetaminophen, aspirin, and other nonsteroidal anti-inflammatory drugs (NSAIDs) including ibuprofen and naproxen—are generally safe, relatively inexpensive, and often very beneficial for arthritis sufferers. However, because even nonprescription drugs can have side effects and some shouldn't be used by certain individuals, you should read the warnings in the box on page 21 and discuss the options with your doctor first. This is especially true for the many arthritis sufferers who need to use one of these drugs on a regular basis. And once you've had that discussion, carefully follow your doctor's directions for use of these products to avoid potentially serious reactions.

Put on a scarf. Not around your neck, but around the elbow or knee joint when it aches; the added warmth may bring some relief. Be careful not to wrap it too tightly, however.

Pull on a pair of stretch gloves. The tightness may help reduce the swelling in arthritic fingers, and the warmth created by covered hands may make the joints feel better. Wearing thermal underwear may help, too.

Get electric gloves. Hunters use these battery-operated mitts to keep their hands toasty on cold mornings in the woods, but they may help people with arthritis, too. Wear them all night while you sleep.

Get "down." Goose-down comforters warm up the joints and help ease pain. For those who are allergic to down, an electric blanket may bring some relief.

Watch your weight. Being overweight puts more stress on the joints. As a matter of fact, a weight gain of 10 pounds can mean an equivalent stress increase of 40 pounds on the knees. So if you are carrying excess pounds, losing weight can help improve joint function.

Question any cure-all. Frustrated by the chronic pain of arthritis, some sufferers pursue a litany of promises for 100 percent relief—whether from a so-called miracle drug, a newfangled diet, or some other alternative treatment. Unfortunately, at this time, arthritis has no cure. So, before you jump at the next hot-sounding testimonial, proceed with caution. Get all the facts. Consult your physician or other health-care provider. Even age-old techniques, such as wearing a copper bracelet, should be viewed with skepticism, agree most experts. And remember, if something sounds too good to be true, it probably is.

Protecting Your Joints

In addition to easing discomfort, you can learn to live well with arthritis by protecting your joints. What's more,

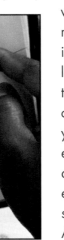

with a little planning and reorganizing, you can learn to do daily tasks more efficiently, so that you'll have more energy to spend on activities you enjoy. Here are some tips from the Arthritis Foundation that can help:

Plan ahead each day. Prepare a realistic, written schedule of what you would like to accomplish each day. That way, you can carry out your most demanding and essential tasks and activities when you think you'll have the most energy and enthusiasm—in the morning, for instance, if that's when you usually feel best.

Spread the strain. As a general rule, you want to avoid activities that involve a tight grip or that put too much pressure on your fingers. Use the palms of both hands to hold and lift cups, plates, pots, and pans, rather than gripping them with your fingers or with only one hand. Place your hand flat against a sponge or rag instead of squeezing it with your fingers. Avoid holding a package or pocketbook by clasping the handle with your fingers. Instead, grasp your goods in the crook of your arm—the way a football player holds the ball as he's running across the field—and you won't be tackled by as much pain.

Avoid holding one position for a long time. Keeping joints "locked" in the same position for any length of time will only add to your stiffness and discomfort. Relax and stretch your joints as often as possible.

"Arm" yourself. Whenever possible, use your arm instead of your hand to carry out an activity. For example, push open a heavy door with the side of your arm rather than with your outstretched hand.

Take a load off. Sitting down to complete a task whenever possible will keep your energy level up much longer than if you stand. But remember not to sit in the same position for too long.

Replace doorknobs and round faucet handles with long handles. They require a looser, less stressful grip (or no grip at all) to operate, so you'll put less strain on your joints.

Build up the handles on your tools. For a more comfortable grip, look for household tools, utensils, and writing implements that have chunky, padded handles. Or tape a layer or two of thin foam rubber, or a foam-rubber hair curler, around the handles of brooms, mops, rakes, spatulas, knives, pens, and pencils.

Let automatic appliances do the work for you. Electric can openers and knives, for instance, are easier on your joints than manual versions are. An electric toothbrush has a wider handle and requires a looser grip than a regular toothbrush does.

Keep your stuff within easy reach. Adjust the shelves and racks in any storage area so that you don't have to strain to reach the items you need. Buy clothes with pockets to hold things you use often and need close by, like a pair of glasses or pen and paper. Use an apron with pockets to carry cleaning supplies with you as you do your household chores.

Use a "helping hand" to extend your reach. For those items you can't store within arm's reach, buy a long-handled gripper, the kind used in grocery shops to grab items from top shelves. Make household chores easier with a long-handled or extendable feather duster or scrub brush. Grab your clothes from the dryer with an

Use Over-the-Counter Painkillers with Care

Over-the-counter (OTC) painkillers, or analgesics, such as aspirin, acetaminophen, and ibuprofen, are generally convenient and safe remedies for occasional minor pain due to a wide variety of conditions. Aspirin and ibuprofen also combat inflammation, and aspirin and acetaminophen (and to a lesser extent ibuprofen) are excellent at reducing fever. Sometimes, a doctor may even prescribe and supervise their long-term use for chronic conditions, such as arthritis.

Still, just because anyone can buy these drugs without a prescription doesn't mean they are safe for every person in every situation. Like almost any drug, used improperly, they can have serious and even deadly effects. That's why it's essential that, before you take any of them—and preferably before the need even arises—you ask your doctor which is safest and best for you. It's important to ask again if you develop a new medical problem, begin taking a new prescription or OTC drug or supplement, become pregnant, or begin breast-feeding (a woman who is or may be pregnant or is nursing should contact her doctor before taking *any* prescription or OTC drug; vitamin, mineral, or other supplement; or herb or other alternative remedy). A doctor should also be consulted before any analgesic is given to a child, and aspirin should never be given to anyone under 19 years old, because of the risk of a rare, fatal condition called Reye syndrome.

In addition, you should not take any OTC pain reliever without your doctor's explicit consent and direction if you:
• Have ever had an allergic reaction to any pain reliever.
• Are taking any other prescription or OTC drug that contains a pain reliever.
• Have kidney or liver disease, diabetes, or gout.
• Have or ever had an ulcer or any bleeding in the stomach or intestines.
• Have a bleeding disorder or take a blood-thinning medication.
• Have more than two alcoholic drinks daily.
• Have high blood pressure, a history of stroke, fluid retention, congestive heart failure, or heart disease or have recently had or are scheduled for the heart surgery called coronary bypass graft surgery (CABG).
• Have asthma or nasal polyps.

When taking an OTC analgesic, read and follow label directions carefully and do not exceed the recommended dose or take it more than occasionally without your doctor's approval and supervision.

extended-reach tool to avoid bending and stooping over and over.

Go with Velcro. Interlocking cloth closures (better known as Velcro) on clothing and shoes can save you the frustration of buttoning or tying with stiff, painful fingers.

Walk this way up and down the stairs. Lead with your stronger leg going up, and lead with your weaker leg coming down.

Bend with your knees. When reaching for or lifting something that's low or on the ground, bend your knees and keep your back straight as you lift.

Dig out that little red wagon. Heavier loads, such as bags of groceries or baskets full of laundry, will be out of your hands if you use a wagon or cart to tote them around instead.

Let loose with loops. You won't need quite as tight a grip if you put loops around door handles, such as those on the refrigerator and oven. Take a strip of cloth or even a short belt, feed one end through the door handle, then tie or buckle it to form the loop. When you want to open the refrigerator or oven door, slip your forearm into the loop and use the strength of your whole arm to pull the door open rather than using your hands and fingers to grip the handle. Have loops sewn on your socks, too, and then use a long-handled hook to help you pull them up.

Sit on a stool in the tub. A specially made stool may give you a steady place to shower and may ease your way in and out of the tub.

Plant yourself on a stool in the garden. Sitting, rather than stooping, over your flowerbeds or vegetable garden may help reduce the stress on your back and legs.

Ask for help. Don't be afraid to ask your family members or friends for assistance when you need it. As the saying goes, many hands make light work. By sharing the load, you'll have more time and energy for the people and activities you enjoy.

Contact the Arthritis Foundation. Learn about all kinds of joint-friendly or energy-saving items specially made for people with arthritis by contacting the Arthritis Foundation. You can write to the Arthritis Foundation at P.O. Box 7669, Atlanta, Georgia 30357-0669; call them at 800-568-4045; or visit their Web site at www.arthritis.org.

Range-of-Motion Exercises

Range-of-motion exercises gently move the joints as far as they can comfortably go in every natural direction they can move. They are aimed at maintaining and/or increasing joint mobility and flexibility and decreasing joint discomfort. With strengthening and aerobic exercises, they are an essential aspect of caring for arthritic joints.

For best results, perform each exercise in a smooth, steady, slow-paced manner; don't bounce, jerk, or strain. Don't hold your breath; breathe as naturally as possible. Start out by doing each exercise five to ten times, if possible, then gradually increase repetitions. If any exercise causes chest pain, other pain, or shortness of breath, stop doing it; don't push your joints to the point of pain. When your joints are inflamed, it's best to skip the exercises and rest until the inflammation eases. If you have any questions, contact your doctor or physical therapist.

Wrist and Fingers

Do these with one hand, then the other. Support your hands/arms on a table during the exercises if it helps.
- Relax your fingers, and bend your wrist upward then downward as far as possible.
- Rest your forearm and hand, palm down, flat on a tabletop. One at a time, lift each finger (including the thumb) as high as it will go while keeping the other fingers on the table. Then, with your fingers together, lift your entire hand while keeping your forearm on the table.
- Open your hand wide, then close it, make a fist, and release.
- With your hand wide open, touch the tip of each finger to the tip of your thumb. The wider you spread your fingers, the more you'll extend your reach.
- Place your hand, palm down, on a table, with your thumb extended to the side. One by one, slide each finger over to your thumb until all your fingers are together.

Neck

These exercises can be done while sitting or standing. Never hyperextend the neck directly backward, as this puts undue pressure on the upper part of your spine.
- Turn your head slowly and look over your right shoulder, then over your left shoulder.
- Tilt your head to the left, moving the left ear to the left shoulder; repeat to the right. Don't be alarmed if you hear a cracking sound; it is likely the sound made by the normal movement of bone against bone, known as crepitus.

Shoulders and Elbows

- Lying on your back with your arms at your sides, bend your elbows and try to move your upper arms away from your body until they are at right angles to it. Keep your arms on the bed or floor throughout the exercise.
- Lying on your back and keeping your upper arms resting on the bed or floor, bend your elbows at right angles so that your forearms are perpendicular to your body. Once in this position, rotate your forearms so that you are alternately looking at the palms and then the backs of your hands.

Back

- Stand with your hands on your hips and your feet shoulder-width apart. Turn your head and shoulders to the right and then to the left. Keep your hips facing forward throughout.

Hips

- Sit on the floor with your legs stretched out in front of you. Roll your legs inward so that your toes/feet point toward each other. Then roll your legs outward so that your toes/feet point away from each other.

Knees

- Lying on your back with your legs extended, bring one knee up toward your chest and then back down to the floor. Do four repetitions, then switch legs.

Feet/Ankles and Toes

- Sit on the floor with your legs extended in front of you. Trace circles in the air with your toes, first clockwise, then counterclockwise. Be sure to rotate your ankles gently. Do several rotations in each direction with each foot.
- Sit on the floor with your legs extended in front of you. Flex and extend your toes. If your toes are too stiff, use your hands to gently bend the toes up and down.

Asthma

28 Ways to Breathe Easier

If you have asthma, you know the dreaded choking sensation, the faintness, the anxiety. It's as if someone made you run around the block, then pinched your nose shut and forced you to breathe through a straw. And you know all too well that once an asthma attack starts, it won't go away by itself.

Some 20 million Americans suffer from asthma. While no two people with asthma are alike in the subtle characteristics of their condition, they do have one thing in common: They have trouble breathing properly because of narrowing or blockage of the airways in their lungs. Their lungs are inflamed and supersensitive—they're easily provoked into constriction by a wide variety of outside factors, called triggers, that do not generally cause problems for people without the disease.

The tendency to develop asthma is inherited, and it is more common among people who have allergies. Indeed, there are two forms of asthma—allergic asthma and nonallergic asthma—with the allergic form being more common. Allergic asthma develops in people who have allergies,

and the same substances (called allergens) that provoke their allergy symptoms also trigger their asthma symptoms. Both the allergy and asthma symptoms are the product of an overreaction by the immune system. Common triggers include dust mites, pollen, mold, and pet dander.

In nonallergic asthma, on the other hand, the triggers that irritate the lungs and bring on asthma symptoms have nothing to do with allergies or the immune system. This type of asthma can be sparked by dry air, cold weather, exercise, smoke (including the secondhand variety), strong perfume, stressful situations, intense emotions, even laughing.

The typical symptoms of allergic and nonallergic asthma are similar. The symptoms may occur immediately following contact with a trigger or may be delayed, and their severity varies among individual asthma sufferers.

While there is no cure for asthma, the good news is that asthma—whether mild, moderate, or severe, allergic or nonallergic—can be managed. Doctors who specialize in treating asthma can be very helpful. Every patient with asthma should see a doctor to be sure another cause of wheezing is not present and, if asthma is diagnosed, to develop a therapeutic program for managing the disorder.

In addition to working with your doctor, you can take measures to help control your asthma. The key is to track down your triggers and, as completely as possible, eliminate them from your life. In short, you can often help counter an asthma attack before it happens. Here are some tips to try:

Smite the mite. Dust mites—or rather the feces and dead bodies of these microscopic insects—are one of the most common allergic asthma triggers. They're everywhere in your home, although they love the bedroom most because they feed on the dead skin cells we constantly shed. Banishing dust mites from your home, or at least reducing their ranks, will help ease symptoms if you have allergic asthma triggered by these little critters (see also ALLERGIES). Here are some tips:

- Enclose your mattress in an airtight cover, then cover it with a washable mattress pad.
- Wash your sheets in hot water every week, and wash your mattress pad and synthetic blankets every two weeks.
- Use polyester or dacron pillows, not those made of kapok or feathers, and enclose them in airtight dustcovers.

- Avoid carpeting, which is difficult to clean thoroughly; stick to bare floors with washable area rugs.
- Choose washable curtains instead of draperies.
- Avoid dust-catchers all over the house, but especially in the bedroom; the less clutter the better. If possible, avoid storing out-of-season clothing or bedding in the bedroom; if you can't, enclose them in heavy plastic.
- Try not to do heavy cleaning, but if you must, use only a vacuum cleaner and damp cloth to clean; dust mops and brooms stir up the dust.
- Wear a mask over your mouth and nose while cleaning, and leave the room when you have finished.
- Run an air conditioner or dehumidifier in warm weather, especially in spring and fall, when mites multiply. Aim to keep the humidity level in your home under 40 percent but above 25 percent.
- Consider using an air purifier in the bedroom to keep the room free from dust particles.

Minimize mold. No matter how vigilantly you clean, mold and other forms of fungi are probably lurking somewhere in your house. Fungus is a parasite that can grow on living and nonliving organic material in several forms, including mold, mildew, and dry rot. Fungi reproduce by producing spores. The spores are the *real* problem, as millions and millions of them float through the air to be inhaled in every breath, touching off an allergic reaction that can contribute to asthma. To stave off the spores, take the following steps:

- Keep your windows closed, because the mold spores can come right in through the windows even if the windows have screens.
- Stay out of attics, basements, and other dank, musty places.
- Wear a face mask and give your bathroom a going-over for signs of mold. The most likely spots for mold growth: dark areas, such as the backs of cabinets and under the sink.
- Examine all closets regularly to see that molds have not set up house inside unused shoes and boots.
- On a regular basis, have a family member or friend investigate the inner workings of air conditioners, humidifiers, and vaporizers in your home where molds like to grow.
- Periodically check houseplants for mold growth. This will help keep your plants healthy, too.

Make peace with pollen. Pollen is released when plants are blooming—trees in the spring, grass in the late spring and early summer, ragweed from mid-August until the first frost. Plants that are pollinated by the wind are much more of a problem for people with asthma than are those pollinated by insects. Since it's just about impossible to escape pollen, learn how to control your exposure to the powdery allergen, instead. Avoid cutting grass or even being outside while grass is being mowed. Keep your windows closed as much as possible—pollen can get through screens, too—and use an air conditioner to cool your home in warm weather. Portable air purifiers are also available that can purify recirculated air, removing particles of all sorts that are suspended in the air and further cleansing the air by passing it through a charcoal filter. After being outside in the midst of pollen, take off your clothes as soon as possible and wash them or run a vacuum over those that can't be washed. Wash yourself, too, and don't forget your hair.

Don't pet a pet. The best approach is to not have a pet that can trigger your asthma, such as a dog, cat, or bird. The problem is not the hair of the animal but the dander—the dead, dry skin that flakes off. When the animal licks the skin, the dander also gets into its saliva. Dander is a powerful allergen, so close contact with the pet can leave you gasping.

Fortunately, taking a few common-sense measures may allow you to coexist with a beloved animal companion. Do not allow your pet into the bedroom—ever. If the animal is in the bedroom at any time during the day, the dander will remain for hours. Leave the pet home if you are going for a car ride that would necessitate very close contact with the animal. If you do have direct contact with your pet (or any animal, for that matter), wash your hands right away. If you simply cannot keep your hands off your pet, at least keep your face away; kiss the air—your pet will still get the idea.

In addition, try bathing your dog or cat once every other week in warm water with no soap. Bathing the animal in this way significantly reduces the amount of allergen on your pet's fur.

Kick the cigarette habit. Tobacco smoke can be an irritant that triggers asthma as well as an allergen that touches off an allergic response leading to asthma. Tobacco smoke is one of the worst irritants known: It para-

lyzes the tiny hairlike cilia along the mucous membranes of the respiratory tract. It also reduces immune response and leaves a smoker much more susceptible to upper respiratory infection. In addition to preventing asthma attacks, quitting smoking will reduce your risk of cancer, heart disease, and many other conditions, as well as save you money.

Nonsmokers who live with a smoker are no better off. So if there's someone in your household who won't quit smoking, ask that individual to take his or her habit outdoors.

Weather the weather. Pay attention to how changes in the weather affect your asthma. You might even keep an "asthma journal" by recording the temperature, wind velocity, barometric pressure, and humidity on days when you suffer attacks. Knowing what types

Beware Quack "Cures"

If you have gone from doctor to doctor in search of asthma relief, you may be frustrated and tempted to explore "alternative" therapies, such as cytotoxicity testing, special diets, herbs, special vitamins, or body manipulation. Tempting as these promised solutions sound, they rarely work.

Cytotoxicity testing, for instance, is supposed to uncover all sorts of "hidden" food allergies that need treatment. It's based on the premise that if the allergenic extract of a food to which you are allergic is mixed with a drop of your blood, certain cells in your blood will attack the food. Your blood cells will thus be altered and look distorted under a microscope. However, science has never shown this technique to be reliable or useful for diagnosing or treating allergies or asthma.

of weather conditions can leave you gasping for air can help you avoid problems. While each person responds to weather differently, some general trends may be noted. For instance, people with asthma should stay indoors when it is very cold outside, since a rush of cold air can cause a spasm in the bronchial tubes. Stay indoors if the wind is strong, too. While gusts of wind can blow pollution and smog away, they can also blow pollen in your direction. If you enjoy walking in the rain, you're in luck, because rain tends to wash away roving allergens, pollutants, and irritants.

Watch what you eat. The question of whether foods trigger asthma has yet to be answered. Some foods, such as nuts, shellfish, milk, eggs, and strawberries, can result in an array of allergic responses, including asthma symptoms. Sulfites in wine can have a

similar effect. Existing scientific evidence suggests that food allergies are probably not a major trigger for chronic asthma in adults. Nonetheless, you may have noticed that certain foods seem to make your symptoms worse. If so, it's best to limit or avoid those foods, but check with your doctor first to be sure you won't be depriving your body of vital nutrients.

Allergies to certain types of food, especially milk and wheat, are more often a trigger of asthma in children. If milk and wheat seem to be causing problems for your child with asthma, eliminate these foods from his or her diet. Check labels, and avoid foods that list milk, milk solids, casein, whey, or caseinate as ingredients. (Talk to your family doctor about alternate dietary sources of nutrients such as calcium.)

Eating away from home can sometimes be a problem. If you are invited to dinner and don't know what meal will be served, eat something at home before you leave so you won't be left hungry should the main course be a trigger food for you. If you are eating in a restaurant, inquire about the ingredients in the dish you want to order. No matter where you have your meal, don't overeat, don't eat too fast, and don't talk while you are eating. Steer clear of alcohol, too, especially if you are taking medications for your asthma. One final reminder: Avoid so-called cytoxicity tests and similar methods that promise to root out hidden food allergies and cure asthma (see "Beware Quack 'Cures'" on page 28).

Protect your health. A problem in the upper airways—such as a respiratory infection—can cause trouble in the lower airways—the bronchial tubes—and precipitate an asthma attack. While taking steps to avoid getting sick makes sense for everyone, maintaining good health can dramatically reduce the frequency and intensity of asthma attacks. Stay away from people who have a cold or the flu, drink plenty of fluids, and avoid getting overtired; otherwise, you will be more susceptible to infections. If, despite your best efforts, you do develop an infection, see your doctor; early use of antibiotics, when appropriate, can be quite helpful.

Exercise your options. For years, people with asthma had been told to avoid exercise because it would induce attacks. Research has shown, however, that getting regular aerobic exercise increases exercise tolerance in people with asthma. Start by warming up with light exercise before a more vigorous workout. Begin with short workouts and gradually increase them. At least at first, keep a bronchodilator with you. If you feel tightness in your chest and can't work through it, use the device. If you are out in cold or dry air, wear a scarf around your nose and mouth to heat and hydrate the air before breathing it in. Cool down with light exercise at the end of your workout. If one type of exercise still brings on attacks, try another form of exercise. You may not be able to tolerate running, for example, but you may be able to swim regularly.

Avoid aspirin. Aspirin can trigger asthma attacks in certain people. Play it safe and avoid aspirin and products that contain it if you have asthma. Even if you have not experienced an asthma flare from aspirin in the past, it's possible for one to occur at any time. Keep aspirin out of your medicine chest, and check labels on every over-the-counter drug you want to purchase. Avoid those that list "aspirin" and those that contain the initials "ASA," "APC," or "PAC"; ask your pharmacist if you are unsure if the medication you want to purchase contains aspirin.

According to an expert report from the National Asthma Education Program, people with asthma should also stay away from certain nonsteroidal anti-inflammatory agents (ibuprofen is one such medication) that have effects similar to aspirin's. Ask your doctor if it's safe for you to try acetaminophen, sodium salicylate, or disalcid for pain relief instead.

You may also need to avoid tartrazine (yellow food dye #5), which is found in a number of soft drinks, cake mixes, candies, and some medications, if it aggravates your asthma.

Take a deep breath. Inhaling through the mouth often produces shallow, unsatisfying breaths that can resemble panting. Practice inhaling slowly through the nose in a controlled way, instead. Before you start breathing exercises, blow your nose to make sure that your air passages are clear. Then sit in a chair in a comfortable position. Take a deep breath and feel your breath going as far down as possible. Your abdomen should expand as you do this exercise. Exhale slowly, feeling your abdomen relax as your breath comes out of your nose. Repeat this exercise at least three times a day (but never right after eating and never in a hurry, which may trigger hyperventilation).

Keep your weight down. Carrying around excess body fat increases the breathing rate and forces the heart to work extra hard to supply blood to all the muscles and organs. If you are overweight, losing weight will ease your heart's burden; unfortunately, asthma medications can cause you to pack on pounds. If you need to lose some pounds, you and your doctor should work together to establish a diet and exercise plan that will help you burn more calories and reduce your calorie intake without depriving you of necessary nutrients.

Mind your mind. The notion that asthma is "all in your head" has gone the way of many medical myths. However, doctors believe that asthma *is* an illness with both physical and emotional aspects. For example, asthma attacks can be triggered by emotional changes, such as laughing or crying, or by stress. While you may not be able to "think away" an asthma attack, keeping your mind at ease may prevent you from panicking at the onset of an asthma attack, which will make a bout with breathing trouble less scary. Develop an upbeat mind-set by committing yourself to feeling better. A positive attitude works wonders to enhance your other coping methods. In addition, be forthright about your asthma; others will respect your directness and, in most cases, try to make things easier for you.

Learn to relax. Since stress and emotional upsets can trigger or aggravate asthma attacks, it may be helpful to set aside time each day—preferably the same time—to practice some form of relaxation.

Athlete's Foot

20 Strategies to Beat Athlete's Foot

Blame the advertising man who mis-named it in the 1930s, but athlete's foot is not restricted to athletes. Also known as *tinea pedis,* or "ringworm of the feet," it has nothing to do with worms either. It's a fungal infection of the feet. The *Trichophyton* fungus that causes the redness, itching, cracking, and scaling of athlete's foot can also infect the scalp, where it causes hair loss and scaly patches; the body, where it causes round, red, scaly patches that itch; and the groin, where "jock itch" causes itching and thicken-ing of the skin.

Athlete's foot is the most common fungal infection of the skin. It affects more men than women, probably

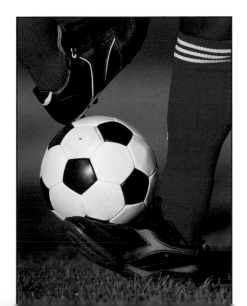

because men typically wear heavy, often airtight shoes, and the fungus loves hot, dark, moist environments.

Contrary to popular myth, athlete's foot fun-gus isn't just found in locker rooms, although the moist locker-room environment is perfect for fungal growth. In fact, most people harbor the

fungus on their skin, but it's kept in check by bacteria that also normally live on the skin.

Most cases of athlete's foot cause only bothersome redness, itching, flaking, and scaling on the soles of the feet and between the toes. In severe cases, however, blisters form on the soles of the feet; fissures, or cracks, that weep fluid can also open between the toes. These fissures can cause a stinging pain and are vulnerable to secondary infection. When the infec-tion involves the toenails, it can cause the nails to become discolored and thick. Also, if left untreated, athlete's foot can infect other parts of the body.

Doctors don't agree on exactly how athlete's foot is spread, although most believe it's passed by direct contact with an infected person or with a contaminated surface, such as the floor of a shower stall. But the real determi-nants of whether or not you'll get the infection are how susceptible you are—doctors believe your genes play a part in whether you'll develop athlete's foot—and how dry you keep your feet.

If you have athlete's foot, follow these simple tips to reduce the risk of spreading it:

- After bathing, wash out the tub or shower with an antiseptic cleaner, such as Lysol.
- Don't share towels.
- Wash your socks twice in hot water to kill fungal spores.
- Wear thongs in public showers.
- Keep your feet dry, and use over-the-counter treatments to clear your infection quickly.

While severe or stubborn cases of athlete's foot may require a doctor's care, most can be effectively treated at home. The following strategies can help you soothe and heal athlete's foot and keep it from returning.

Move away from moisture. All of your treatment and prevention strategies should center around keeping your feet as dry as possible.

Hello, Doctor?

While most cases of athlete's foot can be effectively treated with home remedies, you should see a doctor if:
- You develop cracks in the webs between your toes. Cracks could be a sign of cellulitis, a skin infection.
- Your athlete's foot infection doesn't respond to home remedies or over-the-counter treatments within two to three weeks. You may have eczema, psoriasis, or some other ailment.
- Your infection is getting worse despite treatment. Some fungus strains are very hardy and require prescription medications such as keto-conazole and griseofulvin.
- One or both feet swell.
- Pus appears in the lesions.
- The fungus spreads to your hands. Treatment may require prescription oral medication.
- The toenails appear thick and discolored. This indicates the toenails have become infected with the fungus. Over-the-counter medications often fail to work on toenail fungus.

Soap up. Wash your feet twice a day with soap and water, and dry them thoroughly.

Dry thoroughly between your toes. If you can't get your feet dry enough with a towel, use a handheld hair dryer set on "warm."

Kick off your shoes. Go barefoot or wear sandals or open-toe shoes whenever you can. When you can't, at least sneak your shoes off for short periods, such as during lunch, at break time, or when sitting at your desk.

Medicate 'em. Over-the-counter antifungal preparations are very effective for most cases of athlete's foot. These products come in creams, sprays, or solutions and contain tolnaftate (Tinactin), miconazole (Micatin), or undecylenic acid (Desenex). Creams seem to be more effective, but powders can help absorb moisture. Apply the medication twice a day after washing and drying the feet.

Be persistent. Too often, people stop using the antifungal as soon as symptoms go away. The fungus, however, may still be present, so continue twice-daily use for three to six weeks. Once the infection has cleared, apply the antifungal once a day or once a week—whatever keeps your feet fungus free.

Make tea for toes. To help dry out the infection and ease the itching, steep six black tea bags in a quart of warm water and soak your feet in it. The tannins in the tea may account for the soothing effects of this remedy.

Soak them in Betadine. If the infection has caused redness and cracks between the toes, the fungal infection may be compounded by a bacterial infection. Soak your feet once a day for 20 minutes in a solution of two capfuls Betadine (available over-the-counter at pharmacies) and one quart warm water (skip this remedy if you are pregnant, however). After the Betadine soak, dry your feet well, and apply antifungal medication.

Don't bleach. While the idea is to dry out the infection, avoid home remedies that involve strong chemicals and solvents, such as bleach, alcohol, or floor cleaners, which can severely damage skin.

Treat your shoes. If you have fungus on your feet, you've got fungus in your shoes. To keep from reinfecting yourself every time you put your shoes on, treat your shoes with Lysol spray or an antifungal spray or powder every time you take off your shoes.

Air 'em out. On sunny days, take the laces out of your shoes, pull up their tongues, and set them in a sunny, well-ventilated place. The sunshine and circulating air will help dry out the shoes and kill fungus.

Alternate shoes. Switch shoes every day. Wear one pair for a day while you treat the other pair with sunlight and an antifungal spray or powder. If your feet sweat a lot, change your shoes midway through the day.

Choose shoes with care. Avoid shoes made of plastic or rubber or shoes that are watertight; they trap perspiration and create the warm, moist conditions fungi love. Opt for natural, breathable materials such as leather.

Exercise your sock options. Socks made of natural fibers such as cotton and wool help absorb perspiration and keep feet dry. However, some research suggests acrylic socks may be even better at keeping feet dry by wicking moisture away from the feet. So what kind do you choose? Try a pair of both to see which keeps your feet drier and more comfortable.

If your feet naturally sweat a lot or if you're participating in activities such as sports that make your feet sweat more than usual, change your socks two or three times a day.

Wear thongs. When you're in a public place likely to harbor athlete's foot fungus, such as the locker room of your favorite gym, wear thongs or similar shower shoes to limit your exposure to the fungus. Although this technique isn't foolproof, it will decrease your risk of getting athlete's foot, and it may prevent you from picking up other nasty foot maladies, such as plantar warts.

Back Pain

21 Ways to Keep Back Pain at Bay

Maybe you lifted something heavy or swung a golf club a little too enthusiastically. Or maybe you've been hunched over a desk or computer for two weeks, battling a deadline. Whatever the reason, now your back is "out," and you're wishing for something—*anything*—that will put an end to the agony.

Take heart—you're not alone. Almost every American suffers from back pain at some point in his or her life. The bad news is that unless you have a major injury or disc problem, your doctor may not be able to do much for you other than prescribe some pain medication and advise you to rest. The good news is that by following some simple steps, you can be back in the swing of things in just a few days. Even better, you can help ensure that you won't have to endure similar discomfort in the future.

Easing the Pain

The following remedies are appropriate for anyone who is suffering from back pain due to tight, aching muscles or a strain. However, if you are experiencing pain, weakness, or numbness in the legs or a loss of bowel or bladder control, see a doctor without delay.

Don't take it lying down. Conventional wisdom once held that several days or even weeks in bed were the best cure for a sore back. However, a growing number of doctors today encourage patients to get up and around as soon as they can and to avoid bed rest entirely if possible. That's because mounting research shows that lying down for an extended period not only fails to speed up relief of low back pain but may make it even worse. If you feel you must rest your aching back, the best position is lying

flat on your back with two pillows underneath your knees. Avoid resting or sleeping on your stomach for long periods; it forces you to twist your neck just to breathe and may result in neck pain. Try to get up and move around—slowly and gently—as soon as possible. Any more than three days of bed rest could weaken the muscles and make them more prone to strain.

Ice it. Applying an ice pack to the painful area within 24 hours of a strain can help keep inflammation to a minimum and ease discomfort by decreasing the ability of nerves to send pain signals to the brain. Place ice cubes in a plastic bag, then apply the bag on top of a thin towel on the skin. Leave the ice pack on for 20 minutes, take it off for 30 minutes, then replace it for another 20 minutes.

Take a hot bath. If more than 24 hours have passed since the strain occurred, ice will not help reduce pain or inflammation. After that first day, heat may help increase the elasticity of the muscles somewhat, so try soaking in a tub of hot water for 20 minutes or more. Pregnant women, however, should not sit in a hot bath or hot tub for too long, since raising the body temperature over 100 degrees Fahrenheit for long periods may cause birth defects or miscarriage. If you are pregnant, contact your doctor for advice before trying a hot soak.

Invest in a new mattress. A soft, sagging mattress may contribute to the development of back problems or worsen an existing one. If a new mattress is not in your budget, however, a three-quarter-inch-thick piece of plywood placed between the mattress and box spring may help somewhat. It's not clear whether water beds offer any relief for back pain. No matter what type of bed you have, try to sleep on your back with two pillows propping up your knees.

Get a massage. If you're lucky enough to have an accommodating spouse, friend, or roommate, ask him or her to give you a rubdown. As you lie facedown on a bed or sofa, ask your masseuse to knead your back muscles. Local massage therapists may also make house calls if you don't feel able to visit one of them. Check the yellow  pages for listings or ask your doctor or a friend for a referral.

Relax. Much back pain is the result of muscles made tight by emotional tension. Learn and practice a relaxation technique, such as meditation, or try a deep-breathing exercise, such

Back Office Exercise

If you spend many hours a day hunched over paperwork at a desk, chances are your lumbar, or lower, spine is paying the price. The lower spine's natural curve is slightly inward, toward the abdomen, but hunching forward causes the lower spine to be curved outward, toward the chair back. Such poor sitting posture puts stress on the ligaments and other tissues, which can lead to back pain.

To give your lower back a break, periodically stand up, with your feet shoulder-width apart and your hands on your hips, and slowly lean back to a point of mild tension; hold for a count of ten. Repeat four to five times.

You should also practice getting out of your chair properly: With your feet shoulder width apart, head up, eyes focused straight ahead, and buttocks stuck out, use the strength of your arms, legs, and buttocks, instead of your back, to lift yourself off the seat and into a standing position.

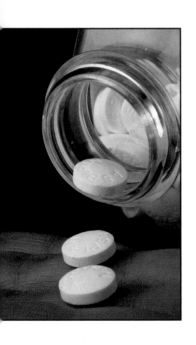

as closing your eyes, breathing slowly and deeply, and counting backward from 100.

Take two aspirin. Taking an over-the-counter analgesic such as aspirin, acetaminophen, or ibuprofen may help relieve your pain. However, be aware that not all medications—not even nonprescription ones—are for everyone. Pregnant women, for example, should not take any medication without first checking with their doctor. And people with ulcers should stay away from analgesics containing aspirin. Don't take any medicine for a bad back without first reading the warnings in the box on page 21 and talking to your doctor.

Preventing Future Pain

Many of the activities you engage in each day—sitting, lifting, bending, carrying—can put a strain on your back. By learning new ways of going about these activities, you can help prevent back pain and ensure the health of your back for years to come. Try the following tips.

Cushion your ride. Most seats in cars and trucks are not designed to support the small of your back, although some these days do provide adjustable lumbar support at least for the driver. If the seat in your vehicle doesn't, buy a small cushion that can be fitted to provide the missing support. Despite what your mother told you about sitting up straight, leaning back at an angle of about 110 degrees is ideal for the back. On long drives, stop and walk around periodically to increase blood flow and decrease stiffness.

Put your arm behind your back. If you get stuck sitting for a long period in a seat that doesn't support your lower back, slip a cushion between your lower back and the chair. If you don't have a cushion, try rolling up a towel or sweater so that it has about the same circumference as your forearm. Then slide the rolled up cloth between your lower back and the back of the seat. In a pinch, you can simply slide your forearm between your lower back and the seat back to ease the strain on your back. Even with the best back support, however, sitting is still stressful on your back, so try to at least make small adjustments in the curvature of your lower back every few minutes or so.

Swim. Many experts agree that swimming is the best aerobic exercise for a bad back. Doing laps in the pool can help tone and strengthen the muscles of the back and abdomen, which help support the spine, while buoyancy temporarily relieves them of the job of holding up your weight. Walking is the next best choice. You can also try the "Back-Saving Exercises" on page 38.

Lift with your knees bent. The large muscles of your legs and buttocks are better equipped to bear heavy weight than your back muscles are. To be sure you're lifting properly, imagine you're balancing a bowl of soup on your head, trying not to spill a single drop: Keep your back straight and bend only your knees, rather than bending at the waist, as you squat to pick something up. Then, as you rise, concentrate on using your leg muscles to push your upper body and the object back up into a standing posi-

tion, again without bending at the waist. Strengthening your leg and buttock muscles will make it even easier to squat and lift properly—whether you're picking up a pen, a bag of groceries, or a small child.

Carry objects close to your body. When picking up and carrying something heavy, pull in your elbows and hold the object close to your body. When reaching for a bulky item on a high shelf, stand beneath it and rest it on your head. That way your erect spine carries the weight, placing less burden on your back muscles.

Stay alert. Careless activity is the number-one cause of back injury, so beware if you have struggled with back pain in the past. As much as possible, avoid bending, twisting, and lifting. Make a mental note of situations that have led to back injuries in the past—and do your best to avoid them. That may mean paying someone to do your lawn work or move furniture for you, but shelling out a few dollars today could keep you pain-free and on the job tomorrow.

Watch your weight. Maintaining a healthy body weight (ask your doctor if you're not sure what that is) may help take the strain off the back muscles by lightening their load. What's more, having a flabby midsection may cause you to become sway-backed, which can worsen back pain.

Back-Saving Exercises

Performing the following exercises once or twice a day—even when back pain is present—will increase your back's strength and flexibility. Although these exercises are safe and effective for most people who experience back pain caused by muscle strain or spasm, those who have or suspect any disc or other structural problem should not engage in any exercise without advice from their doctor.

Single Knee-to-Chest:

Lie on your back with your knees bent and your feet flat on the floor. Grasp the back of one thigh with both hands; gently and slowly pull it toward your chest until you feel mild tension—not to the point of pain. Hold to the count of ten, without bouncing, then release. Repeat four to five times with the same leg, then switch sides. This exercise stretches muscles in the hips, buttocks, and lower back—all muscles that become shortened and tight after a long day of sitting or standing. It is a good warm-up to the other exercises.

Double Knee-to-Chest:

Lie on your back with your knees bent and your feet flat on the floor. This time, grasp both thighs, and gently and slowly pull them as close to your chest as you can. Again, pull only to the point of slight tension, and don't bounce. Hold to the count of ten, then release. Repeat four or five times.

Lumbar Rotation:

Lie on your back with your knees bent, your feet flat on the floor, and your heels touching your buttocks. Keeping your knees together and your shoulders on the floor, slowly allow your knees to rotate to the right, until you reach a point of mild tension. Hold for a count of ten, then return to the starting position. Repeat four to five times to the right, then four to five times to the left.

Partial Sit-Up:

Lie on your back with your knees bent, feet flat on the floor, and hands gently supporting your head. Slowly curl up to the point where your shoulders come off the floor. Avoid bending your neck. Hold for a few counts, then slowly roll back down. Remember to breathe as you do the exercise. Repeat 10 to 15 times, if possible. This exercise strengthens the abdominal muscles, which can help you maintain good posture and reduce the risk of back injury.

Active Back Extension:

Lie facedown on the floor. Put a pillow under your stomach (not under your hips) if that feels comfortable. Put your arms at your sides, with your hands next to your buttocks. Slowly extend your head and neck and raise your upper body off the floor. Hold for a count of five to ten. Slowly lower yourself back to the starting position. Remember to breathe as you do the exercise. Repeat five to ten times.

Posture Enhancer:

Stand with your head, shoulders, shoulder blades, and buttocks held firmly against a wall. Your heels should be about six inches away from the wall. Do not allow your lower back to curve excessively. Start with the backs of your hands against the wall at thigh level. Slowly slide the backs of your hands up the wall, without allowing your elbows, head, buttocks, or shoulder blades to lose contact with the wall. (The movement is similar to making angels in the snow.) Stop when your arms are so high you begin to lose contact with the wall. Repeat five times.

Bad Breath

6 Refreshing Fixes

The problem of halitosis, or bad breath, has plagued humankind for centuries. To conquer bad breath, the ancient Greeks reputedly rinsed with white wine, anise seed, and myrrh, while the Italians mixed up a mouthwash of sage, cinnamon, juniper seeds, root of cypress, and rosemary leaves, according to the Academy of General Dentistry. Today, of course, Americans still worry that their breath smells bad (and swish capful after capful of mouthwashes that often contain little more than alcohol and flavoring to fix it). Indeed, *New York Times* health columnist Jane E. Brody has written that she receives more questions about bad breath than about any other common medical problem.

Maybe one explanation for this preoccupation with oral odor is the simple fact that you can't really tell whether you've got bad breath. This is a time when you have to depend on the honesty and kindness of friends to let you know if your breath smells bad. If you're on your way to that important meeting and you simply *must* know if your breath will precede you through the door, try breathing into a handkerchief or running floss between your teeth and taking a sniff.

Fixing bad breath depends on what's causing it. In 80 to 90 percent of cases, it's due to something in the mouth. Most often, bad breath is the result of nothing more serious than a dirty mouth. Plaque, the nearly invisible film of bacteria that's constantly forming in your mouth, is often responsible. Another possible source of stink can be decaying food that's trapped between teeth.

Persistent bad breath may be due to a treatable dental problem, such as an undiagnosed cavity or periodontal (gum) disease. Sometimes a broken filling can trap food particles. If you visit the dentist and no such problem is found, however, you may want to investigate further and talk to your physician about other possible causes. Occasionally, ongoing bad breath is due to something in the respiratory tract (such as a sinus or lung infection) or gastrointestinal tract or to a systemic (body-wide) condition. Diabetes, for example, can give the breath an unpleasant chemical smell.

Of course, what you eat can contribute to bad breath, too. The strong

What About Mouthwash?

Madison Avenue has played to our fears of bad breath in advertising claims for mouthwashes. But do they really work?

Yes, but only for a short time. Dental researchers agree that commercial mouthwashes mask odors only temporarily (anywhere from about 20 minutes to 2 hours). These products don't prevent bad breath, either. While they may be able to kill bacteria that contribute to bad breath, a new batch of bacteria crops up fairly quickly.

If you do decide to use a mouthwash, choose a product with fluoride for its cavity-fighting potential or one that is accepted by the American Dental Association for removing plaque.

odors of foods like garlic, onions, and alcohol are carried through the bloodstream and exhaled by the lungs. Another big stinker when it comes to turning your breath sour—and harming your health—is tobacco.

Figuring out the cause of bad breath is the first step, obviously, in doing something about it. Here's what you can do to keep your breath as fresh as possible:

Keep your mouth clean. Brush thoroughly at least twice a day, and floss daily. Food and bacteria trapped between teeth and at the gum line can be removed only with floss; if it's left to linger, it's not going to smell nice.

Clean your tongue, too. Bacteria left on your tongue can contribute to less-than-fresh breath, so be sure to brush your tongue after you've polished your pearly whites.

Wet your whistle. A dry mouth can equal smelly breath. Saliva helps clean your mouth; it has a natural antibacterial action and it washes away food particles. (Reduced saliva flow at night explains why your breath smells sour when you wake up in the morning.) Try chewing sugarless gum or sucking on sugarless mints to stimulate saliva production.

Rinse. If you can't brush, at least rinse your mouth with plain water after eating. Swishing the water around in your mouth may help to remove some of the food particles left after a meal.

Munch on parsley. That green sprig of parsley that comes with your meal can do more than decorate your plate. While munching on parsley or spearmint won't cure bad breath, the scent of the herb itself can help temporarily cover up offending oral odor. (You're basically trading an offensive odor for a more acceptable one.)

Eat to smell sweet. Foods that help fight plaque can also help fight mouth odor. Opt for celery, carrots, peanuts, or a bit of low-fat cheese if you want something to snack on.

Belching

9 Ways to Squelch the Belch

Because belching is the body's way of getting rid of swallowed air, you can cut down on unwanted—and potentially embarrassing—belching by cutting down on how much air you swallow. Here's how:

Stifle it. Sometimes, belching produces such an inordinate sense of relief that chronic belchers will encourage themselves to belch many times. It's better not to do this. Repeated belching triggers more belching.

Don't smoke. Here is yet another reason to quit smoking. When you inhale smoke from cigarettes, cigars, or pipes, you swallow excessive amounts of air.

Watch what you put in your mouth. Chewing gum and sucking on hard candy or lollipops stimulate air swallowing, too.

Mind your manners. Mom was right again when she told you not to talk with your mouth full. She wanted to teach you manners, but the fact is, eating with your mouth open makes you swallow air.

Eat slowly. People who gulp down food and beverages are swallowing excessive amounts of air. They're also crowding the stomach with too much food to digest, which causes a gaseous buildup.

Relax. Anxiety and stress can cause you to swallow more often, which increases the amount of air taken in. When you feel stressed, force yourself to breathe slowly and deeply.

Don't catch cold. A cold brings on postnasal drip, and this annoying symptom will probably make you swallow much more frequently. So if you catch a cold bug, try to blow your nose often to keep your nasal passages as clear as possible (see COLDS for more tips on breathing easier). Better yet, try to protect yourself from exposure to cold viruses.

Limit bubbly beverages. Drinking carbonated beverages, including beer, creates air in the stomach that has to come out—one way or the other.

Go strawless. Drinking through a straw increases the amount of air you swallow.

Bites

26 Ways to Fight Bites

Bites can range from itchy to painful to life threatening. And you needn't live in the wilderness to risk getting one. In fact, one of the most dangerous bites can be inflicted in your very own home—by a fellow human being! (Humans have more bacteria in their mouths than most wild animals, no matter how often we brush our teeth.)

Many bites can be treated at home, although others, including a human bite that breaks the skin, require an immediate visit to the doctor or emergency room. The trick is distinguishing the dangerous from the benign.

The following is a guide to treating the most common types of bites, as well as a few tips on how to avoid getting bitten in the first place. Of course, if you've had a run-in with a creature that you suspect is dangerous, don't attempt self-treatment. See a doctor without delay. The same advice holds true if you experience any signs of illness (such as fever, loss of consciousness, nausea, dizziness, or vomiting) following any bite.

Ice it. Bites from mosquitoes and nonpoisonous spiders can benefit from an ice-cold compress. The ice decreases inflammation and reduces pain and itching. Ice the bite for 20 minutes at a time every few hours.

Try an old fail-safe. When you had a mosquito bite as a child, your mother probably used calamine lotion—a thin, chalky, pink liquid—to stop the itch. Sold over the counter (and generally cheaper than hydrocortisone creams and ointments), it is still just as effective today.

Give an antihistamine a go. Over-the-counter antihistamines can also help an itchy bite, since the itch is really a mild allergic reaction. Of course, antihistamines should not be used by sensitive individuals, pregnant women, people with allergies to ingredients in the products, or those taking conflicting medications. Check with your doctor or pharmacist if in doubt.

Recognize the signs of a severe reaction. The bite from a venomous spider can cause a severe allergic reaction. It is important, therefore, to recognize the signs of an allergic reaction before it is too late. Symptoms of anaphylaxis, or severe allergic reaction, include difficulty breathing, hives all over the body, and loss of consciousness. Anyone experiencing such symptoms should be rushed to the nearest emergency room for medical treatment.

Don't panic if you've been bitten by a tick. Lyme disease, a tick-borne illness that can cause chills, fever, headache, and other complications,

Stay Away from Snakes

You can reduce your chances of being bitten by a snake by following these guidelines from the American Academy of Family Physicians:
- Keep your lawn mowed, your hedges trimmed, and brush removed from your yard and any nearby vacant lots. This will reduce the number of places for snakes to live and hide.
- Warn children not to play in vacant, weed-infested lots.
- Always use tongs when moving firewood, brush, or lumber—they're perfect hideaways for snakes.
- When walking through grassy, weedy areas where snakes may live, poke at the ground ahead of you with a long stick or pole to scare away any snakes.
- Wear tall boots and loose, long pants when working or walking in areas where snakes are likely to be.
- Never handle snakes, even if they're dead.
- Sleep on a cot when camping in snake-infested areas.

has received lots of play in the media. But not all ticks carry the disease, and not every Lyme-carrying tick will transmit it to you if you happen to be bitten. Generally, a tick must remain on the skin for 24 to 48 hours to transmit the organism that causes Lyme disease. If you find a tick on your body, remove it using the directions in the remedy that follows, and save it in a small jar of alcohol, so that it can be analyzed for Lyme disease if a suspicious infection develops. There is no need to see a doctor unless you notice any swelling or redness around the bite (a sign of infection), a bull's-eye-shaped rash (often a symptom of Lyme disease), any other skin rash, or a fever.

Remove ticks with care. To remove a tick from your skin, grasp the insect's mouthparts with tweezers as close as

Handling Snakebites

If you've been bitten by a snake that you suspect is poisonous, hightail it to the nearest emergency room. Some snakebites, most notably those from rattlesnakes such as the Eastern diamondback, can be fatal. However, hospital emergency units stock very effective antivenoms to combat them.

One fortunate fact is that snakes only envenomate, or inject their venom, between 25 and 75 percent of the time. The rest of the time they leave nothing more than fang marks and a frightened victim.

If you are far from medical attention, take the following steps while help is being sought or while you are on the way to the hospital:

- Have someone catch the snake and kill it—if the capture can be accomplished without excessive danger. Put the corpse in a bag, and take it to the hospital with you. This way, hospital staff can accurately identify the snake and ensure that you are given the correct antivenom.
- Stay quiet, still, and warm. Do your best not to panic. Getting upset stimulates the heart to pump more blood, which will only speed the spread of venom through your system. Taking long, slow, deep breaths may help you stay calm.
- If you have been bitten on a limb, remove any rings, bracelets, shoes, or socks, since the extremity may swell. If possible, immobilize the limb and elevate it above the level of the heart.
- You may tie a scarf, tie, belt, or piece of fabric above the fang mark, but do not make it tight enough to cut off circulation: Make sure you can slide at least one finger underneath the band.
- If you have a venom-extractor kit with you, apply the suction device for 30 to 40 minutes, or until you get to the hospital.
- DO NOT apply ice, cut the snakebite with a knife, or attempt to suck venom from the wound. These are outdated methods of treatment that may actually do more harm than good.
- Ask for help. If you have been envenomated, you may begin to feel dizzy or ill. Do not attempt to drive yourself to the hospital.

possible to the skin and slowly pull straight upwards. Do not burn, smash, or squeeze the attached tick or pull the tick by the body or head, as it may break off, leaving the mouthparts underneath your skin. Use the tweezers to remove any remaining parts of the tick. Next, apply a local antiseptic, such as alcohol or an antibiotic ointment, to the bite.

Stop the bleeding. If an animal bite has caused severe bleeding, cover the bite with a clean cloth, gauze, or unused sanitary napkin and apply pressure to the area with the palm of your hand. If the wound is large, tie a scarf, towel, or T-shirt tightly around the site to create pressure over a larger area, but don't tie it tightly enough to cut off circulation (you should be able to slide at least one finger between the cloth and skin). Immobilize the area. If the bite is on a limb, elevate the limb above the level of the heart. Seek medical treatment as soon as possible.

Take punctures seriously. A bite that leaves a scratch but doesn't really break the skin may simply be washed with soap and water, then covered with an antibacterial cream or oint-

ment. Not so for a bite that breaks or punctures the skin. A puncture wound requires the expertise of a doctor, in case the animal has rabies. Try to remember how the animal behaved before biting. If it was behaving in a peculiar way—for example, if a wild animal was being unusually placid—the animal may be rabid. Check with doctors or veterinarians in the area to determine if there have been any local outbreaks of rabies in wild or domestic animals.

Get a tetanus booster. If you've been bitten by a wild or domestic animal and the bite has broken the skin, it's probably wise to contact your doctor to see if you need a tetanus booster shot (whether or not you need one depends, in part, on the type of wound and the timing of your last tetanus shot). Bites can become infected easily because of the large amount of bacteria in an animal's mouth. In the days after the bite, watch the site closely for signs of infection, such as redness and swelling.

Report the animal to the authorities. If you've been bitten by an animal in your community, call your local office of the American Society for the Prevention of Cruelty to Animals (ASPCA) or animal catcher to report the incident. If the animal was wild or a stray, the proper agency may want to track it down and capture it for obser-

vation, especially if rabies is suspected. If the animal belongs to a neighbor, report it to the pet's owner, and, if you choose, to the authorities (many communities have laws concerning pet bites).

Don't get bitten in the first place. Stay away from wild animals, even if they let you approach, and don't pester snakes, spiders, bees, or anything else that looks threatening. Most animals and insects will leave you alone unless you bother them.

Know your local fauna. It's best to keep abreast of the insects and animals in your area, so that you know what to avoid. If you live in an area that is home to poisonous snakes or spiders, for example, learn how to recognize and avoid them.

Blisters

19 Ways to Treat—and Beat—Them

You just couldn't resist a bargain. Those shoes looked great with your new outfit, even if they didn't feel so great on your feet. "They'll stretch out," you told yourself, as you patted yourself on the back for getting such a good deal. Unfortunately, you got more than you bargained for—painful blisters to go with your new shoes.

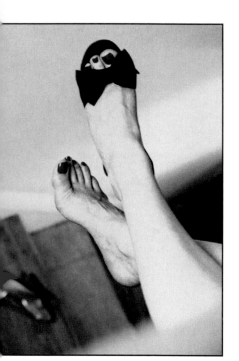

Blisters are tender spots that fill up with fluid released by tiny blood vessels in an area where delicate skin tissues have been burned, pinched, or just plain irritated. Virtually everyone has experienced friction blisters, the kind caused by hot, sweaty feet and/or ill-fitting shoes. If you have one now, read on to find out how to take care of it. Then continue reading to learn how you can help protect your tender tootsies in the future.

Treating Your Blister

A blister is your body's way of telling you that skin and tissues are being injured. So it's important to take steps to relieve the discomfort *and* protect the injured area.

Make a tent. Instead of simply placing an adhesive bandage right on top of the blister, "tent" the bandage by bringing in its sides so the padding in the middle of the bandage raises up a bit. A tented bandage will help protect the blister while exposing it to air, which will speed healing.

Use a double-duty bandage. Another type of bandage, available in pharmacies, contains a gel and antiseptic to cushion and "clean" the blister. Ask your pharmacist if you can't find it on the shelf.

Let it breathe. Some physicians believe a blister needs as much exposure to air as possible and should never be covered. So you may want to give your blister a chance to "breathe" by going without a bandage occasionally, such as when you're sitting around relaxing at home and your blister is less likely to need protection from bumps and debris.

Smear on an ointment. Whether you decide to cover your blister or not, you should apply an antibacterial or antibiotic ointment to it. Doctors generally recommend Bacitracin or Polysporin, which may be less likely to cause an allergic reaction or sensitivity than other over-the-counter ointments.

Pad it. When a blister is in a particularly annoying spot, like the bottom of the foot, padding might provide more of a cushion than a bandage alone would. Try using the circular pads made of foam adhesive found in the foot-care aisle of drugstores. Most pharmacies also sell sheets of padding, which you can trim for a more precise fit. Cut the padding in the shape of a donut, and place it on the skin surrounding the blister. Then gently cover the blister with an antibacterial ointment, and place a bandage over the blister and pad.

Put it up. Elevating the blistered area can help relieve the pressure and temporarily ease discomfort.

Be patient. It usually takes about a week to ten days for the blister's fluid to be reabsorbed by the body.

Drain it. While some doctors believe that a blister should never be popped because of the risk of infection, most agree that a blister causing extreme pressure—such as one on a finger or toe or under a nail—is a candidate for draining. Never open a blister that was caused by a burn. Large blisters that may open on their own through normal activity should be treated by a doctor.

If you decide to pop a blister, first wipe the blister and a sewing needle with alcohol. (Some doctors discourage the common practice of sterilizing needles over flames, since soot on the tip could irritate the blister.) Prick the blister once or twice near its edge; then slowly and gently press out the fluid.

Keep the roof on it. Once you have popped the blister and drained the fluid, do not remove the deflated top skin. This skin, called the blister's roof, protects the blister from infection and forms a "bridge" across which new cells can migrate on their journey to heal the site.

Soak first. You'll find it easier to drain a blister on a tough-skinned area, such as the sole of the foot, if you spend a day or two softening it up. Soak the blister for fifteen minutes three to four times a day in Burow's solution, available from pharmacies in packets or tablets (follow the directions on the package).

Watch for signs of infection. Redness, red streaks, or pus in or around a blister should be treated by a doctor.

Preventing Blisters

The following steps will help prevent friction blisters:

Buy shoes in the afternoon or evening. Pounding the pavement all day can cause your feet to swell by as much as half a shoe size, so you'll want to do your shoe shopping when your feet are likely to be largest. Another tip: When trying on shoes, wear the same type of socks you plan to use with the shoes.

Look for leather. Unlike nonporous vinyl and plastic materials, leather has microscopic pores that allow air to circulate, keeping the foot drier. The clusters of perforated holes primarily found on sports footwear serve the same purpose. Remember: A dry foot is less likely to develop blisters.

Break it in, if you must. Ideally, a shoe should fit well and feel comfortable when you try it on. Often, however, new shoes have stiff areas that take time to soften up. While you may be tempted to wear the new pair right away, your best bet is to break them in gradually. Wear them for limited amounts of time, switching to your old pair of shoes in between.

Don't exercise at midday. The heat of midday, especially in the summer, can make the feet perspire more, making them more blister-prone.

Never wear wet shoes. The wetness can cause more "dragging" between the foot and shoe and can result in blisters. If you jog twice a day, for instance, you may want to have two pairs of shoes, one that you wear for your first run of the day and another for the second; this way, each pair has more time to dry out.

Protect "hot spots." If you have a chronic "hot spot," or place where blisters tend to develop, apply petroleum jelly to it, then slip on your sock. Used alone, adhesive foam or felt pads (sometimes called moleskin) can also absorb the friction and protect a hot spot. For best results, make sure the padding covers more area than you think a blister would take up, since the neighboring areas can become irritated, too.

Wear the right socks. Specially made sport socks with extra padding in typical hot spots can help prevent blisters. Natural fibers such as cotton and wool tend to keep the feet dry by absorbing moisture. However, some research suggests that acrylic fibers may, through a wicking action, move moisture away from the feet, actually keeping them drier and making them less prone to blistering. Your best bet? Try each to determine which type keeps your feet drier and more comfortable. In addition, be sure the socks fit your feet, so they don't bunch up inside the shoes and cause blisters.

Try a sprinkle. Foot powders may aid in keeping feet dry and preventing painful blisters.

Body Odor

7 STEPS TO SWEET-SMELLING SUCCESS

In some cultures and countries, intense body odor is considered a desirable characteristic, signifying greater sexual attractiveness and even prowess. But let's face it, in the United States, a pungent body aroma is not going to make you the life of the party. So powerful is our cultural distaste for body odor that every day, some 95 percent of all Americans over the age of 12 reach for one product or another that will enable them to feel safe and secure in the company of others.

Body odor begins with sweat. The body has two types of sweat glands, and both types produce sweat that is made up largely of water. The eccrine glands, which are located on almost every part of the body, produce the sweat that cools the body. The apocrine glands, which are located in the armpits, around the nipples, and in the groin, produce sweat whose function is not clear. One thing is obvious, however: The sweat from the apocrine glands can make you stink. The reason is that apocrine sweat contains a substantial amount of oil, which provides food for bacteria. It's this bacterial

feeding frenzy that creates the odor that keeps others at a distance.

If you'd prefer that your body odor didn't announce your presence to those far and near, here's what you can do:

Keep it clean. The strength of the odor a person produces depends on how much their glands secrete as well as the number of bacteria on their skin. People with strong underarm odors carry two to three times as many underarm bacteria as others. The best way to prevent body odor is to wash away sweat and bacteria. Clean the underarm and groin areas with water and soap, preferably a deodorant soap, at least once a day—and more often, if necessary.

Bathe your britches. Sweat that seeps into your clothing may remind you of its presence at very inopportune times. What's more,

once it has dried, bacteria-containing sweat can damage the fibers of your clothing. Wear clean clothing, socks, and underwear every day. If you sweat a lot, wear clothing made of cotton, linen, or other natural material, which helps absorb sweat and facilitate airflow.

Try a deodorant. For milder cases of body odor, a deodorant may help. Deodorants are considered cosmetics. Most contain a substance that helps kill the bacteria waiting to feed on your sweat. They may also help mask body odor by substituting a more acceptable scent.

Get tough with an antiperspirant. Since body odor begins with sweat, one of the best ways to control it is to reduce the amount of sweat. That's what antiperspirants are for.

Antiperspirants are classified by the Food and Drug Administration as over-the-counter drugs because they are intended to alter a natural body function—namely, they decrease the production of eccrine sweat. (While apocrine sweat contains the oil upon which bacteria feed, neither an antiperspirant nor a deodorant can decrease apocrine sweat.) By decreasing the production of eccrine sweat, antiperspirants help keep you drier, thus reducing the moisture that creates a fertile breeding ground for bacteria. For added protection, antiperspirants

usually also contain an antibacterial agent that fights odor.

Beat irritation and odor. If you've tried antiperspirants and deodorants and found that they irritate your skin, you might instead try washing with an antibacterial soap such as chlorhexidine (Hibiclens) or applying an over-the-counter antibiotic ointment. Other options for sensitive skin include using talcum powder or baking soda in place of an antiperspirant or deodorant.

Quiet your diet. Certain foods, such as hot peppers, can affect the amount of sweat an individual produces. And the aroma of other pungent foods, such as garlic, onions, spices, and alcohol, can be carried in your sweat.

Tone down that temper. Anger, anxiety, and excitement also increase production of sweat. Consider learning and practicing a technique, such as meditation or visualization, that can help you maintain your calm under stressful circumstances.

Breast-Feeding Discomfort

20 Ways to Beat the Breast-Feeding Blues

Throughout your pregnancy, you probably imagined how wonderful the breast-feeding experience would be for both you and your baby. All you could think about was looking down into that tiny, trusting face and feeling the closeness between you and this new little being. So naturally, when it finally came time to put baby to breast, you were excited. But now, you're in agony. Your nipples may be painful, cracked, and bleeding. Or perhaps your breasts are uncomfortably swollen. The milk may not flow when you need it to and may seem to flow uncontrollably when you most wish it wouldn't (when you're standing in line at the grocery store or sitting at a dinner party). So where are those tender, happy moments you've seen in magazine and television advertisements?

Well, hang in there. Those moments do happen, just not always right away. The problem is, many mothers give up breast-feeding in frustration because they don't realize that things will get better with time and practice. They also don't realize there are steps they can take to decrease breast-feeding discomfort and increase nursing success.

As for what causes breast-feeding pain, it depends on where the pain occurs. Pain in the nipple, for example, is most often caused by the baby latching onto the breast incorrectly. Nipple discomfort can also result from a certain fashion choice and therefore tends to be more prevalent in American women: Women in the United States are more likely to wear bras, which protect the delicate nipples and leave them more sensitive to the friction and exposure that comes with breast-feeding. In contrast, many foreign women go braless much or all of the time and often sunbathe in the nude, which gradually toughen the nipples. As a result, they experience less discomfort when they begin nursing a child. Preexisting conditions, such as inverted nipples or nipple sensitivity that developed during the pregnancy, can also lead to breast-feeding discomfort.

Pain in the fleshy part of the breast, on the other hand, is most often caused by engorgement of the breast with milk. This is most likely to occur during the first few days after your milk comes in, before your body has a chance to adjust its milk production to the needs of your baby. Initially, a woman's body makes enough milk for twins but then gradually changes its milk production based on the amount of milk regularly removed from the breasts. So if you are nursing only one baby, your body gradually lowers the amount of milk it produces to match the amount consumed by the single baby. (You'll discover shortly why this is an important point to remember.)

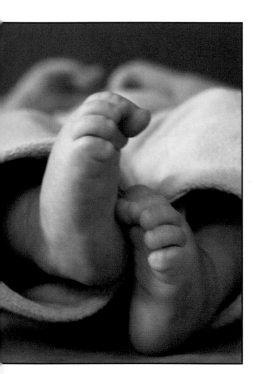

Engorgement can also occur any time the amount of milk produced exceeds your baby's ability to siphon it off, such as when the baby's appetite is diminished due to illness. Mild cases can even occur between feedings, especially if feedings are spaced several hours apart or if a feeding is unexpectedly delayed. Fortunately, no matter the cause, the engorgement will naturally resolve itself within a few days if not sooner (as long as you don't do anything that encourages your body to make too much milk).

To prevent discomfort from turning you off breast-feeding, it helps to keep in mind that breast-feeding is a *learned* skill, and you'll need time, practice, and patience to make it a comfortable, successful experience. It's also important to remember that the early days of nursing may leave your breasts a bit tender and sore, but pain, cracking, blistering, or bleeding means there's a problem that needs to be solved. Fortunately, most breast-feeding problems can be remedied—and the pain either alleviated or prevented—with some fairly simple adjustments. The tips and techniques that follow can help you solve your nursing difficulties so that breast-feeding can truly become that beautiful bonding experience you always hoped it would be.

Make sure the baby latches on correctly. It bears repeating that incorrect positioning of the breast in the baby's mouth is by far the most common cause of nipple pain and damage in breast-feeding women. You DO NOT want your baby to clamp onto the nipple itself. Rather, the nipple should be at the back of the baby's mouth, near the throat, so her lips and gums close around the areola (the circle of skin surrounding the nipple that is a different color than the fleshy part of the breast). Otherwise, you are likely to experience pain or pinching as soon as the baby latches on, and over time, the tender nipple skin is likely to crack and bleed, opening the door to infection.

To help ensure proper form, hold your baby in one arm so that the front of her whole body—not just her head—is facing yours. Using your other hand, place two fingers above the areola and three below to support the breast and "steer" the nipple. Be sure your fingers are behind the areola, so they won't get in the way as your baby latches onto it. Brush the baby's lower lip with the tip of your breast to get her to open her mouth wide. Then quickly pull her in close and slide your nipple into the back of her mouth before she can close her mouth around it. If you feel a general tenderness or a sharp, pinching pain when the baby first latches on, chances are you were not quick enough, and she latched onto the nipple rather than the areola. If so, simply remove her from your breast and try again until her mouth closes around your areola and her sucking no longer causes you pain.

Ease the release. If you need to remove the baby from your breast, don't just pull the two apart. First break the suction that's holding them together. Do this by gently sliding one of your fingers between the corner of the baby's mouth and the breast. Otherwise, it can feel like you're trying to pull a working vacuum cleaner off your nipple.

Use a prop. Try putting a pillow on your lap to help you hold the baby near your breast, so that his mouth is level with your nipple. If you hold him too low, he will tug downward on your breast and will likely end up with your nipple between his gums as he nurses.

Nurse, nurse, nurse. There was a time when new mothers were encouraged to nurse their babies only at set intervals spaced several hours apart. But this approach often left the babies hungry and cranky and left their mothers' breasts painfully full between feedings. Thankfully, most baby doctors now believe that during the first weeks after birth, the baby should be offered the breast whenever she shows the early signs of hunger and should be allowed to continue each feeding until she is satisfied. (Early hunger signals in a newborn include an increase in alertness or activity, rooting, or mouthing; crying is actually a fairly late sign of hunger.) That generally translates into a minimum of 8 to 12 feedings in every 24-hour period (try for a feeding at least every two hours, except perhaps during the night, when you may be able to feed slightly less often), with each feeding lasting at least 10 to 15 minutes. Even a sleeping infant should be woken up to feed if it's been four hours since the start of her last feeding. Having the baby's crib in the same room that the mother is sleeping in during these first few

Hello, Doctor?

If none of these tips seems to help much, it's time to see your doctor to rule out the possibility of a breast infection or other problem. In addition, your local chapter of the La Leche League and most hospital maternity wards can offer over-the-phone or online answers to your breast-feeding questions. (Check your local yellow pages.)

days or weeks can make such frequent feeding a little easier.

Many doctors say that by letting the baby nurse almost continuously, especially during the first 12 to 24 hours after your milk comes in, you may be able to avoid the initial engorgement that normally occurs when the milk comes in; your baby will slowly but steadily siphon off milk, preventing the fullness from reaching the point of pain. But even if you can't completely head off engorgement, frequent feeding will help ease your discomfort during the week or so after birth that the body may need to adjust its milk production to suit your baby's needs.

If you instead trap yourself into feeding the baby on a preset schedule, only offering the breast every three to four hours during the day and letting her sleep as long as she wants, your milk will come in and make your breasts look and feel as if they're going to explode.

Try the "burp and switch" strategy. Always begin feeding the baby on the sorest breast or the one that seems to be the fullest. After five minutes, burp him and switch breasts. Keep switching and burping every five minutes until he is through feeding. This "burp and switch" method ensures that the baby drains both breasts sufficiently, rather than tanking up on one and leaving the other one painfully overfull.

Warm up for feedings. Fifteen minutes before feeding your baby, warm up your breasts. Try soaking a bath towel in hot water, wringing it out, and then laying it across your breasts. You can even cover the towel with a plastic garbage bag to help it retain heat longer. After removing the towel, massage each breast from the fleshy part down to the nipple to encourage the release of milk into the nipple. You'll be glad you did since an empty nipple is much more likely than a full one to be painful during nursing.

Express if necessary to ease engorgement. If breast-feeding on demand has not prevented painful engorgement and your breasts are so full and hard that the baby cannot latch on properly, it is okay to express enough milk by hand to ease your discomfort and allow your baby to suckle. But you should avoid expressing too much milk this way or with a breast pump. That's because the body doesn't know the difference between a pump and a baby's mouth, so whenever milk is siphoned from the breast, the body thinks it's being used by the baby and makes more to compensate for that loss. So the more you express, the more milk your body will produce—not exactly what you want when your breasts are already uncomfortably full. (If your baby is ill and unable to nurse when engorgement occurs, however, ask your pediatrician

Treating Breast Infections

Cracked and bleeding nipples brought on by those first few days of breast-feeding can leave you vulnerable to infection of the breast, called mastitis. While it is rarely serious, mastitis can be quite painful and cannot be cured without the use of an antibiotic.

Signs that you may have mastitis include:

- a reddened area on the fleshy part of the breast that is painful to the touch and ranges from the size of a quarter to the whole side of the breast
- a fever of up to 102 degrees Fahrenheit
- general achiness
- chills

The symptoms tend to come on rapidly, and you may experience only one or two of them or all of them at once. While you will need to see a doctor if you suspect you have mastitis or any other breast infection, there are a few things you should do on your own as your infection is being treated:

Continue nursing, starting with the infected breast each time. This may sound like sheer lunacy when you are in so much pain, but it helps clear the infection. And don't be worried that you'll hurt the baby; it's the area around the milk duct—not the milk itself—that is infected. Try nursing at least every two to three hours, and more frequently if the baby is willing.

Prior to nursing, pack the breast in heat. Use a warm towel with a plastic bag over it to better retain the heat. Once the breast is warm, massage it from the fleshy part where it attaches to the chest down to the nipple. Spend extra time gently massaging the sore spot.

Get in bed. You need to go on full bed rest while you fight the infection. This is your time to take care of yourself and let everyone else nurture you. Usually, it takes only about 24 to 36 hours for the pain to pass. Be sure to continue taking the antibiotics as directed for the full time prescribed, however, even if you feel better before then.

Another problem that can cause breast discomfort is a clogged milk duct. It is characterized by a hard, uncomfortable lump in the fleshy part of the breast that can be very tender to the touch. It isn't usually accompanied by a fever. To relieve the pain of a clogged duct, pack the breast in heat before feedings, get the baby to nurse on the affected breast first, and massage the hard spot the whole time the baby is nursing to loosen up the milk and unclog the duct. A clogged duct usually resolves itself within 24 hours. If the pain and other symptoms of a clogged duct don't clear up in that time, contact your doctor. Milk that remains locked in a duct for more than a day raises the risk of infection, because the fluid may leak into the breast tissue, where it creates a moist environment for bacteria.

It's important to keep in mind that a pattern of problems can occur when a minor problem with breast-feeding is not addressed promptly and properly. This pattern often begins with sore nipples. Unless adjustments are made to the breast-feeding technique and other care is taken to ease the discomfort, the nipple soreness may prompt the mother to limit breast-feeding, which in turn can lead to engorgement. Engorgement may promote clogged ducts that, if slow to resolve, can lead to breast infection. On the other hand, paying prompt attention to sore nipples and engorgement can often prevent clogged ducts and infection from ever developing.

or a lactation consultant for advice on pumping to ensure an adequate supply of breast milk when your infant can once again nurse.) If you can avoid sending your body such a mixed message, it will automatically lower its milk production to suit your baby's needs, and the engorgement will pass.

Stand in a warm shower. Allowing the water to spray directly on the breasts usually causes milk to drip from the nipples, which can relieve some of

the pressure from engorgement. But unlike pumping, this technique doesn't prompt the body to produce more milk. It just provides a little welcome relief. Another option: Take off your bra, fill a sink with warm water, and splash it onto your breasts.

Air them out. Try to expose your nipples to air whenever possible to help toughen them up and to prevent continuous contact with moisture, which can cause nipple irritation, soreness, and even damage. If you finish nursing and immediately put a nursing pad and bra back on, you're likely to get some milk leakage; the pad and bra will then hold this moisture against the nipple. Consider keeping your bra flaps open (on a nursing bra) or going braless under a light T-shirt for at least 15 minutes after feeding. If you were planning to nap after a feeding, you might also consider napping braless.

Wear a supportive bra that breathes. A good-quality bra that fits well will provide support and help protect your breasts from additional trauma. Be sure it's not too tight, which will only add to your soreness. And opt for one made of a natural fiber, such as cotton, that allows air flow and encourages evaporation. Bras made of synthetic fibers may hold in heat, increase sweating, and trap moisture against the breast skin.

Try "cold storage." Between feedings, put ice packs on your breasts, and wear a bra to hold the packs in place (put a thin cloth between the ice pack and the breast skin, however, to prevent frostbite). Some women use bags of frozen peas or carrots as ice packs, but here's an even better idea: Fill four resealable freezer bags with unpopped popcorn, and freeze them for use as ice packs. Not only do the popcorn kernels hold the cold longer, they don't turn mushy as they warm. And unlike most commercial ice packs, the bag of kernels will mold more closely to the shape of your breast.

Skip the soap. Although you don't want the nipple skin to be moist for extended periods, you also don't want it to become dry, chapped, irritated, and cracked, which can leave it vulnerable to infection. So when you bathe, try to avoid using soap directly on the nipples, since this will strip away the natural skin oils that keep the skin supple and hydrated.

Try some olive oil. If you notice that your nipples feel dry or chapped between feedings, smear on a bit of olive oil, some expressed breast milk, or an unscented, dye-free ointment that contains lanolin.

Massage the nipples with an ice cube. It's not a cure, but numbing the tender area will provide temporary relief from pain caused by breast-feeding.

Ice baby's gums. Babies will commonly gnaw on anything they can fit in their little mouths to help relieve the pain of teething. When your baby begins to cut teeth, therefore, don't be surprised if she tries to use your nipples as a teething aid. To help numb your baby's gums and relieve some of the teething discomfort while defending your nipples, try refrigerating or freezing a clean, wet washcloth and allowing baby to suck on it for a few minutes prior to nursing on each breast.

Take acetaminophen if you develop a fever. It is common for women who are breast-feeding to develop a low-grade fever as high as 100.6 degrees Fahrenheit. Acetaminophen should help lower the fever and make you feel a little better, and it is generally recognized as safe for occasional use during breast-feeding. Still, to be on the safe side, check with your baby's doctor before taking this or any medication while you are nursing, and review the analgesic warnings in the box on page 21.

Or take ibuprofen, especially if you feel achy. There's no denying it: Breast-feeding is a workout, and like a tough session at the gym, some days it will leave you with aches and pains. On such occasions, ibuprofen may provide relief (it will also help lower any fever). Again, however, it should be used only occasionally, only with the approval of your baby's doctor while you are breast-feeding, and only after you review the warnings in the box on page 21.

Taking the Pain Out of Weaning

Once you get through the initial discomfort of breast-feeding, nursing generally becomes easy and relatively painless—until, of course, that fateful day when you decide it is time to wean your baby off the breast. Weaning can be more than emotionally uncomfortable for you; it can also cause physical pain. That's because as you decrease feedings, it takes a little time for your body to catch on and produce less milk, so the engorgement of those early days often returns.

There is no consensus among doctors on the best way to wean a baby. Some recommend stopping all at once, while others advise mothers to adopt the more gradual approach. For Mom, it is a little more comfortable to do it slowly, but some babies decide to wean themselves and one day simply reject the breast for good. If you choose to wean the baby gradually, start by eliminating one feeding every two days or so. Make the morning and evening feedings the last ones you drop, since most babies have an intense desire to nurse at these times. It is also important to never drop two feedings in a row. In other words, if you typically breast-feed your baby twice in the morning, twice in the afternoon, and twice in the evening, avoid dropping one morning feeding one day and another morning feeding two days later. Instead, try dropping one morning feeding, then an afternoon feeding, then an evening feeding.

As far as the pain of engorgement that can result, there are a few things you can do. Applying gentle pressure to the glands can limit the amount of milk they hold, so try wrapping an elastic bandage or towel around your chest. You can also reduce engorgement and swelling with ice packs, which will decrease circulation in the breasts. And with your doctor's approval, you can take an over-the-counter anti-inflammatory medication, such as aspirin or ibuprofen, to ease the pain of engorgement (but review the warnings in the box on page 21 first).

Finally, try to avoid any extra stimulation to your breasts, which will cause them to produce more milk—the last thing you want during weaning.

Bronchitis

7 WAYS TO BEAR THE BATTLE

You thought you were finally shaking that cold, but this morning your cough is worse than ever. You're coughing up phlegm by the cupful, and it feels as if someone spent the night tap-dancing on your chest. You've probably developed acute bronchitis, an often painful infection in the major bronchial tubes (airways) leading to the lungs.

Acute bronchitis is most often caused by a virus, frequently the same one that causes colds, although the flu virus is a common culprit as well. (While acute bronchitis can also be caused by bacteria or even fungi, they are only rarely to blame.) Acute bronchitis often follows a cold or the flu, when resistance is down and the lungs may already be slightly irritated. Likewise, anyone whose resistance is low or who has any other type of chronic lung irritation or injury—especially from exposure to cigarette smoke or other toxic gases—is at increased risk of developing bronchitis. And the viruses that cause bronchitis can be passed to others much the same way cold and flu viruses are: An infected person coughs, spraying viral particles either into the air, where they can be breathed in by others, or onto their own hands, where a handshake can pass them to someone else.

The virus attacks the inner walls of the bronchial tubes, which then swell and produce greatly increased amounts of thick, yellow or green mucus (the airways normally produce about an ounce a day of thin, clear or white mucus, which helps trap and remove foreign particles). The lung irritation and mucus trigger a throaty, persistent, productive hacking that is the hallmark of acute bronchitis. It can be accompanied by an irritated throat (from the coughing), burning or aching pain just beneath the breastbone, a feeling of tightness in the chest, wheezing or shortness of breath, and/or a "rattling" sensation in the lungs and chest. A low-grade fever, chills, and achiness may also occur. The irritation caused by the virus also leaves the respiratory tract vulnerable to other complications, such as pneumonia.

If you have an underlying chronic disease or suffer from asthma, allergies, chronic obstructive pulmonary disease (COPD), or any other serious respiratory or heart problem, you need to contact your doctor if you develop symptoms of acute bronchitis. Bronchitis symptoms in infants, the elderly, or anyone else with a weak immune system also require medical attention. If you're otherwise healthy, however, you will likely have to allow the infection to simply run its course. Antibiotics, after all, are useless against viral infections. Fortunately, acute bronchitis generally goes away on its own within a few days or a week, although the cough can sometimes linger for weeks or even months. Until your body has shaken the infection, however, there are some things you can do to decrease discomfort and help your body heal:

Humidify your environment.
Believe it or not, coughing is actually good for you. It's the body's way of eliminating the infection that causes bronchitis. So instead of stifling a cough with an over-the-counter suppressant, help it along by using a warm- or cool-mist humidifier to add moisture to the air. (Take care to use and clean the humidifier according to the manufacturer's instructions.) The added humidity will help bring the sputum up and out of the body. Standing in a steamy shower with the bathroom door closed or keeping a pan of water at a slow boil on the stove (Never leave it unattended!) can also help loosen and bring up phlegm.

Drink plenty of liquids. Taking in extra liquids helps keep the sputum more fluid and therefore easier to expel. It doesn't really matter what type of liquid you drink, although tea, soup, and other warm liquids may feel better than cold ones. As a bonus, warm fluids may also soothe the irritated throat that may result from all that coughing.

Gargle with warm salt water.
Gargling with salt water may provide a double dose of relief by soothing the inflammation in the throat and by cutting through some of the mucus that may be coating and irritating the sensitive throat membranes. It only takes one teaspoon of salt in a glass of warm water (8 to 10 ounces); too much salt causes burning in the throat, and too little is ineffective. Gargle as often as needed, but be sure to spit the salty water out after gargling.

Rest, rest, rest. Since your bout with bronchitis probably followed on the heels of a cold or the flu, you may find it hard to sit still any longer. But walking around with bronchitis will only make you feel worse and slow your body's ability to fight the infection, so you'll need to take it easy a little longer. Those who *won't* be exposed to your germs will thank you, too.

Take aspirin or ibuprofen to relieve the chest pain. If a bout with bronchitis produces muscle pain in the

Bronchitis and Smokers

Smoking is a habit that is continually under fire for its negative impact on a person's health. And rightly so. It has been proven to be a significant contributing factor in emphysema, lung cancer, heart disease, and several other serious illnesses. It leaves you more vulnerable to acute bronchitis and other respiratory infections, aggravates any such infection that does take hold, and slows your body's ability to heal. Because a smoker's bronchial tubes are already irritated, any additional inflammation caused by acute bronchitis may require medical attention. Smoking is also the primary cause of chronic bronchitis—an ongoing irritation of the lining of the bronchial tubes marked by a perpetual cough that brings up mucus, tightness in the chest, and difficulty breathing.

Needless to say, refraining from smoking or at least cutting way back is essential when battling a case of acute bronchitis. To treat or prevent chronic bronchitis, quitting for good and avoiding exposure to other people's cigarette smoke are essential.

chest, these anti-inflammatory pain medications may provide some relief. Acetaminophen also eases pain but does not have an anti-inflammatory effect and so may be less helpful. Because of the risk of a deadly reaction called Reye syndrome, don't give aspirin to children; use acetaminophen instead. And be sure to review the warnings in the box on page 21 before using any analgesic (pain medicine).

Use a cough remedy as a last resort.

Remember, coughing is your body's way of driving out the infection and keeping your breathing passages clear. The best cough remedies for bronchitis contain guaifenesin, which helps bring up sputum. But if you're at the end of your rope and can't bear another minute of hacking—especially if it's been keeping you from getting the sleep you need to recover—you can try a medicine that contains the cough suppressant dextromethorphan. Take it only as often as absolutely needed. Combination products should generally be avoided; decongestants, antihistamines, and alcohol (common ingredients in combination products) have no role in the treatment of coughs and may even increase discomfort by causing side effects. Most of the candy-type cough drops act only as demulcents on the throat—in other words, their soothing properties are due largely to their sugar content.

Keep an eye out for complications. While letting nature take its course is generally the best treatment for acute bronchitis, complications can sometimes occur, so you'll need to stay alert for signs that it's time to see your doctor. The most worrisome complications include pneumonia, sinus infection, and ear infection, which may need to be treated with prescription medications. Signs that one or more of these complications may be present include a persistent high fever (not a typical characteristic of bronchitis), severe shortness of breath, prolonged coughing spells or a cough that lasts more than four to six weeks, severe chest pain, pain behind the eyes, or ear pain. Be on the lookout for blood in your sputum or sputum that changes dramatically in color or consistency, too, and report it to your doctor.

In addition, tell your doctor if you suffer frequent bouts of bronchitis, since you may be suffering from a more serious respiratory problem that requires medical treatment.

Bursitis

10 Ways to Ax the Ache

Bursitis has some funny nicknames. It's called Housemaid's Knee, Clergyman's Knee, and Baker's Cyst, among others. But anyone who has actually experienced the pain of bursitis knows that it's no laughing matter.

The bursa is a fluid-filled sac that helps protect muscle, ligaments, tendons, or skin that rubs across bone. There are bursae throughout our bodies, but the ones most likely to become inflamed are those in the shoulders, elbows, knees, and heels.

The painful inflammation of a bursa is called bursitis. It's caused by bumping or bruising, repeated pressure, or overuse. It can develop after performing an activity you're not used to doing or after increasing a familiar activity.

Sometimes, bursitis can flare up without a clue as to what has caused it. All you know is, it hurts. The good news is, once you tone down your activity, your symptoms should begin to disappear. Here's how to speed your recovery along:

Give it a rest. The pain of bursitis may disappear completely after a few days of resting the affected joint. This doesn't mean ceasing all movement. Particularly in a shoulder, immobilization could "freeze" the joint with adhesions (fibrous tissue) and scar tissue. Just take it easy and try to avoid the movement or activity that brought on the pain.

Get new shoes. If you have bursitis on your heel, you probably got it because of improperly fitting shoes. The solution is simple: Toss the shoes, and put on a better-fitting pair.

Make a change. Search for ways to adjust the activity or habit that sparked the pain to lessen the stress it puts on your joints. If crawling around in the garden or laying flooring has left you with bursitis of the knee, get yourself a low stool to sit on instead or buy a pair of sturdy, well-cushioned kneepads. If leaning on your elbows while reading has caused your elbows to swell and ache, use a book holder to prop up your reading material and take the weight off your arms.

Don't Shrug Off Joint Pain

Don't be too quick to label your joint pain as bursitis, especially if your condition doesn't improve after a few days of rest and home remedies or if the pain is interfering with your everyday activities or your sleep. There are many conditions for which joint pain is a symptom, but absolutely none for which pain and swelling should be ignored. If self-care hasn't brought the pain and swelling under control, if either has gotten worse, or if you have lost any function in the joint, get to an orthopedist, sports-medicine physician, or other medical doctor experienced in treating problems in the affected joint.

Deflate the inflammation. Take two regular-strength aspirin or ibuprofen four times a day to reduce the swelling of the bursa; this will also help ease the pain. Be sure to check the analgesic warnings in the box on page 21 first, however, since even these over-the-counter medicines are not appropriate for everyone. Also, avoid giving aspirin to children.

Skip the acetaminophen. Unlike aspirin and ibuprofen, this over-the-counter pain reliever isn't an anti-inflammatory, so it doesn't do as much to combat bursitis.

Put it on ice. Ice brings down swelling by slowing blood flow to the area. Apply a commercial ice pack or a bag of crushed ice, frozen peas, or frozen popcorn kernels to the joint for about 20 minutes—twice as long if your bursitis is deep in the joint—three or four times a day. Protect your skin by putting a towel or cloth between the ice pack/bag and bare skin.

Warm it up. After the initial swelling has been brought down (usually about three to four days), heat from a heating pad or heat pack will not only feel good but will get rid of excess fluid by increasing circulation.

Use a stepladder. Overhead reaching or pushing and pulling at or above shoulder level may worsen shoulder pain. If you can't reach something easily, use a stepladder, or better yet, have someone else get it for you.

Get in the swing of things. As soon as the pain has eased enough to allow it, you need to begin gently moving the affected joint through its full range of motion. A doctor or physical therapist can prescribe a set of exercises designed to do just that for your affected joint. For bursitis of the shoulder, for example, one effective exercise is the pendulum swing. To do this exercise, bend at the waist, and support your weight by leaning your good arm against a desk or chair back. Slowly swing your sore arm back and forth and then in clockwise and counterclockwise circles.

Play "Itsy Bitsy Spider." Another gentle exercise you can do to restore your shoulder's range of motion is to crawl your hand up the wall, like a spider. Make it a laid-back spider, however. During the healing process, anything other than slow, controlled movement within the joint's natural range of motion may do more harm than good.

Canker Sores

9 SOOTHING STRATEGIES

It may only be the size of a pencil eraser, but a canker sore can be hard to ignore. You know it's there—and it hurts like the dickens, especially whenever you eat or drink.

Fortunately, a canker sore is usually a fairly short-lived misery, and there are a few things you can do to find some temporary relief.

First, however, you need to be able to tell the difference between a canker sore and a cold sore, or fever blister, which is caused by the herpes virus. A cold sore often begins as several tiny blisters that eventually form one larger sore. They appear most often on the lips and face.

In contrast, canker sores usually travel alone. And unlike a sore caused by the herpes virus, a canker sore is not contagious. A canker sore has a yellow or white-gray center with a well-defined red border. It generally measures three to five millimeters in diameter and is usually located on the inside of the lip or cheek or, less commonly, on the tongue.

What causes canker sores? No one knows for sure, though they frequently afflict people who are fatigued or stressed out or who have poor diets. Cankers may also occur as a result of a minor injury in the mouth, such as from a slip of the toothpick or a jab from a taco shell. Certain foods, such as spicy dishes and citrus fruits, have also taken some of the blame.

About 20 percent of the population get canker sores occasionally, and women are more likely than men to suffer from them. Some women tend to get them at certain times of their menstrual cycle.

Here's what you can do for relief. Keep in mind, though, that—as some doctors are fond of telling patients—a canker sore will last seven days with treatment and one week without treatment. In some cases, a canker sore can take up to two weeks to heal; if one sticks around longer than that, see your dentist.

Get out the styptic pencil. Many a barber has used a styptic pencil to stem bleeding from minor nicks and cuts. Used on a canker sore, it will

Hello, Doctor?

If you suffer from frequent canker sores, consult your dentist. Same goes if you have a canker sore that is an inch or more in diameter or leaves a scar when it heals. And definitely get to your dentist or physician if your temperature rises; a fever may indicate that the canker sore has become infected (from poor oral hygiene, dirty fingers in the mouth, or chewing tobacco), in which case you would likely need an antibiotic.

If you've got a sore that doesn't go away, see your dentist, even if it doesn't bother you. Ironically, while a canker sore hurts and stings, a painless ulcer in the mouth may be the first sign of oral cancer. And while a canker sore will usually disappear in seven to ten days, a cancerous lesion will not. About 30,000 new cases of oral cancer are diagnosed each year in the United States.

Other conditions that require medical care can also cause mouth ulcers that resemble canker sores, including iron deficiency anemia, pernicious (vitamin B_{12} deficiency) anemia, folic acid deficiency, gluten intolerance, celiac disease, and Crohn's disease.

numb the nerve endings, temporarily reducing the pain.

Make your own remedy. Several dentists swear by this homemade remedy: Mix together equal amounts Milk of Magnesia or Kaopectate liquid and Benylin or Benadryl liquid. Milk of Magnesia and Kaopectate both contain ingredients that coat wet tissues, such as those in the mouth. Benylin and Benadryl contain ingredients that act as mild topical anesthetics and antihistamines (which reduce inflammation). Every few hours, apply the mixture to the canker sore using a cotton swab. Be careful not to swallow the stuff; you could end up anesthetizing (numbing) the reflex that keeps the windpipe closed when you swallow.

Go over-the-counter. Use a nonprescription product such as Orabase with Benzocaine, which covers the surface of the sore like an oral bandage. Keeping it coated will help prevent infection. Products with xylocaine, a local anesthetic, can dull the pain.

Take two aspirin. A dose of aspirin, acetaminophen, or ibuprofen may help relieve the pain, especially before

meals if the canker sore interferes with eating. Review the warnings in the box on page 21 first, however.

Stick to cool foods. Stay away from foods that are hot—in terms of temperature or spiciness—or acidic. They'll burn and sting a tender canker sore.

Be gentle. Wield that toothbrush extra carefully to avoid irritating a canker sore. You may want to avoid rough, scratchy foods, such as chips, for the time being as well.

Stop bad habits. Alcohol and smoking can irritate a canker sore. A little abstinence may provide a lot of relief.

Check out your diet. One old bit of folk wisdom blames canker sores on tomatoes. And there are experts who admit that some sort of allergic reaction to foods may be to blame. But others point out that food allergies can cause lesions that resemble canker sores. So if you're plagued with frequent canker sores, pay attention to whether an outbreak seems to be linked with any particular food. Likely offenders include nuts, shellfish, chocolate, and tomatoes. If you discover a connection, avoid the offending food.

Learn to handle stress. That's the best advice for preventing canker sores. Try to find some healthy method of relieving or coping with stress, such as engaging in a hobby, an exercise program, yoga, or meditation.

Carpal Tunnel Syndrome

24 TIPS FOR PROTECTING YOUR WRISTS

If your job or hobby requires you to spend a good deal of time punching cash register keys, gripping strings or holes on a musical instrument, twisting a screwdriver, clicking a sluggish computer mouse, or doing any other repetitive, forceful movement with your hands, you may be at risk for a painful condition called carpal tunnel syndrome (CTS). The same appears to be true if you use your hands to control a jackhammer or other powerful, vibrating tool.

CTS is a collection of symptoms that generally includes episodes of numbness, tingling or a pins and needles sensation, burning, and aching in the thumb, index and middle fingers, and thumb-side of the ring finger. Early on, these symptoms tend to appear in the middle of the night or shortly after an extended period of repetitive motion, and shaking out the hand often brings relief. As the condition worsens, the discomfort occurs more frequently and becomes more bothersome. In severe cases, pain may shoot from the wrist up the forearm and even into the shoulder, the numbness in the fingers and thumb may become constant, and the thumb

muscles may waste away, causing a loss of grip strength and coordination.

To understand why CTS occurs, it helps to take a look inside the wrist. The carpal tunnel is a narrow passageway that runs through the wrist. It is only about the size of a postage stamp, but it is crowded with nerves, blood vessels, and nine different tendons—packed in like strands of spaghetti—that control finger movement. Repetitive motions or certain medical conditions can cause the tendons to swell, decreasing blood flow and compressing the median nerve, which controls movement and sensation in the thumb, the index and middle fingers, and one side of the ring finger. (The median nerve does not control the pinky, so if your symptoms extend to your

little finger, carpal tunnel syndrome is most likely not your problem.) This compression is what causes the episodes of numbness, tingling, and burning of CTS. If left unchecked, muscle wasting and permanent damage to the nerve can result.

By far the most common cause of CTS is repetitive, forceful movements of the hand, especially with the wrist bent or the hand in an awkward position, that irritate the tendons and cause them to swell. For this reason, CTS, like tendinitis and bursitis, is considered a "cumulative trauma disorder." How-

ever, medical conditions such as rheumatoid arthritis, hypothyroidism (low levels of thyroid hormone), pregnancy, and overweight can also cause symptoms of CTS by causing swelling within the tightly packed carpal tunnel.

For most people, the key to beating this syndrome is prevention—making changes *before* CTS becomes a problem. If you're already experiencing some minor tingling, numb-

ness, and burning associated with CTS, you may be able to prevent further damage and promote healing by making a few simple changes in your lifestyle. The tips that follow can help you keep your hands and wrists healthy and help reduce symptoms of CTS. However, if your symptoms are severe (if they interfere with your daily activities, for example), if they don't resolve after two weeks of self-care, or if they are accompanied by fever, swelling, a rash or redness on the wrist, or any loss of function or muscle mass, contact your doctor.

Stay in shape. You'll be less likely to suffer injury if your body's circulation and repair systems work well. Help your body out by eating nutritiously, getting adequate sleep and rest, and exercising regularly. Also, be sure to quit smoking, which inhibits circulation to all areas of the body, including the wrists and hands.

Don't lose while you snooze. CTS symptoms often come on at night and may wake you up. Some doctors believe this is because the fluid in the body is redistributed when you lie down, so more of it accumulates in the wrist. But another contributing factor may be your sleeping position: You may sleep with your wrist bent and/or tucked under your head or pillow, which can cause compression of the median nerve. So when you settle down

for the night, rest your wrist flat on the mattress, and don't use it as a prop for your head. You may also want to ask your doctor about a splint (see "Nix flimsy splints" on page 69).

Take some weight off. Excess body weight can compress the median nerve in the wrist, so try to keep your weight within five to ten pounds of your ideal by eating right and exercising. Consult your doctor or a registered dietitian if you're unsure what your ideal weight is or how to achieve it.

Take minibreaks. Fatigue or tiredness in the joints or muscles is a warning sign to change your posture and/or pattern of movement. When your wrist, hand, or fingers begin to feel fatigued or achy, take a break. Shake out your hands, and if possible, get up and

walk around or at least stretch out your arms and adjust your position. Even a one- to two-minute break every 20 or 30 minutes helps, as does a longer break (of about 10 to 15 minutes) every hour or two.

Rotate jobs. Experts at the National Safety Council suggest that you rotate between jobs that use different muscles and avoid doing the same task for more than a few hours at a time. If your job doesn't allow rotation, talk with your supervisor or union about a change. Rotation reduces job stress and minimizes production losses, so it can benefit both employer and employee.

Keep it in "neutral." As you work, keep your body and your wrists in a comfortable, neutral position—straight, not bent or hunched over. Check the height of your computer screen (it should be at eye level). Rearrange the level of your keyboard or workstation so that you don't have to strain, reach, or bend your wrists; it should be at elbow height or just slightly below. Your wrists should always be in a straight line with your forearms. And be sure you are not too close to or far away from your work.

Get the right grip on it. Most of us have a tendency to grip with only the thumb, index, and middle fingers, which can increase pressure on the wrist and cause irritation of the corresponding tendons. If you have to grip or twist something, such as the lid of a jar, use your palm or your *whole* hand to distribute the load.

Alternate hands. Give your dominant hand a break whenever possible. Try using your other hand to do some tasks.

Watch those pressure points. Too often, typists rest their wrists on the sharp edge of a desk or table as they work, which can cause excess pressure on the wrists. Adjust your workstation, if necessary, to keep your wrists straight and off the edge.

Soften up and slow down. It's often powerful, repetitive movements done at high speed that cause carpal tunnel problems. Be mindful as you work, and apply only the force needed to accomplish the task at hand.

Decrease bad vibes. People who use vibrating tools, such as sanders, jackhammers, chisels, chain saws, grinders, riveters, and drills for extended periods appear to be at increased risk of developing wrist problems. If you are one of these folks, take frequent breaks and, when possible, operate the tool at the speed that causes the least vibration.

Go "ergo." Often, CTS can be prevented or treated by adopting tools and workstations that have been ergonomically redesigned to cause less stress on the body. Some tools have been designed to work with less force, while others now feature better grips and handles. Some knife manufacturers, for example, have redesigned meatpackers' knives so they require less wrist bending. Other companies have created aids, such as wrist rests for computer users and computer keyboards that require a lighter touch, which can prevent or reduce CTS problems. Even pens with soft, chubby barrels and smoothly flowing ink, which require less pinching and force from the fingers, are now commonplace. So look for items that can ease the strain on your wrists and hands, but be wary of "miracle" machines and gadgets that promise instant cures.

Watch for symptoms, and take action. Stay alert for the earliest signs of CTS—such as occasional numbness, burning, or a tingling or pins and needles sensation that wakes you up at night or that occurs or gets worse when you are gripping a newspaper or other object between your fingers—and take preventive and self-care steps immediately. Aching in your lower arms and morning stiffness in your fingers can also be early signals of mild repetitive movement injury.

Ice it. If you have CTS symptoms, reduce swelling and inflammation by placing an ice pack wrapped in a thin cloth on the wrist and forearm for 5 to 15 minutes two or three times a day. At the same time, however, be sure to take steps to eliminate the cause of the trauma to your wrist.

Prohibit heat. While ice can reduce inflammation and swelling, heat can worsen a carpal tunnel problem because it causes the tissues in the narrow passageway to swell.

Nix flimsy splints. A properly fitted wrist splint prescribed by a physician can help relieve CTS and may be especially useful when worn at night to keep the wrist in a neutral (unbent) position. Too often, however, people who develop CTS symptoms rush to the pharmacy or sporting-goods store for any old wrist splint as a home remedy. But sometimes the home remedy does more harm than good. If the splint is too flimsy, for example, it can allow the wrist to move, which defeats its purpose. If improperly fitted or worn, it may actually force the wrist into a stressful position and/or cause compression of the median nerve. And, if such splints are worn for too long, the muscles in the wrist area can begin to shrink.

Reach for over-the-counter relief. For minor pain, taking aspirin, acetaminophen, or ibuprofen can be helpful, although only the aspirin or ibuprofen

Stay Loose

Exercise can keep tendons loose, promote blood flow, and strengthen muscles. The National Safety Council suggests performing the following four exercises twice a day or whenever you need a break from a repetitive task. Stop any exercise, however, if it makes your symptoms worse.

Wrist Circles: With your palms down and your hands out, rotate both wrists five times in each direction.

Thumb Stretch: Hold out your right hand, and grasp your right thumb with your left hand. Pull the thumb out and back until you feel a gentle stretch. Hold for five to ten seconds, and release. Repeat three to five times on each thumb.

Five-Finger Stretch: Spread the fingers of both hands far apart and hold for five to ten seconds. Repeat three to five times.

Finger-Thumb Squeeze: Squeeze a small rubber ball tightly in one hand five to ten times. Afterward, stretch the fingers. Repeat with the other hand. (If you have high blood pressure, consult your doctor before regularly engaging in this exercise.)

The following exercises, which call for small handheld weights, can strengthen the wrists. Give them a try, but remember to stop if they make your symptoms worse.

Palm-Up Wrist Curls: Rest your forearm on a table with your palm facing upward and your hand held straight out over the edge of the table. With a light weight (one to two pounds) in your hand, flex your wrist upward ten times. Repeat using the other wrist. Over the course of several weeks, gradually build up to 40 repetitions on each wrist. Increase the weight of the dumbbells each week by one pound to a maximum of five pounds. Don't exceed five pounds with this exercise, however, or you may traumatize the wrist.

Palm-Down Wrist Curls: Adopt the same position as in the previous exercise but with your palm facing downward. Flex your wrist upward ten times. Repeat using other wrist. Gradually increase the number of repetitions over several weeks.

Arm Curls: Stand and hold the weights at your sides, palms facing forward. Slowly curl your arms up, keeping your wrists straight. Do ten curls with each arm; build up to 40 curls each over several weeks.

can decrease inflammation. (See the box on page 21 for important pain reliever warnings and precautions first.)

Chapped Lips

6 Tips for Smoother Lips

If puckering is painful and pursing is too much to bear, you're probably suffering from chapped lips. Harsh winter weather, dry heated air indoors, a habit of constantly licking your lips—all can help dry out the skin of your lips by causing the moisture in them to evaporate. The result: rough, cracked, sensitive lips that leave you little to smile about.

Protecting your lips from chapping is not only important for appearance and comfort, but for health. Cold sores, bacterial infections, and other problems are more likely to strike lips that are already damaged by chapping.

Here's what you can do to keep your lips soft and moist:

Don't lick your lips. It may make your lips feel better temporarily, but you'll be making matters worse. Licking your lips has the same drying effect as constantly washing your hands: The repeated exposure to water actually robs moisture from the skin, causing it to become dry.

Use a lip balm. Numerous products are available over the counter. Pick one that you like so you'll use it frequently. Most lip balms are waxy or greasy and work by sealing in moisture with a protective barrier. Plain old petroleum jelly works just fine, too.

Screen out the sun. The sun's ultraviolet rays can damage and dry the sensitive skin on your lips in the same way they can harm the skin on other parts of your body. Indeed, the lips are a common site for skin cancer, since they

don't contain melanin, a dark pigment (coloring) that helps protect skin from ultraviolet rays. Certain skin cancers that appear on the lips may be more serious and more likely to spread, too, so if you'll be out in the sun, use a lip balm that contains sunscreen. Choose a product that has an SPF (sun protection factor) of 15 or higher.

Wear lipstick. OK, this advice may apply only to female readers. But dermatologists say older women are less likely than older men to have skin damage on their kissers, especially on the lower lips, and lipstick may be the reason. Lipstick appears to offer moder-

ately effective protection against the sun's ultraviolet rays, and these days you can purchase lipstick that includes sunscreen, for even greater protection. Lipstick acts as a moisturizer, too.

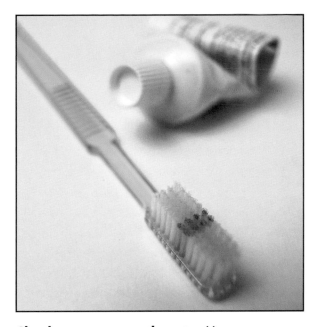

Check out your toothpaste. You might want to consider whether an allergy to your toothpaste or mouthwash could be to blame for the rough, red skin on your lips. Try switching to a different brand of toothpaste or skipping the mouthwash for a few days to see if the condition of your lips begins to improve. (If it does, you've identified the culprit behind your lip irritation and can simply avoid it from that point on.) Also, be sure to rinse your mouth and your lips well after you finish brushing your teeth.

Watch what passes between them. When lips are chapped, they're more sensitive, and certain foods can irritate them. Hold off on pepper, mustard, barbecue sauce, orange juice, and alcoholic beverages to give your lips a break as they heal.

Chronic Fatigue Syndrome

17 COPING STRATEGIES

Chronic fatigue syndrome (CFS) has become one of medicine's most frustrating mysteries. CFS sufferers are plagued with a debilitating and unexplained fatigue that can persist indefinitely. Their flulike symptoms—fatigue (lack of energy), malaise (an overall feeling of being unwell), muscle aches, sore throat, low-grade fever, and swollen lymph nodes—often continue long after what they thought was merely a bout with the flu, mononucleosis, or some other infectious illness. Depression, a common companion to many chronic conditions, can accompany the other symptoms of CFS. So can cognitive problems, such as confusion and forgetfulness, as well as sleep disorders.

Theories abound as to the cause of CFS, but so far, no one has come up with a definitive answer. Is it a virus? Is there a genetic tendency to develop it? Is it triggered by stress? Is it a malfunction of the immune system? No one knows for sure.

Even the diagnosis of CFS can be murky, since there are no currently available blood tests or X-rays to say "Yes, this patient has CFS." Instead, it remains primarily a diagnosis of exclusion—that is, your doctor must first rule out other conditions, such as anemia, multiple sclerosis, thyroid disorders, lupus, and even cancer, that can cause similar symptoms. Chronic fatigue, after all, is one of the most common complaints doctors hear from patients. To help bring some clarity, consistency,

Diagnosing CFS

Comedienne Gilda Radner was mistakenly diagnosed with chronic fatigue syndrome, which delayed the discovery of the ovarian cancer that eventually killed her. That's one of the worst-case scenarios that can occur with CFS. So if you suspect you may have CFS, be sure your physician has ruled out any other condition that can cause similar symptoms.

Because there's no diagnostic test for CFS, the Centers for Disease Control established guidelines in 1994 for diagnosing the condition. According to the guidelines, you must have severe fatigue lasting six months or longer with other known medical conditions excluded by clinical diagnoses. And you should have four or more of the following symptoms concurrently:
• substantial impairment in short-term memory or concentration
• sore throat
• tender lymph nodes
• muscle pain
• pain, without swelling or redness, in multiple joints
• headaches of a new type, pattern, or severity
• unrefreshing sleep
• malaise that occurs after exertion and lasts more than 24 hours.
These symptoms must have persisted or recurred during six or more consecutive months of illness and must not have predated the fatigue.

and confidence to the diagnosis of CFS, therefore, the U.S. Centers for Disease Control and Prevention established guidelines for diagnosing the condition based on the work of international scientists studying the syndrome (see "Diagnosing CFS" on page 72).

CFS is treated with a variety of medications, depending on the symptoms present. Some of the drugs that may be prescribed include nonsteroidal anti-inflammatories (such as aspirin and ibuprofen), low-dose tricyclic antidepressants, selective serotonin reuptake inhibitors (another category of antidepressants), antianxiety drugs, stimulants, and antihistamines.

If you suffer from CFS, what can you do? Unfortunately, there is no known cure. And no one can tell you how long you'll be sick. But the disease does not get progressively worse, and it's not fatal. In fact, you're usually sickest during the first year, often before you're even diagnosed. The challenge is to learn how to cope with CFS.

Here are the coping strategies recommended by the experts—physicians, psychotherapists, and patients. Some deal with the physical side of the condition, some target the emotional side of living with chronic illness, and some are simply practical tips. Together with your doctor's advice and care, they can help you cope day to day with CFS.

Establish a partnership with your health-care team. Find a doctor you trust who takes CFS seriously (since the very existence of CFS as a unique medical condition is not universally accepted in the medical field). Interview several doctors, if necessary, and ask plenty of questions. Then, when it comes to making a choice, trust your gut. Work with your doctor to recruit additional members to your health-care team, such as a dietitian or psychologist, if needed. And become a more effective participant yourself by learning all you can about CFS.

Exercise. An appropriate amount of physical activity helps keep you emotionally and physically healthy. However, it's important to know how much to do and when to stop. Talk with your doctor or consult a physical therapist about what activities are best for you. You may be able to tolerate walking, swimming or water therapy, stretching, yoga, or tai chi better than more high-impact activities.

Do what you can for your body. Practice the basics of healthy living: Eat a nutritious diet, get enough rest, and participate in a suitable exercise program.

Grieve for what you've lost. It's okay to feel sad that you have developed a chronic illness. Grieving over it can help you accept it.

Don't blame yourself. It's not your fault you're sick.

Find support. Talking about your condition with other CFS sufferers can be a big help. They understand what you're going through, and they can offer support, advice, friendship, and information. Ask your doctor or local

hospital about support groups in your area or check the yellow pages or Internet. However, avoid support groups that use the gatherings as sales meetings for alternative products.

You might also want to consider seeking professional counseling, since depression often accompanies any chronic condition.

Spend your energy wisely. Several patients talk of using their precious stores of energy like coins from a piggy bank that they ration carefully and use only when necessary. Sit instead of standing, avoid unnecessary trips up and down stairs, get a handicapped parking sticker so you can park close to your destination, have your groceries delivered, and/or hire someone to clean the house. These are all ways to save energy on everyday tasks.

Set reasonable goals. Be realistic as you set daily goals, keeping in mind how you really feel, not how you wish you felt. If you set your goals too high, you'll feel disappointed when you don't meet them. If you have reasonable expectations, you can meet your goals and enjoy the feeling of accomplishment and control.

Schedule rest periods. Listen to your body, and respect its need to rest before and after activities.

Set priorities. You may have time to do only the top two or three things on your to-do list, so make sure the most important tasks are at the very top of the list.

Keep work and home schedules on the same calendar. That way, you won't overwhelm yourself by scheduling an important work meeting on the same day as your child's birthday party, for example.

Learn to adapt. Find ways to socialize that won't wear you out. Watch a video at home with friends instead of going to the movies, or order takeout instead of meeting in a restaurant. Friends and family members who really care about you won't mind staying in.

Have fun. With less energy to get things done, you may be tempted to work whenever you feel well and to consider socializing an extravagance you can't afford. But you need to keep your life balanced by making time for friends and family, too.

Keep a journal. Even if you don't write in it every day, keeping a journal can help you put your feelings into perspective.

Don't ignore your sexuality. You may have to schedule sex for when you feel good—and that may be in the morning or afternoon, if you're often tired at night.

Alternative Therapies

Dozens of kinds of alternative therapies are marketed for the treatment of CFS: herbal remedies, dietary supplements, special diets, acupuncture, and self-hypnosis, to name just a few. But do they work?

Most have not been scientifically studied, according to the Centers for Disease Control. What is known is that some dietary supplements and herbal preparations can have potentially serious side effects. For example, a supplement may interfere or interact with prescription medications, changing the way they act in your body.

You can protect yourself by using common sense. If a treatment sounds too good to be true, it probably is. Be very suspicious of products that:

- Rely on testimonials rather than scientific studies to prove their worth. A disease can go into remission or the patient may feel better because of the placebo effect (a beneficial effect that occurs but that cannot be attributed to any special property of the substance).
- Are marketed as "exclusive." If you're told that you're one of the lucky few to know about this product, or that it's a "secret" cure that medical professionals don't want to share with the public, it's probably baloney. If a treatment truly worked, it wouldn't be kept secret.
- Include in their packaging or marketing a recommendation that you not tell your doctor that you're using the products.
- Are sold through a multilevel marketing (pyramid) scheme.
- Are marketed with phrases such as "oxygenate your body," "detoxify your system," or "cleanse your body of numerous poisons and toxins."
- Are sold by a practitioner who is clearly profiting from the product—for example, if your doctor insists that you buy vitamin supplements from his or her office rather than from your local pharmacy.

Keep your sense of humor. Seek out funny movies, books, television shows, and people that distract you from your daily stress rather than encourage you to wallow in it.

Live for today. Try not to dwell on the past or the future.

Colds

11 Tips for Fighting the "Cold" War

Sneezing. Stuffy nose. Cough. Watery eyes. Sore throat. Mild headache or muscle aches. A touch of fever. If you're like most people, you know the symptoms of the common cold all too well. Although Americans spend billions of dollars annually on doctor visits and cold remedies—everything from tissues and vitamin C to over-the-counter decongestants and herbal teas—there is no cure for the common cold.

A cold is an upper respiratory infection caused by any one of hundreds of different viruses. Unfortunately, scientists haven't figured out how to wipe out these viruses. The body has to rely on its own natural defenses.

During a cold, virus particles penetrate the mucous layer on the inner walls of the nose and throat and attach themselves to cells there. They punch holes in the cell membranes, allowing viral genetic material to enter the cells. Within a short time, the virus takes over and forces the cells to produce thousands of new virus particles.

In response to this viral invasion, the body marshals its defenses: The nose and throat release chemicals that mobilize the immune system; injured cells produce chemicals called prostaglandins, which trigger inflammation and attract infection-fighting white blood cells; tiny blood vessels stretch, opening up space to allow blood fluid (called plasma) and specialized white blood cells to enter the infected area; the body temperature rises, enhancing the immune response; and histamine is released, increasing the production of nasal mucus in an effort to trap viral particles and remove them from the body.

As the battle against the cold virus rages on, the body counterattacks with its heavy artillery: specialized white blood cells called monocytes and lymphocytes; interferon, often called the "body's own antiviral drug"; and 20 or more proteins that circulate in the blood plasma and coat the viruses and infected cells, making it easier for the white blood cells to identify and destroy them.

The symptoms you experience as a cold are actually parts of the body's natural immune response. In fact, by the time you feel you're coming down with a cold, you've likely been infected for a day and a half.

Many people believe the old adage, "Do nothing and your cold will last seven days. Do everything and it will last a week." (Actually, it's not uncommon for a cold to last a couple weeks.) And, basically, it's true. But the following simple self-care techniques may help you feel more comfortable and help your body heal itself as quickly as possible.

Drink plenty of fluids. Fluids may help thin the mucus, thus keeping it flowing freely and making it easier for the body to expel—along with the viral particles trapped within it. Water and other liquids also combat dehydration. So drink at least eight ounces of fluid every two hours.

Cook up some chicken soup. One of the most beneficial hot fluids you can consume when you have a cold is chicken soup. It was first prescribed for the common cold by rabbi/physician Moses Maimonides in twelfth-century Egypt and has been a favorite folk remedy ever since. In 1978, Marvin Sackner, M.D., of Mount Sinai Hospital in Miami Beach, Florida, included chicken soup in a test of the effects of sipping hot and cold water on the clearance of mucus. To the doctor's surprise, chicken soup placed first, hot water second, and cold water a distant third. Sackner's work has since been

Hello, Doctor?

While most colds can be effectively treated at home, you should call your doctor if:
- You have a headache and stiff neck with no other cold symptoms. (Your symptoms may indicate meningitis.)
- You have a headache and sore throat with no other cold symptoms. (It may be strep throat.)
- You have cold symptoms and significant pain across your nose and face that doesn't go away. (You may have a sinus infection, which requires antibiotics.)
- You have a fever above 101 degrees Fahrenheit (adults) and the aspirin or acetaminophen you've taken has not brought it down.
- Your infant has a rectal temperature of 100.2 degrees Fahrenheit or higher.
- Your child has a rectal temperature of 102 degrees Fahrenheit or higher (See FEVER for more detailed advice on caring for a feverish child.)
- Your cold symptoms seem to be going away, but you suddenly develop a fever. (It may indicate pneumonia, which is more likely to set in toward the end of a cold.)
- You have a "dry" cough—one that doesn't bring up phlegm—for more than ten days.
- You cough up blood.

Don't Pass It On

Unfortunately, modern medicine hasn't invented a cold vaccine that will protect us from the multitude of viruses that can cause a cold. As a result, most people can count on battling the sniffles at least once a year. But that doesn't mean if you get a cold you have to pass it on. By taking a few simple steps, you can keep your cold to yourself.

Most authorities on the common cold are now convinced that cold viruses are passed in two ways—by direct contact (the most common way) and by viral-filled droplets from the nose being inhaled by others (the so-called "aerosol method"). The direct-contact route typically goes something like this: You shake hands with someone in the early stages of a cold. Soon after, you rub your eye or touch your nose, transferring the virus from your hand to your nasal passages (tears wash the virus from your eye into your nose), where a cold takes hold. At some point within the next three days, you touch your nose or sneeze into your hand, contaminating your fingers with virus particles, then open a door, depositing the virus on the knob. Soon after, someone else grabs the doorknob, and the cycle repeats.

Viruses can live on objects such as telephones, doorknobs, and cloth, but no one is really sure how long. To avoid spreading your cold by direct contact, use paper tissues instead of a handkerchief or hand to blow or wipe your nose and to cover a cough or sneeze, dispose of the tissues immediately, and wash your hands frequently.

People can also get your cold by inhaling airborne viral particles. But while most of us feel uncomfortable being near someone with full-blown cold symptoms, the truth is that people with colds are most contagious within the first day or two after their symptoms begin to

appear, when they may be suffering from little more than a scratchy throat and the occasional sneeze. So if you really want to avoid giving your cold to others, you should stay home from work and cancel social engagements when you first begin to feel that you're coming down with something. Pass the tissues, please.

replicated by other researchers. While doctors aren't sure exactly why chicken soup helps clear nasal passages, many seem to agree, "it's just what the doctor ordered."

Rest. Doctors disagree about whether or not you should take a day or two off from work when you come down with a cold. However, they do agree that extra rest helps. Staying away from work may be a good idea from a prevention standpoint, too; your coworkers will probably appreciate your not spreading your cold virus around the office. If you do decide to stay home, forego those chores and take it easy: read a good book, watch television, take naps.

You should probably also skip your normal exercise routine when you've got a cold, at least during the days when you're feeling the worst. Again, let your body be your guide. If you're feeling miserable, the best advice is probably to just stay in bed.

Stay warm. While cold air and drafts don't cause colds, you're likely to feel more comfortable if you stay indoors and keep covered, especially if you have a fever. There's no sense in stressing your body any further.

Use a saltwater wash. The inflammation and swelling in the nose during a cold is caused by molecules called cytokines, or lymphokines, which are made by the body as it fights the infection. Research has shown that washing away these molecules can reduce swelling. Fill a clean nasal-spray bottle with diluted salt water (one level teaspoon salt to one quart water), and spray three or four times into each nostril. Repeat five to six times per day.

Gargle with warm salt water.
Gargling with warm salt water (¼ teaspoon salt in four ounces warm water) every one to two hours can soothe a sore, scratchy throat. Salt water is an astringent (meaning it causes tissue to contract), which can soothe inflammation in the throat and may help loosen mucus.

Consider vitamin C. Although studies suggest that vitamin C may boost the body's immune system, the use of this vitamin in treating colds is still controversial. Many physicians don't recommend vitamin C as a cold remedy. However, some evidence suggests that taking 2,000 milligrams or more of vitamin C daily can lessen the severity of cold symptoms.

If you decide to try boosting your vitamin C intake during a cold, don't overdo it. While vitamin C has been found to be relatively safe at doses up to 10,000 milligrams per day, some people find vitamin C causes diarrhea at the 10,000 milligram level. The safest way to get more vitamin C is simply to choose more foods rich in vitamin C. For example, since you'll

need to increase your fluid intake while you have a cold, fill some of that requirement with orange juice.

Vaporize it. The steam from a vaporizer can loosen mucus, especially if the mucus has become thick. (You can get a similar effect by draping a towel over your head and bending over a pot of steaming-hot water; just be careful not to burn yourself.)

A humidifier will add moisture to your immediate environment, which may make you feel more comfortable and will keep your nasal tissues moist. That's helpful because dry nasal membranes provide poor protection against viral invasion.

Stop smoking. You'll feel better sooner and cut your risk of getting even sicker. Doctors say smokers have a tougher time shaking off a cold than nonsmokers do. Worse, smoking while you have a cold irritates the bronchial tubes, which increases the risk of developing pneumonia and other complications.

In addition to irritating the throat and bronchial tubes, smoking has been shown to depress the immune system. Since you have to depend on your immune system rather than medicine to cure a cold, you'll want it to be in the best condition possible to wage the "cold" war.

Stay away from "hot toddies."
While a hot alcoholic beverage might sound good when you're feeling achy

and stuffy, you're better off abstaining from booze, which increases mucous-membrane congestion and is dehydrating.

Maintain a positive attitude.
Although mind-body science is in its infancy, some researchers suggest that a positive I-can-beat-this-cold attitude may bolster the immune system while you fight a cold. On the other hand, a negative attitude could cause your body's defenses to fall down on the job. Not all doctors are convinced there is a connection between the mind and the immune system, but staying upbeat certainly won't make your cold worse.

What About "Cold Medicines"?

When cold season arrives, doctors' offices fill up with people searching for a "cold cure." Unfortunately, modern medicine doesn't have a drug that is effective against the more than 200 viruses that can cause the common cold. Antibiotics, such as penicillin, don't work against cold viruses. However, that doesn't stop many people from asking their doctors for penicillin shots or antibiotic pills, which—in addition to being ineffective against colds—are expensive and may cause unnecessary side effects that can leave you feeling worse. (Such unwarranted use of antibiotics also contributes to the development of antibiotic-resistant strains of bacteria.)

Okay, then, if the doctor can't help, what about all those "cold remedies" touted on television and radio? Surely some of them must work.

Not really. Some cold experts believe that most popular cold remedies may actually inhibit the body's immune responses as they suppress cold symptoms. All of your cold symptoms are part of your body's natural response in its battle against the viral invaders. To stop or suppress those responses may actually make your cold hang on longer.

For example, some cold experts say a mild fever—below 102 degrees Fahrenheit—enhances the body's ability to fight the cold virus. For that reason, you may want to forego aspirin or acetaminophen to lower a mild fever. (If you are over 60, have heart disease, or have any immune-compromising health condition, however, contact your physician at the first sign of a fever.)

Another example of potentially counterproductive cold remedies are antihistamines, which are common ingredients in multisymptom cold formulas. Antihistamines stop the runny nose, but they may do more harm than good by drying out mucous membranes that are already irritated. What's more, antihistamines thicken nasal mucus, which will make you want to use more decongestant. To top it all off, antihistamines can cause an irritating cough.

One over-the-counter cold remedy that can bring some useful symptomatic relief is pseudoephedrine. Found in products such as Sudafed, this decongestant clears clogged nasal passages by reducing swelling and fluid production while promoting drainage of nasal mucus. People who have high blood pressure or heart disease, however, should avoid this over-the-counter drug.

Cough syrups that contain glyceryl guaiacolate (but not dextromethorphan) can help loosen thick sputum, possibly making it easier to cough up.

If you think you need over-the-counter remedies to cope with your cold, most authorities recommend single-action remedies rather than the "shotgun" approach of multisymptom products. Most people get their cold symptoms serially—sore throat first, cough last. But multisymptom cold remedies say they cure all your cold symptoms at once, even the ones you don't have. Be especially wary of so-called nighttime cold remedies, which cost a lot and do little to relieve symptoms; the prime appeal of these products for many people appears to be the drowsiness they cause, but often that is due mostly to a high alcohol content. You're best off avoiding multisymptom cold remedies altogether. It simply makes no sense to take drugs and risk their side effects for symptoms you don't have.

Cold Sores

7 Ways to Foil Cold Sores

It never fails. Every time you have a big meeting coming up or an important presentation to give, you develop an unsightly cold sore on your lip. First, you get that familiar tingling (called the *prodrome*) and can feel a little hard area beneath the skin on your lip. Then a day or two later, you wake up with a small cluster of tiny, harmless-looking, white blisters that quickly explode into a painful and unsightly sore the size of Rhode Island. (Okay, so maybe it just *looks* that big to you.)

Cold sores, also called fever blisters, are caused by the herpes simplex virus type 1, which is usually acquired in childhood through contact with infected saliva (no surprise considering how young children are forever putting things in their mouths and drooling all over the place). After the initial infection, the type 1 herpes virus is believed to lie dormant (causing no symptoms of infection) in certain nerve cells of the body until it is activated again. A variety of triggers appear capable of "waking up" the virus, including mental or physical stress, anxiety, a cold or fever, the menstrual period, or excessive exposure to the sun. When the virus is reactivated, it causes a cluster of tiny, painful blisters on the lip, usually at or close to the spot of the original outbreak, that last anywhere from 7 to 14 days.

(In contrast to the herpes simplex virus type 1, herpes simplex virus type 2 generally causes sores and ulcers in the genital area—although it can be spread to the eyes and other parts of the body—and is transmitted through sexual contact. The type 2 virus is the cause of the sexually transmitted disease called genital herpes.)

Although many people use the terms "cold sore" and "canker sore" interchangeably, they are different. Unlike cold sores, canker sores are bacterial infections inside the mouth that are characterized by small, round, white areas surrounded by well-defined halos of red. And, while cold sores are highly contagious, canker sores are not (see CANKER SORES).

Unfortunately, attempting to camouflage a cold sore with makeup often aggravates the problem. That's the tough reality of these extremely painful blemishes. Still, while you can't do much about the way a cold sore looks, you can do a few things to help decrease discomfort, speed healing, and keep it from coming back. You can even take steps to prevent passing your cold sore to other people. Here's how:

Cover it with a protective petroleum product. Coating the cold sore with petroleum jelly will speed healing and help protect it from secondary infection with bacteria.

Reach for aspirin, acetaminophen, or ibuprofen. Cold sores can be quite painful. Over-the-counter (OTC) painkillers can help ease some of this discomfort. Be sure to check the painkiller warnings in the box on page 21 first, however, since even these nonprescription medications are not safe for everyone. Follow the package or label directions carefully.

Avoid salty or acidic foods. Salt-coated foods such as potato chips, french fries, and pretzels will irritate a cold sore as they would any open wound. The acidic juices of citrus fruits can do the same. So skip them until your cold sore has healed.

Apply an OTC anesthetic. Putting a local anesthetic ointment containing benzocaine on the cold sore can help numb the pain temporarily. Check your local drugstore for the ointment or ask your pharmacist to recommend one, then follow the package directions.

Protect your lips from the sun. Applying sunscreen to your lips before going outside during the day, no matter what time of year it is, may help prevent sun-induced recurrences of cold sores. Look for a sunscreen designed especially for the lips that has a sun protection factor (SPF) of 15 or higher. Or, if you don't go out without wearing lipstick, choose one that contains sunscreen with the same SPF.

Keep it to yourself. Cold sores are extremely contagious. So avoid kissing, and don't share cups, towels, utensils, or other such items. Wash your hands frequently, especially after touching the cold sore. And take care not to touch your eyes or genitals immediately after touching the sore; be sure to wash your hands thoroughly with soap and water first.

Consult your health-care provider. If you have frequent or severe cold sores, see your doctor. In some cases, an antiviral medication called acyclovir can be prescribed.

Constipation

10 Ways to Keep Things Moving

Irregularity is one of those things that no one likes to talk about. It's personal and, well, a little embarrassing. But if you have ever been constipated, you know it can put a real damper on your day.

The first thing to realize when you're talking about constipation is that "regularity" is a relative term. Everyone has his or her own natural rhythm. Ask four people to define regularity, and you'll likely get at least four different definitions. Normal bowel habits can span anywhere from three bowel movements a day to three a week. If you usually have days without bowel movements but have no other symptoms, you're not constipated; that's just your natural rhythm. However, if you have fewer than three bowel movements a week or if you experience a marked decrease in your normal bowel patterns, you are probably constipated.

People who are constipated often strain a lot in the bathroom, produce unusually hard stools, and feel gassy, bloated, and distended.

A sudden change in bowel habits merits a visit to your doctor to rule out any more serious underlying problems (see "Hello, Doctor?" on page 84). But for the occasional bout of constipation, here are some tips to put you back on track:

Get moving. Exercise not only boosts your fitness level but promotes regularity, as well. When you are active, so are your bowels—and the more sedentary you are, the more slowly your bowels move. That may partially explain why older people, who tend to be less active, and those who are bedridden are prone to constipation. So gear up and get moving. You don't have to run a marathon; a simple walking workout doesn't take much time and can be very beneficial. When it comes to regularity, even a little exercise is better than none at all.

Raise your glass. Drinking an adequate amount of liquid may help alleviate constipation or prevent it from happening in the first place. The reason for this is simple: If you are dehydrated, your stool will become dry and difficult to pass. (Gulping down way more liquid than you need, on the other hand, will just make you urinate more.)

To achieve a balanced intake of liquid, a good rule of thumb is to drink six to eight cups of fluid throughout the day, and perhaps a bit more when you're perspiring heavily during exercise or hot weather. (This general guide doesn't apply, however, if you have a kidney or liver problem or any other medical condition that may require restricting your intake of fluid. In that case, your doctor will need to advise you on how much fluid is appropriate.)

The caffeine in a strong cup of coffee can stimulate the bowels, so a cup or two of java (or tea) in the morning may get things moving. But since caffeine is a diuretic that pulls fluid out of your body, fill most of your fluid needs with water, seltzer, juice, milk, or decaffeinated beverages.

Don't fight the urge. People sometimes suppress the urge to have a bowel movement because they are busy or have an erratic schedule or because they don't want to use public bathrooms. If at all possible, heed the call when you feel it.

Take advantage of an inborn reflex. We're all born with a reflex to defecate a short time after we're fed,

and as babies, that's what we did. With socialization, we learn to control our bladders and bowels, and we tend to inhibit this reflex. Work on reviving this innate tendency by choosing one mealtime a day and trying to have a movement after it—you may be able to teach your body to pass a stool at the same time each day. (Younger people are more likely to be able to "train" their bowels in this way than are seniors.) Don't try to force a movement by straining, however, because this can result in the development of hemorrhoids, which will further complicate your evacuation difficulties (see HEMORRHOIDS). Just give your body the opportunity to have a bowel movement after the chosen meal.

Know your medications. A number of prescription and over-the-counter medications can cause constipation. If you are currently taking any medication, you might want to ask your doctor or pharmacist whether it could be causing your constipation. Among the drugs that can cause constipation are calcium-channel blockers taken for high blood pressure, beta-blockers, some antidepressants, narcotics and other pain medications, antihistamines (to a lesser degree), certain decongestants, and some antacids. Antacids that contain calcium or aluminum are binding and can cause constipation;

antacids that contain magnesium tend not to cause constipation. If you are unsure about what's in your antacid, check the label or consult your pharmacist or doctor.

Bulk up. Sometimes, a little extra dietary fiber is all you need to ensure regularity. Fiber, the indigestible part of plant foods, adds mass to the stool and stimulates the colon to push things along. Fiber is found naturally in fruits, vegetables, grains, and beans (although refining and processing can significantly decrease their fiber content). Meats, chicken, fish, and fats come up empty-handed in the fiber category. The current recommendations for daily dietary fiber are 20 to 35 grams, but most people eat only 10 to 15 grams a day. Fiber supplements may be helpful, but you're better off getting your fiber from foods, which supply an assortment of other essential nutrients as well. To avoid getting gassy, increase the fiber in your diet gradually, and be sure you drink plenty of water so the fiber can move smoothly through your digestive system.

Eat at least five servings of fruits and vegetables daily. Select a variety of fruits and vegetables, including sweet potatoes, apples, berries, apricots, peaches, pears, oranges, prunes, corn, peas, carrots, tomatoes, spinach, broccoli, and cauliflower. And opt for the whole produce over juice as

much as possible; a glass of orange juice, for instance, provides 0.1 grams of fiber, while eating an orange gives you 2.9 grams.

Eat 6 ounces of grain products each day. That's in addition to the five servings of fruits and vegetables just mentioned. Grain products include cereals, breads, and starchy vegetables (such as corn, green peas, potatoes, and lima beans). Whenever possible, choose whole grains such as whole-wheat bread and whole-grain cereal. To get a big dose of fiber early in the day, eat high-fiber cereal for breakfast. Check the labels on cereal boxes; anything with more than five or six grams of fiber per serving qualifies as high fiber. If you don't like high-fiber cereals, try

Laxative Alert

Laxatives seem like an easy solution for constipation woes, but they can cause many more problems than they solve. Indeed, these products can be habit-forming and produce substantial side effects if used incorrectly.

Laxatives work in many different ways. Some lubricate, others soften the stools, some draw water into the bowel, and still others are bulk-forming. One real danger is that people can become dependent on them, needing ever-increasing amounts to do the job. Eventually, some types of laxatives can damage the nerve cells of the colon until the person can't evacuate anymore. Some laxatives inhibit the absorption or effectiveness of drugs. Those with a mineral-oil base can prevent the absorption of vitamins A, D, K, and E. Still others can damage and inflame the lining of the intestine.

If you need over-the-counter help, opt for a fiber supplement rather than a laxative per se. But remember that in the long run, you'll be much better off to depend on exercise, adequate fluid intake, and a high-fiber diet to keep you regular instead.

mixing a small amount in with your usual cereal and increasing the proportion of high-fiber cereal over time.

Read labels when choosing breads as well. Find a bread that has at least two grams of fiber per slice and is labeled "whole grain" or "whole wheat" (the word "wheat" alone on the package or a brown color do not guarantee that the product includes the whole grain). Check the label for portion sizes so you know exactly how much fiber you're getting in each serving.

Don't forget beans. Dried beans and legumes—whether they're pinto beans, red beans, lima beans, black beans, navy beans, or garbanzo beans—are excellent sources of fiber. Many people don't like them because

of the gassiness they can cause. Cooking beans properly (see the "Soak your beans" remedy under FLATULENCE for instructions), however, can ease this problem considerably. Plus, if you add beans to your diet gradually, you'll minimize gassiness.

Cut back on refined foods. Bump up your fiber intake by switching from refined foods to less-refined foods whenever possible. Switch from a highly processed cereal to a whole-grain cereal, move from heavily cooked vegetables to less-cooked vegetables, and choose products made with whole-grain rather than white flour. A serving of white rice has 0.5 grams of fiber; a serving of brown rice contains 2.4 grams. And while a serving of potato chips has only 0.6 grams of fiber, a serving of popcorn supplies 2.5 grams.

Corns and Calluses

23 STEPS TO RELIEF

You may refer to your feet as tootsies or dogs, but the fact remains that feet are highly sophisticated structures. The human foot is a miracle of engineering, designed to stand up under a lot of wear and tear. It's a good thing, too, since your feet are the most used and abused parts of your body. According to the American Podiatric Medical Association, the average American walks 115,000 miles in a lifetime—a distance that would take you all the way around the earth four times. Your feet support the weight of your body, clothing, and whatever extras you might be carrying. And in an average day of walking, your feet are subjected to a force equal to several hundred tons.

Despite how well designed your feet are, however, things can go wrong. In fact, an estimated 87 percent of all American adults have some type of foot problem. Among the most common of these problems are corns and calluses, which are patches of toughened skin that form to protect sensitive foot tissue against repeated friction and pressure.

Corns come in two varieties: hard and soft. Hard corns are usually found on the tops of the toes or on the outer sides of the little toes, where the skin rubs against the shoe. Sometimes, a corn will form on the ball of the foot beneath a callus, resulting in a sharp, localized pain with each step. Soft corns, which are moist and rubbery, form between toes, where the bones of one toe exert pressure on the bones of its neighbor. Both hard and soft corns are cone shaped, with the tip pointing into the foot (what you see is the base of the cone). When a shoe or another toe puts pressure against the corn, the tip can hit sensitive underlying tissue, causing pain.

Unlike corns, calluses generally form over a flat surface and have no tip. They usually appear on the weight-bearing parts of the foot—the ball or the heel. Each step presses the callus against underlying tissue and may cause aching, burning, or tenderness but rarely sharp pain.

The good news is there are some things you can do to relieve the discomfort associated with these two conditions. Try the tips that follow to take the pressure off these sore spots. But if, despite these self-help strategies, your corn or callus continues to cause you discomfort, see your podiatrist. In addition, if you have diabetes or any other disorder that affects circulation, do not attempt to self-treat any foot problem; see your podiatrist right away.

Play detective. Corns and calluses don't just spring up out of nowhere. Excess pressure and friction can produce areas of dead, thickened skin on your feet. The solution? Track down and eliminate the cause of all that rubbing, and take other steps to prevent corns and calluses. Podiatric enemy number one may be your shoes, so read "If the Shoe Fits..." below for some helpful tips on choosing well-fitting footwear.

If the Shoe Fits...

Corns and calluses form when the size and shape of your shoe don't accommodate your foot and the way it works. Here are some guidelines to getting a better fit:

- Have the salesclerk measure each foot twice before you buy any pair of shoes. Don't ask for a certain size just because it's the one you have always worn; the size of your feet changes as you grow older.
- Be sure to try on both the left and the right shoe. Stand during the fitting process, and check that there is adequate space (three-eighths to one-half inch) for your longest toe at the end of each shoe. Remember, your longest toe may not be your big toe; for some people, the second toe extends the farthest. Likewise, your feet may not be exactly the same size. If one foot is slightly larger than the other, buy the shoes that fit the larger foot and use padding, if necessary, for a better fit on the smaller foot.
- Be sure the shoe fits snugly at the heel.
- Be sure the ball of your foot fits snugly into the widest part of the shoe—called the ball pocket.
- If you plan to wear socks with the shoes, bring those socks and wear them while you assess the fit of the shoes.
- Shop for shoes at the end of the day, when your feet are likely to be slightly swollen.
- Don't buy shoes that feel too tight, expecting them to stretch out. If they don't feel right in the store, they will never fit comfortably. They should not need to be stretched.
- Walk around the store in the shoes to make sure they fit and feel right.
- When buying shoes for everyday use, look for ones with fairly low heels.
- Be sure the material of the upper is soft and pliable.
- If you are not sure about the fit, check into the store's return policy. If possible, take the shoes home, wear them on a rug for an hour, and if they don't feel good, take them back.
- Have several different pairs of shoes so that you don't wear the same pair day after day. Alternating your shoes is a wise move, not only for the health of your feet but for the life of your shoes.

You may discover, as most people do, that your left and right feet are not exactly the same size. Or you may have a high instep, a plump foot, or especially long toes. While these characteristics may make it somewhat difficult to step comfortably in every pair of shoes you try on, they do not mean that you must resign yourself to never finding shoes that fit. All it takes is a little time and the determination to walk in comfort.

One last reminder: Like Cinderella, who was the only one able to fit into the glass slipper, the person who buys a pair of shoes is the only one who should wear them.

Trim those toenails. Toenails are designed to protect the toes from injury. However, the pressure of a shoe on a toenail that is too long can force the joint of the toe to push up against the top of the shoe, forming a corn. To take the pressure off, keep your toenails trimmed. Cut each toenail straight across so that it doesn't extend beyond the tip of the toe. Then, file each toenail to smooth any rough edges.

Take a soak. While eliminating the source of the problem is essential, the sharp pain of a corn may demand immediate relief. Soak the affected foot in a solution of Epsom salts and warm water, then apply a moisturizing cream, and wrap the foot in a plastic bag. Keep the bag on for a couple of hours (while you watch television or

read, for example). Then remove the bag and gently rub the corn in a sideways motion with a pumice stone. Bear in mind that soaking will provide temporary relief, but it is not a cure.

Ice a hard corn. If a hard corn is so painful and swollen that you can't even think of putting on a shoe, apply ice to the corn for several minutes to help reduce some of the swelling and discomfort.

Don't cut. There are myriad paring and cutting devices to remove corns and calluses available in your local drugstore, but you should ignore them all in the best interest of your feet. Cutting corns can cause heavy bleeding and lead to infection, so it's not worth the risk.

Soft-step it. Shielding and padding offer another way to get temporary relief from the discomfort of corns and calluses. Padding transfers the pressure of the shoe from a painful spot to one that is free of pain. Nonmedicated corn pads, for example, surround the corn with material that is higher than the corn itself, thus protecting the corn from contact with the shoe.

A similar idea applies when padding a callus. Cut a piece of moleskin (available at your local drugstore or camping supply store) into two half-moon shapes and place the pieces on opposite sides of the callused area to protect it from further irritation.

OTC Corn and Callus Removers

Salicylic acid is the only over-the-counter (OTC) drug that is safe and effective for treating calluses and hard corns, according to the Food and Drug Administration (FDA). For medicated disks, pads, or plasters, the recommended concentration of salicylic acid is 12 to 40 percent. A concentration of 12 to 17.6 percent is recommended for salicylic acid when the corn-and-callus remover is in liquid form.

Many podiatrists, however, advise against the use of these products as home remedies, mainly because the active ingredient is an acid that can burn healthy skin as well as the dead skin of a callus or corn. If you do decide to try one of these products, follow the package directions carefully and be sure to apply the product only to the area of the corn or callus, avoiding the surrounding healthy tissue (one way to do this is by spreading petroleum jelly in a ring shape around the corn or callus before you apply the acid). If your corn or callus does not improve within two weeks, stop using the product and see a podiatrist. If you have diabetes or any medical condition that hinders circulation, do not try any of these products at all—see a podiatrist at the first sign of any foot problem.

The following ingredients are *not* generally recognized as safe and effective for removing corns and calluses, according to the FDA: iodine, ascorbic acid, acetic acid, allantoin, belladonna, chlorobutanol, diperodon hydrochloride, ichthammol, methylbenzethonium chloride, methyl salicylate, panthenol, phenyl salicylate, and vitamin A.

Separate your piggies. To relieve soft corns between the toes, keep the toes separated with lamb's wool or cotton. A small, felt pad, like those for hard corns, may also be used for this purpose.

Baby your soft corn. In addition to separating your toes, sprinkle a little cornstarch or baby powder between them to help absorb moisture and protect the skin from breaking down further.

Mix your own callus concoction. For calluses, mix your own softener.

Make a paste using five or six crushed aspirin tablets and one tablespoon lemon juice, and apply it to the callus. (Be sure to avoid applying the paste to any healthy skin, because it may cause a burn or other irritation. Try smearing petroleum jelly on the healthy skin surrounding the callus *before* applying the paste to the callus itself; the petroleum jelly will shield the healthy skin from the acid in the aspirin paste.) Then, once you've applied the paste, carefully wrap your foot in a plastic bag (again being careful not to smear the paste onto healthy skin), and wrap a warm towel around the bag. Wait ten minutes, then unwrap the foot and gently rub the callus with a pumice stone.

Invite your feet to tea. Soaking your feet in thoroughly diluted chamomile tea has a soothing effect and will temporarily change the pH (the acid/alkaline balance) of the skin to help dry out sweaty feet (excessive moisture can contribute to foot problems). The tea will stain your feet, but the stain can be easily removed with soap and water. (It may also stain fabrics.)

Coat your feet. If you expect to be doing an unusual amount of walking or running, coat your toes with a little petroleum jelly to reduce friction.

Cuts and Scrapes

9 WAYS TO CARE FOR A "BOO-BOO"

You're hurrying along and the front of your shoe catches on a crack in the cement, sending you tumbling to the ground. When you get up, you find that not only is your ego bruised, but you've managed to peel away the skin on your elbows and knees. You've got yourself a collection of painful scrapes.

An amazing number of things happen when you cut or scrape yourself. When you disrupt the skin, a clear, antibody-containing fluid from the blood, called serum, leaks into the wound. The area around the cut or scrape becomes red, indicating that more blood is moving into the wound site, bringing with it nutrients and infection-fighting white blood cells. Nearby lymph nodes may swell. After a few days, pus (which contains dead white blood cells, dead bacteria, and other debris from the body's inflammatory response to infection) may form. And finally, a scab develops to protect the injury while it heals.

A scrape tends to hurt more than a cut because a scrape removes a larger area of skin and exposes a greater number of nerves.

Even being extra careful, you can't always avoid the scrapes and cuts of life. But you can learn how to care for them and speed their healing:

Stop the bleeding. When you get a cut or scrape, the first thing to do (after admonishing yourself for being so clumsy) is to stop the bleeding by applying pressure to the area with a clean cloth or tissue. If possible, elevate the wound above the heart to slow the blood flow. Don't use a tourniquet, which cuts off circulation.

Wash up. One of the most important things you can do in treating a cut or scrape is to clean it thoroughly with soap and water or an over-the-counter (OTC) cleanser such as Hibiclens that doesn't sting. If the wound is really dirty, pour hydrogen peroxide onto it; as it bubbles, it will lift out debris. But apply it carefully, because hydrogen peroxide can damage surrounding healthy skin. A wound that is too deep or dirty for you to clean thoroughly requires medical attention as soon as possible.

Bring on the antibacterial ointment. Antibacterial ointments and solutions can be very helpful. Polysporin, Neosporin, and Bactine are examples of such products available

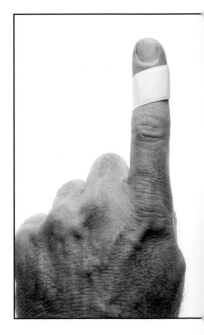

without a prescription. Polysporin is a good choice for people with sensitive skin, because it contains fewer ingredients that may cause allergic reactions.

Close the skin. Properly closing the skin is important in cuts that are ⅛- to ¼-inch wide. (A cut wider than a ¼ inch or with edges that are too ragged to be closed evenly requires prompt medical attention, as stitches may be necessary.) Closing makes the cut heal faster and reduces the chances of scarring. Be sure that you have thoroughly cleaned the cut before attempting to close it. Try to line up the edges of the cut, then apply butterfly strips or a standard adhesive bandage to keep the cut closed.

Cover it. Covering a wound protects it and keeps it clean. Instead of covering with plain gauze, which tends to stick to wounds, use Telfa, a coated, gauze-type bandage. Adhesive bandages often have Telfa on them, but you can also buy larger pieces of Telfa in the pharmacy and cut them to fit. Cover the wound with the Telfa pad, and use adhesive tape to hold the pad in place. Don't cover it too tightly, however, because a bit of air circulation actually facilitates healing.

Keep it clean. To prevent infection, remove the bandage and wash the wound every day with soap and water. Then apply a clean bandage.

Don't let it dry out. By keeping a wound moist (covering it generally accomplishes this, as does applying an antibacterial ointment), you help prevent cracking, speed healing, and reduce the chance of scarring.

If a scab forms, don't pick at it; this disrupts skin repair and can introduce bacteria. Instead, soak crusty scabs using a solution made by adding one tablespoon white vinegar to one pint water; the mildly acidic solution is soothing and helps kill bacteria.

You can keep the wound moist at night without a bandage by using a water/petrolatum regimen before bed: Wash the wound thoroughly, then cover it with a little petroleum jelly to seal in the moisture.

Don't get locked up. Consider having a tetanus shot within 72 hours if you haven't had one in the last five years. Tetanus bacteria cause "lockjaw," a condition that can lead to stiffness in the jaw and other joints, paralysis, and even death.

Protect it from sunlight. To avoid the skin darkening that often occurs when a cut or scrape heals, avoid sun exposure during the healing process and apply OTC hydrocortisone to the wound. Also, for several weeks, be extra diligent about applying a good sunscreen (SPF 15 or higher) to skin that has recently healed.

Dandruff

10 Ways to Shake the Flakes

Don't toss out all those dark suits just yet. There's a better way to deal with dandruff. As a matter of fact, you may be able to simply wash it away.

You may not realize it, but you are constantly shedding dead skin cells from all over your body. It's the skin's natural way to rejuvenate itself. In fact, you get a whole new suit of skin about every 27 or 28 days. The old stuff just sort of flakes away. You simply don't tend to notice the tiny skin cells dropping off your arms, your legs, and even your scalp.

Dandruff results from the same shedding of skin cells. But if the shedding process is normal, what happens to make dandruff so embarrassingly noticeable?

Scientists have discovered that dandruff occurs when a yeast-like fungus called malassezia goes wild on your scalp. The microscopic malassezia fungus, a normal inhabitant on a healthy human head, feeds on the fatty oils secreted by hair follicles in the scalp. But sometimes, for reasons that are as yet unclear, the malassezia fungus grows out of control, causing irritation that actually speeds up cell turnover on the scalp. As a result, the normal process of cell turnover, which usually takes a whole month, may take less than two weeks. The irritated scalp sheds so many dead cells at the same time that, when they mix with the oil from the hair follicles, they form greasy clumps that are big enough to be clearly visible to the naked eye. The oil also makes the clumps more likely to get stuck in your hair (and on your shoulders), rather than float quickly away.

Even if your malassezia has multiplied like wildfire, you don't have to

live with the resulting dandruff. Take the following steps to sweep those flakes away once and for all:

Shampoo each day to keep it away. What easier way to get rid of dandruff than to wash it down the drain? Getting rid of excess oils (which may contribute to the overgrowth of malassezia in the first place) and flakes through daily shampooing may be the easiest way to make dandruff disappear.

Switch shampoos. If your regular shampoo isn't doing the trick, even with daily washing, it's time to switch to an antidandruff shampoo. Check the ingredients in over-the-counter dandruff shampoos, and look for one that contains zinc pyrithione, which can reduce the fungus; selenium sulfide, which can limit cell turnover and possibly even decrease the amount of fungus; salicylic acid, which works as a sort of scrub to slough off dead skin; or ketoconazole, which works against a broad array of fungi.

Go for three. Your favorite dandruff shampoo may stop working after a while, and those little flakes may return. Don't blame the shampoo. You simply may have built up a resistance to its active ingredient. To prevent this, try rotating three brands of dandruff shampoo (each with a different formulation), using each for a month. In other words, use one shampoo for a month, then switch to a second brand for a month, then to a third brand for a month, then back to the original shampoo for a month, and so on.

Lather twice. The first lathering and rinsing gets rid of the loose flakes and the oily buildup on your hair and scalp. It sort of clears the area so that the second lathering can really get to work. Leave the second lathering of

dandruff shampoo on your hair for at least five minutes before thoroughly rinsing it off. That gives the shampoo a chance to penetrate the skin cells and do what it's supposed to do.

Try tar. If the antidandruff shampoos aren't working, it's time to bring out the big guns, namely the tar shampoos, which have been a proven remedy for more than 200 years. The tar decreases cell turnover quite effectively, though there are some drawbacks. Tar shampoos have a strong odor, may stain the shaft of lighter-colored hair (it can take weeks of using a milder shampoo to get rid of the discoloration), and may irritate the skin.

Use a rinse. If you decide to go with a tar shampoo, rinse your hair with lemon juice, a conditioner, or creme rinse to get rid of any lingering odor from the shampoo. Using a hair conditioner after washing with *any* antidandruff shampoo is a good idea anyway, because the medicated shampoos tend to stiffen hair and make it less manageable. Many of them also dry the scalp, which can add to flaking; a conditioner can help seal in nourishing moisture.

Be sensitive to your sensitivity. There are some people who just shouldn't use a tar shampoo. Why? Because they're so sensitive. Rather, their scalp is, and a tar shampoo can irritate and inflame their hair follicles,

Is It Really Dandruff?

You may have something that's like dandruff, but isn't dandruff. Flaking of the skin may also be caused by either seborrheic dermatitis or psoriasis.

Seborrheic dermatitis is a chronic disorder characterized by inflammation of the skin, along with scaling. It may strike the eyebrow and hairline areas, the sides of the nose, the ears, and the central chest.

Psoriasis is characterized by red, scaly patches on the skin and is the result of unusually rapid turnover of cells.

Prescription medications are available to control both conditions. So if you still have trouble with dandruff after attempting the home remedies discussed here, see your doctor.

causing a condition called folliculitis. The cure? Switch to a milder shampoo.

Stop those itchy fingers. Try to resist the temptation to go after those itchy patches like a dog chasing fleas. You may end up with wounds to your scalp caused by your fingernails. If you break the skin on your scalp, discontinue use of medicated shampoo for a while. Switch to a mild shampoo, such as a baby shampoo, and use it daily until the scratches are healed.

Shower away sweat. After exercise or strenuous physical activity that makes you perspire, shower and shampoo as soon as possible. Sweat irritates the scalp and speeds up the flaking of skin cells.

Go easy on the sticky stuff. Although you needn't give up the various mousses, sprays, and gels that hold your hairstyle in place, try to use them less often. These hair products can contribute to oily buildup.

Dermatitis (Eczema)

28 Ways to Escape the Itch

Dermatitis, sometimes also called eczema, can create a vicious cycle. Your skin itches, so you scratch it. It becomes red and swollen, and then tiny, red, oozing bumps appear that eventually crust over. You keep scratching because the itching is unbearable, so the rash gets even more irritated and perhaps even infected.

All too often, you don't even know what's causing the itching. It could be

an allergy to the soap you use in the shower each morning. It could be irritation from a chemical you're exposed to at work. It could even be atopic dermatitis—a mysterious, chronic skin condition that usually begins in childhood and most often strikes people with a personal or family history of allergic conditions.

Dermatitis is sometimes used as a catch-all term for any inflammation or swelling of the skin. The term eczema is used interchangeably with dermatitis by some experts, while others use "eczema" only to refer to the specific condition known medically as atopic dermatitis.

Regardless of the kind of dermatitis you're suffering from, some general rules apply when you're seeking relief. There are also some treatment and prevention tips specific to the type of dermatitis you have. So first, we'll give you some basic strategies for relief—no matter which type of dermatitis has you scratching. Then we'll give you specific helpful hints to protect your skin from the most common types of dermatitis.

Relief from the Itch

Determining what's causing your dermatitis is important in treating it, but if you can't think of *anything* but the itching at the moment, here are some steps you can take for fast relief:

Cool the itch and swelling. Cool compresses will help. Use a folded handkerchief or a piece of bed linen folded several layers thick. Dip the clean cloth into cool water or nonprescription Burow's solution (available at your pharmacy), and place it on the rash for 10 to 15 minutes every hour.

Wet compresses are also appropriate when weeping, oozing blisters are present; ironically, you'll actually dry up the rash by repeatedly wetting it (just as frequent wetting dries out healthy skin if moisturizer isn't applied).

Whole-milk compresses are effective, too, since the protein in dairy products helps relieve itching.

Apply calamine lotion. This old standby can help relieve the itch. Apply it thinly, so the pores aren't sealed, two to three times a day. The downside to calamine lotion is that it leaves your skin the color of bubble gum. At least one manufacturer, however, has come out with a version of this itch buster that will leave you less "in the pink." Check your local pharmacy.

Use a nonprescription hydrocortisone cream. This all-purpose salve is a mainstay in any dermatologist's practice and is also available over the counter (OTC) in 0.5 and 1 percent strengths. It can ease the itch and inflammation of dermatitis (although it won't help—and can even suppress—the body's ability to fight a bacterial or fungal infection, which may develop if excessive scratching has torn the skin). Topical hydrocortisone may be a better treatment choice for allergic dermatitis than for irritant dermatitis, however. (The distinction between these two types of dermatitis is explained shortly.)

> ### Hello, Doctor?
>
> Immediate medical attention is required if:
> - You—or your child—develop a rash accompanied by shortness of breath or difficulty breathing, tightness in the throat, or swelling of the face.
> - Your child develops a purplish skin rash that resembles a bruise.
>
> Call your doctor if a rash develops and:
> - Red streaks appear on the skin.
> - The skin is swollen, puffy, or very tender to the touch.
> - Fever, sore throat, swollen glands, or joint pain are also present.
> - A new medication has recently been taken (do not stop taking the drug, however, unless directed to do so by your doctor or pharmacist).
> - A tick bite may have recently occurred.
> - It has not improved despite the use of home remedies.
> - The symptoms are severe enough to interfere with sleep or normal daily activities.
> - It has gotten worse.

Stay away from products that end in "caine." If a skin product's generic name ends with the letters "caine" (such as benzo*caine*), the medicine is derived from an anesthetic, and anesthetics often cause or aggravate allergic reactions in sensitive individuals. Treating a bad sunburn with one of these products, for example, could produce an itchy allergic rash to go along with the painful burn.

Don't try topical antihistamines. These products can cause allergic reactions, in the form of severe rashes, when rubbed on the skin.

Take an oral antihistamine instead. Try an OTC antihistamine that you take by mouth, such as

Benadryl or Chlor-Trimeton, to help relieve itching. Such products generally cause drowsiness, but that side effect may actually be helpful at night when itching is most severe. If you take an antihistamine during the day and it makes you drowsy, avoid driving or operating heavy machinery.

Don't scratch. Doing so could break the skin and cause a secondary infection. If you simply can't resist the urge, rub the itch with your fingertips instead of scratching with your nails. If a child is affected, trim his or her fingernails short and, if necessary, have the child wear mittens, at least at night, to prevent harmful scratching.

Take a soothing bath. Adding oatmeal or baking soda to bathwater will make it more soothing, although it won't cure your rash. Buy an OTC colloidal oatmeal bath treatment (the oatmeal is ground up so it dissolves better) or add a cup of baking soda to warm—not hot—bathwater.

Allergic Contact Dermatitis

Some people sneeze when confronted with ragweed pollen or dander from cats. And some people break out in a rash, known as allergic contact dermatitis, when their skin comes in direct contact with substances that are normally harmless to most people, such as certain ingredients in costume jewelry or makeup.

In allergic contact dermatitis, the body's immune system reacts to direct contact with an allergen (a substance the body incorrectly identifies as harmful) by producing an itchy rash on the skin where that contact occurred. So, for example, a person with an allergy to the nickel in a bracelet will develop a bracelet-shaped rash on the skin where that piece of jewelry was worn.

The most common allergen in allergic contact dermatitis is poison ivy, which can cause reactions in at least half of the people exposed to it. The next most common contact allergen is nickel, a metal commonly used in costume jewelry. Up to 10 percent of the population may suffer an allergic reaction to this metal.

Other possible causes of allergic contact dermatitis include:

- Neomycin or benzocaine in topical anesthetics
- Leather
- Formaldehyde, which is used in shampoos, detergents, nail hardeners, waterless hand cleaners, and mouthwashes
- Cinnamon flavoring in toothpaste and candies
- PABA, the active ingredient in some sunscreens

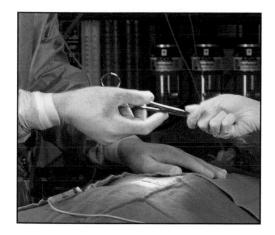

- Chemicals found in hair dyes
- Preservatives in cosmetics

Identifying a rash as allergic contact dermatitis is not always easy, however. An airborne allergen, like ragweed or animal dander, usually elicits sneezing or a runny nose within 15 minutes of exposure. But it may take up to 72 hours after contact with the sensitizing substance before a reaction shows up on your skin. That can make identifying the culprit pretty tough.

Complicating the diagnosis further is the fact that you have to become sensitized to a substance before it can cause a rash. That means you have to come in contact with it at least once before the next contact will provoke an allergic response. And indeed, sometimes it requires repeated contacts with a substance before the body becomes sensitized to it. So, for example, you may wear that nickel-containing bracelet once or even dozens of times without any problems, but then one

day—out of the blue—it causes an allergic rash.

Isolating the cause of a rash can be quite challenging. Part of the reason it can be so difficult is that it may take only a tiny amount of the offending substance to trigger an allergic rash in the first place. What's more, thanks to our concerns with hygiene and appearance, we expose ourselves to a variety of potentially offending substances every day. For instance, the average woman uses more than a dozen different products on her scalp and head each morning.

How can you handle allergic contact dermatitis?

Ferret out the cause. If the rash won't go away or keeps reappearing in the same place, you're going to have to play detective to find out what's causing it. Otherwise, you're stuck with treating only the symptoms. It may help to make a list of everything that came into contact with the affected area of skin within the last three days, including hygiene products, cosmetics, perfumes, jewelry, and even clothing (the clothing itself may not be to blame, but a detergent, fabric softener, or dry-cleaning agent used in cleaning the clothes may). If you're having trouble pinning down the cause, a dermatologist (skin doctor) or allergist (doctor specializing in allergies) can help. Either can do a test using common

Ear-Piercing Alert

If you decide to get your ears pierced but you have an allergy to nickel, make sure those first earring studs have stainless steel posts. Also make sure the needle is stainless steel. Otherwise, the studs or needle may contain nickel, and you'll be risking an itchy, inflamed rash on those recently pierced earlobes.

allergens (called a patch test) and ask you the right questions to zero in on the culprit.

Stay away. Once you've determined the cause, avoid the offender as much as possible. Your rash will remain as long as your skin continues to contact the allergen, and it will return if you again expose yourself to the offending substance.

Don't sweat it. If you are sensitive to nickel, wearing nickel-containing jewelry in a hot, humid environment may worsen the allergy, as perspiration leaches out some of the nickel. So before you start a workout or go out into the heat, take off any nickel-containing jewelry.

Coat nickel jewelry. Paint the surfaces that come in contact with your skin with clear nail polish.

Choose only the best. Even 14 karat gold jewelry has some nickel in it, so if your skin reacts strongly to nickel, you may need to restrict your gold purchases to 24 karat (which is pure gold). Other safe options include platinum and stainless steel.

Become a label reader. If your skin breaks out in a rash when it meets PABA or another chemical common in consumer products, do your skin a favor by reading ingredients lists carefully and choosing only those without the offender. Some products are even conveniently labeled as "free" of certain substances known to cause allergic reactions (you will likely find sunscreens, for example, advertised and labeled as "PABA-free").

Don't depend on the "hypoallergenic" label. It's an ambiguous term with no legal meaning. The Food and Drug Administration has not established a standard to define "hypoallergenic." If you can't tell whether a product contains a substance you're allergic to, try querying the manufacturer or performing your own patch test by applying a little of the product on the skin of your inner forearm and waiting three or four days to see if a rash develops.

Protect your skin. Guard against exposure to poisonous plants by wearing long pants and long-sleeved shirts when you're in areas where these plants are likely to be. Also see POISON IVY for additional prevention tips.

Irritant Contact Dermatitis

Some things in this world are so harsh that frequent or prolonged exposure to them can result in a rash known as irritant contact dermatitis. Numerous industrial chemicals cause problems for workers, but the typical household is not without its share of hazards to your skin. Soaps, detergents, oven cleaners, bathroom cleaners, and many other products can irritate the skin and remove its protective oils.

What's the difference between irritant and allergic contact dermatitis? Soap, for example, can cause either one. Allergic contact dermatitis occurs only in people who have an oversensitive immune system that reacts to the soap's ingredients as if they were somehow harmful. Irritant contact dermatitis occurs when the skin contacts a substance that *is* harmful and that actually causes damage to the skin, especially when that contact is prolonged or frequent; the immune system is not involved.

On the other hand, both irritant and allergic contact dermatitis produce itching, rashes, and inflammation only in the areas of skin that have actually come in contact with the offending substance, so the rash location often points to the cause. Therefore, making a list like the one described for allergic contact dermatitis can be useful in identifying the culprit in irritant contact dermatitis (although the irritating product is often more obvious in this type of contact dermatitis).

If you suspect that an irritant has caused your red, itchy, bumpy rash, there's one very important thing you should do:

Avoid exposure to the irritant.
Until you manage to do that, the rash will continue. If exposure to household products is the problem and it's your hands that are suffering, wear gloves made of vinyl—which doesn't cause allergic reactions—rather than rubber or latex, when using those products. Wearing cotton liners with the gloves will help keep perspiration from further irritating your skin, although this can be a bulky combination. In addition, take a look at the remedies discussed under Atopic Dermatitis, since they may also help you avoid the substances irritating your skin.

Atopic Dermatitis

This type of dermatitis takes its name from "atopy," an inherited condition in which a person is predisposed to developing multiple allergic disorders, including asthma, hay fever, and food allergies. If you or a family member has an allergic disorder, you are at increased risk of developing atopic dermatitis.

Although atopic dermatitis is associated with allergic disorders, it is not itself an allergic reaction to a specific substance, as allergic contact dermatitis is. Rather, atopic dermatitis is a chronic and intensely itchy inflammation of the outer layer of skin. Its cause is unknown, although it appears to be related to an overly sensitive or malfunctioning immune system, and it can be aggravated by a variety of factors, such as temperature changes, skin infections, irritation from clothes or chemicals, and emotional stress.

Atopic dermatitis most frequently develops in children under five years of age, and the majority of cases resolve by adulthood. However, the condition can first appear in adulthood or continue into adulthood after developing in childhood.

The main symptom of atopic dermatitis is an intensely itchy skin rash, although the itchiness may actually precede the appearance of the rash. In infants, the rash may first appear in patches on the cheeks and chin, although it may also occur on the scalp, diaper area, and extremities and eventually cover large areas of the body. In older children and adults, the rash tends to appear in fewer and more limited areas, such as around the mouth and in skin folds, especially at the crook of the elbow and the back of the knee. The rash may appear dry and flaky at first, but the incredible itching often prompts scratching that further inflames the skin, increases itching, and can lead to blistering and crusting or cracking and secondary infection; some areas of skin may

eventually become thick and leathery as a result. The skin of someone who has had atopic dermatitis tends to lose moisture and dry out easily and is more vulnerable to irritant contact dermatitis.

Beyond easing the itching, coping with this condition requires protecting the skin from additional irritation. The following tips may help:

Wash new clothes before wearing. This helps remove formaldehyde and other potentially irritating chemicals used to treat fabrics.

Rinse twice. Even if you use a mild laundry detergent, it's a good idea to rinse your clothes twice to make sure all of the soap is removed.

Wear loose, natural-fiber clothing. You want your skin to be able to "breathe," so choose loose-fitting, open-weave, cotton or cotton-blend clothes.

Keep temperatures constant. Abrupt temperature changes—hot to cold or vice versa—can irritate the skin, so try to avoid them whenever possible. Try to maintain constant humidity levels in your home, too.

Keep your fingernails trimmed. It's hard to scratch effectively—and therefore hard to cause further damage to your skin—if your nails are short.

Hydrate your skin with a bath or shower. Use warm—not hot—water, and soak or shower for at least 15 minutes. Avoid using a washcloth because it's abrasive.

Use soap only where necessary. Choose a gentle soap, such as Dove, Oiltum, Alpha Keri, Neutrogena, Purpose, or Basis; a nonsoap cleanser, such as Aveeno or Emulave; or a liquid cleaner, such as Moisturel, Neutrogena, or Dove. Rinse thoroughly, gently pat away excess moisture, and then apply moisturizer to your damp skin to seal in the water. Plain petroleum jelly is the best after-bath sealant.

Use moisturizer throughout the day. It's extremely important for people with atopic dermatitis to keep their skin from becoming too dry. Some good moisturizers include Aquaphor ointment, Eucerin cream, Moisturel cream or lotion, D.M.L. cream or lotion, Lubriderm cream or lotion, Neutrogena emulsion, Eutra, Vaseline dermatology lotion, or LactiCare lotion. Apply it often, especially right after bathing to lock in moisture.

Use a sunscreen with an SPF of 15 or higher. A sunburn is only going to irritate the skin further.

Wash after swimming. The chlorine and other chemicals in most swimming pools can irritate sensitive skin. So shortly after you've finished your swim, take a shower or bath and use a mild soap all over. Don't forget to reapply your moisturizer, as well.

Check out your diet. Some physicians believe food allergies may play a role in atopic dermatitis, especially in childhood, while others say it hasn't been proven. If you suspect a particular food aggravates your rash, omit it from your diet for a few weeks. If the rash clears up but then returns when you reintroduce the food in your diet, consider permanently avoiding the food. Do not eliminate a large number of foods or an entire food group, however, without consulting your doctor first. If your child has atopic dermatitis and you suspect a food-allergy link, work with the child's pediatrician to investigate this possibility.

Diabetes

22 WAYS TO LIVE WELL WITH DIABETES

Each day in the United States, some 18 million people with diabetes walk a tightrope between too little sugar in the bloodstream and too much. Too little—which may come from a complication of medication—and they may quickly be overcome by dizziness, fatigue, headache, sweating, trembling, and, in severe cases, loss of consciousness and coma. Too much—which can happen after eating too much, especially if the person is older and overweight—and

the person may experience weakness, fatigue, excessive thirst, labored breathing, and loss of consciousness. If diabetes is poorly controlled or left untreated, it may lead to blindness, kidney disease, blood vessel damage, infection, heart disease, nerve damage, high blood pressure, stroke, limb amputation, and coma.

Because the initial symptoms (fatigue, weakness, frequent urination) are usually mild, about 30 percent of all people with diabetes do not realize that they have the disease. And that can have tragic consequences, because with early diagnosis and treatment, the chances of living a long and productive life are higher than if the disease creeps along until irreversible damage occurs.

If you'd like some proof that diabetes is a disease you can live well with, consider the accomplishments of these prolific people with diabetes: jazz musician Dizzy Gillespie, singer Ella Fitzgerald, actress Mary Tyler Moore, and baseball Hall-of-Famer Jim (Catfish) Hunter. Even before treatment was as sophisticated as it is today, author Ernest Hemingway and inventor

Thomas Edison, both of whom had diabetes, managed to leave their marks on the world.

If you are one of the lucky ones whose diabetes has been diagnosed by a doctor, you probably have some idea of what has gone awry in your body. Basically, the disorder stems from a malfunction in the way your body processes carbohydrates from the food you eat.

Normally, the process goes like this: The carbohydrates from your food are converted into a form of sugar called glucose. Glucose is the preferred fuel for your body's cells—and it's the only food your brain can use. The glucose floats along in the bloodstream until the pancreas, a large gland located behind the stomach, goes into action. The pancreas produces insulin, a hormone that signals body cells to take in the glucose. Once inside the cell, the glucose is either used as fuel to produce heat or energy or is stored as fat.

In a person with diabetes, however, the pancreas either produces little or no insulin or the body's cells become resistant to the hormone's action. The result is that the glucose can't get into the cells; it accumulates in the blood and is later expelled in the urine. In short, blood glucose rises while cells starve.

Five to 10 percent of people with diabetes have type 1, or insulin-dependent, diabetes, which usually develops in childhood or young adulthood. People with type 1 diabetes require daily injections of insulin to keep their blood glucose levels under control.

The vast majority of people with diabetes, on the other hand, have type 2, sometimes referred to as adult-onset diabetes even though more and more children these days are developing this type. Lifestyle changes can play a vital role in controlling type 2; they are generally the initial and preferred method for regulating blood glucose levels, although oral medication and even insulin may eventually need to be added to the treatment regimen.

No matter what type you have, you will benefit from taking an active role in your treatment. *But don't make a move without consulting your doctor first.* He or she will advise you on the proper steps; then it's up to you to carry them out. Some or all of the tips that follow may help.

Dish up a special diet. Whether you have type 1 or type 2 diabetes, you can benefit from a healthy diet, which will help improve your blood glucose, blood pressure, and blood cholesterol levels and also help keep your weight on track. Indeed, even if you take medication for your diabetes, watching your diet carefully is essential to controlling your disease and warding off complications. See "Diabetic Diet Choices" on page 106 for some gen-

Diabetic Diet Choices

In general, dietary guidelines for people with diabetes are similar to those for people without diabetes. People with diabetes should focus on eating a wide variety of fruits and vegetables, lean meats and fish, high-fiber whole grains, fat-free or low-fat dairy products, and legumes (dried beans and peas). However, people with diabetes also need to plan meals to avoid wild upward or downward swings in their blood glucose levels. In particular, they have to pay close attention to their intake of carbohydrates.

People with diabetes are often advised to follow one of three main eating plans:

- **The exchange system.** Using this system, you work with a registered dietitian to design a diet based on a series of exchanges. Each food is assigned to a certain category (starch, fruit, milk, and so on); you are permitted a certain number of food exchanges from various categories for each meal. Your dietitian will help you determine the number of exchanges you should eat each day and provide advice on healthy, nutritious choices.

- **Carbohydrate counting.** If you use the carbohydrate counting system, you are permitted a certain amount of carbohydrates per day and per meal. (This eating plan has gained popularity as a weight-loss tool for people with and without diabetes.) Carbohydrate counters work with a registered dietitian to determine how many grams of carbohydrates they should eat at each meal and each snack to keep blood glucose close to normal. (The grams of carbohydrates allowed per day and per meal depend on your weight, activity level, other health problems, medications, and age.) Many people find carbohydrate counting easier than the exchange system, especially now that carbohydrate information is so readily available. Whenever possible, you should choose high-quality carbohydrates such as high-fiber cereals, whole-grain breads, beans, and fresh fruits and vegetables.

- **The diabetic food pyramid** offers daily recommendations of two to three cups of low-fat or fat-free milk or yogurt; four to six ounces of lean meat, fish, nuts, or meat substitutes; three to five servings of vegetables (a serving is 1 cup raw or ½ cup cooked vegetables); two to four servings of fruits (a serving is 1 small fresh fruit, ½ cup canned fruit, 1 cup melon or chopped berries, or 2 tablespoons dried fruit); and six or more servings of grains, beans, and starchy vegetables (a serving is 1 slice bread, 1 ounce bagel, ¾ cup dry cereal, ½ cup cooked cereal, 1 six-inch tortilla, ⅓ cup rice or pasta, and ½ cup potato, yam, peas, corn, or cooked beans). It also allows small amounts of fats, sweets, and alcohol. If this method appeals to you, consult a dietitian for specific, personalized recommendations.

eral recommendations. Be sure to get additional, personalized diet instructions from your doctor, a certified diabetes educator, and/or a registered dietitian experienced in counseling folks with diabetes.

Drop the excess baggage. An estimated 90 percent of people with type 2 diabetes are overweight when diagnosed with the disease. What's more, the burden of added weight can both accelerate the disease process and hasten the development of complications, especially cardiovascular disease and stroke.

Conversely, losing excess weight may be the most important self-help measure you can take if you have type 2 diabetes. First, it helps your body better use the insulin that's available to bring down elevated blood glucose levels, which in turn may allow you to delay, reduce, or eliminate your need for diabetes medication. Second, it lowers elevated blood fat (cholesterol and triglycerides) and blood pressure levels, which are risk factors for heart disease (as well as stroke). Lowering those levels can reduce that risk, which is vital considering that simply having diabetes doubles your chances of developing heart disease.

Even a modest weight loss can produce dramatic effects in someone with type 2 diabetes: High insulin levels drop, the liver begins to secrete less glucose into the blood, and muscle tissues begin to respond to insulin and take up glucose better. It may even help prevent diabetes in people at increased risk for the disease due to overweight. According to the results of the Diabetes Prevention Program, a study of 3,234 people with pre-diabetes (meaning their cells were becoming increasingly insulin resistant), losing just 5 to 7 percent of their body weight sharply lowered the partici-pants' risk of developing diabetes. So, based on those results, if you weigh 250 pounds, for example, losing even 12 to 17 pounds could help lower your risk of diabetes. And if you already have diabetes, it could help bring your blood glucose levels back toward a more normal range and help ward off complications such as blindness. (See "Changing Your Ways" on this page for tips on making weight loss easier.)

But don't "crash." Weight loss that occurs too rapidly, such as from crash

Changing Your Ways

Here are some tips to help you succeed in losing weight:

Learn what triggers your eating. If the sight of a bakery window sets off a craving for cake, make it a habit to walk on the other side of the street. Become aware of any cues like this, and learn to avoid or control them.

Don't keep large amounts of food on hand. For some overweight people, the fact that food is within reach means that it must be eaten. Buy only enough for a few meals at a time.

Prepare your meals from scratch rather than relying on take-out. Take-out foods are likely to be high in calories, fat, and sodium because of the methods used in preparation and because portion sizes are so large. Consuming excess calories and too much fat can pack on pounds, while getting too much of all three ingredients can increase your risk of heart disease and stroke.

diets, is rarely maintained in the long run and is potentially dangerous if undertaken without a doctor's advice. Sometimes a doctor *will,* in fact, pre-scribe a very low-calorie diet to initiate weight loss, but only for a very short period of time and under medical supervision. Generally, the best approach is to lose weight gradually with a low-fat, lower-calorie, nutrition-ally balanced diet combined with increased activity. This approach will not only help you lose the excess weight, it will give you the tools you need to keep it off in the long run. Appetite suppres-sants, fasting, and crash diets won't.

Know your carbohy-drates. The traditional dogma for people with

diabetes was this: Avoid simple carbohydrates, or simple sugars (such as table sugar), because they raise blood glucose quickly, and choose complex carbohydrates (such as the starches and fiber found in grains, potatoes, beans, and peas), because they raise blood glucose more slowly. But researchers have discovered that this is not quite the case. It turns out that simple sugars and the digestible complex carbohydrates known as starches raise blood glucose levels at about the same rate (although fiber is classified as a complex carbohydrate, it is not digested by the body, so it does not raise blood glucose). What is more important is how the food is cooked and what those carbohydrates are eaten with—fat, for example, slows the digestion of carbohydrates and therefore slows the release of glucose into the bloodstream. This new dogma has, in turn, given way to newer dietary rules, which really aren't rules at all in the strictest sense.

Complex carbohydrates that haven't been highly refined or processed are still better dietary choices because of the valuable nutrients they provide (refining and processing often removes nutrients and fiber), but present evidence suggests that sucrose (table sugar) may not need to be "off-limits" for people with type 2 diabetes. As long as you account for the carbohydrates and calories from the sugar and don't go overboard, an occasional sweet treat can fit just fine in a healthy diabetic meal plan.

Get fond of fiber. One of the reasons that unrefined complex carbohydrates, such as whole-grain breads and beans, are so beneficial is that they are high in fiber. Fiber actually slows the rise in blood glucose after a meal.

Graze. Many experts believe that people with type 2 may more easily achieve normal blood glucose levels by not overloading with too much food at one time. Try eating three smaller meals plus two snacks each day—without increasing your total calorie intake—to see if it helps improve your control.

Foot Notes for Folks with Diabetes

A common complaint from many people is, "My feet are killing me!" For a person with diabetes, that statement could be all too true. Loss of nerve function, especially on the soles of the feet, can reduce feeling and mask a sore or injury on the foot that, if undetected and untreated, can turn into an ulcer or gangrene. That's why it's important to take excellent care of your feet. Here are some tips on how to do that:

Look them over. Give your feet a thorough going-over every night to make sure that you haven't developed a sore, blister, cut, scrape, or any other tiny problem that could blow up into big trouble. If your vision isn't good or you have trouble reaching your feet, have someone check your feet for you.

Wash, rinse, and dry. A clean foot is a healthy foot, with a much lower susceptibility to infection. And clean feet feel better, too. Don't forget to clean and dry between the toes.

Avoid bathroom surgery. Under normal circumstances, there is little danger from using a pumice stone to reduce a corn or callus. But for a person with diabetes, such a practice might lead to a little irritation, then a sore, then infection, and finally, a major ulcer. Likewise, over-the-counter caustic agents (such as salicylic acid) for removing corns and calluses can easily cause a serious chemical burn on your skin. Never use them. If you develop a corn, callus, wart, or other foot problem, see a podiatrist.

Take care of the little things. Any time a cut, sore, burn, scratch, or other minor injury appears on your foot, attend to it immediately by washing it and covering it with a protective sterile dressing. If you use adhesive tape, remove it carefully because it can weaken the skin when you pull it off; consider using paper or cloth tape instead. If the sore is not healing or if you notice signs of infection, such as redness, red streaks, warmth, swelling, pain, or drainage, see a podiatrist.

Choose shoes with care. Select shoes that fit both feet well and won't cause blisters or sores (see "If the Shoe Fits..." in CORNS AND CALLUSES for shoe-buying tips).

Have your feet checked. Be sure your doctor examines your feet during your regular checkups; taking your shoes and socks off as soon as you get in the exam room may serve as a reminder for you both. Or, find a podiatrist experienced in treating diabetic feet and together set up a schedule for regular foot checkups, perhaps coinciding with nail trimming if you are unable to take care of this task yourself.

Get a firm foothold. Neuropathy, damage to the nerves, is a common problem for people with diabetes. It occurs most often in the feet and legs, and its signs include recurring burning, pain, or numbness. In addition to being painful, neuropathy can be harmful because if it causes a loss of feeling in the foot, a foot injury may go undiscovered. In extreme cases, even a minor foot injury can lead to serious infection, gangrene, or amputation of the limb. Because of this, people with diabetes must be meticulous in caring for their feet. (See "Foot Notes for Folks with Diabetes" above.)

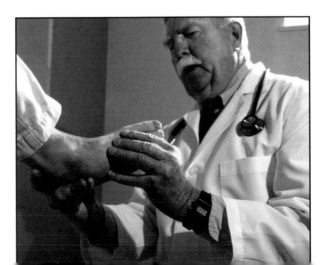

Early Warning Signs

Early diagnosis and treatment is extremely important in helping people with diabetes live healthier, longer lives. If you notice the early warning signs listed below or suspect that you may have diabetes, see your doctor.

Some of the early warning signs of type 1 diabetes include:
- frequent urination accompanied by unusual thirst
- extreme hunger
- rapid weight loss with easy tiring, weakness, and fatigue
- irritability, nausea, and vomiting

Some of the early warning signs of type 2 diabetes include:
- frequent urination accompanied by unusual thirst
- blurred vision or any change in sight
- tingling or numbness in the legs, feet, or fingers
- frequent skin infection or itchy skin
- slow healing of cuts and bruises
- unusual drowsiness
- vaginitis in women
- erectile dysfunction in men

Keep in mind, too, that if you are significantly overweight, you are at a much higher risk of developing diabetes.

Be a sport. Whether or not you have diabetes, exercise is good for your body. It tones up the heart and other muscles, strengthens bones, lowers blood pressure, strengthens the respiratory system, helps raise HDL ("good" cholesterol), lowers LDL ("bad" cholesterol), fosters a sense of well-being, decreases tension, aids in weight management, enhances work capacity, and can confer a sense of control. However, if you have diabetes, exercise provides even more benefits because it can improve your body's ability to use blood glucose and insulin.

Moderate exercise, such as walking, cycling, or swimming, are best for people with diabetes. Because people with diabetes have to take some extra precautions while exercising, you will need to work with your health-care provider to design an exercise program that is right for you. For example, since exercise lowers blood glucose, you will need to learn how to maintain the correct balance of food, exercise, and medication to prevent your blood glucose levels from dropping too low.

Your doctor may recommend that you avoid intense, high-impact activities such as running because of the potential for foot injury. Also, intense exercise could endanger tiny blood vessels in the eyes that are already weakened by diabetes (all that glucose in the blood can damage fragile vessels as well as nerves), potentially leading to rupture, vision problems, and even blindness. Overall, however, the benefits of exercise far outweigh the risks, and if you work with your doctor to create an exercise plan, you should be fine. Keep in mind that if you are over 40 years old, you will need to undergo a general medical examination, including a cardiovascular screening and exercise test, before proceeding with your exercise program.

Once your doctor gives the go-ahead, you need to set realistic goals in order to avoid too-high or too-low blood glucose levels. Begin with small goals, such as exercising for five minutes three days a week, and work up gradually to exercising at least 30 minutes a day most days of the week.

Watch your mouth. People with diabetes must be diligent about oral health. The high levels of sugar in their blood make their mouths extra inviting to oral bacteria, and their decreased ability to fight off infection means they must be especially cautious about preventing tooth decay and periodontal (gum) disease. Keep a supply of soft-bristled toothbrushes on hand so you won't have to deal with old, worn brushing aids. Brush and floss without fail after every meal and before bedtime. And see your dentist regularly (every six months at least) for a checkup and cleaning.

Check your dentures. Ill-fitting dentures or permanent bridgework can cause sores in the mouth that don't heal. If you notice sore spots in your mouth or find that your dentures are moving or slipping, see your dentist to have the problem corrected as soon as possible.

Take charge. The more you know about your disease, the better you can control it. Educate yourself through reputable books, magazines, and Web sites related to diabetes. If you need help understanding what you should do, ask your doctor for a referral to a registered dietitian or a diabetes educator.

Do something nice for yourself. While it's important to learn as much as you can about your diabetes and stay with your treatment regimen, you also need to keep things in perspective. Don't get so caught up in your diabetes that you neglect the rest of your life. Make a list of all the things you would like to do if you had the time—and then *make* the time to do at least some of them.

Do something nice for someone else. It's hard to dwell on your own problems when you are engaged in helping someone else. Doing volunteer work at a nursing home, hospital, school, or church can help others and can make you feel better, too.

Diaper Rash

11 Ways to Get Rid of It—for Good

Hello, Doctor?

If the rash is severe, doesn't improve after about five days of home treatment, or spreads beyond the diaper area (to the arms or head, for example), contact your baby's doctor. Also call the pediatrician if:

- Your baby develops a fever along with the diaper rash.
- Blisters, boils, pimples, or ulcers form on the skin.
- The rash weeps, oozes, or produces pus.

Diaper rash. You hate to see it on your little one's bottom, and your baby doesn't enjoy it, either. While far from being a serious medical problem, it's another of life's little discomforts.

Diaper rash is the result of irritation, usually caused by prolonged exposure to a diaper that is moist with urine or soiled with stool. Chafing from tight-fitting diapers or clothing or contact with an irritating substance in certain disposable wipes or diapers, detergents or other laundry products, soaps, or lotions may also produce a rash in the diaper area.

The good news is, you can usually cure that rash within days. And with some conscientious care, you can say good-bye to it forever. The following steps can help you not only get rid of

diaper rash but protect your baby's tender bottom from future bouts.

Get rid of the diaper... and say so long to diaper rash. The diaper holds the urine and/or feces against baby's sensitive skin and creates a warm, moist environment that can make the skin raw and provides the perfect breeding ground for bacteria, yeast, and fungi. To treat and/or prevent diaper rash, therefore, let your baby go bare-bottomed whenever possible. To minimize mess, put your diaperless baby on a rubber mat covered with a washable cloth.

Change the baby often. When going diaper-free isn't feasible, the best way to avoid diaper rash or cure an existing outbreak is to make sure the baby is always clean and dry. Check the baby's diaper often, and change it as soon as possible after it is soiled.

Avoid commercial baby wipes. Many brands of store-bought baby wipes contain alcohol and other chemicals that can irritate your child's skin and strip it of the natural protective oils that keep it soft and supple. Water, perhaps with a little mild soap, and a

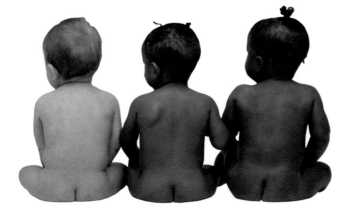

soft washcloth are actually the best tools for cleaning baby's bottom if you want to prevent a rash. If you do use soap, rinse thoroughly with a clean, wet cloth or plain water to remove any residue. You may want to skip the soap if a rash is already present, though, since it may cause stinging.

Dry that bottom. Once you've removed a soiled diaper and cleaned your baby's bottom, make sure you thoroughly pat the area dry (no rubbing!) with a soft towel. To ensure a completely dry bottom, leave the area exposed to air for a few minutes before putting on a new diaper.

Put on a barrier. Many pediatricians recommend applying a thin layer of nonprescription diaper-rash cream or ointment containing zinc oxide, such as A+D or Desitin, every time you change your baby. Used on healthy skin, it forms a barrier that can help protect the diaper area from the irritating effects of urine and feces. If a rash is already present, however, you don't want to completely seal the skin with an ointment or thick layer of cream, since air reaching the skin will keep the irritated area dry and help it heal. So you may need to either skip the salve until the skin clears or apply only a thin layer of cream, which will soothe and help protect the skin while allowing some air to penetrate.

The Great Diaper Debate

Are cloth diapers or disposable diapers better at preventing diaper rash? A 1990 study conducted at the Department of Design at Colorado State University in Fort Collins found that diapers labeled "super absorbent" kept the skin drier and retained more moisture than cloth or conventional disposable brands. In most cases, the regular disposables were less effective than cloth diapers at keeping the skin dry. Among cloth diapers, the most effective were those that contained an inner layer of nonwoven fabric, researchers found. Another study conducted at the Department of Dermatology at the University of Rochester in New York found that babies who wore diapers containing substances to absorb urine and make it "gel" had significantly less diaper rash than babies who wore regular disposable diapers.

Research notwithstanding, most pediatric experts say that it doesn't really matter which type of diaper parents choose and that they should pick the kind that works best for their particular situation. To prevent diaper rash, they say, the most important thing is to make sure that the baby's diaper gets changed as soon as possible after it is soiled.

Use only baby-friendly skin products. Choose soaps, shampoos, creams, and ointments specifically designed for use on baby's tender skin. Don't use products meant for adults, which often contain strong detergents, fragrances, dyes, and other chemicals that can irritate a baby's skin. Never use a cream that contains camphor, phenol, methyl salicylate, benzoin tincture, or boric acid on your baby unless specifically directed to by a pediatrician. Also, wash your infant's diapers, clothes, sleepwear, bedding, towels, and washcloths separately from those of other household members, using a laundry soap designed for this purpose. Residue of harsh detergents, bleaches, and fabric softeners on material that comes into prolonged contact with baby's skin may be enough to cause irritation.

Give powder a pass. In the past, the accepted way to keep a baby's bottom dry was to sprinkle talcum powder or cornstarch on the diaper area to soak up moisture. However, studies have shown that if babies inhale talcum powder, it can be dangerous, even fatal. And cornstarch or cornstarch-based powders foster the growth of yeast. So this is one old remedy to leave in the past.

Put the diapers "on line." Some moms have been taught that diapers are less likely to cause a rash if they are hung out to dry on a line instead of tossed into a dryer. Call it mother's intuition, but they may have something there: Some doctors say this trick works, although no one is sure why. If you have a place to hang diapers, you may want to give it a try. If you use a clothes dryer instead, skip the dryer sheets, which are likely to contain chemicals that can easily irritate sensitive baby skin. No matter how you dry cloth diapers, however, be sure to wash them in hot water without bleach and, if your baby already has diaper rash or seems

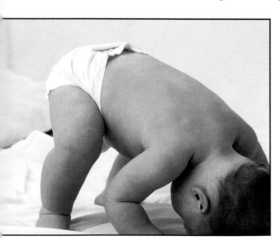

prone to getting it, rinse them twice without adding fabric softener.

Try a vinegar solution. Stale urine is extremely alkaline—the bacteria that colonize it release ammonia—and can burn the skin the same way acid can. To neutralize it, add ½ cup white vinegar to the rinse water when you wash the baby's diapers. If you use disposables, you can try wiping the baby's bottom with a solution of eight parts water to one part vinegar for a similar effect.

Avoid plastic pants. Diaper rash clears up faster when the skin remains dry. Plastic pants worn over a diaper, however, keep moisture in. If a rash is present, also avoid tight-fitting diapers and clothing, which may cause chafing as well as restrict airflow. You may even need to switch, at least temporarily, to looser or larger-size diapers if you usually use more-fitted diapers that have tight, elastic leg holes and other "leak guards" that hold urine in and keep out air.

Try a different disposable. Some babies may be sensitive to materials or substances in one brand of disposable diaper but not in another. So if diligent changing of soiled diapers and other home remedies haven't completely cleared the rash or kept it from coming back, you might want to experiment with another brand to see if it does the trick.

Diarrhea

15 Ways to Go with the Flow

You may blame it on a 24-hour bug or something you ate, but if you're like the average American, you'll suffer once or twice this year from diarrhea—frequent, watery bowel movements that may be accompanied by painful cramps, nausea, and/or vomiting.

Diarrhea is uncomfortable and unpleasant, but generally no big deal in otherwise healthy adults. However, if diarrhea becomes a chronic condition, the situation changes. Or if it affects the very young, the elderly, or the chronically ill, it can be dangerous. And if you're not careful to drink enough fluids, you could find yourself complicating what should have been a simple enough situation.

What causes diarrhea? Because the condition generally lasts only a few days, doctors don't usually test the stool to diagnose what started it in the first place. It's most often due to a viral infection, which antibiotics can't fight, so you just have to tough it out for a couple of days. If a virus is the cause, you may also experience cramping, nausea and vomiting, headache, fever, malaise, and even upper respiratory

Hello, Doctor?

See a doctor for your diarrhea if:
- You see blood in your stool.
- You experience symptoms of dehydration, including dizziness when you stand up, scanty and deep-yellow urine, increased thirst, and dry skin. Children who are dehydrated may also cry without producing tears.
- You've got a fever or shaking chills.
- Your diarrhea persists for more than 48 to 72 hours.
- The person with diarrhea is very young, very old, or chronically ill (see "The Young and the Old" on page 118).

tract symptoms, such as a runny nose. One clue: If members of your family all get sick, but at different times, a virus is likely the culprit. Bacteria, which often cause traveler's diarrhea in certain parts of the world, can also be responsible for diarrhea, usually as the result of food poisoning.

Much rarer are microbes like amoebae and giardia that try to set up house permanently in your bowel, causing diarrhea that lasts for weeks or months. You can get these from contaminated food or water, lakes and streams, public swimming pools, and communal hot tubs.

Certain drugs, especially antibiotics, can cause diarrhea as a side

When Diarrhea Lasts and Lasts

Sometimes diarrhea goes on...for weeks. That's when a more serious problem is probably responsible. Your doctor can ferret out the cause. Here are some of the possibilities:

Lactose intolerance. If you get diarrhea after drinking milk, your body may have lost some or all of its ability to digest lactose, the sugar in milk and dairy products. Lactose intolerance is the most common cause of chronic diarrhea. If you can't drink milk, you'll probably need to take calcium supplements or to drink calcium-fortified juice or soy milk. (See LACTOSE INTOLERANCE.)

Celiac disease. In this case, you can't digest gluten, which is a part of wheat.

Irritable bowel syndrome (IBS). Some people with IBS have constipation and some have diarrhea. Others alternate between the two.

Parasitic infections. These can hang on indefinitely.

Crohn's disease or ulcerative colitis. These two conditions are similar, and no one knows their cause. But the end results are bowel inflammation and diarrhea, often accompanied by pain.

Systemic illnesses. Chronic diarrhea can be a complication of diseases such as diabetes, scleroderma, and hyperthyroidism.

Cancer. The cause of diarrhea is usually more benign, but one of the warning signs of tumors in the bowel is diarrhea, especially if blood is present.

effect. Magnesium-containing antacids and artificial sweeteners, such as sorbitol, are often overlooked culprits, as well.

Unless diarrhea persists—which can signal a more serious problem (see "When Diarrhea Lasts and Lasts" on this page)—you usually don't find out its cause. Treatment for a temporary bout is aimed at easing the symptoms and preventing dehydration, the most serious consequence of diarrhea.

So what can you do?

Ride it out. If you're not very young or old or suffering from any chronic illness, it may be safe just to put up with it for a couple of days. After all, it's often your body's natural way of getting rid of something that shouldn't be there to begin with.

Keep hydrated. You can lose a lot of liquid in diarrhea, but you also lose electrolytes—minerals such as sodium and potassium that are critical in the running of your body. To help replace what you're losing, you need to drink plenty of fluids.

Aim to consume two quarts (eight cups) of fluids a day, three quarts (12 cups) if you're running a fever. Plain water lacks electrolytes, but it's a good, gentle-on-the-tummy option that can help you replace some of the fluid that you've lost. Other choices include weak tea with a little sugar, sports drinks such as Gatorade, flat soda pop (decaffeinated flavors such as ginger ale are best), and fruit juices other than

apple and prune, which have a laxative effect.

Use an over-the-counter electrolyte replacement. Pedialyte, Rehydralyte, and Ricelyte are examples of rehydration solutions that also help replenish the electrolytes lost through diarrhea. These formulas, available without a prescription from your local drugstore, contain fluids and minerals in the proper proportion. Follow the directions on the package.

Keep your liquids cool but not ice-cold. Whatever you choose to drink, keep it cool; it will be less irritating that way. Sip, don't guzzle; it will be easier on your insides if you take frequent sips of liquid instead of guzzling down a glass at a time.

Sip some chicken broth. Or any broth, but have it lukewarm instead of hot, and add a little salt to it if it's not already salted.

Rest in bed. Give your body a chance to fight the bug that's got you "on the run."

Put a heating pad on your belly. It may help relieve abdominal cramps.

Try yogurt. Choose a brand that contains *live* lactobacillus cultures, which are friendly bugs that normally live in the gut. (Even people with lactose intolerance can often handle this type of yogurt.)

Eat easy-to-digest foods. Good choices include soup, gelatin, rice, noodles, bananas, potatoes, toast, cooked carrots, soda crackers, and skinless white-meat chicken.

Take the pink stuff. Stopping the diarrhea with an over-the-counter (OTC) medication may not be the best thing for your body, since the diarrhea probably reflects your body's attempt to get rid of a troublesome bug. If you do feel it's necessary, however, bismuth subsalicylate (the most well known brand-name version of this is Pepto-Bismol) is probably the safest OTC antidiarrheal medicine. It also appears to have a mild antibacterial effect, making it useful against traveler's diarrhea, which is usually bacteria related (see TRAVELER'S DIARRHEA).

Take something stronger if you must. Again, you're probably better off going without antidiarrheal medication if you can possibly stand it because your body is likely trying to

The Young and the Old

For most people, diarrhea is nothing more than a minor inconvenience. But for the very young and the elderly, it can be life threatening, even fatal. Diarrhea causes fluid loss, and babies and seniors are more vulnerable to fluid loss than are adults and older children.

Dehydration can take days to occur in an adult, hours to days for a child, and seconds to minutes in a newborn. Unfortunately, diarrhea is harder to recognize in infants because they have anywhere from six to nine bowel movements a day, and if they are breast-fed, the movements may normally be very loose. But parents generally learn fast what their baby's normal stool looks like. If it becomes more liquid, if it's explosive, or if the odor changes, it's probably diarrhea. Call the doctor.

Breast-feeding is the best way to prevent diarrhea in babies. The colostrum, the special kind of milk the mother produces during the first few days after childbirth, is loaded with substances that help prevent gastrointestinal infections later in life.

There's also less chance of contamination with breast-feeding, since bottles don't have to be washed. And formula itself can cause allergic reactions that include diarrhea.

Diarrhea is less serious in children between the ages of 18 months and 8 years, but it still warrants a call to the doctor.

The elderly can't afford to lose much fluid, either, but that's because their circulatory system has changed with aging. Fluid loss can reduce the body's ability to circulate blood, raising the risk of stroke, heart attack, or kidney failure.

When the elderly have diarrhea, it's often difficult to know when they're becoming dehydrated. Elderly people are less likely than younger people to feel thirsty, and changes in the skin that signal dehydration aren't very apparent in aged skin.

The best clue: Are they still passing urine every hour or two?

If you're older and in good health but have a history of congestive heart failure and/or are taking diuretics, you should call your physician as soon as the diarrhea starts. Your doctor may want to adjust your diuretic use because diuretics increase fluid loss.

About half of the cases of diarrhea in the elderly are probably due to infections, the majority of which are viral. Ironically, medical care can lead to some of the cases of diarrhea in the elderly that are not the result of viral infection. Older people are more likely to be on antibiotics, which can cause diarrhea as a side effect. They're also prone to constipation and may self-medicate or have a physician recommend several types of laxatives, which can end up causing diarrhea.

flush out a nasty bug. If you absolutely need some relief, however, you can try OTC loperamide hydrochloride (sold under the brand names Imodium A-D and Kaopectate II, among others). It decreases intestinal motility, slowing the movement of the contents of the intestines through the gut. Elderly patients should use this medication only with their doctor's approval, because decreased motility can be especially dangerous for them when an infection is present and can lead to bigger problems.

Don't do dairy. Avoid milk, cheese, and other dairy products (except yogurt, unless you don't usually tolerate it well) while you have diarrhea as well as for one to three weeks after it stops. The small intestine, where milk is digested, is affected by diarrhea and simply won't be able to do its job as well for a while.

Cut out caffeine. Just as it stimulates your nervous system, caffeine jump-starts your intestines. And that's the last thing you need when you have diarrhea.

Say no to sweet treats. High concentrations of sugar can increase diarrhea. The sugar in fruit is no exception.

Steer clear of greasy or high-fiber foods. These are harder for your gut to handle right now. It needs foods that are kinder and gentler.

Dry Hair

11 TIPS FOR TAMING IT

Your hair feels like straw—dry, fly-away, unmanageable. How could you have been cursed with such a mane? You probably can't blame your genes. While some people are born with naturally dry hair, the problem is most often caused by abuse.

That's right. Those dry locks are most likely your own fault. Exposing your hair to harsh chemicals such as hair dyes, permanent-wave solutions, and the chlorine in swimming pools and hot tubs dries out the hair. So does shampooing too often and using styling tools such as hot combs, hot rollers, and blow-dryers. Even too much sun and wind can dry out your tresses.

You can learn to treat your hair with TLC and teach your dry hair to be more manageable. Here's how:

Don't overdo the shampoo. Shampooing too often is one of the most common causes of dry hair. Many people believe that squeaky-clean hair is healthy hair, so they wash it one or more times every day. But shampoos often contain harsh cleaning agents that can strip away your hair's natural oils, which help hold in moisture.

On the other hand, a gentle shampoo will stimulate the oil glands, so you probably shouldn't go longer than three days without a good lather.

Be kind to your hair. Dry hair is the most fragile type of hair and is subject to breakage, so it must be handled with care. When lathering, be gentle. Avoid any pulling or yanking on your hair in any way, which strains the hair shafts. Don't scrub with your fingernails, which can not only break the hair but irritate your scalp. Work up a lather using your fingertips, instead.

Use a gentle shampoo. Dry hair needs a gentle, acidic cleanser. The ideal shampoos for dry hair have a pH of between 4.5 and 6.7, but here's a good rule of thumb: Don't use any hair cleanser that you wouldn't put on your face. Some people recommend baby shampoos, but their pH is usually far too high—such alkaline shampoos dry out the hair. Acidic shampoos are better for your hair.

Pour on the conditioner. Strawlike hair needs conditioning. Look for

products that contain little or no alcohol, which will dry out hair even more. Reading labels will help, but it might be simpler just to take a whiff before you buy: Conditioners with little or no fragrance tend to be low in alcohol or contain none at all. If your hair is really dry, consider using an overnight conditioner, which you apply before going to bed (you sleep wearing a shower cap) and rinse off in the morning.

For severely dry, damaged hair, you may want to use a body lotion that contains petroleum jelly and glycerin (such as Moisturel) instead of a conditioner. Apply the moisturizer to damp hair, and leave it on overnight beneath a shower cap. Rinse it out thoroughly in the morning.

Pour on hot oil. Hair-care professionals often recommend hot-oil treatments to repair dry, damaged hair. Over-the-counter hot-oil products are available that you heat and place on the hair for 5 to 20 minutes (according to package instructions). Wear a plastic bag or shower cap over your hair while the hot oil is on, then wash the hair thoroughly with a gentle shampoo.

Slather on the mayo. Mayonnaise is another excellent moisturizing treatment for dry hair. Begin by shampooing your hair, then working in a tablespoon of regular (not low-fat) mayonnaise. Cover your hair with a plastic bag for about a half hour, then shampoo again and rinse thoroughly.

Nix the 100 strokes. Despite what you may have heard, too much brushing can actually fracture the hair, causing it to fall out. Fragile, dry hair is even more vulnerable to excessive or aggressive brushing.

Give yourself a scalp massage. Gently rubbing your scalp with your fingertips stimulates the oil glands.

Be an egghead. For another homemade hair treatment, beat an egg in a cup and, with tepid water (not hot—it cooks the egg!), lather the egg into the hair and then rinse it out with tepid water. There's no need to shampoo afterward. The egg cleans the hair and gives it a lovely shine.

Pace your hair treatments. If you perm on Tuesday, dye your hair on Thursday, and put it in hot rollers on Saturday, your hair is destined to be dry and damaged. You don't have to abandon styling practices such as dyes, permanent waves, or hair straightening if you have dry hair. Just space those treatments out as much as possible.

Hold the heat. Using hot combs, hot rollers, and blow-dryers is asking for dry hair. Hot rollers are the worst because they stretch the hair while the heat shrinks it. Hot combs tend to do the same. If you must use artificial heat, keep your blow-dryer on a low setting and avoid pulling or stretching the hair while drying.

Dry Skin

16 WAYS TO FIGHT MOISTURE LOSS

Everyone occasionally suffers from dry skin. To a degree, your genes and the climate you live in influence the moisture content of your skin. But lifestyle choices, such as taking too many hot showers, can cause dry skin, too.

When there's not enough water in the skin's top layer (called the stratum corneum), the skin becomes flaky, itchy, and unsightly. In extreme cases, this layer can become rough, raw, cracked, and painful, and chronic dermatitis (skin irritation) can develop.

Normally, the outer layer of the skin is kept moist by fluid from the sweat glands and from underlying tissues. Oil, produced by the sebaceous glands in the skin, helps to seal in that fluid.

Hello, Doctor?

While dry skin can usually be dealt with at home, you should consult your doctor if:
- Your dry skin hasn't improved after you've diligently applied these home remedies for two to three weeks.
- You have persistent cracks or open sores in your skin or notice signs of infection, such as red streaks, swelling, or pus.
- Your dry skin causes itching that prevents you from falling asleep or interferes with your normal daily activities.
- You have large patches of scaley skin with a red or silvery appearance.

But lots of things rob moisture from the skin's outer layer. Some people simply have an outer skin layer that doesn't hold water well. Others may have less-active sweat glands. Age is also a factor: The older you get, the less oil the sebaceous glands produce, and the drier your skin is likely to be.

One of the greatest thieves of skin moisture is low humidity. Dry air, common in many areas during the cold winter months, sucks water from the skin. (Add the drying effects of the sun and/or high altitude to low humidity and the

Sun and Your Dry Skin

If you're a sun worshipper who is always "working on your tan," you're also drying the outer layer of your skin and setting the stage for wrinkles and age spots. Far worse, excessive sun exposure increases your risk of skin cancer. People who are fair-skinned are at greater risk of developing such cancers than are darker-skinned individuals. To avoid the dry skin, wrinkles, and increased cancer risk from sun exposure, follow these tips:

Wear sunscreen. Sunscreens are rated by their sun protection factor, or SPF. The higher the SPF number, the greater the level of sun protection. Opt for an SPF of at least 15.

Cover up. Wear a lightweight, long-sleeved shirt and a hat when you're in the sun.

Avoid the sun between 10:00 A.M. and 3:00 P.M. This is the time of day when the sun's burning rays are strongest, so try to plan outdoor activities for earlier or later in the day.

Use lotions. If you refuse to give up sunbathing, apply a cream-type tanning lotion and occasionally "spritz" your skin with mineral water to keep it moist. Keep your tanning sessions as short as possible, and moisturize afterward.

parching is compounded.) Heated or air-conditioned air also tends to be dry and thus readily steals valuable moisture from skin.

And as odd as it may sound, repeated exposure to water can actually dry out your skin. Washing your hands frequently or bathing several times each day causes repeated wetting and drying of the tissue that holds the outer layer of skin together. Over time, this process robs the skin of proteins that help to keep it moist. Soaking in steaming-hot water for long periods can have a similar effect.

Harsh soaps, detergents, household cleansers, and chemical solvents can also take their toll on the skin. All by themselves, these products can damage the skin's outer layer. For people who must frequently wash and dry their hands, such as nurses and hair stylists, their hands suffer from the combined drying effects of frequent contact with water *and* exposure to strong soaps. This double whammy can cause red, chapped skin, often called "dishpan hands."

While you can't keep skin away from all external moisture-robbers, here are some tips to keep your skin moist, comfortable, and looking youthful for years to come:

Moisturize, moisturize, moisturize. Use skin lotion or cream every day. For best results, apply moisturizer as soon as you step out of the bath or shower, before your skin has a chance to dry:

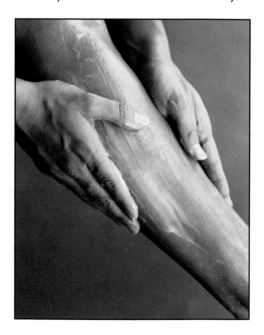

Pat, don't rub, yourself dry-damp with a soft towel, then apply moisturizer all over. Re-apply moisturizer throughout the day when your skin feels dry and again before bed. Avoid heavily scented salves, which may contain drying alcohol, and runny moisturizers, which are mostly water. Thick moisturizers, such as cold cream, are more effective since they contain more oil than water. For an inexpensive, extra-thick moisturizer, mix petroleum jelly (which is all oil) with a little water.

Take short, cool showers and baths. Hot water actually removes oil, the skin's natural barrier to moisture loss, and can make itching worse. Bathe or shower only as often as *really* necessary and no more than once a day. If you insist on long, hot soaks,

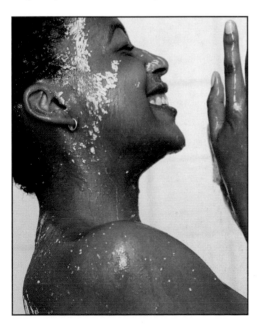

always apply a moisturizer immediately afterward.

Use soap sparingly. It's natural to associate cleanliness with good health, but dermatologists think washing too often with soap and water damages the outer layer of skin. People who suffer from chronically dry skin should take brief baths or showers and lather up only the groin, armpits, and feet.

When you use soap, opt for milder, oilated or superfatted soaps such as Dove, Basis, or Aveenobar. For super-dry skin, you may have to use a soap substitute to cleanse your skin.

Don't be abrasive. Trying to scrub off dry, scaly skin with washcloths, loofah sponges, or other scrubbing products dries and irritates your skin even more.

Oil that bath. When used properly, bath oils can help restore moisture to dry skin. If you put the bath oil in the water before you get in and get wet, the oil can coat your skin and prevent it from becoming saturated with water. Instead, add the oil to the bath after you've been in the water for a while— or apply it directly to your wet skin after bathing. (Take care getting in or out of the tub, however, since the oil will make the tub slippery.)

Mineral oil makes an excellent bath oil. However, do not soak, even in an oil bath, for longer than 20 minutes.

Raise the humidity. The higher the humidity, the less dry your skin. That's why dry skin is virtually unheard of among people who live in tropical climates where the humidity surpasses 90 percent much of the time. Once the temperature drops below 50 degrees, the humidity tends to drop off, too.

Sixty percent humidity is perfect for the skin. It's the point at which the skin and the air are in perfect balance and moisture isn't being drawn from the skin into the air. If you live in a dry climate or if the humidity in your office or home is less than 60 percent, consider using a humidifier. Even a vaporizer or kettle of water on slow boil can raise the humidity in a room somewhat.

Avoid detergents, cleansers, and solvents. Common household products such as cleansers, window cleaners, ammonia, turpentine, lighter fluid, and mineral spirits, can dry and damage the skin's outer layer. Avoid directly exposing your skin to such products by wearing vinyl gloves or using less-harsh alternatives (for example, vinegar and water make a great window cleaner) whenever possible. Use a long-handled brush to keep your hands out of dishwater.

Nix alcohol-based products. Some people like to cleanse their facial skin with alcohol wipes or other astringents. They leave the skin feeling clean and make it tingle, but the alcohol dries the skin, so avoid them.

Use cream- or oil-based makeup. If you wear foundation and blusher, choose oil-based types that help retain moisture rather than water-based products. In the evening, wash off makeup with mild soap. Then, rinse thoroughly, blot dry with a soft towel, and moisturize well with a heavy, cream-type moisturizer.

Go easy on the heat. During the winter months, the hot, dry indoor environment produced by forced-air heating systems and woodstoves pulls moisture from your skin. So try to maintain the air temperature in your home a few degrees lower—and add a layer of clothing, if necessary–to lessen the drying effect on your skin.

Toss off the electric blanket, pile on the comforter. The heat from electric blankets can dry out your skin, too. If you have chronically dry skin, opt for an extra blanket instead of an electric one.

Avoid too much alcohol on the inside, too. Beer, wine, and other liquor lower the water concentration of the blood, robbing the skin of moisture, which helps keep it looking youthful. Doctors say that alcohol abusers often have parched, wrinkly skin. If you drink alcohol, limit your intake to no more than a drink or two a day.

Earache

7 SOUND WAYS TO HEAD OFF PAIN

Most people don't think about their ears much, unless they're self-conscious about their size. But when an earache develops, the affected ear—no matter its actual size—can feel as if it has taken on monster proportions, making it difficult to think of anything else.

For all the unspeakable pain caused by earaches, they are rarely life threatening. Still, they can be serious, especially if they are caused by infection. Signs of an ear infection include ear pain and hearing loss. In a young child, clues that an ear infection may be present include rubbing or tugging at the ear, excessive crying or fussiness, fever, nausea, and vomiting. Since an untreated ear infection can lead to permanent hearing loss, and since ear pain can sometimes reflect a problem in another part of the body (see "Earaches that Aren't" on this page), it is important to have any earache checked out by a doctor. (For information on preventing ear infections, see MIDDLE-EAR INFECTION and SWIMMER'S EAR.)

Other than infection, the most common cause of earache is a blocked eustachian tube. The eustachian tube is

Earaches that Aren't

Sometimes, diseases and disorders in other parts of the head and neck can sound an alarm in the ear. This is called referred pain, because it originates elsewhere in the body but is felt in the ear. That's one reason why it's important to have ear pain evaluated by a doctor.

To otolaryngologists (doctors who specialize in ear, nose, and throat disorders), the most common culprits in referred ear pain are the "five Ts": tongue, teeth, tonsils, throat, and temporomandibular (jaw) joint.

a thin, membrane-lined tube that connects the inside-back portion of the nose with the middle ear. Normally, when you swallow, the eustachian tube opens so that the air pressure in the middle ear is equalized with the air pressure in the atmosphere. Sometimes, however, the eustachian tube can become blocked, usually as a result of a cold, a sinus or throat infection, or an allergy. When this happens, a vacuum occurs in the middle ear, sucking the eardrum inward and stretching it painfully taut.

When Your Eardrum Takes a Beating

If you feel a sudden, sharp pain in your ear following a trauma such as an explosion or a scuba-diving accident, you may have a perforated eardrum.

While the pain may occur only at the time of the accident, the injury itself needs evaluation by a specialist to head off permanent disruption of the middle-ear mechanism. Most injury-related eardrum perforations are small and will heal spontaneously within a few weeks, provided middle-ear infections are prevented or controlled (which is why you still need to see a doctor). Large perforations may require surgery.

This type of earache is especially common in people who travel by air. As the plane takes off, the air pressure in the plane's cabin decreases, and as the plane lands, the air pressure in the cabin increases; in each instance, the pressure change occurs very rapidly. While normally the air in the eustachian tube manages to equalize on its own, if there is congestion in the upper respiratory tract—such as a stuffy nose caused by allergies or a cold—the tube may not behave so naturally. (This type of earache can also occur as a result of pressure changes during an elevator ride in a tall building and during scuba diving.) Fortunately, there are some tricks you can try to ward off ear pain that results from the ups and downs of air travel.

Swallow hard. When you swallow, you activate the muscle that opens the eustachian tube. On an airplane, when the pilot announces that it's time to fasten your seat belts for landing, get your mouth set to swallow. Frequent swallowing can also bring some temporary relief from earache pain until you can get to the doctor.

Keep your mouth moving. You swallow more often when you chew gum or suck on a hard candy, so pop some into your mouth just before the plane descends.

Don't stifle a yawn. Yawning is an excellent way to keep the eustachian tube open.

Stay awake. If you're sleeping, you're not going to be swallowing, so ask your seatmate or a flight attendant to wake you before descent.

Hold your nose. If your ears still become uncomfortably blocked as the plane descends, the American Academy of Otolaryngology, Head and Neck Surgery suggests that you try this: With the thumb and forefinger of one hand, pinch your nostrils tightly closed, and use the forefinger of your other hand to press closed the external opening of the unaffected ear. Now, with your mouth closed, try to blow out through the pinched nostrils, blowing as forcefully as you would blow your nose. Repeat if necessary. You should experience a cracking sensation or a loud pop and relief of the pain if the maneuver works. Don't try this trick if you have a sore throat, fever, or other signs of brewing upper respiratory infection, however, because the infection might be forced into your ears. And don't attempt it if you have a heart or circulatory disorder.

Reach for relief. Frequent flyers should tuck away a decongestant pill or nasal spray to use an hour or so before landing. This shrinks the nasal membranes, making it easier to keep the eustachian tube open. Over-the-counter medications like these are not for everyone, however. People with heart disease, high blood pressure, irregular heart rhythms, or thyroid disease should avoid them. Pregnant women and individuals subject to anxiety should stay away from them, too. And the nasal sprays or drops should not be used for more than three days in a row, because such overuse

Detecting Earaches in Babies

Kids get more ear infections than any other ailment except the common cold. In fact, according to the American Academy of Pediatrics (AAP), most children have at least one ear infection by the time they are three years old.

Babies, toddlers, and preschoolers can't always tell you when their ears hurt, so you sometimes have to be a medical detective to figure out what's bothering them. The following symptoms may suggest that your child has an earache, according to the AAP:

- Pain. In younger children who can't tell you they have an earache, pain can cause irritability, crying, and overall fussiness.
- Loss of appetite
- Trouble sleeping
- Fever ranging from 100 to 104 degrees Fahrenheit
- Drainage from the ear. Look for foul-smelling yellow or white fluid, sometimes tinged with blood.
- Difficulty hearing

can lead to rebound congestion. Still, if you suffer from allergies or sinusitis, you can reduce the risk of ear pain by taking your medication at the beginning of the flight.

Take the train. If, despite all your best efforts, you still end up with an uncomfortable stuffed feeling and pain following air travel, you might consider traveling by land rather than air.

Fever

7 WAYS TO MANAGE THE UPS AND DOWNS

You're drenched in sweat. Your head is filled with a dull, throbbing ache, and, worse, you feel like someone is pressing their thumbs against your eyelids. One minute you feel afire; the next minute you are overcome with shaking chills. You reach for a thermometer and discover your temperature has climbed to 102 degrees Fahrenheit. Yep, you have a fever.

To understand what having a fever means, and what you should or should not do about it, it helps to know some-

thing about how the body controls temperature. There is quite a range in what is considered normal in body temperature. The body's natural temperature-control system, managed by a tiny structure at the base of the brain called the hypothalamus,

generally keeps body temperature at an average 98.6 degrees Fahrenheit (measured orally). But the normal or usual body temperature for any particular person can naturally range a degree or two above or below that. What's more, an individual's body temperature can vary by a degree or more during the course of a day, with the lowest reading usually occurring in the early morning and the highest in the evening.

Fever is not a disease in itself but simply a symptom of some other condition, usually an infection caused by a bacteria or virus. When such an enemy invades, white blood cells attack, releasing a substance called pyrogen. When pyrogen reaches the brain, it signals the hypothalamus to set the body's temperature to a higher point; if that new set point is above 100 degrees Fahrenheit, you have a fever.

When a fever develops, what should you do? Here's some advice:

Don't force yourself under cover. Shivers are your body's way of creating heat to boost your temperature, so if your teeth are chattering or you feel chilled, by all means, cover up to make

yourself more comfortable. However, once your fever is established and you start feeling hot, bundling yourself in bed under a pile of blankets will only hold the heat in and likely make you feel worse. You can't "sweat out a fever," or get a fever to break by forcing your body temperature up even higher. So if you feel as though you're burning up, toss off those covers or use a single, light sheet.

Undress. With your body exposed as much as possible, your sweat glands will be better able to release moisture, which will make you feel more comfortable if you're burning up. Strip down to your skivvies—that means a diaper for an infant and underpants and thin undershirt for an older child or adult.

Dip. Sponge yourself with tepid water or, better yet, sit in a tub of coolish

water (definitely not ice-cold water, which can induce shock) for half an hour. If you put a feverish child in a tub or sink of water, be sure to hold the child at all times. Don't apply an alcohol rub, because it can be absorbed into the skin and cause alcohol poisoning.

Sip. Fever, especially if it is accompanied by vomiting or diarrhea, can lead to fluid loss and an electrolyte imbalance, so it's important to keep drinking. Cool water is best, but unsweetened juices are okay if that's what tastes good. Getting a child to drink plenty of water is sometimes difficult, so try Popsicles or flavored ices that are made primarily of water.

Starve a fever. The old folk advice to "feed a cold, starve a fever" may not have been off the mark. Medical experts now believe that during periods of fever caused by infection, the body may do better without outside nutrition (pro-

Hello, Doctor?

An untreated fever in an adult or a child older than six months of age tends to be self-limited, relatively benign, and—contrary to popular belief—not likely to escalate to the point that it causes harm. Nor does lowering a fever mean that you are lessening the severity of the illness itself; indeed, some experts believe that fever may actually help the body fight infection.

Letting a fever run its course is not the best idea for everyone, however. Here are some basic guidelines to follow, although it's best to clarify with your doctor or your child's doctor ahead of time (such as during a regular checkup) when you should seek medical attention for an elevated temperature.

Call for medical advice immediately for:

- An infant under two months of age with a rectal temperature of 100.2 degrees Fahrenheit or higher (or lower than 95 degrees)
- A child two months of age or older with a rectal temperature of at least 102 degrees Fahrenheit (or, in an older child, an oral temperature of at least 101)
- A child two months of age or older with a rectal temperature between 100 and 102 degrees Fahrenheit (or, in an older child, an oral temperature between 99 and 101) that is accompanied by:
    - unexplained irritability
    - listlessness or lethargy
    - repeated vomiting
    - severe headache, stomachache, or earache
    - croupy "barking" cough
    - difficulty breathing
- Any fever that lasts more than one day in a child under two years of age or more than three days in a child two years old or older
- Whenever you're in doubt about the severity of your child's fever/illness. Pediatricians are not annoyed by such calls—they welcome them. So if you're concerned or unsure, day or night, make the call.
- A pregnant woman with any above-normal body temperature (generally 100 degrees Fahrenheit or higher)
- An adult with a temperature higher than 104 degrees Fahrenheit (oral) who is otherwise healthy; a temperature of 102 (oral) or higher who also has a serious underlying illness, such as heart arrhythmia or lung disease; or a temperature of 100 (oral) or higher that lasts for more than three days or is accompanied by:
    - severe headache
    - neck pain or stiffness
    - chest or abdominal pain
    - swelling of the throat or difficulty breathing
    - skin rash
    - sensitivity to bright light
    - confusion or unexplained irritability
    - listlessness
    - repeated vomiting
    - pain during urination
    - redness or swelling of the skin

vided you were reasonably well nourished before you got sick). During infection, your body actually sends

certain nutrients such as iron and zinc into hiding, because it turns out that these nutrients are essential for the growth of many infectious organisms. So by stoking up with foods and nutritional supplements during an infection, you may be helping disease-causing organisms to flourish. (Your body will tell you when it's time to start eating again; for your recovery diet, see "Eat Yourself Well" on this page.)

Resort to over-the-counter relief. If a fever is making you or your child very uncomfortable, a nonprescription antipyretic (fever-reducing) drug can be used. Antipyretics seek out the trouble-making pyrogen and put it out of commission. Aspirin, ibuprofen, and acetaminophen are all antipyretics. Aspirin and ibuprofen also have an anti-inflammatory action, which can be an advantage when battling certain conditions, such as an abscess, that may cause fever. However, do not give aspirin products to children under 19 years of age because of the risk of a potentially fatal condition known as Reye syndrome; stick with acetaminophen for children. Also, be sure to check the warnings in the box on page 21 before using any of these medications, and then follow the package directions carefully.

Let it run. Bear in mind that antipyretics are designed to make you (or yours) feel more comfortable during the course of a fever. The fact is, however, that fever may do an ailing body some good by making it less hospitable to

Eat Yourself Well

As your fever breaks and you start feeling better, your appetite will improve. You may even feel ravenously hungry for a while. That's because your body's stores of protein and many vitamins and minerals were depleted during the siege of fever, and now your body is demanding that they be replaced. Protein and calories are the most important elements in a recovery diet. Try not to fill yourself up on empty calories, however; nutrition is still a high priority. Water-soluble vitamins such as B and C need to be restored quickly. Iron, too, needs to be replenished, although this should be done slowly in case there are any lingering infectious organisms that would fuel up on iron-rich foods.

To restock your body's nutrient shelves, try eating a variety of foods, including fruits and vegetables, whole grains, low-fat dairy products, and small amounts of low-fat meats, fish, and poultry. The more variety in your diet, the likelier it is that you will provide your body with all of the nutrients it needs.

In spite of a sudden onset of appetite, however, remember one thing: If you haven't eaten much for a few days, your digestive system may need to reacclimate, too. Eat slowly, so your stomach can signal fullness before you overdo it.

How to Measure Body Temperature

The trusty old mercury-filled glass fever thermometer is no longer the recommended tool for measuring body temperature, especially in households with children. There's just too much risk of exposure to the mercury—which is toxic—should the glass break. And despite Mom's or Grandma's best intentions, kissing or touching the forehead is not a precise enough gauge. So what's the best tool to use? A digital thermometer appears to be the way to go.

Many digital thermometers are designed for oral, rectal, and even axillary (armpit) use. Checking temperature orally, by placing the thermometer under one side of the tongue (as far back as possible) and closing the lips around it, is probably the most familiar method. However, the most accurate reading is obtained rectally by inserting the thermometer about a half-inch to an inch into the rectum; a rectal reading will be one-half to one degree higher than an oral temperature taken at the same time. The American Academy of Pediatrics recommends taking a rectal temperature with a digital thermometer in children younger than three years of age. For most adults and for children who are old enough to be able to hold the thermometer properly (usually around four or five years of age), the oral method is safe and generally accurate enough if done correctly.

A less invasive but also less precise way to measure body temperature in a young child is by placing the thermometer in the armpit; this axillary reading will be one-half to one degree lower than an oral temperature taken at the same time. While this method can give you an idea if a fever is present, an axillary reading that is above normal should be confirmed by a rectal reading whenever a more exact measure is essential (such as in an infant under two months of age, since even a slight fever in this age group requires medical attention).

Digital thermometers are fast, often providing a reading in a minute or less, compared to the three minutes necessary for mercury thermometers. Be sure to read the instructions that came with your digital thermometer, however, to find out how long to keep it in place (most send out a beep or series of beeps to indicate when it can be removed) as well as how to handle, place, and care for the instrument.

Another type of thermometer, a tympanic thermometer, is placed in the ear to measure body temperature. Tympanic thermometers have become commonplace in medical settings. They can also be purchased for home use, although they are considerably more expensive than other digital thermometers. They can provide fast and accurate

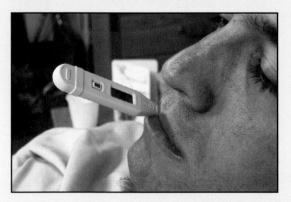

results in adults, older babies (over six months of age), and children but only if inserted properly in the ear canal (read and follow the directions carefully and ask your pharmacist for a demonstration if you are unsure). Also, the results may be affected if there's too much earwax in the ear. The temperature measured in the ear may be as much as a degree higher than an oral temperature taken at the same time.

No matter what type of thermometer you use, wait at least an hour after vigorous physical activity or a hot bath before measuring body temperature. Before taking an oral temperature, wait at least 20 minutes after smoking, eating, or drinking something hot or cold. And never leave a child unattended with any thermometer.

the infecting organism, so you may want to let it run its course rather than rush to bring it down with medication.

(See "Hello, Doctor?" on page 130 for advice on when a fever warrants medical attention.)

Flatulence

13 WAYS TO COMBAT GAS

Everyone passes a certain amount of flatus—or "breaks wind," as we delicately describe it. Normally, 400 to 2,000 milliliters of oxygen, nitrogen, carbon dioxide, hydrogen, and methane are expelled each day from the anus. Most of the time, this happens without inviting notice through sound or smell. But under some circumstances and in some people, undigested food products pass from the small intestine into the large intestine (colon), where the mass is fermented by the large amounts of bacteria normally present there. The benign bugs of the colon are not choosy: Whatever comes their way goes right on their menu. It is the bacterially produced gas that gives human flatus its characteristic odor when expelled.

If you are a stoic or a recluse, you may simply be able to ignore that gaseous excess and its audible effects. If you're neither, there are some things you can do to prevent or relieve flatulence. Here's how:

Eat to beat it. Carbohydrates cause gas in some people. But certain carbohydrates provide vital nutrients, and it would be nutritionally unwise to elimi-

nate them from your diet. A healthier approach: Trim the simple sugars and refined carbohydrates (such as cakes, donuts, cookies, white breads, and other products made with refined flour), and opt for nutrient-rich, high-fiber and/or whole-grain carbohydrates instead. It takes smaller amounts of high-fiber carbohydrates to make you feel full, so you'll be able to lower your total carbohydrate intake without feeling hungry or missing out on valuable fiber, vitamins, and minerals. If you're new to high-fiber or whole-grain foods, however, switch to them gradually so your digestive system can adjust; otherwise, you could end up producing *more* gas.

Minimize milk consumption. Some people don't have enough of the enzyme lactase in their gut to digest lactose, the sugar in milk. If you are

Gassers

The following foods are the most common gas-causing culprits:

Extremely flatulogenic:

Beans

Beer (dark)

Bran

Broccoli

Brussels sprouts

Cabbage

Carbonated beverages

Cauliflower

Onions

Milk (for those who are lactose intolerant)

Mildly Flatulogenic:

Apples (raw)

Apricots

Bananas

Bread and other products containing wheat

Carrots

Celery

Citrus fruits

Coffee

Cucumbers

Eggplant

Lettuce

Potatoes

Pretzels

Prunes

Radishes

Raisins

Soybeans

Spinach

lactose intolerant, replace the milk in your diet with calcium-fortified orange juice or with calcium-fortified soy milk. Or, try yogurt or buttermilk, which can sometimes be consumed by lactose-intolerant people without causing gas or discomfort. To find out if lactose intolerance is responsible for your gassiness, cut down on or eliminate milk from your diet for a few days to see if your flatulence diminishes.

Add a little enzyme. If you are lactose intolerant but don't want to give up milk, you can try one of the over-the-counter (OTC) products, such as Lactaid or Dairy Ease, which contain lactase, the enzyme that helps to break down lactose. Be sure to follow the package directions carefully. (You'll find other coping tips in LACTOSE INTOLERANCE.)

Banish the offenders. Some foods are notorious for causing gas (see "Gassers" on this page). To find out whether these foods affect you in this way, give them up until you feel that the flatulence problem has been relieved, then start adding the foods back into your diet one by one. If your

body can tolerate small quantities, gradually increase your intake to determine how much you can handle without becoming uncomfortably gassy.

Soak your beans. Beans are a great source of fiber and protein, but for many people, eating them can be an "explosive" enterprise. Rather than give up beans, however, you can try adjusting the way you prepare them: Soak dried beans overnight, then dump out the water. Pour in new water, and cook the beans for about half an hour. Throw that water out, put in new water, and cook for another 30 minutes. Drain the water for the last time, put in new water, and finish cooking.

Try Beano. This OTC food modifier contains an enzyme that breaks down some of the sugars that can cause gassiness. You may find that it helps make valuable foods such as beans, cabbage, broccoli, carrots, oats, and other vegetables and legumes more tolerable. Follow the package directions.

Stay calm. Emotional stress can play a role in worsening a flatulence problem. The gastrointestinal tract is exquisitely sensitive to anxiety, anger, and depression. A network of nerves connects this area of the body to the brain, and when you are under stress, muscles in the abdomen tighten. The results are painful spasms. Eating while under stress can also contribute to flatulence because you tend to swallow air.

Get physical. Sometimes, flatulence is less a matter of a faulty diet than of a faulty digestive process; the smooth passage of foods down the digestive tract may be hindered. Exercise helps regulate the process; so when things get uncomfortable, take a walk. Likewise, engaging in even such low-key exercise most days can help keep your digestive system working smoothly and may prevent some episodes of excessive gassiness.

Press on, or get down for some rock and roll. You can apply pressure to your abdomen or lie facedown on the floor with a pillow bunched up under your abdomen to help relieve discomfort from gassiness. Sitting on the floor—with your knees drawn up to your chest and your arms wrapped around your legs—and rocking back and forth may also help, as might a heating pad placed on your abdomen.

Loosen up. If you'll be taking a long airplane flight, wear loose clothing. Tight-fitting pants can compress the abdomen and cause pain.

Bust the belch. Habits that can lead to excessive belching, such as swallowing air and chewing gum, can also increase flatulence. See BELCHING to learn how to squelch the belch.

Get activated. Activated charcoal tablets, available without a prescription at drugstores, may help to absorb some excess gas and calm your flatulence problem. If you are taking any prescription medications, however, first ask your pharmacist whether the activated charcoal will interfere with them.

Reach for relief. If you just couldn't resist the spicy bean dish at the restaurant but are dreading the car ride home with your friends, stop off at the nearest grocery store or pharmacy. You're likely to find a variety of nonprescription preparations containing simethicone (such as Mylanta, Maalox, and Phazyme), which may help ease gassiness and make that trip a little quieter.

Flu

6 Ways to Cope with the Flu-Bug Blahs

Yesterday, you felt fantastic. Today, you feel 100 years old and counting. Your head aches, your skin feels sore to the touch, and you're chilled to the bone even though your forehead is on fire. Welcome to the wonderful world of the flu virus.

While "the flu" has become a catch-all term for any affliction of the upper respiratory tract (and is also often improperly used for infections of the gastrointestinal tract), the condition it refers to—influenza—is a specific viral infection that strikes every year, typically between October and April.

As far as who gets the flu, it seems to occur initially in children. Absenteeism in schools soars, as does the number of kids admitted to hospitals with respiratory illnesses. The infection quickly spreads to adults, who also begin filling hospital beds, sometimes with pneumonia or worsening of heart or lung conditions.

While there are two major strains of the flu virus—influenza A and influenza B—each strain changes slightly from year to year, so being infected one year doesn't guarantee protection against the flu the following year. Every now and then, a new influenza virus emerges that causes an unusually high number of infections and deaths. The last so-called "pandemic" struck the United States in 1977.

Regardless of the strain, the symptoms are generally the same. They include a high fever, sore throat, dry cough, severe muscle aches and pains, fatigue, and loss of appetite. Some people even experience pain and stiffness in the joints. Usually, the aches, pains, and fever last only three to five days. The fatigue and cough, however, can hang on for several weeks.

The change in flu strains from year to year also makes it hard to develop 100 percent effective flu vaccines. The shot in the arm you receive to guard against the flu is typically effective against the previous year's flu strain as

Hello, Doctor?

Signs that it's time to see your doctor include a high fever that lasts more than three days, a cough that persists or gets worse (especially if associated with severe chest pain or shortness of breath), or a general inability to recover. These things could signal a secondary bacterial infection that would need to be treated with prescription antibiotics. If you have underlying lung or heart disease, consult your physician at the first sign of the flu.

well as the strain(s) researchers predict will hit during the coming flu season, but it likely cannot fight new strains that may evolve. Still, flu vaccines manage to be about 80 percent effective when received before the flu season begins (ideally you should get the vaccine in September or October). So, if you really can't afford to get sick, a flu shot may not be a bad idea. And, if you fall into a high-risk group (see "Should You Get a Flu Shot?" on page 139), a flu shot is a priority.

On the other hand, if you don't manage to outrun this relentless bug, you can do a few things to ease some of the discomfort and help your body fight back.

Get plenty of rest. Plan on sleeping and otherwise taking it easy for a few days. This shouldn't be hard to do considering fatigue is one of the main symptoms, so you won't feel like doing much other than lounging in bed or on the couch, anyway. Consider it a good excuse to take a needed break from the daily stresses of life. And if you absolutely must continue to work, at least get to bed earlier than usual and try to go into the office a little later in the morning.

Take aspirin, acetaminophen, or ibuprofen—if you must. The flu is often accompanied by a high fever that can range from 102 to 106 degrees Fahrenheit. You can count on a doozy

of a headache, too. Lowering the fever will help prevent dehydration and will cut down on the severe, shaking chills associated with fever. On the other hand, since a fever may actually help your body fight the bug (see "Influenza Myths" on page 138), you may want to try to let the fever run its course if it's safe for you to do so (see "Hello, Doctor?" on page 130 in FEVER to determine if you need medical treatment for your fever). Aspirin and ibuprofen are generally better at easing aches and pains; acetaminophen is most effective at fighting fever. However, before you take any of these, check the warnings in the box on page 21.

Drink, drink, drink. This doesn't mean alcoholic beverages, of course. But drinking plenty of any other nonalcoholic, decaffeinated liquid (caffeine and alcohol both act as diuretics, which increase fluid loss) will help keep you hydrated and will also thin

Influenza Myths

There are a few myths about the flu that continue to prevail despite evidence that disproves them. One myth has to do with what people often refer to as the "24-hour flu" or "stomach flu." This is an illness characterized by the sudden onset of vomiting and diarrhea, accompanied by a general feeling of malaise. It can be quite intense in the first few hours but tends to subside completely after 24 hours. While this illness is indeed caused by a viral agent, it is not caused by the influenza virus and therefore is not a form of the flu at all. The correct term for this type of upset is "gastroenteritis," which indicates an infection of the gastrointestinal tract.

Another common myth about influenza is that being cold or chilled makes us more susceptible to it. Several scientific studies on humans have shown that those exposed to temperature extremes for several hours fare no worse as far as getting the flu than those who are kept comfortably warm and dry. The myth is perpetuated because severe chills are one of the first symptoms of the flu, leading people to believe that they "caught a chill" that somehow led to their illness.

An additional myth is the belief that using medicine to keep the fever down helps us get over the illness. Although you may feel a bit better after taking something to lower your fever, you may also be extending your bout with the flu. Animal studies suggest that it takes the body longer to eradicate the flu virus if its core temperature is lowered with medication.

mucous secretions. The flu can cause a loss of appetite, but patients often find warm, salty broth agreeable. If you're not eating much, juices are a good choice, too, since they provide some nutrients you may be missing.

Humidify your home in winter. Ever wonder why the flu tends to strike in the colder months? Part of the reason is your furnace. Artificial heat lowers humidity, creating an environment that allows the influenza virus to thrive. (Colder outside air also pushes people together in confined indoor spaces, making it easier for the flu bug to spread.) Adding some moisture to the air in your home during the winter with a warm- or cool-mist humidifier may not only help prevent the spread of flu, it may also make you feel more comfortable if you do get it.

Suppress a dry cough. For a dry, hacking cough that's keeping you from getting the rest you need, you can reach for over-the-counter relief. When shopping for a cough remedy, look for products that contain dextromethorphan, a cough suppressant.

Encourage a "productive" cough. A cough that brings up mucus, on the other hand, is considered productive and should generally not be suppressed with cough medicines. Drinking fluids will help bring up the mucus of a productive cough and will ease the cough a little as well.

Should You Get a Flu Shot?

Anyone who wants to reduce their chance of getting the flu should consider being vaccinated against it. However, it is especially important for the following groups of individuals to get a flu shot:

Individuals with chronic heart or lung disease. The flu virus can aggravate these conditions to the point of causing serious complications and even death.

People over the age of 65, especially if living in a nursing home or chronic-care facility. Viruses spread more rapidly in such environments. What's more, when the flu virus attacks the already weakened immune systems of elderly people, it can lead to pneumonia and even death.

Individuals with other chronic diseases. This includes asthma, diabetes, kidney disease, and cancer. Any time the body is already fighting a disease, getting another illness can cause serious problems.

Children who take aspirin regularly for problems such as chronic arthritis. Reye syndrome, a potentially fatal illness, may be triggered by the flu virus in children who are on aspirin therapy.

Health-care providers. While catching the flu may not seriously endanger these individuals, it can be deadly to the patients they are treating.

Pregnant women who fall into any of the high-risk groups mentioned. According to the U.S. Centers for Disease Control and Prevention, pregnant women can receive inactivated influenza vaccine during any trimester of pregnancy. Pregnant women should not receive live, attenuated influenza virus (LAIV) vaccine. Before receiving a flu shot, be sure to inform the medical personnel administering the vaccine if you are or might be pregnant or if you plan to become pregnant during the coming flu season.

But what if you don't want a shot in the arm? Then how about a whiff up your nose? Doctors (and even pharmacists, in some states) can now offer an alternative to the traditional injected vaccine to people who want to ward off the flu. Nasal-spray flu vaccine, called FluMist, is about as effective as a flu shot, but as its name implies, the drug is delivered to the body in a less painful manner. Patients visit the doctor and receive one blast of the vaccine up each nostril. Not everyone can be vaccinated with FluMist. Children under 5 years of age and adults over 50 cannot receive the nasal spray, since its safety hasn't been established in such individuals. Other conditions may also make you ineligible for nasal-spray flu vaccine; ask your doctor if it's right for you.

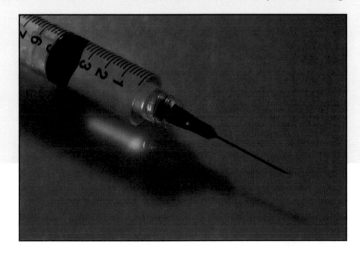

Food Poisoning

7 COPING TIPS

As anyone who's had a bad case of food poisoning can attest, it is an experience so thoroughly awful that you wouldn't wish it upon your worst enemy. Not only does everything you've eaten for the last 24 hours seem to want to escape from both ends of your body simultaneously, but the cramps and overall discomfort you experience can make you want to just crawl into a hole and die.

The good news is that food poisoning is rarely life-threatening. In most cases, it passes within 24 hours. The bad news is that once it's started, there's no real way to put the brakes on it until it has run its course.

The following tips, however, may help minimize your discomfort and shorten the duration of your symptoms.

Replace your body's fluids. If your stomach will tolerate it, be sure to keep taking liquids, especially if you have diarrhea. Try eating gelatin or drinking decaffeinated soda, decaffeinated tea with sugar, or water.

Hello, Doctor?

In some instances, food poisoning may be dangerous. Immediate medical assistance is required for food poisoning:
- in an infant or young child
- in a pregnant woman
- in an older adult
- in someone with a chronic illness, such as heart disease or diabetes
- in someone with a depressed immune response, such as occurs in AIDS or from radiation or chemotherapy
- if you have severe cramps
- if you haven't been able to keep fluids down for 12 hours
- if you have a fever above 102 degrees Fahrenheit (when measured orally)
- if you are dizzy or you faint
- if vomiting continues for more than 12 hours or diarrhea continues for more than 24 hours
- if you see any blood in your stool or vomit
- if you experience paralysis, double vision, difficulty breathing, inability to urinate, or weakness in a limb

Avoid rich or spicy foods. When your stomach is feeling irritated, eating fatty or highly seasoned foods may send you right back to the bathroom. If you feel hungry, it's probably best to stick with clear liquids, plain toast, mashed potatoes, bananas, or other bland foods.

Go with the flow—literally. If you have been poisoned by contaminated food and your digestive system is reacting with diarrhea or vomiting, you can trust your body's impulses. Don't reach for antidiarrheal or antinausea medications, because they will only interfere with your body's own defenses, which include expelling the invader.

Be careful with pain medications. Some people make the mistake of taking prescription or over-the-counter pain medications to reduce the discomfort of intestinal cramps. These drugs—especially those containing aspirin or ibuprofen—may irritate the gastrointestinal tract and increase discomfort. Acetaminophen is usually okay, but check the warnings in the box on page 21 before taking it.

Try a hot-water bottle. A not-too-hot hot-water bottle placed on the abdomen may help ease the pain of cramps.

Hibernate for a day. There's really not a whole lot you can do to end your misery; just be good to yourself and wait it out. Cancel your plans, rest,

Prevention Is the Best Medicine

The best way to treat food poisoning is to avoid getting it in the first place. Although you can't control the conditions in the restaurants you patronize, you can take several precautions at home by following these tips:
- Keep mixed foods, such as salads with mayonnaise dressing and foods that contain dairy products, refrigerated.
- Thaw meat in the refrigerator, not at room temperature.
- Stuff turkeys or roasts just before cooking—or cook the stuffing separately.
- Keep perishable foods cold.
- Cook chicken, pork, and beef very thoroughly.
- Wash hands, utensils, and surfaces with soap and very hot water after handling meat or eggs.

and take solace in the fact that it will pass in 24 hours or so.

Replace your potassium. Vomiting and diarrhea may deplete your body's supply of potassium, which may leave you feeling even worse. An extreme potassium imbalance can even be fatal. Twenty-four hours after your symptoms started (and hopefully when you're feeling a bit better), replenish your potassium stores with a sports drink or a banana.

Foot Aches

20 Ways to Ease the Agony

Our poor, overworked feet. In a single day, they absorb about 1,000 pounds of force. And we mistreat them terribly—standing on them for hours; walking on hard, unyielding surfaces; and cramming them into shoes that may be fashionable but are often far from comfortable. It's no wonder that four out of five adults eventually suffer from foot problems.

While certainly not as glamorous as the heart or the brain, the feet are amazing pieces of engineering, perfectly designed to give years of service—if you treat them right. Each foot has 26 bones—together the feet have almost one-quarter of the bones in the entire body. Thirty-three joints make the feet flexible, and 19 muscles control movement of foot parts. Tendons stretch tautly between muscles and bones, moving parts of the feet as the muscles contract. Two arches, in the midfoot and forefoot, constructed like small bridges, support each foot and provide a springy, elastic structure to absorb shock. Numerous nerve endings in the feet make them sensitive (and ticklish). And the whole structure is held together by more than 100 ligaments.

As incredible as our feet may be, few of us ever think about them until they hurt. Fortunately, if your dogs are barking, there are several things you can do to pamper them and prevent

High-Heel Hell

Remember your grandmother's feet? Chances are good they were misshapen with corns, bunions, calluses, and curled toes. Chances are equally good your grandfather had long, well-formed feet. A genetic difference? No, it's probably due to high-heel hell, the punishment women's feet are put through by high-heeled shoes.

Nature didn't intend for women (or anyone else, for that matter) to walk in high heels. And towering stilettos are not the only culprit—any heel higher than one inch forces weight forward, shortening the Achilles tendon and shifting the pelvis forward. This precarious sliding forward can cause all kinds of structural problems, including back pain and foot pain. Podiatrists often see women for "forefoot shock"—pain, fatigue, and a wobbly gait caused by the body's weight being centered on the ball of the foot.

Sometimes, we just can't get around the convention of wearing high-heeled shoes at work or social gatherings. But here are a few ideas to help you minimize the strain on your feet:

- Wear the lowest heel you can find.
- If you must wear high-heeled shoes at work, wear lower-heeled or flat shoes when you're traveling to and from work and during lunch and breaks.
- Look for shoes that are more rounded in the toe area; avoid pointy shoes that pinch the toes.
- Buy shoes that are large enough to accommodate added padding or an arch support. A half insole can help keep your foot in place and prevent your toes from slamming into the pointy tip when your foot hits the ground in high-heeled shoes. Experiment and see what works for you.
- Buy the thickest heel possible for the greatest stability.

serious problems from developing. If you have diabetes or any problem with circulation, however, your feet require extra special care, and you should run these remedies (and any other foot-care steps you're considering) by your doctor or podiatrist for approval before trying any of them at home.

Take a load off. Much of the foot pain we experience comes from over-worked lower limbs. Movement of the foot is controlled by four groups of muscles in the leg. These muscles get a workout not only when our feet are visibly moving (such as when we walk or run) but even when we stand still, because they help keep us balanced and upright. And like nearly all mus-cles (the heart muscle is an exception), these muscles can become fatigued, decreasing their ability to properly support the feet and causing discom-fort. Standing in place for long periods also tends to result in a pooling of blood in the lower extremities, which can cause uncomfortable swelling.

If you have to stand a great deal, take breaks to take the weight off your feet. Whenever you can, elevate your feet at a 45 degree angle to your body, and relax for 10 to 15 minutes. Elevating your feet will move blood away from the feet and help reduce swelling.

Give them a soak. Put two table-spoons of Epsom salts into a basin of

warm water, and give your feet a relaxing bath for 15 minutes. Then, pat your feet dry with a soft towel, and moisturize them with your favorite cream or lotion.

Alternate hot and cold. Sit on the edge of the bathtub and alternately run cold water then (comfortably) hot water for one minute each on the feet; end with cold water.

Give them the squeeze. There's nothing quite as relaxing as a foot massage. Have a partner massage your feet with massage oil, baby oil, or moisturizing lotion (then put socks on before you stand up to prevent slip-ping). Or treat yourself by massaging your own feet. First, apply oil and condition the foot with medium-light

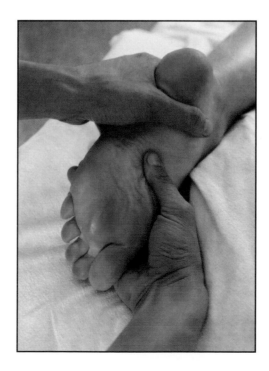

strokes, using your thumbs and fingers. Next, starting with the ball of the foot, work across and down the entire foot using the thumbs to make small, circular motions. Use the thumbs to make long, deep strokes along the arch of the foot, moving in the direction of the toes. Gently squeeze, rotate, and pull each toe. End by cupping the foot between both hands and gently squeezing, going up and down the length of each foot.

Ice 'em. A cool way to refresh your feet after a long, hard day is to ice them down with a washcloth filled with ice. It'll make them feel wonderful and decrease swelling.

Exercise your feet. Like any part of the body, the feet stay healthiest if they're kept strong and flexible with regular exercise. Walking regularly, in shoes that provide good support and cushioning, is excellent exercise for the feet.

Feet also benefit from specific foot exercises. Try these:

- Golf-Ball Roll: Sit in a chair with your shoes off, place one foot on top of a golf ball on the floor in front of you, and roll (don't stand) on the ball using only the weight of the foot; repeat with the other foot.
- Spill the Beans: Sit in a chair, scatter beans or marbles on the floor just in front of you, and pick them up with your toes.

- Circle and Stretch: Sit in a chair with one of your feet raised off the floor in front of you, and make four or five small circles in the air in both directions with that foot. Next, point your toes as much as you can; then stretch them up toward your knee. Repeat six times with each foot.

Trim your toenails. The tendency to develop ingrown toenails may be inherited, but improper nail trimming can make the problem worse. The correct method is to trim the nails straight across and only to the end of the toe, then file the corners to remove sharp edges that might cut into the skin (see INGROWN TOENAILS).

Maintain a healthy weight. Being overweight puts excess strain on your feet, as well as on all of the other weight-bearing joints of the body.

Buy shoes that fit. Too often, people buy shoes that don't fit their feet. They opt for fashion rather than fit or comfort. A good-fitting pair of shoes will improve virtually any foot problem. Look for shoes that:

- have plenty of room in the toe area (toe box).
- don't slip. The foot should not slide around in the shoe.
- are wide enough. Your foot shouldn't bulge over the edges of the sole.
- fit in the store. Don't buy too-small shoes believing you'll "stretch them out" over time.

And do your shoe shopping in the afternoon or evening, when your feet tend to be slightly larger.

Know your feet. Different types of feet require different kinds of shoes. For instance, if you have high arches, your feet tend to be rigid. Shoes with lots of cushioning will help absorb shock. Flat-bottomed feet are less rigid but also less stable, so they require shoes that control excess motion.

To find out what kind of foot you have, wet your bare feet and stand on a concrete floor or piece of paper. If you have high arches, the outline of your foot will appear very narrow and curved like a half-moon. If the outline looks like a slab, you're probably flat-footed.

Wear the right shoes for the activity. Wearing the wrong type of shoes can cause a long list of problems, including knee tendinitis, chronic foot pain, heel spurs, and stress fractures. Choosing the right shoes is especially important when it comes to fitness footwear. Different sports and exercises have unique repetitive movements that require special support and cushioning. You wouldn't play basketball in a pair of heels. Likewise, don't rely on that old pair of sneakers if you're going climbing or hiking. Spend the extra money to buy shoes that are specific for the activity you're doing.

The investment could save you and your feet a lot of pain.

Replace worn shoes. It's tough to give up those old favorite shoes, but often, we wear shoes long after they've lost their ability to support and cushion the foot. Keep in mind that looks can be deceiving: A pair of shoes may show few signs of wear-and-tear but no longer absorb the shock of pounding the pavement. Instead, pay attention to your body. If your feet are killing you, knees ache, or hips hurt after spending time on your feet, your shoes may no longer be doing their job.

Foot Odor

11 Steps to Sweeter-Smelling Feet

If removing your footwear at the end of the day calls to mind the scent of a postgame locker room, you may be suffering from what is scientifically known as bromhidrosis—sweaty, smelly feet.

While neither painful nor contagious, foot odor causes unmitigated social suffering to those who are burdened with it. Under normal conditions, each of your feet produces half a pint of sweat through some 20,000 sweat glands each day. In most people, this perspiration evaporates. In people with bromhidrosis, however, more sweat is produced, and it doesn't evaporate as easily. The result: odoriferous feet.

If you suffer from this problem, don't worry. You don't have to stand for it anymore. Simply follow these suggestions for keeping your feet drier and sweeter smelling:

Wash well. Those sweat glands on the soles of your feet produce perspiration composed of water, sodium chloride, fat, minerals, and various acids that are end products of your body's metabolism. In the presence of certain bacteria, these sweaty secretions break down, generating a foul smell. Washing away the bacteria with deodorant soap (and drying them well) will short-circuit this process.

How often should you wash your feet? Enough to remove the offending bacteria but not so often that you remove all the protective oils from your skin. For strong foot odor, you may need to bathe your feet several times a day. However, if you notice that your feet are becoming scaly and cracked, cut back on the number of washings.

Salt your tootsies. For extra-sweaty feet, try adding half a cup kosher salt (it has larger crystals than ordinary table salt, although in a pinch, table salt will do) to one quart water and soaking your feet in the solution. After soaking, don't rinse your feet; just dry them thoroughly. As anyone who has ever taken a dip in the ocean has likely discovered, salt has a drying effect on the skin.

Pretend they're the pits. Believe it or not, the deodorant and/or antiperspirant that you use under your arms can be used on your feet, too. Pay attention to the label on the product, though. Deodorants contain antibacterial agents that can kill bacteria—they won't stop the sweat, but they will eliminate the odor that ensues when sweat meets bacteria. Antiperspirants, on the other hand, stop the sweat and the smell at the same time.

Take a powder. Shake on deodorizing foot powder that contains aluminum chloride hexahydrate.

Give 'em a good sock. Wear socks that let your feet breathe. Some people find that natural fibers such as cotton and wool are best, but others prefer acrylic; try different fabrics until you find the one that seems to keep your feet driest. If possible, change your socks at least once during the day, and don't wear the same pair two days in a row without laundering them. Contrary to conventional wisdom, white socks are not sterile and do contain dye, so they are not necessarily preferable to colored socks.

Shoe it away. Choose open shoes such as sandals whenever possible, because they allow air onto the feet, which helps evaporate sweat and slows the growth of odor-causing bacteria. If sandals aren't an option, choose leather or canvas shoes, which breathe a bit, and avoid shoes with uppers made of solid rubber or synthetic materials.

Wash your sneakers. Some shoes— such as sneakers and other canvas footwear—can go right in the washing machine. Let them air-dry rather than throwing them in the dryer, though.

Let your shoes breathe. Try airing out your shoes between wearings, too. If you can, alternate shoes on a daily basis so that you don't wear the same pair two days in a row. Loosen the laces and pull up the tongue on the pair you're not wearing, and let them dry out in the sunshine.

Sprinkle your shoes. Sprinkle cornstarch inside your shoes to help absorb moisture and keep your feet drier.

Eat wisely. Avoid strong-flavored foods such as garlic, onions, scallions, and peppers, because the substances that give them their powerful flavor and aroma can pass through the bloodstream and eventually concentrate in your sweat. While this effect is not restricted to foot perspiration, it certainly won't help a case of smelly feet.

Keep calm. Stress and anxiety increase production of sweat, giving those nasty little bacteria even more to feed on. If you're so stressed that it's making your feet smell, it's time to make some changes in your life or, at the very least, learn some stress-reduction techniques.

Gingivitis

15 Hints for Healthier Gums

You're brushing your teeth, and when you rinse and spit, you see a little blood. No big deal, you think to yourself. It happens all the time. Well, it's time to think again, because that bit of blood may be a much bigger deal than you think. It may be a sign of gingivitis, the first stage of gum disease. According to the American Dental Association, gum disease—not dental caries, or "cavities"—is the leading cause of tooth loss among adults.

Gingivitis is inflammation, swelling, and bleeding of the gum tissue caused by the bacteria that naturally coat the teeth. The bacteria form a sticky, whitish film on the teeth called plaque. If plaque isn't thoroughly removed every day, the bacteria produce toxins that irritate the gums, making them red, swollen, and likely to bleed easily. Eventually, the toxins destroy gum tissue, causing it to separate from the tooth and form pockets. The pockets hold more bacteria and detach even further. This is periodontitis, an irreversible stage of gum disease that can destroy the bone and soft tissue that support the teeth.

If you have gingivitis, you're not alone. According to the American Dental Association and the American Academy of Periodontology, three out of four adults have gingivitis. Most gingivitis results from poor oral hygiene—not brushing and flossing correctly or often enough and not having teeth professionally cleaned on a regular basis. However, a number of factors can increase your risk. Dentists say that people who are chronically stressed seem to develop gum problems more often than laid-back types. Hormones influence risk, too, which is why the condition often flares up in women who are pregnant or menstruating. Likewise, adolescents, whose hormones are going crazy, may develop gingivitis. Some diseases, such as diabetes, and some drugs, including phenytoin (an antiseizure drug) and oral contraceptives, are associated with gingivitis. Finally, if you tend to breathe through your mouth rather than your nose, you may be at increased risk, because this habit dries out the mouth and gums—saliva helps kill bacteria—and could result in an overgrowth of gum tissue.

Still, the most common cause of gingivitis is poor oral hygiene. Fortunately, gingivitis is reversible, and better oral hygiene is the solution. Here are some tips to prevent gingivitis and, if you already have it, to "clean it up":

Use the "three-three" rule. The American Dental Association says that most people spend less than one minute *per day* on dental hygiene. That's far from adequate, say dentists. Here's a good rule of thumb: Brush your teeth three times a day for at least three minutes each time. That may seem like a lot of brushing—not to mention the flossing that should follow—but those nine minutes each day could spare you a great deal of time in the dentist's chair, money, and oral distress in the long run.

Try brushing dry. "Dry" brushing—brushing without toothpaste—while doing other activities such as watching television can help remove dental plaque.

Be consistent. You will be less likely to miss teeth as you brush if you develop a routine and stick with it. Start with the same part of your mouth every time you brush, always moving from one section to the next in the same order.

Lighten up. One of the biggest mistakes people make when they brush is pushing too hard with the toothbrush. Try the following experiment: Apply the bristles of your toothbrush to the back of your hand. Push as hard as you normally would for toothbrushing, and try to move the brush around. Then apply only a tiny amount of pressure and try to move the brush. You'll find that too much pressure doesn't allow the tips of the bristles—the part of the brush that cleans the teeth—to move.

In addition, avoid a "traveling" stroke. Instead of swiping the brush rapidly across several teeth, brush a couple of teeth at a time, moving the brush up and down in one place before moving on to the next couple teeth.

Use a softie. Using a toothbrush with stiff bristles can damage the sensitive tissue in your mouth and even cause gingivitis. Always use a toothbrush labeled "soft."

Brush your tongue and palate. Many dentists advise patients to brush the tongue and the roof of the mouth when they clean their teeth to cut down on the amount of bacteria present and increase circulation in the tissue.

Electrify 'em. Okay, so you hate to brush. It's awkward and boring, or maybe it's too difficult because you don't have as much dexterity as you used to. Try a "rotary" electric toothbrush. Beware, however, that not all electric toothbrushes are created equal. Ask your dentist for a recommendation.

Floss, and floss again. Toothbrush bristles are not designed to clean

Hello, Doctor?

Most cases of gingivitis can be effectively treated at home with the remedies described here. But some symptoms need to be checked out by your dentist. The American Dental Association recommends calling your dentist if:

- You have persistent bad breath.
- There is pus between the teeth and gums.
- Your "bite," the way your teeth fit together, has changed.
- You have loose or separating teeth.
- Your gums consistently bleed.
- The gums at the gum line appear rolled instead of flat.
- Your partial dentures fit differently than they used to.
- Your gingivitis doesn't improve after three or four days of diligent home care.

between teeth. That's a job for dental floss, which—despite what you might prefer to think—is not an optional tool in your daily dental-care arsenal. Try using a waxed floss, since it's easier to move between the teeth without getting hung up, and be sure to floss at least once a day.

Irrigate it. While water-irrigation devices like the Waterpik don't take the place of flossing, they do help clean out debris from pockets in the gums and from between teeth. They also massage the gums.

Brush with baking soda. Once or twice a week, brush your teeth with baking soda. The white powder is just abrasive enough to help clean your teeth without harming their enamel. Make a paste with a little baking soda and water, and brush thoroughly, especially around the gum line. Not only will the baking soda help gently scrub off the plaque, it will also neutralize acidic bacterial wastes, deodorize your mouth temporarily, and polish your teeth.

Rinse it. Most antiplaque rinses and antimicrobial mouthwashes (such as original Listerine) contain alcohol, which kills bacteria in the mouth. Fewer bacteria mean less plaque on your teeth. However, rinsing your mouth is not a substitute for regular, thorough brushing and flossing.

Bring on the salt water. Try rinsing your mouth with a warm saltwater solution (add half a teaspoon salt to four ounces warm water). Swish it around in your mouth for 30 seconds, then spit (don't swallow). The salty solution will soothe your inflamed gums; as a bonus, it will also kill some bacteria.

Try hydrogen peroxide. If the bleeding persists when you brush your teeth, try rinsing your mouth with an oral 3 percent hydrogen peroxide solution (not the 20 percent hydrogen peroxide used for cuts). It's available without a prescription at pharmacies and in the dental section of some stores. Mix equal parts hydrogen peroxide and water, rinse with it for 30 seconds, then spit (don't swallow).

Eat a carrot. Anytime you can't brush after eating, you're giving bacteria in your mouth the opportunity to cause gingivitis. But face it, sometimes you just can't brush. When you can't brush, try to end your meal with an abrasive food, such as a raw carrot or even popcorn, which will scrape some of the plaque from your teeth and stimulate the gums.

Swish. If you can't brush right after eating, at least rinse your mouth out thoroughly with water. A little H_2O therapy can wash away debris and provide some relief if your gums are inflamed.

Headaches

16 WAYS TO KEEP THE PAIN AT BAY

Headaches. We've all had them. From the morning-after-celebrating-too-much headache to the tough-day-at-the-office headache to the you-might-as-well-kill-me-now-because-I'm-going-to-die-any-way type of headache. Sometimes, a dose of aspirin or another analgesic may alleviate the pain, while other times, nothing short of simply waiting it out seems to help.

If you suffer from frequent, severe headaches that put you out of commission several times a month, you need to seek medical attention. Likewise, if your headaches are associated with physical exertion, changes in vision, or weakness, numbness, or paralysis of the limbs, skip the urge to self-treat and see a doctor. If you're already seeing a physician and aren't getting relief, think about getting a referral to a headache specialist or headache clinic.

However, if you are prone to occasional headache pain, read on. The tips that follow can help you feel a lot better—fast.

Try—but don't overdo—pain pills. A dose of an over-the-counter (OTC) analgesic, such as aspirin, acetaminophen, or ibuprofen, is often enough to

alleviate the occasional headache (be sure to review the analgesic warnings in the box on page 21 before trying one though). But if you need to take more than two doses a day frequently or for more than four or five days in a row to relieve headache pain, contact your doctor. Taking pain relievers too often can actually worsen your headache pain.

Lie down. Lying down and closing your eyes for half an hour or more may be one of the best treatments for a bad headache. For some types of headaches, such as migraines, sleep is the only thing that seems to interrupt the pain cycle. Recognizing the early signs of a headache can keep the pain from getting out of control, since doctors say the sooner you get to bed or lie on a sofa, the sooner a headache will fade.

An Antiheadache Diet?

It's been estimated that perhaps 10 to 30 percent of headaches are related to food sensitivities. The dietary triggers seem to vary considerably among individuals, however, making it difficult to create a trigger-free diet that would work for all. Indeed, the reported food suspects range so widely that if they were all prohibited, you might end up with little or nothing to choose from—not a good thing, since fasting itself is a headache trigger. Still, some foods or ingredients do seem to cause trouble for a number of headache sufferers, and they are discussed below.

To determine if a food sensitivity might be triggering your headaches, begin by recording the foods you eat, along with other environmental factors (it's possible an interplay of food and another trigger, such as a hormonal change, is necessary to trigger your headaches), in your headache diary (see page 155). Look for patterns in the foods you've eaten within the 24 hours prior to getting each headache. If a food or ingredient consistently shows up in your diet just prior to a headache, try cutting out that food or ingredient for two or three weeks. Then add it back for two to three weeks. If your headaches fade and resume with the removal and return of the food, then you've discovered a food trigger that you should try to avoid. (If this experimenting seems to indicate that you're sensitive to a large number of foods or an entire food group, discuss it with your doctor or a registered dietitian to ensure your adjusted diet will provide all the nutrients you need for health.)

Tyramine and other amines. Tyramine is an amino acid known to promote headaches, nausea, and high blood pressure in certain individuals. (People who take antidepressant drugs called monoamine oxidase, or MAO, inhibitors are especially prone to accumulating high amounts of tyramine.) Tyramine is found in a wide variety of foods, including aged cheeses, processed meats, peanuts, broad beans, lentils, avocados, bananas, fresh baked bread, red wine and other alcoholic beverages, and pickled foods. A related amine that can be troublesome for some headache sufferers is phenylalanine, which is found in chocolate, among other foods. Even citrus fruits contain an amine that can serve as a headache trigger for some folks.

Monosodium glutamate (MSG). This purported flavor enhancer is also found in a wide variety of foods, although it is not always clearly identified on food labels. It is most commonly found in Chinese foods, canned foods, soy sauce, seasonings and tenderizers, and processed foods.

Nitrates and nitrites. These preservatives are often added to luncheon and other processed meats, such as bologna, salami, hot dogs, bacon, and ham, as well as smoked fish.

Don't let the sun shine in. Especially if your symptoms resemble those of a migraine (such as severe pain on one side of the head, nausea, blurred vision, and extreme sensitivity to light), resting in a darkened room may alleviate the pain, experts agree. Bright light may also cause headaches. Even staring at a glowing computer screen may be enough to trigger pain on the brain. Wearing tinted glasses or using other means to filter bright light and minimize glare may help prevent headaches.

Use a cold compress. A washcloth dipped in ice-cold water and placed over the eyes or an ice pack placed on the site of the pain can also help ease headache pain. You might also see if your pharmacy sells special ice packs that surround the whole head (known as "headache hats") or frozen gel-packs that can be inserted into pillows. Whatever you use, keep in mind that speed is critical: Using ice as soon as possible after the onset of the headache will relieve the pain within 20 minutes for most people.

Try heat. If ice feels uncomfortable to you, or if it doesn't seem to help your headache, try placing a warm washcloth over your eyes or on the site of the pain. Leave the compress on for half an hour, rewarming it as necessary.

Think pleasant thoughts. Many headaches are brought on or worsened by stress and tension. Learning to handle life's difficulties by tuning out unpleasant thoughts may keep the volume down on a bad headache. When you feel your body shifting into crisis mode—after you have a serious disagreement with your spouse or coworker, for example—force yourself to think pleasant thoughts. Relaxing your mind may help you figure out a way to resolve the problem, which can help ward off headache-causing tension.

Check for tension. Along with the preceding tip, stop periodically during the day and check your body for tension. Are you clenching your jaw or wrinkling your brow? Are your hands balled-up into fists? If you discover these signs of tension, stop, relax, and take a slow, deep breath or two (don't go beyond a couple of deep breaths or take them too quickly, because you may begin to hyperventilate). Occasional body checks like this could nip a tension headache in the bud.

Quit smoking. Smoking may bring on or worsen a headache, especially if you tend to suffer from cluster headaches—extremely painful headaches that last from 5 to 20 minutes and come in groups.

Recipe for Relaxation

One easy, pleasant technique that can be used to combat the headache-promoting effects of stress is progressive relaxation. It only requires a few minutes and a comfortable chair, sofa, or patch of floor in a quiet spot away from people, phones, television, and other distractions.

Progressive relaxation consists of alternately tensing and then releasing the tension in each muscle or muscle group from one end of your body to the other. For the purposes of headache relief or prevention, you can focus on the muscles from your forehead to your shoulders. Purposely tense the specific muscle or group as tightly as you can, hold the tension for a few seconds, and finally release the tension, allowing the muscles to slowly relax. Then proceed to the next muscle or group and repeat. Try the following steps to work the headache zone.

1. Scrunch up, then release, your forehead muscles (or furrow your brow).
2. Close your eyes tightly, then open them slowly.
3. Make a wide smile, then allow it to fade.
4. Clench your jaw, then relax it.
5. Press your tongue against the roof of your mouth, then let it fall back down.
6. Press your lips together tightly, then relax.
7. Press your head against the floor or the back of the chair, then relax.
8. Shrug your shoulders, bringing your shoulders up as close to your ears as you can, then let them fall.

If you have additional time, you can proceed all the way down to your toes, for a whole-body relaxation exercise. Be sure to breathe slowly and deeply throughout the exercise.

Don't drink. Drinking more alcohol than you're used to often causes a notorious morning-after effect—the pounding headache. But even a single serving of some alcoholic beverages can trigger headaches, including the migraine and cluster varieties, in certain people. For example, dark alcoholic beverages, such as red wines, sherry, brandy, scotch, vermouth, and beer, contain large amounts of tyramine, an amino acid that can spark headaches in people who are sensitive to it (see "An Antiheadache Diet?" for more on tyramine). And some people appear to be sensitive to the histamine in beer and wine. So if you're struggling with headaches, abstaining may be your best choice.

Start a program of regular exercise. Regular exercise helps release the physical and emotional tension that may lead to headaches. Walking, jogging, and other aerobic activities help boost the body's production of endorphins (natural pain-relieving substances).

Cut down on caffeine. The same chemical in coffee and tea that perks you up in the morning can also make your muscles tense and send your anxiety level through the roof. Consuming too much caffeine can also cause insomnia, which can in turn trigger headaches. Another problem is that many people drink several cups of coffee a day during their work week but cut their consumption on Saturdays and Sundays. This pattern can lead to caffeine-withdrawal headaches on weekends and holidays.

If you suspect caffeine may be giving you headaches, wean yourself off the stimulating stuff by cutting your intake slowly. Start by eliminating the equivalent of one-half cup coffee per week until you are only drinking one cup of caffeinated coffee (or its equivalent) per day. One five-ounce cup of drip coffee contains about 150 milligrams of caffeine. A five-ounce cup of tea brewed for three to five minutes may contain 20 to 50 milligrams of caffeine. And cola drinks contain about 35 to 45 milligrams of caffeine per 12-ounce serving. Look out for stealth sources of caffeine, too, particularly in the OTC drugs in your medicine cabinet.

Fight the nausea first. Some headaches may be accompanied by nausea, which can make you feel even worse. What's more, the gastric juices produced by stomach upset may hinder the absorption of certain prescription and OTC analgesics, which may make these drugs less effective at relieving the pain of your headache. So by first taking care of the nausea, the pain of the headache may be easier to treat. Many patients find that drinking peach juice, apricot nectar, or flat cola helps alleviate nausea. OTC antinauseants such as Emetrol and Dramamine may also be useful.

Rise and retire at the same time every day. Oversleeping can create changes in body chemistry that set off migraines and other headaches. Going to bed and getting up at the same time every day—including weekends— keeps your body in a stable rhythm.

Keep a headache diary. If you get frequent headaches, try to tease out the factors that seem to be responsible. Get a notebook and keep track of your headaches. Rate each one on a scale of 0 to 3, starting with no headache (a score of 0) and moving up in intensity to mild headache (a score of 1), moderate to severe headache (a score of 2), and incapacitating headache (a score of 3). Record details about potential headache triggers. Were you under an unusual amount of stress? What did you eat? Was your usual sleep schedule thrown out of whack? If you're a woman, did you have your period? Did you use medications that contain hormones, such as oral contraceptives? Now look for patterns connecting these factors to days when you had bad headaches. This information may help you avoid triggers and can also help your physician devise a better treatment plan if these self-help strategies are not successful against your headaches.

Heartburn

20 Ways to Beat the Burn

Heartburn. The word evokes a frightening picture: your heart on fire, sizzling and smoking, without a firefighter in sight. Fortunately, it's a misnomer. It's not your heart that's on fire, it's your esophagus. But heartburn is easier to say than "esophagusburn."

The "burn" part, however, they got right. Your esophagus, the food tube that carries what you swallow down to your stomach, can literally be burned by the acids released by your stomach. Those acids are industrial-strength and are meant to stay where the tough stomach lining can handle them.

Unfortunately, we can experience something called reflux. That's when some of the stomach contents, includ-

ing the acid, slip back up through the esophageal sphincter, the valve that's supposed to prevent the stomach's contents from reversing course. Reflux causes an uncomfortable, burning sensation between the stomach and the neck. Most people feel the discomfort beneath the breastbone.

Doctors call chronic heartburn by another name: It's gastroesophageal reflux disease, or GERD. Despite the silliness in some TV commercials for heartburn medications, GERD is serious business. If untreated, frequent exposure to acid can damage the esophagus, making it difficult for food to pass and in extreme cases leading to cancer of the esophagus.

But you don't have to have GERD to be bugged by heartburn. Here are some ways to put out that fire and keep it from flaring up again.

Block the problem. Acid in your stomach helps digest food, but your body makes much more than it needs. Shutting down production of this stinging stuff means there will be less of it swishing around in your stomach, just waiting to wash upward and burn your esophagus. Pharmacies sell low-dose, over-the-counter (OTC) versions of medications that block stomach acid from forming. (The higher doses of these drugs are available only by prescription.) These so-called H2 (or histamine) blockers, such as cimetidine (Tagamet HB) and ranitidine (Zantac 75), seem to help about half of heartburn sufferers.

Medications called proton pump inhibitors (PPIs) are even more effective at reducing acid. Most of these drugs require a prescription, however. And even though one PPI, omeprazole (Prilosec), is available OTC, most gastroenterologists recommend patients undergo endoscopy (a diagnostic procedure in which a lighted, flexible tube is inserted through the mouth and down the throat to visualize the upper gastrointestinal tract) before beginning treatment with a PPI.

Take an antacid. OTC antacids in tablet or liquid form can help cool the burn. Take a dose about every six hours as needed. Don't overdo it, though, because too much antacid can cause constipation or diarrhea.

Don't forget your bedtime dose. Even if you forget to take an antacid during the day, you should try to remember to take one at bedtime if you suffer from frequent heartburn. You need to protect your esophagus from the pooling of stomach acids that commonly occurs at night, when you are horizontal for hours on end. Heartburn that occurs during the night causes more damage than daytime heartburn.

Keep your head up. Another way to protect your esophagus while you sleep is to elevate the head of your bed. That way, you'll be sleeping on a slope, and gravity will work for you in keeping your stomach contents where they belong. Put wooden blocks under the legs at the head of your bed to raise it about six inches.

Get rid of your waterbed. In a waterbed, your body basically lies flat on the water-filled mattress. You can't effectively elevate your chest and therefore can't prevent your stomach contents from spilling into your esophagus.

Say no to a post-dinner snooze. Tempting as it may look, the couch is not your friend after you eat a meal. People who lie down with a full stomach are asking for trouble. Wait at least an hour before you lie down.

Don't eat before bed. Avoid bedtime snacks. In fact, it's best if you can wait two to three hours—the time it takes the stomach to empty—after a meal to go to bed. While you're waiting, stay upright.

Pass on seconds. A stomach ballooned by too much food and drink may partly empty in the wrong direction.

Loosen your belt. Tight clothing can push on your stomach and contribute to reflux.

Lose the fat. Abdominal fat pressing against the stomach can force the contents back up.

Look forward to delivery. Pregnancy can cause heartburn, particularly in the third trimester when your growing baby is pushing up against

Is It Really Heartburn?

If symptoms don't subside, you may have something other than a simple case of heartburn. The symptoms of more serious problems, such as heart disease, can mimic those of heartburn. And if it is heartburn, it may be caused by a hiatal hernia (in which part of the stomach slips up into the chest cavity), inflammation of the esophagus, ulcers in the stomach or small intestine, or even cancer. So if you're still suffering even after following the self-help advice here, see your doctor.

Heimlich Maneuver Won't Help This

In people with serious, chronic heartburn, acid reflux can sometimes burn the lining of the esophagus so badly that scar tissue will build up. The resulting strictures can cause food to get stuck in the esophagus.

A person with a piece of food stuck in his or her esophagus can still breathe and talk. However, he can't swallow his saliva.

The Heimlich maneuver, used for dislodging an object that is obstructing the airway, is not the appropriate treatment in this case. Usually, a doctor must use a special instrument that is inserted into the esophagus to dislodge the food. So if it feels as if you have food stuck in your esophagus or if you are having trouble swallowing your saliva, see a doctor.

your stomach. If you still have heartburn after making lifestyle changes, such as eating smaller meals, talk with your doctor about taking an antacid.

Get in shape. Even mild exercise done on a regular basis, such as a daily walk around the neighborhood, may help ease digestive woes. However, avoid working out strenuously immediately after a meal; wait a couple of hours.

Watch your diet. Avoid high-fat and fried foods, because they take longer to digest. (The longer they're in your stomach, the more chance they'll back up.) Spicy foods and black pepper cause trouble for some people, too. Opt for a diet of fresh fruits and vegetables, lean meats, fat-free dairy products, and plenty of complex carbohydrates, such as whole-wheat bread and high-fiber cereal. Dietary fiber helps keep things moving throughout the digestive system.

Don't smoke. Nicotine from cigarette smoke irritates the valve between the stomach and the esophagus, as well as

the stomach lining, so smokers tend to get heartburn more often.

Be careful of coffee. The caffeine in coffee relaxes the esophageal sphincter, which can lead to reflux. But even decaffeinated coffee may cause reflux problems: Research suggests the oils contained in both regular *and* decaffeinated coffee may play a role in heartburn. Experiment to see if cutting your coffee intake lessens your heartburn.

Be wary of peppermint. For some people, peppermint seems to cause heartburn. Try skipping the after-dinner mints and see if it helps.

Take it easy. Stress can prompt increased acid secretion and cause the esophageal sphincter to malfunction.

Skip the cocktail. Alcohol can relax the sphincter and irritate the stomach, too, which can lead to reflux.

Slow down on soda. The carbon dioxide in soda pop and other bubbly drinks can cause stomach distention, which can push the contents of the stomach up into the esophagus.

Check your painkiller. If you're about to pop a couple of aspirin in your mouth, think again. Aspirin, ibuprofen, and products that contain them can burn the esophagus as well as the stomach. Opt for acetaminophen for pain relief (but check the warning box on page 21 first).

Hemorrhoids

14 Ways to End the Torment

Hemorrhoids are swollen and stretched-out veins that line the anal canal and lower rectum. Internal hemorrhoids may either bulge into the anal canal or protrude out through the anus, in which case they are called "prolapsed." External hemorrhoids occur under the surface of the skin at the anal opening. Regardless of type, hemorrhoids cause cruel distress: They hurt, burn, itch, irritate the anal area, and, very often, bleed.

About one-half to three-fourths of all Americans will develop hemorrhoids at some time in their lives. There are a number of factors that contribute to them, some of which can be avoided.

- Gravity. Humans stand upright, which causes a downward pressure on all of the veins in the body, including those in the anal canal and rectum.
- Family history. If one parent has hemorrhoids, it is more likely that his or her child will develop them in adult life; if both parents have hemorrhoids, it is a near certainty.
- Age. While hemorrhoids usually begin to develop when an individual is 20 years old or even earlier, symptoms usually do not appear until the 30s and beyond.
- Constipation. Difficulty in passing fecal matter creates pressure on and may even injure veins in the anal canal and rectum.
- Low-fiber diet. Highly refined foods (white-flour products, sugar, foods high in fat and protein and low in complex carbohydrate) result in a fiber-deficient diet, with resulting constipation and hemorrhoids.
- Obesity. Added pounds put more pressure on veins. What's more, overweight individuals may be more likely to favor refined foods and a sedentary lifestyle.
- Laxatives. Ironically, improper use of nonprescription laxative products is a major cause of constipation and therefore likely plays a leading role in the development of hemorrhoids.
- Pregnancy. As the fetus grows in the womb, it puts additional pressure on the expectant mother's rectal area. Thankfully, pregnancy-related hemorrhoids

Could It Be Something Else?

Hemorrhoids aren't the only cause of itching in the anal area. Poor anal hygiene, perianal warts, intestinal worms, medication allergies, psoriasis, other forms of dermatitis or local infection, or even too much coffee can cause itching. Pain can result from fissures—small cracks in the skin around the anus.

If you find blood in the area, don't assume it's from hemorrhoids. Bleeding can be a symptom of colorectal cancer, which kills 56,000 people every year, according to the American Cancer Society. While bright-red blood usually heralds hemorrhoids, don't try to make a diagnosis yourself. If you notice blood, see your doctor.

usually retract after the baby is born, unless they were present before the woman became pregnant.

- Sexual practices. Anal intercourse also puts pressure on and can injure veins in the anal canal.
- Prolonged sitting. Without some form of regular exercise, the heart muscle is less efficient at returning blood from the veins to the heart.
- Prolonged standing. The pull of gravity continues unabated on the body's veins in individuals who are on their feet all day.

Fortunately, most cases of hemorrhoids respond to basic self-care methods, so you may never have to tell a soul about them. (If you notice blood, however, see "Could It Be Something Else?" on this page.) Here are the most effective steps you can take to soothe your achy bottom and keep hemorrhoids from flaring:

Rough up your diet. Dietary fiber—the fiber found in foods such as fruits, vegetables, whole grains, and dried beans—passes through the human digestive tract untouched by digestive enzymes. As it travels, it absorbs many times its weight in water; by the time it reaches the colon in combination with digestive waste, it produces a stool that is bulky, heavy, and soft—all factors that make it easier to eliminate without straining. Straining, remember, is a major cause of hemorrhoids. In about half of hemorrhoid cases, consuming

more dietary fiber is the only treatment necessary to fix the problem. (See "An Apple a Day" on page 161 for dietary fiber sources.)

Drink up. Be sure to drink plenty of water to keep things moving right along. At least eight large glasses of water or other noncaffeinated fluid throughout the day is recommended. Fruits and vegetables, which are important sources of dietary fiber, are naturally packed with water and can also help keep you hydrated.

Avoid sweat and strain. Don't try to move your bowels unless you feel the urge to do so. And don't spend any more time on the toilet than it takes to defecate without straining. Once your bowels have moved, don't strain to produce more or sit there reading the newspaper.

Heed the call of nature. On the other hand, don't wait too long before responding to the urge to eliminate.

The longer the stool stays in the lower portion of the digestive tract, the more chance there is for moisture to be lost, making the stool hard and dry.

Try a different position. It has been suggested that squatting is a more natural position than sitting for moving one's bowels; unfortunately, Western toilets are not designed to make this possible for most people. Some people find that propping their feet up on a small footstool and pulling their knees in the direction of their chest helps.

Soften it. If eating more fiber-packed food and increasing water intake aren't enough to solve a severe constipation problem, you might want to talk to your doctor about taking a laxative known as a stool softener (such as Colace or Correctol) or one that contains a natural bulking agent (such as Metamucil or Effer-Syllium). These are only short-term solutions, however—the best way to add fiber is through food (see "Laxative Alert" on page 86). Do not—repeat, do not—use laxatives that act on the muscles of the colon and rectum unless specifically directed to by your doctor; prolonged use of such products, which typically contain bisacodyl, senna, cascara sagrada, or castor oil as their active ingredient, can cause permanent malfunction of the bowel in addition to severe irritation of the anal area. Avoid taking mineral oil, as well, since it can interfere with the absorption of some essential nutrients, such as vitamin A.

Take a walk. Regular exercise helps your digestive system work more efficiently. Strenuous exercise isn't necessary, however; a lengthy walk at a brisk pace will do quite nicely.

An Apple a Day

One of the most important moves toward healing hemorrhoids is a change in diet. However, it's best to add fiber to your diet gradually. Too rapid an increase can cause gas, abdominal cramps, or diarrhea. As it is, you can expect some increase in intestinal gas at first, but this will subside in a week or two as your system and the bacteria that inhabit your colon adjust to your new diet.

Here are some foods that can increase the fiber content of your diet when eaten regularly:

Grains
Wheat, whole
Rye, whole
Rice, brown
Corn, milled
Oatmeal, unprocessed
Oats, rolled
Bran, unprocessed miller's

Legumes
Lima beans
Soy beans
Kidney beans
Lentils
Chick peas

Vegetables
Carrots
Brussels sprouts
Eggplant
Cabbage
Corn
Green beans
Lettuce

Fruits
Apples
Oranges
Pears
Figs
Prunes
Apricots
Raisins

Those Over-the-Counter "Shrinks"

Drugstore remedies for hemorrhoid discomfort usually achieve part of what they promise: temporary relief of pain and itching (of the skin in the anal area, that is; rectal nerves can't sense pain). Claims that they can shrink hemorrhoids or reduce inflamed tissue, however, don't hold up when put to the test.

Over-the-counter aids are available in several forms: cleansers, suppositories, creams, and ointments. The cleansers, although effective, are more costly than ordinary warm water, which works very well. Suppositories may be of little help because they can slide into the upper rectum, bypassing the area they are meant to soothe. Ointments are greasy and tend to retain moisture, which can lead to increased irritation. Creams, especially hydrocortisone creams, are effective, although their prolonged use may lead to dependency and can also cause thinning of the skin.

Some of these products, however, should not be used by individuals who have certain medical conditions, such as heart disease or diabetes, so you'll need to check the label of any product you are considering to see if there are warnings that apply to you. In addition, many preparations contain a number of ingredients, including anesthetics, astringents, counterirritants, and skin protectants, which may cause an allergic reaction in some people that is far worse than the discomfort of the hemorrhoids themselves.

The Food and Drug Administration has also made some specific rulings about products marketed for hemorrhoid use:

- Boric acid is no longer allowed. While it's safe enough for ordinary skin, it is toxic if absorbed by the mucous membranes.
- Painkilling ingredients for use in the rectum or on internal hemorrhoids (which originate in the lining of the lower rectum) are out, too, because rectal nerves sense pressure but not pain; therefore, such ingredients are unnecessary. (Painkilling agents may soothe discomfort from external hemorrhoids, which originate in the lining of the anus, because the nerves in the anal area sense pain as well as pressure.)
- Lanolin alcohols, cod liver oil, and Peruvian balsam are banned as ineffective rather than unsafe.
- Product labels must say "If your condition worsens or does not improve in seven days, consult your doctor."
- Product labels claiming to shrink tissue must also caution: "Do not use this product if you have heart disease, high blood pressure, thyroid disease, diabetes, or difficulty in urinating due to an enlarged prostate gland unless directed by a doctor."

Keep in mind that using petroleum jelly or zinc oxide ointment or powder may be just as beneficial as any "hemorrhoid preparation" that you can buy.

Keep it clean. Keep your anal area clean at all times. Residual fecal matter can irritate the skin, but so can vigorous rubbing with dry toilet paper. Use plain water to rinse the area, then pat it dry and dust with cornstarch powder.

Rinse well. Soap residue can also irritate the anal area.

Skip the soap. If you find that, even with thorough rinsing, soap still irritates the anal area, look for a special perianal cleansing lotion in your drugstore. Follow the package directions.

Soften your seat. If your job demands that you sit all day, try sitting on a doughnut-shaped cushion—an inexpensive device that takes the pressure off the sensitive area. And be sure to take short walking breaks several times a day.

Sitz around. Take a sitz bath for 30 minutes, three or four times a day: Sit in six inches of warm water on an inflatable doughnut cushion or on a towel twisted into a circle big enough to support your bottom.

Take the heat. Even if you can't manage a full-scale sitz bath, a washcloth moistened with warm water can soothe the painful area.

Slim down. If you are overweight, you'll be doing your bottom a favor by getting your weight closer to the desirable range. Of course, you'll be doing the rest of your body good, too.

Hiccups

13 Techniques Worth a Try

Hiccups are little more than a reflex, like the way your knee jerks when a doctor taps it with a hammer. They result when the vagus nerve or one of its branches, which runs from the brain to the abdomen, is irritated. And the vagus lets you know by tweaking the phrenic nerve, which leads to the diaphragm, the muscle below the lungs that helps you breathe. The diaphragm then spasms, causing the "hic" sound true to the condition's name.

Experts say hiccups are most often a reaction to common digestive disturbances. And luckily, they're usually more a nuisance than anything else. But what about the times when we seem to hiccup for no apparent reason? No one knows for sure why these seemingly unprovoked bouts occur. What experts do know is that even infants hiccup, and the reflex continues to be triggered, about three to five times a year, throughout life.

The home remedies used to stop a hiccupping bout are believed to work on two principles. Some basically rely on overstimulating the vagus nerve. Like all nerves, it processes a variety of sensations, ranging from tempera-ture to taste. One way to stifle hiccups is to overwhelm the vagus nerve with another sensation; in turn, the vagus nerve signals the brain that more important matters have arisen, so it's time to knock off the hiccupping. Other methods, which interfere with breathing, increase the amount of carbon dioxide in the blood, probably causing the body to become more concerned with getting rid of the carbon dioxide than making hiccups. Here are some tried-and-true remedies from both camps.

Sweeten the hiccups.
Mary Poppins sang that a spoonful of sugar helps the medicine go down. But does it help hiccups? Many experts think over-loading nerve endings in the mouth with a sweet sensation can do the trick. Have a teaspoonful of sugar, and if you can, place the sugar on the back of the tongue, where "sour" is tasted. This way, the sugar overload will pack the most punch.

When You Can't Stop the Hiccups

In rare cases, chronic hiccupping may be a symptom of a more serious health problem. Possibilities include infection; renal (kidney) failure; liver disease; cancer, including lung cancer; nervous system or abdominal problems, such as ulcers; and even heart attacks. Virtually anything that affects the head, chest, or abdomen can be implicated.

A common bout of hiccups usually lasts no more than an hour, and the hiccups occur at a rhythmic interval of about every 30 seconds. It's time to see a doctor if the hiccups continue with frequency for much more than an hour, keep you awake at night, or don't respond to home remedies.

In some cases, a physician will prescribe antacids or a sedative to help calm the digestive system. And in instances of severe, nonstop hiccuping, surgery may be performed to cut the phrenic nerve's link to the diaphragm in order to stop the spasms.

Play "hear no evil." Some doctors recommend that you put your fingers in your ears—and not because they don't want you to hear yourself hiccup. It seems that branches of the vagus nerve also reach into the auditory system, and by stimulating the nerve endings there, the vagus nerve goes into action. (You could also try sticking a finger in the back of your mouth, which has a similar effect as creating pressure in your ears—but gagging is even less fun than the hiccups.) Of course, other doctors insist that you should never put anything smaller than your elbow in your ear in order to avoid irritating or damaging the ear canal. So if you do decide to try this hiccup reliever, be gentle, and don't stick your fingers too far into your ears.

Get scared silly. Have you ever, out of frustration, yelled at a crying child who, as if on cue, suddenly stopped? Scaring your vagus nerve may shut it up, too. Having someone surprise you can overwhelm the vagus nerve, though this method is probably best reserved for the stout-hearted who enjoy a good scare.

Drink water. Swallowing water interrupts the hiccupping cycle, which can quiet the nerves. Gargling with water may have the same effect.

Pull on your tongue. Sticking out your tongue and yanking on it may stop hiccups.

Tickle it away. Tickling the soft palate of the roof of your mouth with a cotton swab may do the trick. Or, if you're the type who enjoys getting tickled, it may be more fun to have someone find your ticklish spots.

Hold your breath. Hold your nose and close your mouth—the way you would when you're ready to jump in a pool—for as long as you can or until you sense that the hiccups are gone.

Bag those hiccups. The old standby, breathing into a paper bag, is believed to work on the same principle as the breath-holding method. Both increase the amount of carbon dioxide in the bloodstream, and the body becomes preoccupied with getting rid of it.

Take an antacid. This method may be more effective if you choose one that contains magnesium, since the mineral tends to decrease irritation and quiet the nerves. One or two tablets should do the job.

Eat slower. Scarfing down your dinner in a hurry causes two problems. First, if you're eating fast you are probably not chewing food thoroughly, which seems to cause hiccups. Furthermore, rapid-fire feeding causes air to get trapped between pieces of food, which may also set off the vagus nerve. Chew deliberately, and while you're at it, take smaller sips of drinks, to keep your air intake to a minimum.

Don't pig out. Overloading the stomach with food is another cause of

hiccups. Some experts theorize that hiccups are your body's way of telling you to quit eating so your digestive system has time to process all the food you've forced down your gullet.

Avoid spicy foods. Some spices can irritate the lining of the esophagus (the food pipe) and stomach. At the same time, they can cause acid from the stomach to leak into the esophagus. The irritation and acid can bring on a bout of hiccups.

Drink only in moderation. Like spices, alcoholic beverages can cause a simultaneous irritation of the esophagus and the stomach. And over time, excessive drinking can damage the lining of the food pipe. The result: an embarrassing "hic" after "hic," reminiscent of the down-and-out bum with a brown-bagged bottle and a red nose. But chronic alcoholism isn't the only cause. At parties, like the kind some college students attend, people are sometimes dared to consume a lot of alcohol as quickly as possible, and that can lead to what is called acute ingestion. The digestive system not only becomes irritated by the alcohol, but the esophagus expands rapidly because of the big gulps, resulting in hiccups. (In truth, hiccups are the least worrisome of the effects such binge-drinking can have; acute ingestion can lead to alcohol poisoning, which can be fatal.)

High Blood Cholesterol

21 HEART-HEALTHY WAYS TO LOWER IT

Heart disease is the leading cause of death in the United States, claiming the lives of more than 700,000 Americans each year.

The heart is a muscle that pumps blood throughout the body. Like any muscle, the heart requires a steady, plentiful blood supply to thrive. Heart attacks happen when the arteries that deliver blood to the heart become blocked. Starved of the oxygen and nutrients carried in the blood, heart cells die. If you don't receive swift medical attention, so will you.

The heart's arteries, better known as the coronary arteries, can become narrowed or even completely blocked by a buildup called plaque, which is made up of excess cholesterol and other bits of detritus floating in the blood. Cholesterol is a soft, waxy, fat-like substance found naturally in animal products, such as meat and dairy foods. The human body requires a certain amount of cholesterol to form hormones and vitamin D, among other things. Indeed, it's so important that the body can make all the cholesterol it needs. An overabundance of cholesterol in the body, however, can

result in high levels in the blood, where it can add to the plaque on artery walls. Scientists are still trying to figure out what causes plaque to form, but there is no question that having high blood cholesterol is a major cause of heart attacks.

The risk to your heart is affected not only by the total amount of cholesterol in your blood, but also by how it is packaged. It's well known that water and oil don't mix. The same is true for blood, a watery substance, and cholesterol, an oily one. For cholesterol to move through the blood, it must be packaged with protein into a molecule called a lipoprotein. There are two primary types of lipoproteins, high-density and low-density. High-density lipoproteins (or HDLs) are considered the "good" form of cholesterol because they help shuttle excess cholesterol out of the body. Low-density lipoproteins (or LDLs), in contrast, tend to deposit their cholesterol into plaque, where it hinders blood flow. So the more of your total blood cholesterol that's packaged as HDLs, the better for your arteries and heart; the more that's bundled in "bad" LDLs, the greater the danger to your heart. The levels of LDLs and HDLs in your blood can be determined through a blood test, just as your total cholesterol level can, and it's important you get this additional information if you've been told you have high blood cholesterol.

Some other major risk factors for cardiovascular (heart and blood-vessel) disease—in addition to high total and high LDL cholesterol levels—include heredity, increasing age (55 percent of all heart attack victims are 65 or older, 45 percent are under 65 years of age, and 5 percent are under 40), and being male (although after menopause, a woman's risk rises to almost equal that of a man). But while there's nothing you can do about your genes, gender, or age, you can control your cholesterol. Doctors can prescribe powerful drugs, including a class called statins, which produce dramatic reductions in blood cholesterol. (To learn how low you need to go, see "Low, Borderline, High—What Do the Numbers Mean?" on page 168.) But there are plenty of steps you can and should take on your own to improve your cholesterol profile, including the following:

Know it's never too early—or too late—to act. Although people with a total blood cholesterol level over 240 are considered to have the greatest risk of heart disease, the numbers can be a bit misleading, because most heart attacks occur in people whose cholesterol is below 250. So if your total cholesterol level puts you in the low- or borderline-risk group, don't assume you can ignore your lifestyle habits. Likewise, if you've already had a heart attack or been diagnosed with heart disease, there's no need to throw in the towel, because there's still plenty you can do to prevent another attack and keep your disease from getting worse.

Make some permanent changes. Making a commitment to lowering blood cholesterol and improving heart health requires a change of mind-set and daily habits for the long haul, not a temporary fad diet. Adopting a healthier lifestyle also means avoiding "yo-yo" dieting—losing weight and gaining it back repeatedly. Yo-yo dieting has been shown to cause cholesterol levels to rise.

Heart-Smart Glossary

The following are definitions of terms commonly used in discussions of cholesterol and cardiovascular health:

Atherosclerosis: The deposition of fatty plaques upon the walls of the arteries that supply blood to the heart. These plaques can block the flow of blood and cause a heart attack. Although doctors still don't know exactly why it occurs, having a high blood cholesterol level is thought to be a contributing factor.

LDL: Low-density lipoprotein, the "bad" cholesterol often implicated in the development of atherosclerosis.

HDL: High-density lipoprotein, the "good" cholesterol thought to protect against atherosclerosis.

Triglycerides: A type of fat in the blood that is measured to help evaluate heart-disease risk.

Ignore the magic bullets. This week it's rice bran, last week it was garlic, the week before it was oat bran and fish oil. All were touted as *the* solution to your cholesterol problem. While it's the American way to search for shortcuts, such an approach just doesn't cut it when you're dealing with your health.

Stay away from saturated fats. It might seem counterintuitive, but while the amount of cholesterol in your diet has some effect on the level of cholesterol in your blood, it's actually the amount of saturated fat you consume that has the greatest dietary influence on your blood cholesterol levels. The

Low, Borderline, High—What Do the Numbers Mean?

So you've had the blood test and received your lipoprotein profile. But what do all those numbers mean? Only your doctor can say for sure. Below you'll find guidelines established in 2001 by the National Cholesterol Education Program, a part of the National Heart, Lung and Blood Institute. (All measurements are in milligrams per deciliter of blood.) But these guidelines provide only a general view. What your numbers mean in terms of your heart-disease risk and your treatment options and goals depend on whether you already have heart disease or have any other risk factors for it. In addition to elevated total and LDL cholesterol levels, other risk factors for heart disease include:

- previous heart attack
- age (risk rises with age)
- gender (men have a higher risk than women, although women's risk begins to catch up at menopause)
- family history (your risk is increased if you have/had a close male relative who developed heart disease before age 55 or a female relative who developed it before age 65)
- cigarette smoking
- high blood pressure
- diabetes
- overweight (the more excess body fat, the greater the risk)
- physical inactivity

Even cholesterol numbers in the "optimal" range may need lowering if other risk factors put you at very high risk of heart disease. So you and your doctor must take into account each of your cholesterol numbers in conjunction with all of your risk factors to truly estimate your heart-disease risk, decide how to begin and progress with treatment, and plan how often and closely to monitor your levels.

Total Cholesterol
Optimal: Less than 200
Borderline-high risk: 200 to 239
High risk: 240 and above

LDL Cholesterol
Optimal: Less than 100
Near or above optimal: 100 to 129
Borderline-high: 130 to 159
High risk: 160 to 189
Very high risk: 190 or above

HDL Cholesterol
Optimal: 60 and above
Acceptable: 40 to 59
Higher risk: Less than 40

Triglycerides
Optimal: Less than 150
Borderline-high risk: 150 to 199
High risk: 200 to 499
Very high risk: 500 or above

more saturated fat—the kind found in dairy products made from whole milk, the marbling in red meat, the skin of poultry, and certain oils commonly used in commercially prepared baked goods—in your diet, the more cholesterol in your blood. Be sure to check food labels to compare the saturated-fat content, and choose products with the lowest amounts.

Avoid *trans* fats. Another culprit is partially hydrogenated vegetable oil, which contains *trans* fatty acids, substances that increase the cholesterol-raising properties of a fat. *Trans* fats are found in processed baked goods, margarines, and many other foods. Check margarine labels and buy *trans*-fat-free margarine. (You might also ask your doctor if it is worthwhile for you to try one of the new margarines spiked with substances called plant sterols and stanols. They tend to be more expensive than regular margarines, but consuming one of these special margarines may lower LDL cholesterol by up to 14 percent when it replaces other sources of fat in your diet.) Choose snack foods without partially hydrogenated fats; again, be sure to check labels.

Let TLC guide you. The TLC, for Therapeutic Lifestyle Changes, Diet is a dietary plan from the National Heart, Lung and Blood Institute designed to help people with heart disease or those at high risk for developing it (such as those with high blood cholesterol levels). It is a diet low in saturated fat and cholesterol that will help reduce your blood cholesterol level and in turn decrease your chance of developing heart disease or experiencing future heart attacks. (See "Therapeutic Lifestyle Changes (TLC) Diet" below.)

Learn to count grams of fat. The TLC Diet outlines the percentages of daily calories that should come from saturated fat and total fat. And it's true that most package labels these days indicate what percentage of a 2,000-calorie-a-day diet the specific food would contribute in calories, fat, and saturated fat. But what do you do if your recommended daily calorie intake is well above or below 2,000? You can do some minor calculations to determine the maximum number of

Therapeutic Lifestyle Changes (TLC) Diet

According to the TLC Diet, you should get:

- Less than 7 percent of the day's total calories from saturated fat
- 25 to 35 percent of the day's total calories from fat
- Less than 200 milligrams of dietary cholesterol a day
- No more than 2,400 milligrams of sodium a day
- Just enough calories to achieve or maintain a healthy weight and reduce your blood cholesterol level

To find out what a reasonable calorie level is for you, ask your doctor or a registered dietitian. Another option is to go to the Web site of the National Heart, Lung and Blood Institute, where you'll find a tool that calculates a recommended calorie level for you, taking into account your weight, height, gender, and activity level. (Go to www.nhlbi.nih.gov and enter TLC in the "search" box to link to the TLC section, which will walk you through the steps.)

grams of total fat and saturated fat you should consume in a day; then compare the grams of fat listed on the food label to your personal limits to decide if a food will fit in your daily diet.

How many grams of fat, and how many grams of saturated fat, can you have each day? First multiply your total number of calories per day by .25 (depending on your activity level, age, gender, and weight, you may be allowed 30 or even 35 percent of calories from fat—in which case you would multiply by .30 or .35, respectively; ask your doctor or a registered dietitian what level you should aim for). Next, divide that result by 9, which will give you the maximum grams of total fat recommended for you. (You divide by 9 because each gram of fat provides 9 calories.) Because you should get less than 7 percent of your day's total calories from saturated fat, you can multiply your total number of calories per day by .07 and then divide by 9 to determine that limit as well.

Eat as much like a vegetarian as possible. Dietary cholesterol is found only in animal products; animal products also tend to be higher in fat (skim milk products are exceptions), especially saturated fat. Foods derived from plant sources, on the other hand, contain no cholesterol and tend to be lower in fat. The fats they do contain are generally polyunsaturated and monounsaturated, which are healthier than the saturated kind. (The exceptions are coconut oil, palm oil, palm kernel oil, and partially hydrogenated oils, which contain higher amounts of saturated fatty acids.) You'll be doing your arteries a favor if you increase your intake of vegetable proteins, such as beans, whole grains, and tofu, and keep servings of high-fat animal products to a minimum.

Increase your complex carbohydrate intake. Eating plenty of complex carbohydrates will fill you up and make you feel more satisfied, leaving less room for fatty meats and desserts. Complex carbohydrates include fruits, vegetables, dried beans, whole-grain pastas and breads, brown rice, and other grains.

Read your meat. The small orange labels stuck to packages of meat at the grocery store aren't advertisements or promotions; they're actually grades of meat. "Prime," "Choice" and "Select" are official U.S. Department of Agriculture shorthand for "fatty," "less fatty" and "lean." Prime is 40 percent to 45 percent fat by weight, choice is 30 percent to 40 percent fat, and select or "diet lean" is 15 percent to 20 percent fat. So when you do add meat to your meal, opt for "select" cuts.

Change the way you cook. Broiling and steaming are heart-smart ways to cook food. Unlike frying, these methods require no added fat.

Skin your poultry. The skin of chicken (and turkey, too, for that matter) is an absolute no-no for people who are watching their fat intake. It contains high amounts of saturated fat.

Skip the pastry. One hidden source of saturated fat is pastry—donuts, Danishes, piecrust, eclairs, and so on. These confections are often made with shortening, butter, and/or hydrogenated fats—just the kinds of ingredients that should be limited by people striving to eat less saturated fat. Stick with whole-grain breads and rolls, and read labels to be sure you know what's in the package.

Eat fish. Although fish oil does not lower cholesterol, it has a dual benefit for the heart. In the simplest sense, if

you choose halibut instead of prime rib, you're avoiding a huge amount of saturated fat and cholesterol, since fish is low in both. But your heart gets a bonus, since fish is a rich source of omega-3 fatty acids, unsaturated fats that have been shown to protect the heart. The American Heart Association recommends eating fish twice a week. Fatty fish have more of those healthful omega-3 fatty acids, so the best varieties to add to your menu are mackerel, lake trout, herring, sardines, albacore tuna, and salmon.

Don't fear eggs. But don't think you can raid the henhouse anytime you like, either. Eggs were long considered no-no's if you were concerned about heart disease, since eating just one provides a bit more than the recommended daily limit of cholesterol

(200 milligrams). But in recent years, cardiologists have relaxed the rules a bit. Eggs can fit into a healthy diet if you omit other sources of cholesterol on days when you indulge.

Eat smaller meat portions. One way to trim your saturated fat intake without giving up the steaks you love is to keep your portions to about three ounces, the size of a deck of cards. Also, make whole grains the center of your meals, and use meat as more of a garnish or side.

Give up organ meats. Although rich in iron and protein, these meats are also tremendously high in fat and cholesterol. That goes for pâté, too.

Increase your fiber intake. Fiber, especially the soluble kind found in fruits and brans, has been shown to lower cholesterol levels. If you follow the recommendation to eat more complex carbohydrates, you'll naturally boost your fiber intake. You might also consider punching up your fiber consumption with a daily one-teaspoon dose of a psyllium-husk powder, such as Metamucil. Women should aim for 25 grams of fiber each day, and men should try to get 38 grams. You don't want to go much above that, but that's unlikely, since we average only about half the recommended intake as it is. Be sure to increase your fiber intake gradually to give your system time to adjust, and drink plenty of fluids, so that fiber doesn't end up plugging your internal plumbing.

Quit smoking. Although most of us are aware that smoking can cause lung cancer and can raise the risk of experiencing a heart attack, few people know that smoking can actually affect cholesterol levels. When you quit the habit, your HDL, or "good," cholesterol goes up.

Add exercise to your daily routine. Studies have shown regular aerobic exercise (the type that gets your large muscles moving and your heart pumping faster for sustained periods) can boost levels of HDL in the blood. Exercise also helps reduce weight and lower triglyceride (another type of fatty molecule in the blood that, when present in high levels, can increase the risk of heart disease) and LDL levels. Aim for at least 30 to 45 minutes of moderate exercise, such as brisk walking, most days.

Move, move, move. In addition to scheduling regular heart-pumping exercise, you need to graduate from a sedentary lifestyle to a more active one. That means fitting in extra physical movement whenever you can, such as taking stairs instead of elevators, running errands on foot or by bicycle rather than by car, and parking at the far end of parking lots. Consider getting a pedometer as a mini-motivator, and aim to take 10,000 steps a day.

High Blood Pressure

10 WAYS TO REDUCE THE PRESSURE

Blood pressure is the force that keeps blood circulating through the body. When blood pressure is too high, however, it strains your heart and blood vessels.

One in three Americans has high blood pressure, also known as hypertension, according to the American Heart Association (AHA). Uncontrolled high blood pressure can lead to heart attack, heart failure, stroke, kidney failure, and blindness. Unfortunately, a third of the people who have high blood pressure don't know it. That's why high blood pressure is often called the "silent killer."

High blood pressure is defined as a pressure equal to or higher than 140 systolic (the top number) over 90 diastolic (the bottom number). Between 120 and 139 systolic over 80 to 89 diastolic is considered "prehypertension." Readings below these are considered normal.

High blood pressure is particularly prevalent in African Americans, middle-aged and elderly people, the obese, heavy drinkers, and women who are pregnant or taking oral contraceptives, as well as people with diabetes, gout, or kidney disease.

The good news is that, together with your doctor, you can control hypertension. It will take some effort on your part, however. You'll have to make some changes in the ways you think and act. You may have to take medication. You'll definitely have to cut out some old habits and begin some new, more healthful ones. However, your efforts are likely to pay off in a longer, healthier life.

Here are some of the adjustments you can make to keep high blood pressure in check:

Lose weight. Slimming down lowers blood pressure in most people. In fact, for each pound lost, blood pressure may drop by two points. Losing weight may help you decrease the amount of medication you take or even get you off medication completely. Even a small amount of weight loss is beneficial.

Invest in a home blood pressure monitor. If you have been diagnosed as having high blood pressure,

Symptoms of a Stroke

If you are experiencing any of the following stroke symptoms, get immediate medical assistance. Waiting too long or not recognizing the signs could mean the difference between life and death. If you experience any of these symptoms and then feel better within 24 hours, you may have had a transient ischemic attack, or TIA. A TIA is a warning sign that a full-blown stroke is on its way. Again—call for an ambulance or have someone take you to the emergency room at once.

- Sudden weakness or numbness of the face, arm, or leg on one side of the body
- Sudden impairment or loss of vision, particularly in only one eye
- Loss of speech, or trouble talking or understanding speech
- Sudden, severe headache with no apparent cause
- Unexplained dizziness, unsteadiness, or sudden falls, especially along with any of the above symptoms

or if your doctor wants more blood pressure readings before making a definitive diagnosis, you may have been advised to buy a home blood pressure monitor. At-home monitoring has several benefits—first and foremost, warning you if your pressure becomes dangerously high, so you can get medical attention early. Second, a monitor can save you money, because it can save you trips to the doctor. (Check with your health insurer, because the cost of the monitor may be covered.) And it involves you more intimately in your own care, allowing you to see for yourself the benefits of lifestyle changes and treatments.

You can measure your blood pressure yourself, or you can have someone else do it. Try to check your blood pressure at the same time each day (or as often as your doctor recommends), because blood pressure normally fluctuates throughout the day.

Start an exercise program. Exercise lowers blood pressure and helps you lose weight. Check with your doctor before exercising, however—if your blood pressure is very high, your doctor might want to get it under control before you begin an exercise regimen. This is especially important if you have been sedentary. The types of exercise that are most likely to benefit your blood pressure are aerobic activities, such as walking, jogging, stair-climbing, aerobic dance, swimming, bicycling, tennis, skating, cross-country skiing, or anything else that elevates your pulse and sustains the elevation for at least 20 minutes.

Nonaerobic exercise, such as weight lifting, push-ups, and chin-ups, may actually be dangerous for people with hypertension. These types of exercise should not be done without the explicit consent of your doctor.

Take your medicine. Unlike other chronic illnesses, such as diabetes, you'll probably feel fine even if you don't take your medicine. However, inside your body, the disease will continue to progress, damaging the arteries in your eyes, destroying your kidneys, straining your heart, and so on. Another problem that can occur if you suddenly stop taking your medicine is a rebound phenomenon, in which your blood pressure rises to a higher level than it was before you started taking the drug.

Eat less salt. Consuming less sodium and salt can help some people lower their high blood pressure. A small amount of sodium is essential for life; the estimated safe and adequate daily amount for adults is 500 milligrams. But most of us get far more sodium than we need—the average intake for typical American adults has been estimated to be anywhere from 3,200 milligrams to more than 6,000 milligrams. So there's little to lose and potentially much to gain by reining in your intake.

Sodium is part of additives such as MSG (monosodium glutamate) and baking soda (sodium bicarbonate), but one of the largest sources of sodium in our diets is table salt (sodium chloride). There are 400 milligrams of sodium in 1 gram of table salt, and there are 6 grams of salt in a level teaspoon, so just a teaspoon of salt provides 2,400 milligrams of sodium. That amount—2,400 milligrams—is actually the recommended upper limit of daily sodium intake for an adult. It's not just the upper limit for salt you add at the table—it's the maximum amount taken in from *all* sources of sodium. And you'd probably be amazed at all the foods and food products that contain sodium.

Pregnancy and Hypertension

If you have been diagnosed as having high blood pressure and you become pregnant, you should see your doctor as soon as possible to discuss ways to control your condition during pregnancy. If possible, talk with your doctor before you become pregnant. Your chances of having a healthy pregnancy increase if your blood pressure is well controlled before you conceive.

During pregnancy, your blood volume increases by 40 to 60 percent, placing a great deal of additional strain on your heart. Perhaps because of this increase in blood volume, many pregnant women who never had a problem with blood pressure develop high blood pressure, a condition called pregnancy-induced hypertension.

The concerns about hypertension in pregnancy are twofold: First, the condition is extremely dangerous, posing a risk of stroke, preeclampsia (a condition that causes sudden weight gain, extreme water retention, blurred vision, and other symptoms), stillbirth, premature delivery, and low birth weight. Second, blood pressure may be difficult to control without medication, and many medications may pose a danger to the developing fetus.

But you can do your best to limit these risks by getting good prenatal care—starting as soon as you learn you are pregnant, or even before—and carefully following your doctor's instructions. Also be sure to check with your doctor before trying any self-care measures or making any dietary changes during your pregnancy.

Sodium is naturally found in a wide variety of foods, and we can likely get all that we need from eating plain foods that have had no sodium added to them. Unfortunately, sodium *is* added during processing and/or preparation to many, many foods, and its presence is not always obvious (sugary breakfast cereals and canned vegetables, for example, can contain loads of sodium). As a result, we have become so used to the taste of salty food that when food is made without salt, it tastes strange to us. Fortunately, your taste sense is adaptable, and over time you can adjust to a less-salty diet.

To limit your sodium intake, read and compare food labels—you want to take in no more than 2,400 milligrams each day and preferably even less. Remove the saltshaker from the table; get familiar with the many herbs, spices, and sodium-free seasonings that can take salt's place in cooking; and take advantage of the many low-sodium and sodium-free versions of common foods that have become available. Keep an eye out for foods that don't taste salty but still contain sodium sources such as MSG, baking soda, and baking powder. And ask your doctor or pharmacist to check the medications you take regularly, since some over-the-counter and prescription drugs also contain sodium.

Cut down on alcohol. More than one alcoholic drink a day may cause a rise in blood pressure. What constitutes a drink? A 1 ounce shot of hard liquor, a 6 ounce glass of wine, a 12 ounce beer—all of which contain 1 ounce of alcohol.

Eat bananas. According to the National Heart, Lung and Blood Institute, the mineral potassium has been shown to lower blood pressure. That's not to say you can stop taking your blood pressure medicine and stock up on potassium instead. (Never stop taking your blood pressure medication without talking to your doctor first.) But you may want to discuss with your doctor the potential benefits of increasing your potassium intake. Potassium supplements are available, although your doctor may advise against them since they can be hazardous in individuals with certain medical conditions. Instead, your doctor may recommend that you consume three or four potassium-rich foods each day. Good dietary sources of potassium include bananas, raisins, currants, milk, yogurt, and orange juice.

Drink your milk. Some studies have shown that extra calcium added to the diet may have a small beneficial effect on blood pressure. Since calcium is essential for strong bones and since most of us, especially women, don't get enough anyway, try including plenty of calcium-rich foods—such as skim milk, low-fat or nonfat yogurt, leafy green vegetables, and calcium-fortified orange juice—in your diet.

Quit smoking—now. Cigarette smoking is the number one taboo for people with hypertension. Not only does the nicotine contained in the smoke cause blood pressure to rise, but it dramatically raises your risk of having a stroke. Cigarette smoking can thicken the blood and increase its propensity to clot. Blood clots in the arteries leading to the heart can cause a heart attack, while blood clots in the artery leading to the brain may cause a stroke. The good news is, you get an immediate benefit by giving up the habit. Within two years of quitting, your risk of developing coronary artery disease drops as low as that of someone who doesn't smoke. (In contrast, it can take much longer for a person's risk of lung cancer to drop to that level.) Your doctor can recommend local resources to help you quit. You might also want to try the nicotine patch or nicotine gum, both now available over the counter, as an aid to kicking the habit.

Learn to relax. Many people misunderstand the term hypertension, believing it to mean a condition where the patient is overly tense. This isn't true. The term is defined solely by blood pressure levels. However, many people with hypertension *do* have the consummate "Type A" personality—aggressive, workaholic, hostile, frustrated, or angry. For these people, some form of relaxation, be it meditation, yoga, biofeedback, or massage, or just making time for rest may be an important component of treatment. Chronically stressed individuals release a lot of adrenaline into their systems. That rush of hormone can constrict the arterioles (tiny blood vessels), causing them to go into spasm. It is difficult for the heart to push blood through constricted arterioles. The effect? Higher blood pressure.

Hives

14 ROUTES TO RELIEF

Just about anything can make you break out in hives: Foods such as peanuts or strawberries, drugs such as penicillin or aspirin, vitamin supplements, heat, cold, sunlight, exercise, fever, stress, and even scratching or rubbing the skin are among some of the possibilities.

Some substances actually cause an allergic reaction that results in hives, while other hive triggers have absolutely nothing at all to do with allergies. Strawberries, for example, contain a chemical that can cause cells in your body to release histamine, a

chemical also produced during allergic reactions, which allows blood plasma to leak into the skin and form the hives.

And sometimes only a tiny amount of the culprit is needed to set off a reaction. For example, you may have a sensitivity to seafood but break out after eating a steak—simply because the steak was cooked in a pan that had earlier been used to fry fish.

Don't confuse hives with other skin eruptions. Hives (or urticaria, the medical term for them) occur when blood plasma leaks into the skin, causing "wheals," or swollen areas. They can be as small as a pencil eraser or as large as a dinner plate, and they usually last only a few hours. But new wheals may form continuously. And as they form, they often itch.

An attack of hives generally lasts a short time, often just a few days. Some people, however, may be plagued with recurrent outbreaks. Such individuals may want to do some detective work to find the trigger that keeps their hives coming back. Still other unfortunate folks have chronic hives—hives that can persist for years. But whether it's your first attack of hives or one of a string of outbreaks, when you're suffering from them, the only thing you can think of is finding some relief. Here are some tips:

Take an antihistamine. The most recommended remedy is over-the-counter (OTC) oral Benadryl (available generically as diphen-hydramine). But be forewarned: It may cause drowsiness. However, since hives tend to be worse at night, a medication that makes you sleepy may help you ignore the itching.

Don't scratch. Raking your skin with your fingernails may feel good at first, but you'll regret it later. Scratching can actually increase the local inflamma-tion, or swelling, and even cause more hives to develop. It can also tear the skin, opening a path for infection.

Wear gloves to bed. If you don't trust yourself not to scratch in your sleep, put on a pair of gloves or mit-tens before you bed down for the night to help prevent any damage.

Wrap up the affected area. Wrap an elastic bandage around the area with hives or cover it with clothing—but only loosely—so you can't reach it with your fingernails.

Use a milk compress. Wet a cloth with cool milk and lay it on the affected

Hello, Doctor?

Many episodes of hives are inconveniences that go away on their own in a day or two. But sometimes hives indicate a more serious condition, such as anaphylaxis, which is a medical emergency. Get immediate medical attention if, in addition to hives, you:

- have a lot of swelling around your face and throat
- feel nauseated or dizzy
- have trouble breathing
- have a fever

In some cases, diseases such as thyroid disorders, hepatitis, lupus, or even some cancers can produce hives as a symptom. See a doctor if you develop hives that persist for four to six weeks or that are accompanied by weight loss and a feeling of being unwell.

area for 10 to 15 minutes at a time. Do not use ice-cold milk, which can freeze the skin.

Chill the itch. Hold an ice pack or ice cubes in a thin towel on the skin for five minutes at a time, three to four times a day.

Take a bath. Put half a box of baking soda or one cup of oatmeal in the water first. Soaking in this solution may help bring some relief.

Try cortisone. A 1 percent topical cortisone preparation, available with-out a prescription, may help. Follow the directions on the package.

Try to ferret out the cause. But don't get frustrated, since doctors are only able to identify a specific cause in 20 to 30 percent of patients. Do remember that hives generally show up

Top Triggers of Hives

According to the American Academy of Dermatology, here are the most common foods that cause hives*:

Peanuts
Eggs
Nuts
Beans
Chocolate
Strawberries
Tomatoes
Condiments such as mustard, ketchup, and mayonnaise
Spices
Fresh fruits, especially citrus
Corn
Fish
Pork

The drugs most likely to cause hives are*:

Aspirin (check the labels on OTC drugs, because many contain aspirin)
Penicillin
Sulfa drugs
Tetracyclines
Codeine

*This is not an all-inclusive list.

within half an hour of eating, so if you break out today, you probably can't blame the strawberries you had for dessert last night.

Avoid the trigger. This one's pretty obvious, but if you know that cold sets off hives, don't put your hands in the freezer. In fact, jumping into cold water could be life-threatening for some hives sufferers. And there's no question that if you're prone to hives, stress will trigger them. So learn or develop ways to ease or manage stress.

Treat any underlying infection. If hives turn into a chronic problem, they may be due to an infection. For instance, an undetected dental or yeast infection could trigger an outbreak. Consider these possibilities and have them checked out.

Relieve the pressure. Hives often form where clothing is tight, such as under bra straps or waistbands. Hives on your forehead? Reconsider that old baseball cap you love to wear.

Use a moisturizer. If dry skin contributes to the itch, apply a moisturizer to relieve it.

Don't make the problem worse. Nonprescription anti-itch lotions or creams may seem like the perfect solution but can themselves cause allergic reactions. If you end up having a reaction to topical diphenhydramine or to one of the topical products ending in "caine," you'll be in worse shape after using them. Calamine lotion, that old standby for so many itches, doesn't do much for hives either.

Impotence (Erectile Dysfunction)

18 WAYS TO IMPROVE YOUR SEX LIFE

Impotence. The word somehow sounds like failure, weakness. If you feel that you are impotent, you may also feel that you have somehow lost part of your dignity, your masculinity, your wholeness. But you shouldn't feel that way—impotence, also known as erectile dysfunction (ED), can almost always improve with treatment.

There are many degrees of erectile difficulties. Some men are able to achieve an erection but are not able to maintain it. Others become erect, but not extremely rigid. Still others only have problems when they are with a new partner or with a long-time partner. And there are those who cannot achieve an erection at all.

Do not despair. You may be suffering from a medical or emotional problem (or both) for which there are definite solutions. Behavior modification can help if your ED is the result of emotional issues. If it is caused by a medical condition—and some 70 percent of ED cases are—there are new therapies that can help restore your sexual health (see "Medical Causes and Treatments" on page 182).

Whatever the nature of your problem, remember that almost every man has difficulties with erection at some point in his life. About 5 percent of 40-year-old men and between 15 and 25 percent of 65-year-old men experience erectile dysfunction. You are not abnormal, nor are you alone. There is no need to suffer in silence. Don't let embarrassment keep you from sexual health and happiness. Try the self-help steps here, but if the problem doesn't resolve, don't hesitate to seek professional help.

Check your prescriptions. A variety of medications can cause ED, including blood pressure drugs, antihistamines, antidepressants, tranquilizers, appetite suppressants, and cimetidine, an ulcer drug. Ask your doctor or pharmacist whether any of the drugs you take could be contributing to ED. If one of the medications you take has ED as a side effect, your doctor may be able to prescribe a different one.

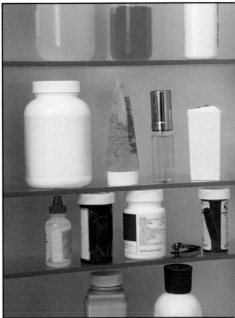

Remove the performance demand. It's not unusual for a man to have an occasional episode of ED—

Medical Causes and Treatments

A variety of medical conditions can cause or contribute to erectile dysfunction. The most common diseases that cause ED are diabetes, kidney disease, chronic alcoholism, multiple sclerosis, atherosclerosis, vascular disease, and neurologic disease. These diseases account for about 70 percent of ED cases, according to the National Institutes of Health (NIH). Between 35 and 50 percent of men with diabetes experience ED. In younger men, accidents, such as gunshot wounds to the spinal cord, car crashes, and skiing wipeouts, are often responsible. Other problems can include hormonal imbalances.

Doctors treat ED with psychotherapy, behavior modification techniques, oral medications, locally injected drugs, vacuum devices, and surgically implanted devices. In rare cases, surgery on the blood vessels in the region may be necessary, according to the NIH. (Keep in mind that even when a physical cause can be identified, emotional or psychological factors often play a role as well.)

Oral medications for ED include Viagra (sildenafil) and Levitra (vardenafil), which work by enhancing the effects of nitric oxide, a chemical that increases blood flow in the penis. They should not be used more than once a day, and men who take nitrate-based drugs such as nitroglycerin for heart problems should not use them because they can cause a sudden drop in blood pressure.

If you suspect your erection difficulties may be related to a disease, accident, or medication or if you're simply unsure of the cause, contact your doctor.

after drinking alcohol or after a particularly stressful day, for example. However, if he places too much emphasis on the incident and harbors fear that it

may happen again, the anxiety itself may become a cause of erectile difficulties. Behavior modification can help with this, though. One strategy that sex therapists often use is to have couples abstain from intercourse altogether, telling them instead to engage in cuddling and nonsexual touch. Gradually, over a period of weeks or months, depending on the couple, the partners work toward more sexual touching, then intercourse. The idea is to make sex a less-threatening experience.

Break out of a rut. Add some spice to your lovemaking: Go to a hotel or a different setting. Vary the routine. Try new positions. Buy your partner some new lingerie.

Learn to relax. Stress, arising either from performance anxiety or from other life situations, can exacerbate ED. Regardless of the cause, it's difficult to enjoy yourself when you've got too much on your mind. Try relaxation exercises such as deep breathing or progressive muscle relaxation, where you consciously tense and relax each part of the body in sequence.

Express your feelings. Marital or relationship difficulties are notorious contributors to sexual problems. Anger, resentment, and hurt feelings often spill into a couple's sex life, turning the bedroom into a battlefield. This situation is especially likely to develop if partners don't communicate. Work to share your feelings with your partner. Use "I" statements, and keep the focus on your feelings, instead of your partner's actions. Doing a thorough housecleaning of the relationship, instead of storing up emotional debris, may very well clear the way for a healthier sexual union.

Talk about sex. Sometimes, erectile problems occur because you simply don't feel aroused. In these cases, sex therapists often work to help patients communicate more openly about their sexual relationship—what they like, what they don't like, whether they'd like to do some experimenting. Again, to avoid defensiveness and hurt feelings, "I" statements are key. Choose to make assertive, rather than aggressive, comments.

Don't hit the bottle before sex. Consuming alcohol or being drunk can significantly impair your sexual functioning.

Remember your successful experiences. If performance anxiety has undermined your confidence, thinking about positive sexual relationships or experiences you have had in the past may help boost your self-esteem. It may also help reassure you that you can have a fulfilling sex life in the future.

Involve your partner. Although erectile difficulties originate with the man, they are a couple's problem and have couple solutions. If the problem is not a medical one, there are many strategies, such as the ones discussed here, that can help. However, your chances for improvement are much better if your sexual partner is involved in the solution.

Know that you are not abnormal. It can never be stated enough: Having problems with erection does not mean that you are physiologically or psychologically abnormal in any way. It is not your fault and you shouldn't feel guilty or allow your self-esteem to suffer.

Read, then talk. Take advantage of the many sources of information about sex. There are countless books as well as sex manuals and even videos that can help you and your mate solve your problems and work toward a more mutually satisfying sex life.

Prevention Tips

You can help prevent ED in the following ways:

Quit smoking. Studies have shown that smoking is associated with blockages in the blood vessels of the penis that obstruct the blood flow necessary for an erection. If you smoke, quit. It won't reverse existing damage, but it can help prevent it from worsening.

Protect your crotch from injury. One very common cause of ED, especially in young men, is an injury to the crotch area. Often, these injuries (and the erectile problems they cause) do not heal on their own and must be treated with surgery. Crotch injuries can be caused by all kinds of sports, such as bicycling, karate, and horseback riding. If you believe that your erectile difficulties were caused by an accident, see a doctor.

Make sure your aim is true. Believe it or not, another cause of ED is...brace yourself for this...a broken penis. This type of injury—which is thankfully quite rare—can occur when your partner is on top, your penis slips out of her vagina, and she sits on it. This can actually cause a hole in the erection chamber, along with bruising and swelling from internal bleeding. When this happens, you'll need surgery to repair the hole.

Skip the aphrodisiacs. So-called aphrodisiacs are usually little more than placebos—sugar pills or inert substances that have no actual physical action within the body. If a man believes the substance will enhance his sexual prowess, however, it may provide a confidence boost that *can* help him overcome anxiety-related ED. Unfortunately, some substances touted as aphrodisiacs, such as Spanish fly, can actually be dangerous and even deadly. So it's not worth the risk. Avoid alternative or herbal remedies.

Employ fantasy. Many men with erectile problems engage in "spectatoring," or constantly observing their own sexual performance. This takes the individual out of the moment and leads to being overly critical. Instead of judging yourself, focus on the pleasures of being with your partner. Fantasizing about and with your partner can take the focus off you.

Try masturbation. Performance anxiety is just that—anxiety over performing for your partner. But don't forget that while it's important to please your partner, you're also there to please yourself. Masturbation—bringing yourself to orgasm while you are alone—may be helpful by reteaching you how to achieve your own pleasure (as long as it's not overdone). The next step is to bring that ability into a sexual situation with your partner. In this way, you can change the focus from performance to mutually pleasurable interaction.

Don't be afraid to seek help. If your ED has no medical cause, psychological issues may be involved. Guilt, shame, anger, fear, sadness, and other emotions can impair your ability to perform sexually. Help is available from therapists who specialize in sexual issues. Ask your regular doctor or a urologist for a referral.

Incontinence

20 STEPS TO GREATER SECURITY

Have you stopped taking an aerobics class because you're afraid you might have an "accident"? Do you identify all the restroom locations in a mall before you dare to begin shopping? Do you dread sneezing, coughing, even laughing, because you're not sure if you'll stay dry?

Rest assured, you're not alone. According to the National Institutes of Health, more than 13 million Americans suffer incontinence, oftentimes in silence. Indeed, it's a problem that's only been recognized relatively recently in America as a common, treatable condition and not an unavoidable symptom of aging. As a matter of fact, other cultures in times past seemed to have been much more aware and accepting of the problem. The ancient Egyptians developed products for incontinence, and in Great Britain around the turn of the twentieth century, it was perfectly acceptable for a woman to hold what was called a "slipper" under her dress to relieve herself during a long church service.

The loss of bladder control is not a disease but a symptom with a host of possible causes. It can affect anyone at any age—from children to the elderly, both women and men. Women, however, are three times more likely than men to be incontinent, due in large part to the physical stresses of childbearing and a decrease in estrogen after menopause.

There are four kinds of incontinence. Stress incontinence results from damage to or weakening of the muscles of the pelvis, especially the pelvic-floor muscles. This set of muscles at the bottom of the pelvis supports the lower internal organs and helps them maintain their shape and proper function. Childbirth, menopause, a fracture of the pelvis, and certain types of surgery, such as a hysterectomy (removal of the uterus) or prostatectomy (removal of the prostate gland),

can cause these muscles to become deficient. (See "Exercises for Incontinence" on page 189 for advice on toning the pelvic-floor muscles.) As a result, any activity that puts a sudden stress or pressure on the bladder—anything from sneezing to hitting a tennis ball—can cause urine leakage.

Someone who has urge incontinence, on the other hand, experiences a sudden need to urinate but is unable to get to the toilet in time. Urge incontinence (sometimes called overactive bladder) occurs when there is damage to the nerves that connect the brain and the bladder, resulting in uncontrollable bladder-muscle contractions that force urine out. The nerve damage itself may be caused by a stroke, trauma to the spinal cord, or a disease such as multiple sclerosis that causes nerve dysfunction.

Some people suffer from both urge and stress incontinence. They are said to have "mixed incontinence."

And finally, some people suffer from overflow incontinence, in which the body produces more urine than the bladder can hold, causing leakage, or "dribbling" of the excess urine. It results from either an obstruction or poorly functioning bladder muscles, either of which prevents the bladder from emptying completely and causes an overflow of urine. An obstruction may be caused by a tumor or an enlarged prostate,

while certain medications, diseases such as polio or multiple sclerosis, spinal-cord damage, or pelvic trauma or surgery can prevent the bladder muscles from working properly.

The National Association for Continence (NAFC) estimates that approximately 80 percent of people who have urinary incontinence can find relief or even a cure. Depending on the type of incontinence, treatment may include changes in lifestyle or behavior, medication, special muscle exercises, surgery, or various devices and products to manage incontinence; often, a combination of these is used. So while you'll need to see a doctor for proper diagnosis and a treatment plan, the following steps can help you cope:

Keep a diary. Maintaining a voiding diary, or uro-log, will create a record of when you urinated and the circumstances surrounding it. The diary should include the time of day of urination or leakage, the type and amount of fluid intake that preceded it, the amount voided in ounces (pharmacies carry measuring devices that fit right inside the toilet bowl), the amount of leakage (small, medium, or large), the activity engaged in when leakage occurred, and whether or not an urge to urinate was present. Keeping such a diary for at least four days, if not a full week, before you see a doctor can help him or her determine what type of incontinence you have and the course of treatment. When you see a doctor, take along a list (or the actual bottles) of any prescription or over-the-counter medicines you have been taking, because some medications can cause incontinence.

Watch what you drink. Experts are not entirely sure why some beverages seem to irritate the bladder lining and, as a result, cause bladder leakage. But you may want to eliminate certain substances from your diet or at least decrease your intake of them to see if your urine control improves. The caffeine in coffee, for instance, may irritate the bladder, and the ingredients that give coffee its distinct aroma (also found in decaffeinated varieties) can be irritating too. Tea, another favorite breakfast drink, is not only a diuretic, which promotes fluid loss through urination, but also a bladder irritant. (As a substitute for your morning cup of coffee or tea, try one of the hot grain beverages found in your grocer's coffee and tea aisle.) Citrus fruits and juices, such as grapefruit and tomato, can be a problem. Carbonated sodas may be irritating, too (although you might be able to tolerate seltzer water, because it's not as highly carbonated as sodas). And, finally, alcoholic beverages should be avoided. Your safest beverage bet is water, perhaps with a twist of lemon for flavor (a few drops of lemon should not

be enough citrus to cause or aggravate an incontinence problem).

Try these juices. Grape juice, cranberry juice, cherry juice, and apple juice are not irritating to the bladder and may, in fact, help control the odor of your urine.

Keep drinking. It seems logical enough: Drink less and you'll urinate less, right? Unfortunately, not only is this strategy unhealthy, but it can be counterproductive. Depriving yourself of fluids can cause dehydration, which may make you constipated. This unpleasant condition can irritate nearby nerves that will trigger the bladder to void. Instead of cutting back on how much you drink, schedule the time that you drink. A normal bladder holds about two cups of fluid; problem bladders may hold as little as half a cup or as much as a quart and a half. Having liquids at set intervals during the day will keep your bladder from becoming empty or too full; bladder irritation usually occurs when fluid levels are too high or too low. Some experts suggest an average total fluid intake of six to ten 8-ounce cups a day. If you find yourself constantly waking up in the middle of the night to go to the bathroom, you might try to taper off your fluid intake between dinner and bedtime.

Watch what you eat. Again, experts don't know what it is about certain foods that seems to aggravate the bladder, but you may want to try cutting back on the following foods to see if your bladder control problem improves: hot spices and the foods they're used in, such as curry powder and chili; tomato-based foods; sugars, such as honey and corn syrup; and chocolate.

Try a recipe for success. If constipation is contributing to your urinary incontinence, adding fiber to your diet may relieve the constipation, and in turn, the incontinence. Here's an easy-to-make snack from the NAFC (previously known as Help for Incontinent People, or HIP) that may help. Combine one cup applesauce, one cup oat bran, and a quarter cup prune juice. Store the mixture in your refrigerator, or freeze premeasured servings in sectioned ice-cube trays. Begin with two tablespoons every evening, followed by a six- to eight-ounce glass of water or juice (one of the acceptable varieties mentioned previously). After seven to ten days, increase this to three tablespoons. Then, at the end of the second or third week, increase your intake to four tablespoons. You should begin to see an improvement in your bowel habits in about two weeks. The extra fiber may cause increased gas or bloating, but this should decrease after a few weeks as your body adjusts. Be sure to keep up your daily fluid intake in addition to using this fiber recipe.

Lose weight. Carrying extra fat in the abdominal region puts pressure on the bladder and stresses the pelvic muscles.

Do not smoke. Here's another reason to give up the habit. Nicotine can irritate the bladder, and for heavy smokers, coughing can contribute to stress incontinence.

Buy yourself some insurance. There are numerous products on the market today that will absorb any accidents and, at the same time, protect your clothing or bedding from wetness. Specially made disposable or washable briefs, diapers, liners, inserts, and linen protectors can add a measure of confidence. For some people, sanitary napkins or panty liners may be an acceptable alternative that provides enough protection. You may also want to ask your doctor about medical devices that can prevent leakage, including urethral inserts (small plugs placed in the urethra that can be removed when you need to urinate) and urine seals (tiny disposable foam pads that are placed over the urethral opening).

Be confident on the road. External collecting devices that are specially designed for use by females or males can make traveling a little more comfortable. These on-the-go urinals, which are also convenient for bedside use, are available at medical-supply stores and pharmacies and through mail order and Web sites.

Go before you go. Try to empty your bladder before you leave home, whether you feel the urge to go or not.

Then go again. After voiding, stand up and sit down again. Then lean forward, which will compress the abdomen and put pressure on the bladder, to help empty it completely.

Wear clothes that are easy to remove. Women's clothing, in particular, can pose a problem, especially for those with urge incontinence. Jumpsuits, unitards, and one-piece swimsuits can slow you down when you're in a hurry to go because these one-piece outfits must be removed from the top down. Skip such suits or look for ones with a snapped opening at the crotch for quick and easy removal. (You should also probably skip the skintight pants or skirts and control-top hose, which put unnecessary pressure on your lower abdomen in addition to being difficult to pull down.)

You might also want to carry extra clothing with you so that you can change if an accident occurs. If your clothes happen to become stained with urine, soak them for three hours in a mixture of one gallon water and one cup dishwashing detergent.

Exercises for Incontinence

The pelvic floor is made of muscles at the bottom of the pelvis that support the lower internal organs, such as the bladder and uterus, and control the sphincters, which open and close the urethra and rectum. When you stop and start your urine stream, you're working these muscles. When this set of muscles becomes weak, incontinence may occur. Since these muscles can be controlled voluntarily, exercises may help strengthen them and in turn help control leakage, especially in cases of stress incontinence. This is true only if the exercises are done properly, however.

Here are a few simple exercises recommended by the NAFC that should be done on a daily basis for best results. If you need additional instruction, the NAFC can help you obtain more information, or you can consult your doctor. In addition, your doctor may recommend exercises of increasing difficulty, depending on your specific case.

1. Lie on your back with your knees bent and feet slightly apart. Contract all the openings in the pelvic floor—the rectum, urethra, and, in women, the vagina, too. To help you isolate the muscles, first squeeze as if you were trying to keep from passing gas. Then (for women) contract the vagina as if trying not to lose a tampon. Finally, tighten the urethral opening as if trying to stop urine flow. In each case, hold the tension while slowly counting to three. Then slowly release the tension. Repeat five to ten times. You should feel a "lift" inside you. Be sure to breathe smoothly and comfortably and do not tense your stomach, thigh, or buttocks muscles; you want the various sphincter muscles to do all the work instead. Check your abdomen with your hand to make sure the stomach area is relaxed.

2. Repeat the first exercise while propping your lower legs on a low stool. Raising your legs will help further relax the pelvic-floor muscles for the exercise.

3. Repeat the first exercise while kneeling on the floor with your elbows resting on a cushion. In this position, the stomach muscles are completely relaxed. If you are unable to kneel, roll up a blanket and place it under your groin while you lie on your stomach, then perform the exercise.

Weight for results. Resistive exercise—when force is exerted against a weight—can be used to strengthen the sphincter muscles of the urethra and other muscles in the pelvic region that are important to regaining continence. Cones that are about the size of a tampon and that come in varying weights are designed for use in the vagina (women) or rectum (men). When a cone is inserted, the muscles in the region must contract in order to hold the weight and not let it drop. When done properly and consistently, these exercises should begin to show results within a few months. These weight sets are available from physicians, who can guide your use of the cones, or from medical-supply stores. Be sure to carefully read and follow the accompanying instructions on proper use for best results. Start by holding in the lightest weight for 15 minutes, two times a day. Once successful at that weight, try the next heaviest weight for the same amount of time. Some versions of these cones come with an electronic biofeedback system, called a perineometer, which reports the amount of pressure you're applying to the inserted cone.

Take control of your muscles every day. To prevent leakage, contract the pelvic-floor muscles when you feel a cough or sneeze coming on (pretend you're trying to stop urinating midstream, since you are contracting your pelvic-floor muscles when you do that). Also contract them when you lift or carry something.

Be wary of exercise gimmicks. Carefully investigate any exercise contraption that claims to help

decrease incontinence. A company may promote the fact that its gadget will tone the pelvic-floor muscles, but the device may actually exercise an unrelated muscle group, if it does anything at all. An exerciser for use between the thighs, for instance, will not strengthen the pelvic-floor muscles. If you're not sure if a certain exerciser will help with your incontinence problem, ask your doctor about it before you spend your time or money.

Make a phone call. Call 1-800-BLADDER, NAFC's toll-free number, for details on how to receive a free packet of information on services and products for people with incontinence; you can also order the packet from the NAFC's Web site at www.nafc.org.

Ingrown Hair

10 Ways to Get It Straight

Curly hair looks cute on a little boy. When he gets old enough to shave, however, those same curls can become a curse, causing uncomfortable, unsightly ingrown hairs.

Curly-haired men, particularly African Americans, get curls on the cheeks and neck as well as on the head. The hair sometimes just curls right back on itself. When the tip of the hair re-enters the skin, it's called an ingrown hair.

Ingrown hairs are also known as razor bumps, because they're usually aggravated by shaving. Another term for them is *pseudofolliculitis barbae.* Pseudo means false: The bumps appear to be infections of the oil gland or hair follicle (folliculitis), but they aren't. The skin does, however, become irritated at the point the hair actually curls into the skin.

Women are not immune to this shaving malady. It happens sometimes after shaving the places a skimpy bikini won't cover.

The most effective solution for both men and women: Stop shaving altogether. Short of that, here are a few other tips to consider:

Go with the grain. Shave in the direction your hair grows. Facial hair grows downward on the cheeks, straight out on the chin, downward below the jawbone, and upward along the lower neck, usually below the Adam's apple.

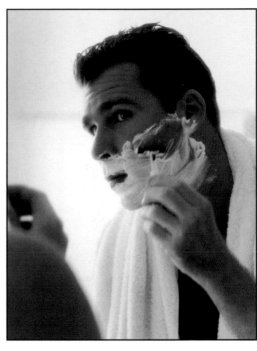

Hang up your razor for a day or two. Particularly if your razor bumps have become infected, you will do more damage if you shave over them. Giving the skin a break from the razor, and washing the affected areas with an antibacterial soap in the meantime, will usually end the inflammation.

Shave more often. After the inflamed razor bumps have gone down, shaving more frequently, but with a lighter touch, can help prevent them from coming back. This applies especially to young men whose beards are just coming in.

Lift them out. Before shaving, take a clean straight pin, a pair of tweezers, or a beard pick and carefully lift out any ingrown hairs. Don't pick or dig at them, which can damage the skin further and open the door to infection.

Get ready to shave. To lessen the trauma from shaving, prepare your beard (or other stubble) and your skin before you pick up that razor. First, soften them by soaking them with warm water in the shower or by holding a towel soaked in warm water against your face for a few minutes. Then, make sure your skin and beard are wet when you apply your shaving cream; whether you use foam, gel, or soap, never apply it to a dry surface.

Avoid electric. Electric shavers sometimes cause the hair to go in all sorts of directions—up and down, back and forth, round and round. That's no help at all when you're trying to shave with the grain.

Train your whiskers. Shave in the exact same direction (using the directions given in the first remedy) every day, and don't press too hard. After a few weeks, your whiskers will be growing out straight. Well, at least they won't be so curly.

Change your blade. If you're using a double- or triple-track razor, you're probably shaving too close for the good of your skin. Switch to a single-track, disposable razor or, better still, an old-fashioned safety razor, so you can adjust the closeness of your shave.

Sharpen up. A dull razor blade will make the problem worse. Use a new razor blade every time you shave.

Change your collar. Avoid wearing shirts with stiff, high collars that rub against the skin of your neck. The neck is the site of most ingrown hairs and razor bumps, so try not to wear clothing that will aggravate the problem. If you have no choice, at least opt for a shirt with a larger neck hole.

Ingrown Toenails

14 WAYS TO CURB THEM

Here's the good news: Treating ingrown toenails is easy and relatively painless. Now for the bad news: A simple nail infection, if not treated properly, can swiftly lead to further complications. When a sharp edge of a toenail grows into the skin folds at its edge, it results in pain and discomfort, especially if the wound gets infected.

People with diabetes or vascular disease in particular should get immediate medical treatment for ingrown toenails (see "Hello, Doctor?" on this page). People without nerve or circulatory problems, however, can usually take care of an ingrown toenail themselves, if they follow these tips from the experts:

Go soak your toe. To relieve the soreness, soak your foot in a basin of warm, not hot, water mixed with a tablespoon or two of Epsom salts. Soak your toe for five to ten minutes, once or twice a day.

Try a different solution. Some doctors recommend a product called Domeboro Astringent Solution, an antibacterial, anti-inflammatory soak that you can buy without a prescription at most drugstores. Soaking the affected foot in this solution for 20 to 30 minutes each night should help bring down inflammation so that the nail can grow out naturally.

Apply ointment. If the nail has already broken the skin (or is close to doing so), spread a topical antibiotic dressing, such as Neosporin, on the wound to prevent infection.

Don't play surgeon. You won't help matters by performing bathroom

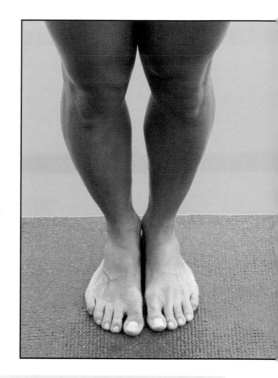

Hello, Doctor?

If you have diabetes or any other condition that affects circulation, don't even think of trying to treat a nail infection yourself. In folks with poor circulation, any foot wound or infection takes longer to heal. If not properly treated, an injury could worsen quickly and cause other complications; at worst, it could result in amputation. Reduced circulation also affects the foot's sensitivity to pain, which can delay detection of a minor injury. To complicate matters even more, people with diabetes often have nerve damage in the feet that further limits their ability to sense the pain caused by a worsening wound. So leave your foot doctoring—and even your nail cutting, unless you have your doctor's okay—to a trained health-care professional. But be sure to clean, dry, and examine your feet every day, and call the doctor at the first sign of a nail or foot problem.

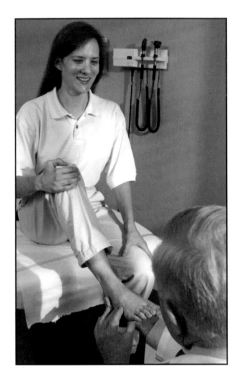

surgery on your toe. You'll risk giving yourself an infection, since the implements in your medicine cabinet are probably chock-full of bacteria and who knows what else. And if the nail has grown in deeply, your skin may already be infected. So see a podiatrist.

Go straight. No more curved toenails! When trimming your toenails, get in the habit of cutting them straight across. If the corners seem too sharp, it's okay to file them down a bit.

Don't cut too short. When you stand up, the weight of your body places pressure on your feet. That pressure pushes up the skin in front of each toenail. If you cut a nail too short, it may dig into the skin as it grows. To prevent this, always trim a nail so it is flush with the front end of your toe.

Wear the right covering. Dye-free socks only, please, if the nail has cut into the skin. Dyes used in colored and even white hosiery can run and may leak into the wound. This could cause further complications, especially if you are allergic or sensitive to dyes. If you have to wear dyed socks, cover the affected toe with sterile dressing before slipping it into the sock.

Step into a different shoe. An ingrown toenail may be nature's way of telling you to go shopping for new shoes that don't pinch your toes. If you're a woman, avoid high heels; try a lower heel (about one inch high) to relieve the pressure on your toes. Men and women alike should shop for shoes with roomier toe boxes.

Get some sandals, too. If the weather and terrain allow, wear open-toed sandals to give your ailing toe extra room and allow it to breathe. Put yourself in your toe's place: If you were sick, would you want to be cooped up all day in a dark, damp, hot room? And whenever possible, slip off your shoes for a while when you're sitting at home or at your desk. Healing will be speedier in the open air.

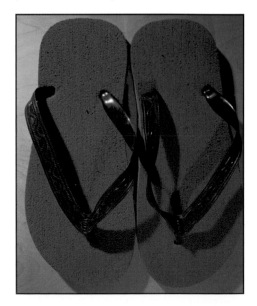

Protect it from mean streets. While padding around in sandals can be a great help, open-air footwear isn't suited for all terrains. In particular, avoid wearing sandals in the city, where the sidewalks may be covered with bacteria that could enter your injured toe, or on uneven ground, where an open toe is more vulnerable to bumps and cuts. Wear sandals around your home, but choose shoes with closed toes for urban or cross-country excursions.

Guard your toes. Even while wearing shoes, accidents and mishaps can hurt your toes pretty badly. For instance, drop a bowling ball on your toe and you could lose the nail, which may grow back as an ingrown toenail. If your job poses any danger to your feet, or if you have a habit of dropping things, wear steel-toed shoes.

Don't stub. Stubbing your toe can produce injuries that cause the nail to thicken or grow inward. So try to lift your feet, rather than dragging or shuffling them, when you walk, and watch where you're going.

Ignore folk cures. An old bit of folk wisdom says that cutting a V in the top center of the nail will keep the corner of the nail from pressing into the skin. But doctors point out that nails grow from the base, so this folk treatment makes little sense. Some people with ingrown toenails swear by rubbing coal oil into

Too Much Nail, Too Little Toe

If you had to wear braces as a kid, you may recall feeling as though you suddenly sprouted more teeth than would fit in your mouth. Sometimes, a similar thing can happen with toenails: The growth pattern of a toenail may change for some reason, and the nail may grow wider than it used to. The result can be a persistent ingrown-toenail problem.

A podiatrist can solve the problem with minor surgery that permanently narrows the nail. After applying a local anesthetic, the doctor removes part of the nail's side border, as well as some of the cells that line the base of the toenail (this area is known as the matrix). Removing these cells at the root of the nail eliminates the corner of the nail that burrows into the skin.

the affected area, though there's no medical reason for this therapy to work and it could be dangerous if there's already a break in the skin.

Pass on some pedicures. If you intend to have a pedicure, be sure the person who is performing it does not use metallic cutting instruments to remove dead skin; pumice stones are okay. And make sure all of their tools are sterilized before being used on you.

Insomnia

20 Ways to Sleep Tight

You know the story: It's 5:00 A.M., and the first traces of dawn have begun to appear in the night sky. You've been awake since 2:00 A.M. and are beginning to feel hopeless. How will you function at work tomorrow (make that today)? How will you cope with your presentation at the board meeting? How will you make it through another day after yet another night without sleep?

Adults need an average of seven to nine hours of sleep a night, but insomnia can keep them from getting the sleep they need. Insomnia is the most common sleep disorder in North America and Europe. A whopping one-third of the U.S. population cannot sleep well enough to function well during the day. Half of those people have only one or two bad nights a week. The other half spend countless sleepless nights tossing and turning, feeling miserable. They also spend countless days exhausted.

Insomnia is one of the least-understood sleep disorders. Still, sleep experts have come

up with many tried-and-true ways to relieve it. The results of their work appear in the tips that follow. Try them out, and see what works for you. If they don't help, consult your doctor for a recommendation for a sleep clinic near you, or contact the National Sleep Foundation (www.sleepfoundation.org or 202-347-3472) for a referral to a sleep specialist.

Don't torture yourself. The worst thing that an insomniac can do is to lie in bed tossing and turning. If you can't fall asleep after 15 to 20 minutes, get up and do a quiet activity, such as reading or listening to relaxing music. Then, go back to bed and try again.

Say no to naps. If you nap, you'll have more trouble getting to sleep the next night, thereby compounding your insomnia. It's best to let yourself get good and sleepy during the day so it will be easier to get to sleep at night.

Change your interpretation of the problem. Several misconceptions about sleep can make people overly concerned about their sleep and can actually keep them awake. One example is when people wake up out of what seems like a deep sleep and feel wide awake. They think that because they feel so alert they will never be able to get back to sleep. However, this is not the case. The key is to understand that your awakening is natural and that you just have to wait it out. Another instance of mistaken perception is that often when people wake during the night, they feel as though they were never asleep at all. But most people actually sleep much longer than they think they do.

Try earplugs. Sometimes, insomnia is caused by being awakened repeatedly by loud noises. Often, the sleeper is not aware of what triggered his or her awakenings. Try sleeping in a quieter room, or wear earplugs.

Exercise. Regular aerobic exercise, such as walking, cycling, jogging, or swimming, helps with sleep. Don't exercise too close to bedtime, though; exercising in the morning or afternoon is best.

Get a comfortable bed and pillow. Sleep may elude you if your bed is too hard or too soft, or if your pillows aren't just right.

Don't drink alcohol. Although alcohol can make you feel drowsy and may actually put you to sleep, it has the unpleasant side effect of waking you up later in the night with a headache, stomachache, or full bladder. In addition, once alcohol's sedative effect wears off, there's a rebound effect that actually makes you more likely to have trouble falling back to sleep.

Cut down on caffeine. Limit your coffee intake to two cups a day. Starting at noon, consume no foods or beverages that contain caffeine.

Don't switch beds or move to the couch. It is important to associate your bed, and only your bed, with sleep.

Maintain a normal schedule. Perhaps the most important rule for people with insomnia is to keep a strict sleep-wake schedule, even on weekends. If you can't sleep one night, get up at your usual time the next morning and don't take any naps. Chances are you'll be ready for a sound sleep by the next night.

Confine work to the office. Use your bedroom only for sleep and sex. No work, no eating, no television, and no arguing with your bed partner.

Take a hot bath. A hot bath taken two hours before bedtime is a wonderful way to relax your body and make it ready for sleep. For most people, taking a bath closer to bedtime may be stimulating and may delay sleep (of course, there are always exceptions, so experiment with the timing if you need to).

Adopt a relaxing ritual. When mothers bathe their children or read to them every night before bedtime, they are reinforcing a signal that it's time to get ready for sleep. Establishing such a ritual may also be helpful for adults.

Prepare your bedroom for sleep. The best sleep environment is dark, quiet, comfortable, and cool.

Drink warm milk. Some people find it soothing. However, if you wake frequently to urinate, avoid all liquids for a few hours before bedtime.

Don't eat before bed. Finish eating two or three hours before bedtime.

Try a sleeping pill. You're not admitting defeat by asking your doctor for a prescription sleeping pill or by trying an over-the-counter (OTC) remedy. It may help you through a tough time, but you should still take steps to remove the source of your sleep trouble.

Most prescription sleep aids should not be used for more than a month at a time. They should also not be used for insomnia at high altitudes—which may be caused by trouble breathing and a lack of oxygen—because taking sleeping pills at high altitudes may slow your breathing rate even further.

Some doctors don't endorse OTC sleeping pills, since they can dry out the mucous membranes in your mouth, nose, and throat and leave you drowsy the next day. And if you are pregnant, are nursing a baby, or have a serious medical problem, you should consult your doctor before taking such drugs. Sleep medications may also worsen snoring and sleep apnea, a dangerous condition in which breathing is labored during sleep. If you do try an OTC sleep aid, follow the label directions carefully and use it only for occasional insomnia; these drugs often become less effective the more you use them.

Never take sleeping pills throughout the night. If you choose to take a sleeping pill, only take a dose before you go to bed. If you take one when you wake during the night, it may not wear off by morning, and you may be dangerously groggy the next day.

Evaluate your other medications. Certain prescription drugs, such as those for asthma and thyroid problems, may cause insomnia. Check with your doctor if you suspect that one of your medications is causing your insomnia.

Be your own sleep scientist. There is no one formula for perfect sleep—different things work for different people. The important thing is to give everything a fair trial (for at least a week or two, not just one night) and see what works best for you. Keep a sleep log, a notebook of what works and what doesn't. It can help you identify factors interfering with your sleep and will prove helpful if home remedies aren't successful and you need to see a sleep doctor.

Lactose Intolerance

9 Ways to Manage It

Many folks relish the taste of frosty-cold milk, creamy ice cream, or cheesy pizza. For 30 to 50 million Americans, though, the aftereffects of these dairy delights may force them to take a pass or suffer unpleasant consequences.

The common condition these people share is lactose intolerance. That means they don't properly digest lactose, the sugar found in all milk products. This problem is usually due to a shortage of the enzyme lactase, which normally breaks down milk sugar in the small intestine so it can be absorbed into the bloodstream. The end result of this lactase deficiency may be gas, stomach pains, bloating, and diarrhea. The severity of the symptoms varies from person to person.

Who is lactose intolerant? It's not an equal-opportunity problem. It affects some ethnic groups much more than others. The National Institute of Diabetes & Digestive & Kidney Diseases estimates 75 percent of African American and 90 percent of Asian American and Native American adults have this condition. (Only about 10 to 15 percent of adult Caucasians do.) Though you may not fall into any of these ethnic groups, keep in mind that as we get older we all lose some ability to digest lactose.

Some people figure out they're lactose intolerant on their own; for others, it takes a trip to a doctor.

If you suspect you are lactose intolerant but you're not sure, it may be worth a visit to a physician to rule out other possible problems (see "Hello, Doctor?" on page 200). Once you know you are indeed lactose intolerant, try these tips to ease your symptoms:

Determine your level of lactose intolerance. The degree of intolerance differs with each person. The best way to assess your tolerance is first to get all lactose out of your system by avoiding all lactose-containing foods for three to four weeks. Then start with very small quantities of milk or cheese. Monitor your symptoms to see how much or how little dairy food you can handle without experiencing discomfort. Once you know your limits, management becomes a little easier.

Stick with small servings. While you may not be able to tolerate an

Hello, Doctor?

If you're feeling digestive distress that you think may be lactose intolerance but you're not certain, try this simple test: Lay off all milk products for a few weeks and see if your gut gets better. If things don't improve, it's time to contact your doctor. Other glitches in the digestive system may be causing your problems. For instance, you may have an intolerance to caffeine. Or, you may have irritable bowel syndrome, another common digestive disorder that can produce symptoms similar to lactose intolerance. So play it safe and get an expert's opinion, especially if you notice a major change in bowel patterns.

eight ounce glass of milk all at once, you may have no discomfort from drinking a third of a cup in the morning, a third of a cup in the afternoon, and a third of a cup at night.

Don't eat dairy foods alone. If you eat some cheese or drink a little milk, plan to do so with a meal or a snack. Eating dairy on an empty stomach can worsen your symptoms.

Supplement your diet. Lactase-enzyme supplements can supply your body with some of what it lacks. They're sold in tablet and liquid forms without a prescription. The tablets are chewed with or right after you consume a dairy product; you add the drops directly to milk. You can also try lactose-reduced milk.

Try yogurt. It doesn't cause problems for many lactose-intolerant people. This holds true, however, only for yogurt with active cultures, so check labels. If you can tolerate yogurt, it's to your advantage to include it in your diet, because like other dairy foods, yogurt is a great source of calcium.

Choose hard cheeses. If you won't give up cheese, pick hard, aged varieties such as Swiss, cheddar, or Colby. They contain less lactose than soft cheeses.

Check processed foods. Lactose is used in a lot of processed foods where you might not expect to find it. To iden-

tify hidden sources of lactose, check labels for any of the following words that indicate the presence of lactose: milk, whey, curds, milk by-products, dry milk solids, nonfat dry milk powder, casein, galactose, skim milk powder, milk sugar, and whey protein.

Get calcium from other foods. Lactose-intolerant people, especially women and children, should make sure their calcium intake doesn't plunge. Green, leafy vegetables, such as collard greens, kale, turnip greens, and Chinese cabbage (bok choy), as well as oysters, sardines, canned salmon with the bones, and tofu provide lots of calcium, as does calcium-fortified orange juice and soy milk. If your diet is calcium poor, you may need a supplement; ask your doctor for a dosage recommendation.

Watch out for medications. Lactose is used as a filler in more than 20 percent of prescription drugs (including many birth control pills) and in about 6 percent of over-the-counter medicines. It may not bother you if you take medication only occasionally, but if you take it every day, it could cause symptoms. Lactose may not be listed under the inactive ingredients on the label, however. So, to find out if your medication contains lactose, contact your doctor or pharmacist or the drug's manufacturer.

Laryngitis

18 WAYS TO TAME A HOARSE THROAT

Your voice makes you sound more like a frog croaking than a human talking. Chances are, you can figure out the cause—whether it was all the yelling you did at last night's hockey game or that cold you've had for the past couple of days.

Don't confuse laryngitis with a sore throat, though. True laryngitis is the loss of the voice or hoarseness, and it's the result of inflammation (swelling) of the larynx, or voice box, and the voice folds. The most common cause of temporary laryngitis is an upper respiratory infection such as the common cold, which is caused by a virus. If the infection is bacterial, you may need to see a doctor to get antibiotic treatment.

The second most common cause of laryngitis is abuse or overuse of the voice—such as yelling at that hockey game—which can leave you hoarse.

The symptoms of acute, or short-term, laryngitis can include pain in the throat or around the larynx, hoarseness, raspiness, the loss of range (noticed especially by singers), tiring easily, and a scratchy feeling in the throat. The constant need to clear your throat can be another symptom.

If you suffer from chronic (long-term) laryngitis, smoking may be the culprit. Inhaling tobacco smoke increases the mass of the larynx, lowering the pitch of the voice.

One surprising cause of laryngitis is gastroesophageal reflux disease (GERD). That's a long name for what a lot of us think of as heartburn, except that only about half of GERD sufferers actually feel any pain or burning in their chests. A GERD sufferer who feels no chest discomfort is unlikely to be aware that the acid-rich contents of

Hello, Doctor?

Laryngitis is usually a temporary inconvenience without serious consequences. But sometimes persistent hoarseness or voice loss is your body's way of telling you something is wrong.

When should you see a doctor?

- If pain is present
- If the hoarseness continues for more than 72 hours
- If you've got an upper respiratory infection with a fever that lasts more than a couple days
- If you have any trouble breathing
- If you notice a permanent change in the pitch of your voice, especially if you are a smoker
- If you cough up blood

The problem may be as minor as a bacterial infection that needs antibiotics. You could have polyps or nodules on your vocal folds that cause them to vibrate more slowly, changing the sound of your voice. Or you could have cancer of the larynx, which can be treated with radiation if caught early.

their stomach are coming back up in their throat, especially during the night. Laryngitis caused by GERD (which is very common among the elderly) can make you feel like you have something stuck in your windpipe. People often mistake it for the mucus of postnasal drip. Symptoms are worse in the morning: You may wake up with a bad taste in your mouth, do a lot of throat clearing, and have hoarseness that gets better as the day goes on. If you suspect GERD is causing your laryngitis, you should see your doctor (also see HEARTBURN).

If you're experiencing laryngitis, here's what you can do to soothe your voice:

Drink. Water, that is. Take frequent sips of water to stay hydrated and keep your throat moist. Other fluids are fine, too, though warm drinks may feel more soothing than cold.

Cut out the caffeine. The caffeine in coffee, tea, and colas dehydrates you.

Sip noncaffeinated tea with lemon. Make sure the tea isn't too hot or too cold. The lemon helps stimulate the flow of saliva.

Suck on lemon drops. Again, lemon gets those juices flowing, keeping the throat tissues moist.

Use artificial saliva. It may sound unpleasant, but you can buy over-the-counter (OTC) products that help keep your mouth and throat moist.

Speak softly. Talk as though you are seated with a friend in a café. More importantly, avoid yelling or speaking loudly.

But don't whisper. Contrary to what you might think, whispering is more stressful on your voice box than a softly modulated voice.

Limit conversation. Give your voice a rest, as you would an injured limb. Become a person of few words so your voice can recover.

Don't clear your throat. No matter how tempting it feels, clearing your throat actually increases irritation.

Stop smoking. Chalk up one more reason to avoid tobacco. If you can't kick the habit completely, at least cut way back while your throat is healing.

Avoid smokers. Even passive smoke irritates the larynx. If you live with a smoker, ask him or her to take their habit outside.

Say no to recreational drugs. In addition to their other dangers (and their illegal status), marijuana and cocaine are extremely rough on the larynx.

Abstain from alcohol. Alcohol dehydrates you—the opposite of what you and your voice need.

Humidify the air. Indoor heating takes moisture out of the air. Use a humidifier or vaporizer (just be sure to follow the manufacturer's directions for keeping it clean). If nothing else, breathe in the steam from a teapot or pan of boiling water, but be careful not to burn your face.

Avoid dusty environments. The dust is irritating, and such places are often also dry, which compounds the problem.

Beware of certain drugs. Medications such as antihistamines and diuretics can dry your mouth and throat. Don't stop your prescription diuretics (often prescribed for high blood pressure), but think twice about taking OTC antihistamines. Ask your doctor or pharmacist if any other medications you take could be drying.

Gargle with salt water. Add one-half to one teaspoon salt to 8 to 10 ounces warm (about body temperature) water. Don't make the water too salty, or it will actually worsen the irritation.

Protect your voice. To help your voice heal and to prevent future attacks of laryngitis, learn how to take care of your voice. Staying well-hydrated is the first step. Avoiding voice abuse is the next. And if you depend on your voice in your career—whether you're an opera singer or a traveling salesman—you may want to invest in some voice training.

Menopausal Symptoms

9 Tips for Coping with "the Change"

Menopause is a phase of four or five years, usually two years before the last menstrual period and two to three years after. For most women, menopause occurs between the ages of 45 and 55, although some women experience it earlier and others go through it at a later age. Women generally experience menopause at about the same age their mothers did.

Menopause begins with changes in the menstrual cycle—shorter or longer periods, heavier or lighter bleeding, decreased or increased premenstrual symptoms—until the menstrual periods cease altogether. You are considered to have reached menopause when you have not had a period for one year.

You should keep track of your irregular bleeding so your physician can be sure that these changes are normal and not an indication of abnormal changes in the uterine lining. If you have spotting after your periods have ended, your doctor will want to do an exam to rule out cancer.

During menopause, levels of the hormones estrogen and progesterone decrease. As you go through menopause, you may experience one or more of the following symptoms, according to the U.S. Department of Health and Human Services Office on Women's Health: abnormal bleeding or spotting; hot flashes; night sweats; insomnia; vaginal changes; vaginal infections; thinning of the bones; mood changes; urinary problems such as leakage or burning/pain while urinating; problems with concentration or memory; loss of interest in sex; weight gain; increase in body fat around your waist; and hair thinning or loss.

But menopause signals more than hormonal changes. It usually signals other kinds of life changes—some positive, some negative. Postmenopausal women are free of the discomforts of menstruation, free of the need for contraceptives, and in many cases, free of child-rearing responsibilities. For some women, those freedoms are exciting, but others struggle with them. It's normal to feel conflicted over these midlife changes.

Luckily, most women experience few if any menopausal symptoms, with hot flashes and vaginal dryness being the most common. Here are some tips to make menopause more bearable:

Dress for hot flashes. Eight in ten women experience periods of sudden, intense heat and accompanying sweating often called "flushes" or "hot flashes." These flashes occur because of changes in hormone levels. You can cool off quickly when a hot flash strikes by wearing layers of loose clothing that are easily removed, such as cardigan sweaters.

Douse it. If you're at home or in a place where it's convenient, you can "spritz" your face with cool water from a squeeze bottle or you can blot your face with a cool washcloth or moist towelette for instant heat relief.

Avoid caffeine and alcohol. If your hot flashes seem to be triggered by caffeine and alcohol, avoid them. Try substituting noncaffeinated teas or decaffeinated coffee for caffeinated beverages. (Keep in mind that caffeine withdrawal may cause headaches and fatigue for several days.) Excess caffeine also causes the kidneys to excrete more calcium, a factor in bone-thinning in postmenopausal women.

Estrogen Replacement Therapy

Most menopausal symptoms are a nuisance, but many women figure out how to cope with them, and the symptoms go away eventually. However, some women find the symptoms to be very disruptive. Until recently, physicians commonly prescribed hormone-replacement therapy (HRT) for those women. HRT makes up for the decrease in estrogen levels that occurs during menopause and can reduce or eliminate the hot flashes and vaginal soreness and, in some women, can decrease the risk of osteoporosis. However, a large research study, the Women's Health Initiative, found that HRT can increase the risk of blood clots, heart attacks, strokes, breast cancer, and gallbladder disease.

Because of the findings of the Women's Health Initiative, doctors are much more cautious about prescribing HRT. However, for some women, the benefits outweigh the risks. These days, women who take HRT are advised to take the lowest dose possible and stay on it for the shortest time possible. Also, women on HRT are advised to see their doctors every three to six months to reevaluate whether it is still necessary.

Carry a personal fan. Many women find they can get relief from the sudden heat of hot flashes by using a battery-powered personal fan; it's small enough to be carried in a purse and can be used anywhere.

Make small adjustments in your lovemaking. Hormonal changes associated with menopause often cause a woman's vaginal mucous membranes to become thin and secrete less moisture. The result can be painful sexual intercourse. Some of this lack of moisture can be overcome by taking more time to make love. Using an over-the-counter lubricant, such as Astroglide or K-Y Jelly, can also help. Avoid using petroleum jelly, because it's difficult to wash off.

Natural Treatments for Menopause

You may have heard of herbal products and other "natural" treatments for menopause that promise to reduce symptoms. There is little proof that any of these treatments works, and some may cause harm, particularly if they interact with any of your prescription medications. Before you take black cohosh, wild yam, dong quai, valerian root, or other plant-based treatments touted for relieving menopausal discomfort, talk with your doctor.

Exercise regularly. Regular aerobic exercise such as brisk walking or swimming can do much to increase your general health level, fight fatigue, and raise your spirits. Exercise also appears to slow changes such as loss of strength that many people believe to be age-related but are actually more associated with a sedentary lifestyle.

Regular, weight-bearing exercise such as walking or jogging can also help stave off the bone thinning of osteoporosis, a problem for many menopausal women. Bones get stronger with regular exercise no matter what your age.

Get support. Menopause can be a time of emotional upheaval. It can shake the image you have of yourself because your body and your roles in life are changing. You might find it helpful to talk with others who are going through it. Consider joining a menopause support group sponsored by a local hospital, community college, or professional group. Or you might want to form your own support group with friends who are experiencing menopause. Another option is to discuss your feelings with a licensed clinical therapist, such as a psychologist or social worker.

Get plenty of calcium. Estrogen levels drop during and after menopause, and as a result, bone loss increases. You can help keep your bones strong by making sure you get 1,500 milligrams of calcium each day from foods, supplements, or a combination of the two.

Dairy products are good sources of calcium, although you'll be doing your heart health and waistline an even bigger favor if you choose those that are low in fat, such as skim milk, non-fat yogurt, and low-fat cheeses. For example, an eight-ounce glass of whole milk and an eight-ounce glass of skim milk contain the same amount of calcium (350 milligrams), but the whole milk contains more calories (150 *vs.* 80) and more saturated fat

(8 grams *vs.* 0 grams). To add to your calcium stores, eat a diet that also includes more of the nondairy food sources of calcium (see "Calcium-Rich Foods" at right).

If your diet isn't rich in calcium or if your stores of calcium are seriously depleted from a lifetime of poor eating habits, consider taking a calcium supplement. Keep in mind that the number of milligrams of calcium listed on the label of a supplement may not reflect the amount of elemental calcium in the product, which is what counts toward your calcium requirement. For example, it takes 1,200 milligrams of calcium carbonate to get 500 milligrams of elemental calcium. Ask your doctor or pharmacist for advice on choosing a calcium supplement.

Eat a balanced, low-fat diet. Once a woman enters menopause, her risk of heart disease as well as osteoporosis begins to rise sharply. The decrease in estrogen allows LDL, or "bad," cholesterol levels to increase.

Diet can go a long way toward preventing serious health problems like osteoporosis, cancer, and heart disease in menopausal women. Diets high in protein and sodium, for example, cause the body to excrete more calcium, which contributes to osteoporosis. So choose lots of fresh fruit and vegetables, whole grains, fat-free dairy, and moderate amounts of lean protein. If you

Calcium-Rich Foods

Calcium is important at any age, but it becomes even more important for menopausal women in order to prevent the bone-thinning of osteoporosis. Include these calcium-rich foods in your diet to ensure you're getting enough of this important mineral:

Almonds
Brewer's yeast
Calcium-fortified orange juice
Calcium-fortified soy milk
Dandelion greens
Ice milk or ice cream (opt for lower-fat varieties)
Kelp
Mackerel, canned
Milk (opt for skim or low-fat varieties)
Mustard greens
Oysters
Salmon, canned with bones
Sardines, canned with bones
Soybean curd (tofu)
Yogurt (opt for nonfat or low-fat varieties)

eat a lot of meat, try to replace some of it with nonmeat protein, such as tofu, dried beans, or fish.

Middle-Ear Infection

9 Tips for Prevention and Treatment

Middle-ear infection (known medically as *otitis media)* is the most common illness in babies and young children. Researchers estimate that at least 75 percent (and possibly more than 90 percent) of children experience at least one such infection during the first three years of life, and close to 50 percent get three or more ear infections during those early years.

Of course, children aren't the only ones who get ear infections. But they are, by far, the most common victims. Adults are more likely to get an infection of the outer ear, which is aptly referred to as "swimmer's ear" because it usually gets its start when water containing bacteria or fungi seeps into the ear and gets trapped in the ear canal (see SWIMMER'S EAR).

In order to understand how middle-ear infections develop, it helps to know how healthy ears function. The outer ear is connected to an air-containing space called the middle ear. The eardrum, a thin membrane, is stretched across the entrance to the space, and three tiny sound-conducting bones are suspended within it. The pressure within the middle-ear space is equalized with the atmosphere through a narrow tube called the eustachian tube. The eustachian tube opens into a space behind the nose where air or fluid may enter or escape. The air pressure in the middle ear is equalized more than one thousand times a day—every time you swallow—usually without you noticing it. The eustachian tube also carries fluid away from the middle ear.

When a cold or an allergy is present, the eustachian tube swells and air is absorbed by the lining of the middle ear, creating a partial vacuum. The eardrum then gets pulled inward, and fluid weeps from the lining of the middle ear. Bacteria or viruses from the nose and throat can travel up the eustachian tube and infect the stagnant, warm fluid in the middle ear, which provides a perfect environment for them to live and multiply.

Children may be more prone to middle-ear infections for a variety of reasons. For example, their eustachian tubes are shorter and straighter than those in adults, which may make it easier for bacteria and viruses to penetrate. Children also get colds and sore throats more often than adults do. And the immune system is not as fully developed during childhood as it is in adulthood.

Preventing Ear Infections

As a parent, there are some things you can do to decrease the chance your child will develop a middle-ear infection.

Steer your child clear. Since middle-ear infections generally start with a cold or other upper respiratory infection, you'll help protect your child from ear infections by keeping him away from other kids who have infections. Making sure that any nasal allergies that your child has are well controlled can also be beneficial. And if you are in the process of choosing a day-care facility for your child, check into the center's policy for dealing with children who are ill.

Teach proper nose-blowing technique. Once your child is old enough, teach her to blow her nose softly rather than with excessive force, so as not to drive infection into the ears. And teach your child not to stifle a sneeze by pinching the nostrils, since this, too, may force the infection up into the ears.

Don't smoke. Here's another reason not to smoke: Children who live with smokers seem to be more susceptible to middle-ear infections than are those who live in smoke-free homes. Cigarette smoke irritates the linings of the nasal passages and middle-ear cavity, which in turn interferes with the normal functioning of the eustachian tube. If you cannot quit, at least take your habit outside.

Be careful with bottle-feeding. Avoid giving a bottle of milk or formula to a baby who is lying on his back, because the nutrient-rich liquid can flow into the eustachian tube during swallowing and pool there, creating a luxurious breeding ground for infectious organisms.

Stay alert to the signs. It is essential to get your child to the doctor as soon as you suspect an ear infection, but to do that, you need to be aware of the symptoms that can signal an ear infection. An older child who has an ear infection may complain of ear pain or aching or stuffiness in the ear. In a younger child who cannot yet describe an earache, you need to be alert to other signs that may signal an imminent ear infection, such as pulling on or rubbing the ear, any trouble with hearing or balance, crying more than usual, or fluid draining from the ear. (Signs that an infection has taken hold include fever, crying, rubbing the ear, nausea, and vomiting.)

Treating an Ear Infection

If you suspect your child has an ear infection, you should take the child to the doctor at once. If a middle-ear

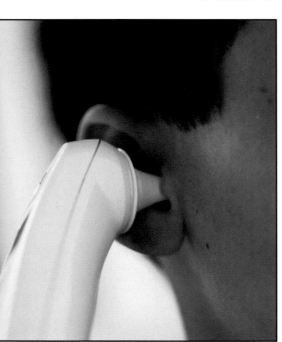

infection is treated promptly, serious complications can be avoided. If it is not treated right away, your child could potentially suffer hearing loss and, as a result, a delay in learning and speech development. Once your child has seen the doctor, however, there are some things you can do to help make your little one more comfortable.

Follow through on the doctor's instructions. Your job doesn't end with a visit to the doctor. You will need to be sure that your child receives any medication prescribed by the doctor. Be sure, too, that you understand and follow the directions for administering the medicine (call your doctor or pharmacist with any questions). If an antibiotic has been prescribed, it's especially important that your child take the medication for the full time prescribed.

Keep your child's chin up. If your child is lying down, prop her head up on pillows. Elevating her head will help keep her eustachian tubes draining into the back of her throat.

Try mild heat. Applying a heating pad set on warm—not hot—to the affected ear may make your child more comfortable.

Give acetaminophen. With the doctor's okay, give your child acetaminophen to help relieve pain and fever. Do not give your child aspirin. Aspirin use in children with a viral illness has been associated with Reye syndrome, an often fatal condition characterized by sudden, severe deterioration of liver and brain function.

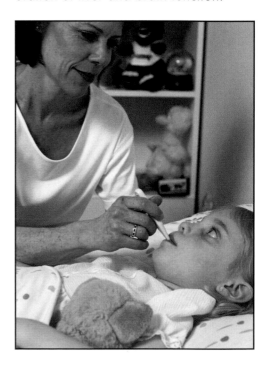

Morning Sickness

14 WAYS TO EASE THE QUEASINESS

The nausea and vomiting of early pregnancy were written about as early as 2000 B.C. Unfortunately, the ancient Egyptians didn't have a cure for the condition, either.

More than half of American women will suffer from nausea, vomiting, or both during the first three months (also known as the first trimester) of pregnancy, according to the March of Dimes. The occurrence and severity, however, vary not only from woman to woman, but from pregnancy to pregnancy in the same individual.

Some women never have even the slightest touch of queasiness. Some are ill in the morning and recover by lunch. And some stay sick all day for days on end, wondering why it's called "morning sickness" when it lasts 24 hours.

No one knows what causes morning sickness. It is less common among Eskimos and native African tribes than in Western civilizations. But today's doctors emphasize it's not psychological, as was once believed.

Since hormones run amok during early pregnancy, researchers theorize that they somehow contribute to the existence of morning sickness. A sus-

pected culprit is human chorionic gonadotropin (HCG), the hormone tested for in home pregnancy kits, which hits an all-time high in those first months. But other hormones may play a role as well. High levels of progesterone, for example, result in smooth-muscle relaxation, slowing down the digestive process.

If you're suffering from morning sickness, you probably don't care what causes it. You just want relief. Time will eventually take care of it; the condition usually subsides after the third month. (Scant words of comfort.) While you're waiting for the second trimester to arrive, however, here's what the experts suggest you try for relief:

Don't worry about crumbs in the sheets. Keep crackers by the bed. Eating a few low-sodium crackers as soon as you wake up—and before you get out of bed—is the first line of defense against morning sickness.

Eat protein-rich snacks. Nuts, peanut butter, dairy products, and other high-protein foods may help.

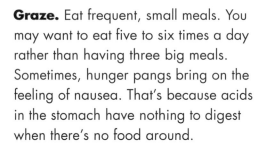

Hello, Doctor?

If morning sickness persists past the third month or you find yourself so ill you're losing weight, see your physician. Watch out, too, for becoming dehydrated; you'll feel dizzy when you stand and/or your urine output will be scant and dark colored.

Graze. Eat frequent, small meals. You may want to eat five to six times a day rather than having three big meals. Sometimes, hunger pangs bring on the feeling of nausea. That's because acids in the stomach have nothing to digest when there's no food around.

Don't drink and eat at the same time. In other words, drink your fluids between meals, instead of during meals, to avoid too much bulk in the stomach.

Stay fluid. You need at least eight glasses of fluids a day—it's important not to become dehydrated during pregnancy.

Go for a liquid diet. You may find it easier on your stomach to emphasize liquids over solids when morning sickness is at its worst. Get your nutrients from bouillon, juices, and other liquids. (Confirm that this approach is okay with your obstetrician first.)

Stick to bland foods. This isn't the time to try that new Thai restaurant. Spicy foods just don't cut it right now.

Choose complex carbohydrates. Pasta, bread, potatoes—the foods you think of as starches—are easier to digest and they're soothing.

Avoid fatty foods. Fats are harder to digest than carbohydrates or pro-teins, so high-fat foods may not sit well right now.

Don't sniff. Certain odors often trigger the feeling of nausea, so try to identify any scents that have that effect on you and avoid them as much as possible.

Avoid sudden moves. Don't change your posture quickly. In the morning, for example, sit up slowly first, then gently slide your legs out from under the covers, and take your time rising from the bed.

Take vitamin B₆. A number of physicians recommend taking a supplement of this vitamin—the usual dose is 10 to 25 milligrams three times a day—to combat the nausea of morning sickness. Talk to your doctor before trying a supplement, however, and be sure not to exceed 75 milligrams of the vitamin each day.

Take a walk. Exercise can sometimes help alleviate symptoms. Plus, it's good for your body. Be sure to check with your doctor before trying anything more strenuous than a walk, however.

Don't forget to brush. If you do succumb to vomiting, take good care of your teeth by brushing afterward (at least rinse your mouth if you can't brush right away). Otherwise, the prolonged contact with the harsh acids in your vomit can eat away at tooth enamel.

Motion Sickness

14 Ways to Still the Savage Beast

Oh that queasy feeling, when the world won't stop swaying, bobbing, or just plain moving. No matter what the mode of transport, the result can be motion sickness. While many experts believe there may be a genetic tendency involved, they aren't exactly sure why some people get sick from riding in a car, boat, plane, or train, while others don't. If you do, you're not alone. Motion sickness caused some pilots to drop out of training during World War II. And to this day, NASA astronauts struggle to combat this side effect of space travel.

Normally, the eyes, inner ears (which contain fluid that sloshes around in reaction to movement), skin, and muscles send sensory information to the brain that allows it to determine the body's position in space and to track whether and in what direction it is moving. Motion sickness is believed to occur when this balancing system gets overwhelmed by contradictory messages sent from the eyes and inner ears. The resulting symptoms of motion sickness can include sweating, light-headedness, hyperventilation, nausea, and vomiting.

For some people, the symptoms of motion sickness can be brought on merely by walking down the aisles in a supermarket or watching telephone poles whipping by a car window. Some people can even get motion sickness sitting in a theater and watching an action-packed film on one of those super-sized movie screens.

With a few simple steps, you may be able to prevent motion sickness from developing in the first place or help quell your queasiness once it's begun. Here's how:

Pick the right seat. If possible, sit in an area with the smoothest ride, where motion is least likely to be felt in the

Patch Up the Problem

Another option for preventing motion sickness is to use a transdermal (skin) patch. Available with a prescription from your doctor, the patch adheres to the skin behind the ear or on the neck or forehead and dispenses small amounts of scopolamine, a drug that suppresses the body's balancing mechanisms. In order to be effective, however, you must take care to use the patch properly. If you are prescribed patches, the first one must be applied at least 12 hours before departure. Be sure to carefully follow all the directions for use. And do not dispense them to anyone else. Children and the elderly, in particular, are more likely to be sensitive to the medication in the patch and should never use it unless a physician has specifically prescribed it for them. Children, for example, can become hyperactive as a result of wearing the patch. And in older adults, the medicine can cause severe confusion.

first place. When making a plane reservation, ask for an aisle seat over a wing. On a train, opt for a car toward the front. Sit in the front seat of an automobile. And on a ship, ask for a cabin toward the center of the vessel.

Avoid standing. The last thing you need when you're trying to keep your stomach settled is to be tossed around during the trip.

Face forward. Choose a seat that faces in the direction you are traveling, so that the forward motion your body feels will match what you see.

Minimize head movements. Try to avoid sudden movements of your head, which can aggravate motion sickness.

Stay up. While you may be tempted to go below when you're feeling queasy on a boat, stay on deck as much as possible, so your eyes can confirm the movement that your body is feeling.

Look off into the distance. Not to daydream, but to focus on a steady point away from the rocking boat, plane, or car. If there isn't a tree or barn or other specific object in the distance to focus on, stare out at the horizon, where the sky meets the earth (or water). Again, this will allow your eyes to see that you are moving—to match the movement your body feels—without making you dizzy, the way that watching telephone poles or mile markers whizzing by can make you feel.

Leave your reading at home.
If you read in a car, your eyes stay fixed on a stationary object, yet your body feels the motion of the car—again setting up that sensory contradiction. Instead, focus on the road in front of you or at a distant object so all your senses can confirm that you are on the move.

Volunteer to drive. Drivers are so busy watching the road that they're less apt to get carsick.

Eat a little or don't eat at all.
Sometimes eating helps, sometimes it doesn't. Experiment to see what works for you. About an hour before you leave, eat some plain crackers or a piece of bread or toast. If it makes you feel worse, don't eat next time—keep your stomach calm and empty, in case you should start to get nauseated.

Avoid heavy foods and odors. The smell of spicy or greasy foods and strong odors can prompt motion sickness before or during a trip. So skip the stop at the roadside diner.

Say no to alcohol. Avoid alcoholic beverages before and during a trip. Booze can worsen motion sickness.

Stay calm, cool, and collected.
Sometimes, just the thought of getting sick can make you sick. The same goes for those who are anxious about what they're about to do, like flying in a plane or riding in a boat. Try to stay as calm and relaxed as possible. Take a couple slow, deep breaths, and tell yourself that you will not get sick.

Try over-the-counter remedies.
Antihistamines are the active ingredients in nonprescription motion-sickness medications, such as Dramamine, Bonine, and Marezine. If you plan to try one of these, you should take it at least an hour before the trip for maximum effectiveness. Always check the label for warnings and possible side effects, such as drowsiness or blurred vision, and take necessary precautions, such as not driving a car.

Stay away from others who are sick. The power of suggestion is very strong, especially if you have a tendency to get a bit "green" yourself. As callous as it may sound, let someone with a sturdier stomach tend to the sick; you should be looking at the horizon or at another steady point in the distance.

Muscle Pain

21 Steps to Relief

It was just a pickup game of basketball with the guys, not a marathon. And it felt great to finally get back on the court. But a day-and-a-half later, you can barely move. You're so stiff, it feels like you've aged 100 years nearly overnight. Every time you try to move, your muscles cry out in pain. What's going on?

Well, weekend warrior, you've overdone it, and your body is letting you know. Overworking muscles, especially muscles that aren't accustomed to much work in the first place, causes the muscle fibers to actually break down, and that's what's causing your pain. If you had been exercising regularly all along, slowly and gradually increasing the duration and intensity of your workouts, chances are that game of round ball wouldn't have left you feeling like you got hit by a truck.

In addition to the tiny tears that occur in

muscle fibers during intense exercise, the muscles swell slightly, and by-products of muscle breakdown accumulate. Together, they contribute to the feeling of stiffness and soreness.

Another common source of muscle pain is a cramp, an acute spasm of the muscle that can send you to the ground clutching the offending muscle and howling in pain. Muscle cramps can be caused by anything that interferes with the mechanisms that cause muscles to contract and relax. The tight contraction of the muscle restricts the blood flow to the area, causing the intense pain of a muscle cramp.

Knowing how muscles contract and relax can help you understand why muscle cramps occur and how to prevent them. To cause a muscle to contract, the brain sends an electrical "contract" message through nerves to the muscle. When this signal reaches the muscle, the minerals sodium and calcium inside the muscle and potassium outside the muscle move, causing the signal to flow along the muscle and making it contract. For muscles to contract and relax properly, they need the right concentrations of these minerals as well as adequate supplies of sugar (glucose), fatty acids (components of fat), and oxygen.

If a muscle uses up its energy supply (called glycogen, which is the storage form of glucose), and if too many waste products have built up in the muscle, it may go into spasm. The spasm, in turn, slows the blood flow, causing pain.

While muscle soreness and cramps aren't generally life-threatening, they can be uncomfortable and annoying and can dim your enthusiasm for physical activity, which in turn can negatively affect your overall health and well-being. Here are some tips to ease the pain and prevent the problem from recurring:

Stop. If your muscle cramps up while you're exercising, STOP. Don't try to "run through" a cramp. Doing so increases your chances of seriously injuring the muscle.

Give it a stretch and squeeze. When you get a cramp, stretch the cramped muscle with one hand while you gently knead and squeeze the center of the muscle (you'll be able to feel a knot or a hard bulge of muscle) with the fingers of the other hand. Try to feel how it's contracted, and stretch it in the opposite direction. For example, if you have a cramp in your calf muscle, sit on the ground with that leg extended, and with one hand, reach

Muscles that Go Cramp in the Night

You're sleeping peacefully in your bed when suddenly your leg is seized with a painful cramp. You're no longer sleeping and you're certainly no longer peaceful. You weren't even dreaming about exercise, so what happened?

Cramps that occur during the night are usually due to a pinched nerve or an exaggeration of a normal muscle-tendon reflex. A particular sleep position, for example, may cause a nerve to be compressed. Or, in changing positions, you may contract a muscle, causing an attached tendon to stretch. The stretched tendon sends a message to the spinal cord, which, in turn, sends a message to the muscle, causing it to contract even more forcefully and resulting in a cramp.

No matter what the cause of the muscle cramp, the bottom line is that muscles that cramp at night have somehow gotten "stuck." The key is to short-circuit this cramping before it happens and disturbs your rest. Here's how:

Stretch before bed. Take a few minutes before retiring to stretch the muscles that are subject to cramping. Calves are often victims of nighttime cramping. Stretch them out with the "runner's stretch": Stand facing a wall, your feet positioned two to three feet away from it. Place your palms on the wall at about shoulder height. Keeping your legs straight and your heels pressed against the floor, slowly bend your elbows and lean your upper body toward the wall until you feel a stretch in your calves. Hold for a count of eight, then return to the starting position.

Be sure you get enough calcium. Nighttime cramps are often associated with a lack of calcium in the diet. Eat plenty of calcium-rich foods like broccoli, spinach, and dairy products (opt for low-fat or fat-free varieties if you're trying to limit your fat or calorie intake). If cramping is still a problem, talk to your doctor about using a calcium supplement.

Lighten the load. Sometimes, cramps in the legs and feet can be caused by a pile of heavy blankets. Toss off all those covers and try either an electric blanket set on "warm" or a lightweight down comforter.

Massage the muscle. If you develop a cramp despite using prevention tips, massage the cramped muscle with long strokes toward the heart. Or do so even before you turn off the light for the night; sometimes a massage before you go to sleep can keep those muscles loose and free of cramps until morning.

forward and grab the toes or upper portion of the foot, and pull the top of the foot toward the knee. With the fingers of your other hand, squeeze and knead the calf muscle. Another way to stretch out the calf muscle is to put your foot flat on the ground, then lean forward without allowing your heel to lift off the ground. With this method, however, you'll probably need someone else to massage the knot out of the muscle for you.

Walk it out. Once an acute cramp passes, don't start exercising heavily right away. Instead, walk for a few minutes to get the blood flowing back into the muscles. Then gradually return to your original activity and pace.

Sip quinine tonic. Quinine was once used to prevent and treat malaria. These days, many competitive swimmers drink tonic water—which gets its flavor from a small amount of quinine—to prevent muscle cramps. While there may not be much in the way of scientific research to support drinking quinine tonic for muscle cramps, you might want to give it a try to see if it works for you.

Go bananas. Muscle cramps can sometimes be caused by a lack of potassium. If you're plagued by frequent cramping, try eating a banana a day—bananas are rich in potassium—to see if it helps keep the cramps at bay.

Chill out. If you know you've overworked your muscles, immediately take a cold shower or a cold bath to help prevent or minimize inflammation and soreness. World-class Australian runner Jack Foster used to hose off his legs with cold water after a hard run. He told skeptics if it was good enough for racehorses, it was good enough for him! Several Olympic runners are known for taking icy plunges after a tough workout, insisting that it prevents muscle soreness and stiffness. If an icy dip seems too much for you, ice packs work well, too. Apply cold packs for 20 to 30 minutes at a time every hour for the first 24 to 72 hours after the activity. Cold helps prevent muscle soreness by constricting the blood vessels, which reduces blood flow and thus inflammation in the area.

Avoid heat. Using a heating pad or hot water bottle after a tough workout may feel good, but it's the worst thing for sore muscles because it dilates blood vessels and increases circulation to the area, which in turn leads to more swelling. Heat can actually increase muscle soreness and stiffness, especially if applied during the first 24 hours after the strenuous activity. If you absolutely can't resist using heat on those sore muscles, don't use it for more than 20 minutes every hour. Or, better yet, try contrast therapy—apply a hot pad for four minutes and an ice pack for one minute. After three or four days, when the swelling and soreness have subsided, you can resume hot baths to help relax the muscles.

Take an anti-inflammatory. Taking aspirin or ibuprofen can help reduce muscle inflammation and ease pain. Follow the directions on the label, read the warnings in the box on page 21, and check with your doctor or pharmacist if you have any questions about whether the medication is safe and appropriate for you. If aspirin upsets your stomach, try the coated variety.

Over-the-counter salicylate (the active ingredient in aspirin) creams can also reduce pain and inflammation. They're greaseless, usually won't irritate the skin, and won't cause the stomach problems often associated with taking aspirin by mouth.

Avoid "hot" or "cold" creams. The pharmacy and supermarket shelves are loaded with topical "sports" creams designed to ease sore, stiff muscles. Unfortunately, they don't do much beyond causing a chemical reaction that leaves your skin (but not the underlying muscles) feeling warm or cold. If you do use the topical sports creams, test a small patch of skin first to make sure you're not allergic, and never use these topicals with

hot pads, because the combination can cause serious burns.

Do easy stretches. When you're feeling sore and stiff, no doubt the last thing you want to do is move, but it's the first thing you should do. Go easy, though, and warm up first with a 20-minute walk.

Take a swim. One of the best remedies for sore muscles is swimming. The cold water helps reduce inflammation, and the movement of muscles in water helps stretch them out and ease soreness.

Anticipate second-day soreness. You may feel a little stiff or sore a few hours after overexercising, but you'll probably feel even worse two days afterward. Don't panic. It's perfectly normal.

Drink plenty of fluids. One cause of acute cramps, especially when you're exercising intensely during hot weather for an hour or longer, is dehydration. So be sure to drink enough fluids before, during, and after exercising. If you're running, aim to drink about a cup per hour. Don't overdo it, however, because drinking too much water can cause a dangerous imbalance in the body's mineral stores.

What about those sports drinks? You really don't need them unless you're exercising intensely for longer than an hour at a time. Water is better.

Massage it. As long as it's gentle, massage can help ease muscle soreness and stiffness.

Wrap up. In cold weather, you can often prevent muscle cramping by keeping the muscles warm with adequate clothing. Layered clothing offers the best insulating value by trapping air between the layers. Some people like the compression and warmth offered by running tights.

Warm up your muscles. One way to prevent muscle cramping and injuries is to warm up muscles adequately before exercise. Instead of stretching first, walk a little or bike slowly to "prewarm" the muscles. Then do a series of stretches appropriate for the exercise you're going to be doing. Even if you're only chopping wood or working in the garden, warming up before the activity will get your muscles ready for work and help prevent muscle cramping and injury.

Learn your limits. The key to preventing muscle pain, soreness, and stiffness is to be aware of your limits. You know you did too much if it makes you feel stiff and sore the next day, so use that as your guide. Better yet, instead of being a weekend warrior, aim to exercise regularly throughout the week. Start at a low intensity and short duration, and gradually, over a period of weeks or months, increase how hard, how long, and how often you exercise. That way, your muscles won't be so "shocked" when you put them to use on the weekend.

Nausea and Vomiting

9 Soothing Strategies

We've all been there, and it's no fun. Perhaps, you think, it's some kind of 24-hour bug, or maybe it was something you ate. Whatever the cause, now you're feeling queasy and sick.

The tips that follow are designed to reduce your discomfort and help relieve your symptoms as quickly as possible. If vomiting is violent or persists for more than 24 hours or if your vomit contains blood or looks like coffee grounds, see a physician without delay.

Evaluate the cause and treat the symptoms accordingly. Nausea and vomiting are two vague symptoms that can be caused by many illnesses and conditions. How you respond to and treat them depends on what's causing them. For example, if your nausea is the result of a migraine, treating the migraine (with medication, a cold compress, rest, quiet, and darkness) will also help with the nausea and vomiting. If your upset stomach is caused by gastroesophageal reflux (see HEARTBURN), you can alleviate your symptoms by taking an over-the-counter (OTC) medication and doing whatever else your doctor has advised

you to do when your reflux flares up. There are other possible causes of nausea and vomiting, too. (See MOTION SICKNESS, MORNING SICKNESS, and FOOD POISONING).

Stick to clear liquids. If your stomach is upset, it probably doesn't need the additional burden of digesting food. Stick to fluids until you feel a little better and have stopped vomiting. Clear, room-temperature liquids, such as water or diluted noncitrus fruit juices, are easier to digest, and they are also necessary to prevent the dehydration that may result from vomiting or diarrhea.

Let it run its course. The best cure for the 24-hour "stomach flu" (it isn't truly "the flu"—or influenza—which is an upper respiratory infection caused by specific microorganisms) is bed rest mixed with a tincture of time, doctors agree. The more rest you get, the more energy your body will have to devote to fighting the invader.

Don't drink alcohol. As anyone who has suffered a hangover knows, alcohol can be very irritating to the stomach. If you already have an upset stomach, now is certainly not the time to imbibe. (And if your current stomach upset is the result of drinking alcohol, forget the old saw about having "a hair of the dog that bit you"; more alcohol will only make you sicker.) The same goes for fatty foods, highly seasoned foods, beverages containing caffeine, and cigarettes.

Opt for easy-to-digest foods. When you are ready to start eating again, choose soft, plain foods, such as bread, unbuttered toast, steamed fish, or bananas. Avoid fatty foods and foods that are high in fiber. What about Grandma's chicken soup? It's fine if it is low in fat. Another tip is to start with very small amounts of food and slowly build up to full meals.

Let it flow. The worst thing you can do for vomiting is to fight it, because vomiting is your body's way of getting rid of something that is causing harm in your stomach. Trying to hold back the urge can actually cause tears in your esophagus.

Think pink. OTC stomach medications that contain bismuth, such as Pepto-Bismol, claim to coat the stomach and may help relieve some of the discomfort you feel. Avoid Alka-Seltzer and other aspirin-containing products, however, because aspirin can irritate the stomach.

Try a cold compress. A cold compress on your head can be very comforting when you are vomiting. It won't stop you from spewing, but it may help you feel a little better.

Maintain your electrolyte balance. Along with replacing the fluids you lose through vomiting, it is also important to maintain the balance of sodium and potassium (the electrolytes) in your system. If you spend more than a day or so unable to keep food down, have a sports drink, such as Gatorade, which is easy on the stomach and designed to replace electrolytes. Try diluting it with water if drinking it straight bothers your stomach.

Oily Hair

5 TIPS FOR CUTTING THE GREASE

You wash and style your hair every morning, but within a few short hours, it looks stringy and dirty. You, like millions of others, have oily hair.

A certain amount of oil secretion from oil glands on the scalp is healthy and necessary. The oil, called sebum, protects your hair shafts from breaking and gives hair luster and shine. But with oily hair, you've got too much of a good thing.

If your mother or father had oily hair, chances are good you will, too. The problem usually doesn't emerge until the teen years, when sex hormones stimulate the sebaceous glands in the scalp to produce more oil. Fluctuations in hormone levels make matters worse, which is why women often complain of oilier hair around the time of their periods.

While you can't change your family history or do much about your hormones, there is plenty you can do to get your oily locks under control:

Shampoo often. Don't worry about overdoing it. If you have oily hair, shampooing every day is a good idea.

Use a "no-nonsense" shampoo. Skip shampoos with additives and conditioners. Oily hair requires a good solvent-type shampoo, one that will cut the grease. There are plenty of shampoos that will cut through the excess oil, including old standbys such as Prell and Suave and any number of generic and store-brand shampoos labeled for use on oily hair. To give your shampoo a boost, you can even add a few drops of dishwashing liquid.

Rinse thoroughly. Soap residue will only collect dirt and oil more quickly.

Forget conditioners. Conditioners coat the hair, something oily hair doesn't need. Apply a small amount of conditioner only to the ends if they've become dried out.

Try an acidic rinse. One way to decrease the oil is to rinse with diluted vinegar or lemon juice after shampooing. Add two tablespoons white vinegar to one cup water, or mix the juice of one lemon (strained) with one cup water. Pour the mixture on your hair, then rinse with warm water.

Oily Skin

9 WAYS TO MANAGE IT

If you have oily skin, you may feel as though you're forever fighting a losing battle to remove the shine from your chin and forehead. You can probably thank your genes for the sheen: Overly oily skin is a problem that is often handed down through generations within a family.

Changes in hormone levels, such as those that occur during the teen years and early 20s, can cause skin to become oily and trigger outbreaks of acne (see ACNE). But it's not just a problem for teenagers and young adults. Many women notice oily skin problems around the time of their menstrual periods, during pregnancy, or at menopause. Some types of birth control pills can also increase skin oiliness.

The good news about oily skin is that it keeps the skin looking younger. Over time, people with oily skin tend to wrinkle less than people with dry or normal skin.

While you can't alter your genes or completely control your hormones, there are plenty of things you can do to manage your oily skin.

Keep skin squeaky clean. As anyone with oily skin knows, the oilier the skin, the dirtier the skin looks and feels. To help combat this feeling, it's important to keep the skin clean by washing it at least twice a day. Some doctors recommend detergent-type soap. You might even try adding a drop or two of dishwashing detergent to your regular soap; the extra kick will act as a solvent for the oil. However, other dermatologists say detergent soaps are just too harsh even for oily facial skin, recommending instead twice-daily cleansing with a glycerine soap. If you try a detergent soap and find it too irritating for your skin, try the glycerine variety, generally available in the skin-care aisle of most drugstores.

Try aloe vera. Apply aloe vera gel (available in many drugstores as well as health-food stores) to your face to absorb oil and clear out pores. Dab the gel onto your face two to three times a day (especially after washing), then let it dry. The gel will feel more refreshing if it's cool, so keep it in the refrigerator.

Wipe with astringents. Wiping the oily parts of the face with rubbing alcohol or a combination of alcohol and acetone (a mixture found in products such as Seba-Nil Liquid Cleanser) can help degrease your skin just as well as more-expensive, perfumey astringents. Many drugstores even sell premoistened, individually wrapped alcohol wipes that you can keep in your pocket or purse for quick touchups throughout the day.

Carry tissues. Even if you don't have an astringent with you, paper facial tissues can help soak up excess oils in a pinch. You can also purchase special oil-absorbing tissues at the cosmetics counter that are very effective in removing excess oil between cleansings.

Chill out with cold-water rinses. If you don't want to apply chemicals to your skin, simply splashing your face with cold water and blotting it dry a couple of times a day can help remove some excess oil.

Ban moisturizers. While advertisements are forever urging women to apply facial moisturizers, oily-skinned folks shouldn't use them—their skin is already doing a more-than-adequate job of keeping itself supple and warding off dryness. Applying a sunscreen to the face before going outdoors in daylight is still a very good idea, however. Check labels for products that are designed for oily skin or that are noncomedogenic (meaning they'll be less likely to plug up pores; this is especially important for oily skin, which is already more susceptible to acne blemishes).

Make a scrub. Giving your face a very light scrub can remove excess surface oil. Try this almond honey scrub: Mix a small amount of almond meal (ground almonds) with honey. Then *gently* massage (don't *scrub*) the paste onto your skin with a hot washcloth. Rinse thoroughly. You can also make a scrub from oatmeal mixed with aloe vera gel. Rub gently onto the skin, leave on for 15 minutes, then wash off thoroughly. If you have acne on your face, however, you should probably skip the scrub, since it can aggravate your already-irritated skin.

Mask it. Masks applied to the face can reduce oiliness. Clay masks are available, or you can mix Fuller's Earth (available at pharmacies) with a little water to make a paste. Apply to the face and leave on for about 20 minutes before thoroughly rinsing off.

Use water-based cosmetics. Better yet, learn to live without makeup—or at least without foundation—since it will simply add to and trap the oil against your skin and help set the stage for blemishes. If you feel you simply must use makeup, choose water-based products over oil-based types, and opt for spot concealers rather than coating your entire face. In general, stick with powder or gel blushers, and avoid cream foundations.

Hello, Doctor?

In most cases, oily skin can be treated at home. However, you'll want to call a doctor if you develop acne that doesn't respond to home remedies (see ACNE) or notice any sudden and/or unusual change in your skin (if it goes from dry to oily seemingly overnight but it isn't time for your period, for example).

Osteoporosis

13 Ways to Combat Brittle Bones

You probably don't think of your bones as growing once you reach adulthood. After all, you don't keep getting taller as you age. But in truth, your body continuously breaks down old bone and builds new bone throughout your life. More bone is added than lost during childhood and young adulthood, and somewhere around age 30, your bones reach their peak bone mass (when your bones are at their strongest and most dense). After that point, the tables turn, and the breakdown of bone begins to slowly outpace the building of new bone. For women, that net bone loss really speeds up right after menopause, when levels of the bone-protective hormone estrogen drop.

That's the way the process normally works. But in some people, bone breakdown occurs too rapidly and/or bone-building moves too slowly, and osteoporosis develops. Osteoporosis is a disease in which bones become so porous and low in mass that they are fragile and easily broken. It strikes mainly women, partly because they have a lower bone mass than men do to begin with, although many men suffer from it, too. And it's more likely to strike a person who never obtained optimal bone mass in their bone-building years.

Osteoporosis is sometimes referred to as a silent disease, because many people don't discover they have it until a minor fall results in a broken hip or something as seemingly harmless as raising a stuck window sash or open-

Are You at Risk?

Risk factors for osteoporosis include:

Gender. Women are at higher risk than men.

Age. The older you are, the more porous your bones get.

Body size. Women who are small and thin are at higher risk.

Ethnicity. Osteoporosis is more likely to strike if you are Caucasian or Asian, although Hispanics and African Americans are also at risk.

Family history. Osteoporosis is believed to be hereditary.

Low levels of hormones. Estrogen and other hormone levels drop after menopause; they are also low in women who don't menstruate because of low body weight.

Diet. A diet that is low in calcium and vitamin D can take a toll on your bones.

Use of certain medications. Ask your doctor or pharmacist if any of the medications you take on a regular basis can increase your risk.

Sedentary lifestyle. Physical activity—especially weight training and weight-bearing activities in which your bones are forced to support or move weight—is essential in keeping bones solid and strong.

Cigarette smoking.

Excessive use of alcohol.

ing a tight jar lid results in a broken wrist. Some 10 million Americans have osteoporosis, and 34 million more are at high risk of developing it because they have low bone mass. According to the National Institutes of Health, one in two women and one in four men over age 50 will have an osteoporosis-related bone fracture at some point.

The best preventive measure? Building and maintaining strong bones throughout life to prevent fractures and other complications later. The earlier you begin, the better, although it's never too late to start taking better care of your bones. And many of the self-help strategies that can build stronger bones can also help protect bones that have become fragile. Here are some ways to arm yourself in the war against brittle bones:

Exercise regularly. Exercise is one of the most important things you can do to fight osteoporosis. Here's why: Forcing a bone to carry a load or work against an opposing force (such as gravity) prompts the body to produce more bone cells, increasing the bone's mass and making it stronger. (You can actually see the bone-building results of such loading in the significantly developed swinging arms of many tennis pros.) Weight-bearing exercises, such as walking, jogging, dancing, and aerobics, in which your bones work against the force of gravity to keep you

upright, are just the kind of exercises that fit the bill. Of course, for some folks, jogging and similar high-impact activities pack a bit too much punch for their joints. For them, walking is a great option. Walking is a bone-strengthener that puts much less stress on the joints, *plus* it can be done by almost anyone, almost anywhere, without expensive equipment.

Familiar exercises such as swimming, in which the water supports much of your weight, and cycling, in which the bicycle seat carries a lot of the load, are less effective at building bone mass. However, they do provide other important exercise benefits, including controlling weight and improving heart health. So if you love to swim or cycle, just be sure to mix in some walking or jogging.

It's best to check with your doctor before beginning an exercise program, especially if you have any chronic medical condition or have been sedentary. Start out slowly, and gradually increase the frequency, duration, and intensity of your workouts. Aim to reach a goal of exercising at least 30 minutes a day, five to seven days a week.

For Dairy Lovers: How to Boost Calcium Intake

- Use milk instead of water to mix up hot cereals, hot chocolate, and soups.
- Substitute plain yogurt for half the mayonnaise in dressings.
- Add liquid or powdered skim milk to coffee instead of oily nondairy creamer or fattening cream.

Give yourself strength. Weight lifting, strength training, resistance training—these are all names for exercises in which you strengthen your bones and muscles by lifting weights or otherwise working against resistance (such as using an exercise band). Women and men of any age can strength-train. You don't even need to join a gym—you can buy a couple of weights at a local sporting-goods store or general merchandiser and exercise at home. On the other hand, if you've never used weights before, a session with a personal trainer or a short weight-training course at your local community center, hospital, or YMCA can help ensure that you are using proper form and safely getting the most out of your weight training. As with any exercise plan, get your doctor's approval and advice before beginning weight training. Start with weights as light as three pounds each and gradually increase the repetitions and/or weight from there. Aim for at least two weight-training sessions per week, in addition to your regular weight-bearing-exercise routine, to be sure you're building and protecting the bones of your arms and upper torso.

Aim to maintain a healthy weight. If you are underweight (say, more than 10 percent lighter than the average weight for your age and height), you are at higher risk for a deficiency of calcium and other important vitamins and minerals, which can affect your bones' health. On the other hand, being overweight is no guarantee of bone health either, because even though the extra weight puts a greater load on the bones, it also tends to discourage regular bone-building physical activity.

Get the right amount of calcium. Our calcium needs vary throughout our lives. An adequate intake, as recommended by the Institute of Medicine of the National Academy of Sciences, is 1,300 milligrams (mg) for boys and girls ages 9 to 18; 1,000 mg for men and women ages 19 to 50; and 1,200 mg for people over 50 (the intake for older adults is higher because with age the body naturally loses some of its ability to absorb the mineral). Most of us don't come close to reaching the recommended adequate intake.

Dairy foods, such as milk and milk products (such as ice cream), yogurt, and cheese, are the major sources of calcium in the American diet. Eight ounces of milk provide about 290 to 300 milligrams of calcium; one-and-a-half ounces of cheddar cheese supply a little over 300 mg; and eight ounces of plain, low-fat yogurt provide more than 400 mg (fruit yogurts usually provide less). And, fortunately, low-fat and nonfat dairy products provide just as much calcium (sometimes a bit more) as full-fat varieties. For people who don't consume enough dairy products to fulfill their calcium needs, there are other food options (see "How to Get Calcium Without Drinking Milk" at right).

Carefully consider calcium supplements. It's best to get calcium from food, but if your diet lacks adequate calcium, consider a supplement. There are a few different compounds that are used in calcium supplements, two common ones being calcium citrate and calcium carbonate; they deliver different amounts of calcium, so while either compound is acceptable, be sure to check the label to determine the actual amount of elemental calcium in each pill or dose. Never take more than 2,500 mg of supplemental calcium per day, unless your doctor prescribes it, since excessive calcium intake can lead to kidney stones. In addition, consult your doctor or pharmacist to be sure a calcium supplement won't interfere with any other medication or prescribed supplement you are taking.

Your body will absorb the calcium best if you divide your daily dose into smaller doses that you take throughout

How to Get Calcium Without Drinking Milk

Some people don't drink much milk—they don't like the taste, they have trouble digesting the lactose in milk (see LACTOSE INTOLERANCE), or they just never get around to drinking the three glasses a day that are needed to provide adequate amounts of this mineral. Are these "dairy deserters" destined to a life of brittle bones? Not necessarily. There are many other sources of dietary calcium. To get the most calcium, eat foods in the raw; as foods are cooked, calcium can leach into the cooking water. Here are some nondairy, calcium-rich options:

Orange juice. The calcium-fortified variety, that is. It contains as much calcium as milk.

Broccoli. Yet another good reason to munch a few stalks—preferably in the raw.

Beans. Kidney and pinto head the list.

Soy. Choose tofu, soy milk, and other soy products that are fortified with calcium.

Nuts. Hazelnuts, Brazil nuts, and almonds are among the best nuts to choose.

Fruit. Figs and prunes are high in calcium.

Leafy greens. Romaine lettuce, spinach, collards, and kale are good choices.

Salmon and sardines. Salmon is a good source of vitamin D as well as calcium.

Yogurt. The lactose, or sugar, in yogurt, has already been broken down, so even many people who are lactose intolerant can eat it. Eat it with fresh fruit or substitute it for sour cream in recipes.

the day. And while calcium citrate can be taken without regard to meals, the body absorbs calcium carbonate better when it is taken with food.

Make sure you're getting enough vitamin D. Vitamin D works with calcium to keep bones healthy. Indeed, the body can't absorb calcium from the diet without it. Without adequate vitamin D to absorb dietary calcium, the body begins to pull the calcium it needs for vital functions from its own bones, making them weaker.

The two main ways to get vitamin D are through sun exposure and from dietary sources. Vitamin D is sometimes called the sunshine vitamin, because the body can make its own vitamin D when the skin is exposed to sunlight. In general, 15 minutes of exposure on the hands, lower arms, and face (without sunscreen, which blocks the rays necessary to trigger vitamin-D production) is enough to allow your body to produce and store all the vitamin D it needs. However, there are some people who may need longer exposure times or additional vitamin D from foods and/or supplements, including people who live in northern regions (higher latitudes) during the darker winter months, those over 65, darker-skinned individuals (who require more sunlight than lighter-skinned people to make the same amount of vitamin D), people who are overweight (vitamin D is a fat-soluble vitamin that can get trapped in the excess body fat, leaving too little in the bloodstream), and people who simply do not spend enough time outdoors without wearing sunscreen (such as those at increased risk for skin cancer or those who are housebound).

People who may not make enough vitamin D can get additional amounts from vitamin-D-rich foods, such as fatty fish, egg yolks, mushrooms, and liver, and from products that have been fortified with vitamin D, such as most milk and some breads and breakfast cereals (check labels). And, if necessary, a supplement of vitamin D can be added to ensure a daily intake of 400 to 800 IU (international units, the standard measure for vitamin D). Do not take a supplement of more than 800 IU per day unless it has been specifically prescribed by your doctor. Consuming more than 2,000 IU can cause kidney damage and have other harmful effects. (You can't overdose on vitamin D that is made by your body, no matter how much sun you get, because your body automatically regulates this process.)

Stop smoking. Smokers absorb less calcium from foods. In addition, women who smoke have less estrogen in their blood (estrogen helps protect bones) and tend to go through menopause earlier.

Shake your taste for salt. Salt can increase the amount of calcium your body loses through urine. The more sodium that flows out this way, the more calcium that flows out with it. Likewise, diuretics, which some people take to combat the fluid retention caused by excess salt intake, may pull calcium out of the body.

Be wise about protein. For healthy bones, protein is a double-edged sword. Consuming too much protein increases the amount of calcium excreted in the urine. Yet protein is needed to help maintain a component of bone called collagen, which is made up of proteins. It's not so much a question of eating too much protein, but of not getting enough calcium to balance out the amount of protein in the diet. If you have an adequate calcium intake, you probably don't need to worry about getting too much protein. However, if you don't get much calcium in your diet, you'd be wise to avoid consuming an excess amount of protein.

Make your own soup. When preparing stock from bones, add a small amount of vinegar to leach the calcium from the bones.

Limit booze. Alcohol interferes with the body's ability to absorb calcium.

Check your medicines. A loss of bone density can result from long-term use of certain medications, including some of those prescribed for arthritis, asthma, cancer, Crohn's disease, lupus, and other diseases of the lungs, kidneys, or liver. Other drugs that can cause bone trouble when used for a long time or in large amounts include some antiseizure medications, barbitu-

rates, gonadotropin-releasing hormone analogs used to treat endometriosis, antacids that contain aluminum, and thyroid hormone. Ask your doctor or pharmacist if any medication you take on a regular basis could have bone-thinning effects and what you can do to counter those effects.

Talk with your doctor about osteoporosis meds. There are several medications that are prescribed for the prevention and treatment of osteoporosis. They include Fosamax (alendronate), Actonel (risendronate sodium), Evista (raloxifene), Forteo (teriparatide), and calcitonin.

In addition, hormone therapy has been shown to reduce bone loss, increase bone density, and reduce the risk of hip and spine fractures in post-menopausal women. However, hormone therapy can also increase a woman's risk of blood clots, heart attacks, strokes, breast cancer, and gallbladder disease, according to the National Institutes of Health. Your doctor may prescribe hormone therapy if the benefits to your bones outweigh the risks of the medication, but be sure the two of you discuss the risks and benefits thoroughly first. Women who take hormone therapy for bone health should be prescribed the hormone progestin in combination with estrogen because estrogen alone increases a woman's risk of developing endometrial cancer.

Poison Ivy, Oak, and Sumac
11 PREVENTION AND TREATMENT TIPS

The itching can drive you absolutely crazy. You try to ignore it, but you can't. All you want to do is scratch like a maniac. Getting a rash from poison ivy, oak, or sumac is maddening. It's almost enough to make you want to give up going outside ever again. Fortunately, you don't have to. You simply need to know how to take steps to avoid these foes and what to do to get relief if your preventive steps fail.

When you get a rash from poison ivy, oak, or sumac, you're having an allergic reaction to the oil, or sap, inside the plant. This oil, which is clear to slightly yellow, is called *urushiol*. It oozes from any cut or crushed part of the leaves or stem, so just brushing a plant may not elicit a reaction. Oil content in the plants runs highest in the spring and summer, but cases are reported even in the dead of winter.

Poison ivy, oak, and sumac are hardy weeds that can be found throughout the United States, except in Hawaii, Alaska, and some desert areas of Nevada. Poison ivy is found east of the Rockies, poison oak grows in the West and Southwest, and poison sumac thrives east of the Mississippi River. All three produce similar reactions, and if you're allergic to one, you'll probably react to the others, as well.

Cases of poison ivy, oak, and sumac affect 10 to 50 million people in the United States each year. In fact, these plants constitute the single most common cause of allergic reactions. A lucky 10 to 15 percent of Americans don't react to these plants, but another 10 to 15 percent are quite sensitive to them. The rest of us fall somewhere in between, with varying levels of sensitivity.

What muddies the waters is that a person's sensitivity can change over

time, even from season to season. You could be quite sensitive to poison ivy as a child but seem immune to the weed as an adult. Or you may not have your first bad reaction to one of these poisonous plants until late in life, though sensitivity tends to decline with age.

Your level of sensitivity determines how bad a reaction you'll have. Once the oil touches the skin, it starts to penetrate in minutes. Within 12 to 48 hours, a red, itchy rash appears, followed by blisters that may weep and later get crusty. The area usually heals in about ten days. Among the very sensitive population, affected areas of skin will quickly swell up, the rash can be severe and painful, and the reaction may take up to three weeks to clear if left untreated. If you are highly sensitive to these plants, see a doctor as soon as you come in contact with one.

Even for people who are only mildly sensitive, a rash from poison ivy, oak, or sumac is no fun. So what follows are tips for preventing the problem in the first place and simple ways to treat the rash if it does occur. (While the remedies often refer to poison ivy, the steps are generally appropriate for poison oak and poison sumac, too.)

Know the plant so you can avoid it. Find out what the plant looks like in the area you live or plan to visit, because appearance will vary, even within a state. For instance, poison oak that grows in Northern California doesn't look like poison oak native to Southern California. Typically, poison ivy is a vine or a low shrub with grayish white berries and smooth, pointed leaves that are usually clustered in groups of three. The reddish leaves turn green in the summer and redden again by autumn. Poison oak is a shrub or small tree with greenish-white berries and oak-like leaves that, again, usually appear in groups of three. Poison sumac is a woody shrub found in swampy, boggy areas that has smooth-edged leaves and cream-colored berries. The leaves of poison sumac retain their reddish color year-round and aren't grouped in threes.

Spotting the plants isn't always easy. Poison ivy can mimic other plants, such as Virginia creeper, and can twine itself around English ivy. Even doctors who warn their patients to avoid these plants can't always identify them. You'll decrease your chance of being exposed to one of these plants, however, if you become familiar with their typical appearance.

Cover up. Long pants, long-sleeved shirts, boots, and gloves provide a barrier between you and the plant's oil. This is especially important if

you're sensitive and you know you're going to be in an area that could contain poison ivy.

Don't let your pets romp in wooded areas. If you get a rash from poison ivy but can't remember being near the plant, you may have your pet to thank. If your dog or cat strolls through a patch of poison ivy, the oils may cling to the animal's fur. Stroke or pick up the pet, and the oils can rub off on you. The same is true of anything that comes in contact with oil from poisonous plants, including gardening tools, bicycle tires, and golf balls. Once there, the oil can remain active for a long time. That means you can get poison ivy again and again without touching the plant itself if you don't use care when handling these outdoor items and rinse them off after each use.

Rinse your clothes outside. If you think you've had a close encounter with poison ivy, the oil may be all over your clothes. If you walk inside your home without rinsing your clothes, you may transfer the oil to rugs or furniture. Water deactivates the oil, so once your clothes are soaked, they're safe.

It's also a good idea to rinse off camping, hunting, and fishing gear so you don't start off your next vacation with a case of poison ivy. Don't forget your shoes, which can pick up oils from twigs or vines. At night, if you take your shoes off by grabbing the sole or the heel, you may grab onto more than you bargained for and end up with a nasty case of poison ivy.

Head for water fast. This should be your first step if you suspect you've come in contact with poison ivy. Don't hesitate—the sooner you rinse off, the better. Whether it comes from a stream, lake, garden hose, or faucet, if you can get to water within five to ten minutes after contact with the plant, you may be able to wash off the oil before all of it sinks in.

Carry rubbing alcohol with you. The oil from poison ivy isn't absorbed into the skin all at once; it sinks in fairly gradually. If you move quickly enough, you may be able to use rubbing alcohol to extract some oil from the skin. If you think you've been exposed to the weed and you're heading back inside for the day, pour rubbing alcohol on the exposed areas and then rinse well with water. Don't use a cloth wipe, which may simply pick up the oil and transfer it somewhere else. And don't use the alcohol near your eyes.

Cool off the itch. If preventive steps failed and you've got a rash, a cool bath or shower may help ease the itch. Placing ice-cold compresses on the rash for a few minutes every hour may also provide relief.

Smooth on some calamine lotion. Your mother probably painted your skin pink with this goop if you had a brush with poison ivy as a kid. Smart thinking, Mom: Calamine lotion can be mildly soothing and help dry the rash. Apply it in a thin layer, however, so that the pores in your skin are not sealed.

Apply Burow's solution. This lesser-known product (sold without a prescription) can soothe and relieve mild rashes when put on compress-style. It's often sold under the name Domeboro in a tablet or powder form that you mix with water (according to package directions). Ask your pharmacist if you're having trouble locating it.

Soak in oats. Bathing in lukewarm water mixed with oatmeal or baking soda may help dry oozing blisters and soothe irritated skin.

Try a hydrocortisone cream. Sold without a prescription, these creams may offer some relief for mild rashes. However, for more serious cases, hydrocortisone creams are not strong enough to help. If you have a rash that is severe enough to take you to the doctor, he or she may prescribe more-potent steroids.

Poison-Ivy Myths

A number of widely held beliefs about poison ivy simply aren't true. Here's the real story on some long-standing myths:

Scratching poison ivy blisters will spread the rash. The oil in the plant, not the fluid in the blisters, spreads the rash. If you get the oil on your hands, for instance, and you touch different parts of your body, it will spread to those areas. This happens long before the blisters have even formed. It is true that you should avoid scratching the blisters, but only because your fingernails may have germs on them that could start an infection.

The old saying "Leaves of three, let them be," always holds true. This is *usually* the case for poison ivy and oak—but not every time. Leaflets may come in groups of five, seven, or even nine.

You can catch a poison ivy rash from someone else. The rash can't travel from person to person through the blister fluid or any other way. Only the oil can be spread by contact.

Dead poison ivy plants can do you no harm. This may seem logical, but it's not true. The oil from the leaves and stem can remain an active allergenic chemical for up to several years after the plant itself dies. The oil even remains a threat in winter, when it's possible to pick up poison ivy while gathering kindling and firewood.

The juice from crushed plantain leaves will prevent a case of poison ivy rash. There's no scientific proof to back this claim, although hikers often try this preventive strategy.

You can't be immunized against poison ivy. You can, but the procedure requires a great deal of time, effort, and commitment from both the patient and doctor, and there are side effects. If you're considering immunization, talk to an expert and get the facts. Some patients end up deciding that undergoing the treatments is worse than putting up with the occasional poison ivy rash. Doctors usually suggest immunization as a last resort for people who experience very troublesome reactions.

Premenstrual Syndrome

11 WAYS TO EASE THE DISCOMFORTS

You've heard the line before. A woman flies off the handle at work or at home and some joker says, "It must be that time of the month."

The remark, of course, ignores the fact that women sometimes have good reason to get upset or fed up with the demands made on them by husbands, children, and jobs. For some women, however, comments such as this, although made in jest, hold more truth than they'd like to admit. For these women, "that time of the month" really is a period of emotional imbalance

and seemingly unprovoked or out-of-proportion anger, sadness, and anxiety. Situations that they normally cope well with suddenly become insurmountable. And the energy and health they enjoy most of the time give way to fatigue, discomfort, and weight gain almost overnight.

These women have what is known as premenstrual syndrome, or PMS, a condition with an unknown cause and no complete cure. Research into the condition has suggested

several theories as to what may make some women more vulnerable to PMS, although none has yet been proved. Some doctors speculate the condition occurs because of an imbalance of the hormones produced by the ovaries, either estrogen or progesterone. Others suggest hormone fluctuations or deficiencies in the brain cause PMS. Still, no one really knows why certain women develop PMS, and research has produced contradictory evidence.

Whatever the cause, the symptoms can include anxiety, irritability, mood swings, and anger. Indeed, the emotional symptoms, which occur in more than 80 percent of PMS sufferers, are what often drive women to their doctor's office. Other symptoms may include sugar cravings, fatigue, headaches, dizziness, shakiness, abdominal bloating, breast tenderness, and overall swelling (from edema, or fluid retention). Much less common are depression, memory loss, and feelings of isolation. The symptoms of PMS appear to occur in a cycle, and their severity varies from woman to woman. As a rule, PMS symptoms fade once the woman's menstrual period begins.

As for what you can do to relieve the discomfort of PMS, there are several home remedies. Some probably work as well as, or better than, the medical treatments available. Here's what you can try:

Maintain a well-balanced diet. Include lots of fresh fruits and vegetables, starches, raw seeds and nuts, fish, poultry, and whole grains.

Go easy on sugar. You may find yourself yearning for chocolate and other sweets, but giving in to sugar cravings can cause reactive hypoglycemia (an abnormal decrease of sugar in the blood), which will make you feel even worse and intensify feelings of irritability and anxiety. If you can't give up the sweets completely, try eating only small amounts at a time, and opt for treats such as fruits or apple juice that can help satisfy your sugar craving *and* provide nutrients.

Eat small, frequent meals. Waiting too long between meals could cause blood sugar to drop, triggering reactive hypoglycemia. Plus, sometimes hunger pangs alone are enough to make a person grumpy.

Avoid alcohol. You may think a glass of wine or two will help get you through a bout of PMS blues, but alcohol is a depressant that will only make you feel more down and fatigued. Booze also depletes the body's stores of B vitamins and minerals and disrupts carbohydrate metabolism. What's more, it disrupts the liver's ability to metabolize hormones, which can lead to higher-than-normal estrogen levels. So if you need to be holding a beverage at that dinner party, try a nonalcoholic cocktail, such as mineral water with a twist of lime or lemon.

Cut down on caffeine. You may be tempted to increase your intake of caffeinated coffee, tea, or soda to battle PMS-related fatigue, but all that caffeine can intensify anxiety, irritability, and mood swings. It may also increase breast tenderness. Try substituting water-processed decaffeinated coffee; grain-based coffee substitutes such as Pero, Postum, and Caffix; or ginger tea. And make time for adequate rest and sleep.

Cut the fat. Eating too much dietary fat can interfere with liver function. And some beef contains small amounts of synthetic estrogens. Too much protein can also increase the body's demand for minerals. So opt for smaller servings of lean meats, fish or seafood, beans, peas, seeds, and nuts. Use more whole grains, rice, vegetables, and fruits to fill out your meals.

Put down the salt shaker. Table salt and high-sodium foods such as bouillon, commercial salad dressings, catsup, hot dogs, and a host of other processed foods can increase fluid retention, bloating, and breast tenderness.

Practice stress management. PMS symptoms feel worse when life's daily frustrations rattle your nerves and try your patience. Keep anxiety and tension under control by joining a stress-management or stress-reduction program at your local hospital or community college, learning biofeedback techniques, meditating, exercising, or doing anything that helps you to relax and cope more effectively with stress.

Exercise aerobically. Working up a sweat not only eases stress, it causes your body to release feel-good hormones called endorphins that act like natural opiates. And increasing blood circulation in the pelvic region can help the body flush out some of the extra fluid often retained during PMS. Choose an activity that will get you huffing and puffing, such as jogging, stair-stepping, or bicycling. Better yet, sign up for an aerobics class—a little socializing at the health club is an added bonus that may help improve your mood. Try to exercise for 20 to 30 minutes at least three times a week. If you are just too fatigued to exercise when your PMS is at its worst, don't. Being active the rest of the month should help.

Try not to plan big events during PMS time. Throwing a party? If possible, schedule it for a date when PMS won't be a problem. The added stress of special engagements can make your moodiness and physical symptoms seem worse.

Talk it over. Dealing with members of your family can be one of the biggest sources of stress for a woman coping with PMS. Feeling guilty about snapping at a spouse or child, then finding the strength to apologize for your outburst, can be emotionally draining. Try to limit the fallout by explaining to your loved ones and close friends the reason for your erratic behavior. Ask them to understand the problem and realize that when you lash out at them during such times, you are not as in control as you would like to be. This openness about your condition could help not only lower your stress level, but avoid hurt feelings. For example, if a rambunctious child has you climbing the walls, explaining that it's a bad time for him or her to make you upset may serve as a cue for the child to give you some peace and quiet by playing outdoors. Keep in mind, however, that PMS is a medical condition, not an emotional crutch. In other words, don't use your menstrual cycle as a defense for being nasty. If the emotional symptoms of PMS are causing serious problems in your relationships, consider getting some counseling from a mental-health professional. Ask your doctor for a referral.

Psoriasis

28 COPING TECHNIQUES

Psoriasis is a noncontagious, chronic skin condition that produces round, dry, scaly patches of varying size that are covered with white, gray, or silvery-white scales. If you suffer from this incurable disease, you're certainly not alone. According to the National Psoriasis Foundation, between four and five million American adults have the disease, and between 150,000 and 260,000 new cases are diagnosed every year.

Not only is psoriasis common, it's very mysterious—there seem to be few "absolutes" about the condition. Doctors aren't sure what causes psoriasis, although they believe it tends to run in families. On the other hand, you may have psoriasis yet have no family history of the disease. It most often strikes between the ages of 20 and 50, but it can appear at any age and has even been diagnosed in children and infants.

Psoriasis also behaves mysteriously. Sometimes, it can be very mild, appearing in only a few small areas. The next day, however, large patches of scaly skin may cover the body. Treatment is difficult, because what works for one person may not work for another, and treatments that were once effective for an individual often become ineffective, or vice versa.

Despite not knowing exactly what causes psoriasis, doctors do know that it involves a mixup in the immune system. (It is considered an autoimmune disorder, in which the immune system mistakenly targets the body's own healthy cells.) Certain white blood cells, called T cells, become overstimulated and trigger an acceleration in the normal growth and turnover of skin cells. In normal, healthy skin, new cells take about a month to migrate to the surface, as dead cells slowly slough off. In the skin of someone with psoriasis, this process takes a mere three to four days.

This speeded-up cell growth is what causes the red, scaly, flaking patches of skin, called plaques. In addition to being unsightly, these plaques often cause itching and discomfort. Although there are several other types of psoriasis, this plaque-forming variety (called plaque psoriasis) is the most common. The plaques can appear anywhere on the body. However, they most commonly occur on the scalp and lower back and over the elbows, knees, and knuckles. When psoriasis affects the fingernails and toenails, it causes pitting and brownish discoloration and sometimes cracking and lifting (detaching) of the nail.

While there currently is no cure for psoriasis, there are medical treatments and self-help steps that make living with psoriasis easier. The following are simple strategies used successfully by many people with psoriasis; with your doctor's approval, try some or all of them to create a self-care regimen that works for you.

Moisturize. Dry skin can crack, bleed, and become infected, so it's important to keep your skin from drying out. Moisturizing not only helps prevent dry skin, it also reduces inflammation, helps maintain flexibility (dried plaques can make moving certain parts of the body difficult), helps keep psoriasis from getting worse, and makes plaque scales less noticeable. The heaviest, or greasiest, moisturizers work best at locking water into the skin. Thick moisturizers like Eucerin, Aquaphor, and Neutrogena Norwegian

Formula Hand Cream are all effective. But inexpensive alternatives, such as cooking oils, lard, or petroleum jelly, offer equally strong protection.

Get out in the sun. Sound like surprising advice? While doctors want most of their patients to avoid the sun to prevent skin cancer and wrinkles, many people with psoriasis are encouraged to seek out the sun's ultraviolet (UV) light, since the rays often cause psoriasis to clear up. Although doctors aren't sure exactly how sunlight works to heal psoriasis, it seems to slow skin cell replication. There is a limit to the sun's beneficial effects on psoriasis, however; getting a sunburn can actually cause the disease to flare.

For many years, people have flocked to the Dead Sea to treat their psoriasis. The sun shines 300 days a year at the Dead Sea, which allows for near-constant exposure to its healing rays. More importantly, the Dead Sea is located 1,300 feet below sea level, creating an atmospheric filter that allows psoriasis patients to remain in the sun longer without burning. The high salt content of the Dead Sea water allows for effortless floating, too. (Some cosmetic companies even sell products containing salt and minerals from the Dead Sea.)

While you may not be able to schedule your next vacation at the Dead Sea, you can take advantage of the healing effects of the sun. Before you expose yourself, the National Psoriasis Foundation suggests applying a thin layer of mineral oil to affected areas of skin, which will enhance the sun's effects and keep the skin moist. However, the oil will also increase your risk of sunburn, so keep your bouts in the sun relatively brief. Likewise, to protect plaque-free skin from the detrimental effects of sun exposure, coat it with sunscreen that has a sun protection factor (SPF) of at least 15; apply the sunscreen 20 to 30 minutes before you expose yourself to the sun, and reapply often, especially after swimming or sweating heavily. (Do not apply sunscreen to the plaques, since it will block out the UV rays that can help them disappear.) And if you use UV light exposure to treat your psoriasis, be sure to have your dermatologist check your skin regularly for signs of skin cancer.

Light up your life. UV light therapy (or phototherapy, as it is sometimes called) can also be administered rain or shine in your doctor's office or even in the privacy of your own home. That's right. You can harness the benefits of the sun using a home light unit that shines ultraviolet B (UVB) light.

The sun's rays are actually made up of two types of UV light, known as A and B. UVB rays have been shown to slow the unusually quick skin-cell

Buying Sunlight

If your doctor has prescribed a UVB light unit for home use, the National Psoriasis Foundation suggests that you:

- Look for safety features such as special switches that keep the machine from being used when the owner is not around. (Children should never be allowed to use a phototherapy unit unless a physician has prescribed light therapy to treat their psoriasis, in which case the therapy should be supervised and administered by a responsible adult. Never allow children to play on or near the light machine.)
- Make sure the unit has a reliable and accurate timer.
- Check to ensure there are safety guards or grids over the lamps.
- Look for equipment that is stable, to prevent accidental tipping, and durable.
- Ask about replacement bulbs, their cost, and how and where they can be purchased.

growth that is the hallmark of psoriasis. (UVA light does not appear to help except when it is used concurrently with an oral medication called psoralen, in a treatment called PUVA, which is usually prescribed for more resistant or severe cases of psoriasis.) According to the National Psoriasis Foundation, studies have shown that 80 percent of psoriasis sufferers get good results with UVB light therapy.

You'll need to discuss using at-home UVB light therapy with your doctor first; usually, the doctor will administer the therapy in the office until your condition is stable before prescribing a light box for home use. See "Buying Sunlight," above, for tips on selecting a home light box. (The light boxes for home therapy do not use the same type of UV light that's used in tanning booths and salons, by the way.) And just as when you are soaking up the sun's rays, you'll have to take care to avoid burning your skin when using home light therapy, and you'll need to have your skin checked regularly by your dermatologist for signs of skin cancer.

Take a soak. Showering, swimming, soaking in a tub, and applying wet compresses all can rehydrate very dry skin and help soften and remove thick psoriasis scales without damaging the skin. Since thick scaling can act as a barrier to both medications and UV light, it's important to gently remove as much scale as possible. Regular soaking also helps reduce itching and redness of lesions. Keep the water tepid rather than hot (hot water can increase itching).

While soaking helps remove plaque scales, however, be aware that frequent wetting and drying also removes the skin's oils, its natural protection against moisture loss. Therefore, to get the benefits of soaking without overdrying the skin, be sure to moisturize with a heavy emollient immediately (within three minutes) after soaking, washing, or wetting your skin.

Apply aloe. The gel from the aloe vera plant has long been known for its skin-soothing properties and for helping the skin heal from minor wounds and burns. Research in the 1990s appears to have extended the plant's repertoire of possible benefits to include clearing psoriasis plaques. If you want to try aloe, you can buy the plant itself, split open one of its leaves, and smear the gel onto the plaques. For larger areas of plaque or a more portable balm, you can instead purchase a bottle of pure aloe vera gel at many pharmacies and health-food stores.

Try a vinegar dip. Like aloe, apple cider vinegar has a long history of being used to soothe minor burns and other skin inflammations, and it's also a disinfectant. According to the Psoriasis Foundation, some folks with psoriasis have reported success in using it to treat their condition. As a liquid, it makes a great soak for affected fingernails and toenails—just pour some in a bowl or cup and dip your nails in for a few minutes—and apparently has even been effective when applied to plaques using cotton balls. It might just be worth a try.

Beat the tar out of it. Tar-containing shampoos, creams, and bath additives can help loosen psoriasis scales. Tar-containing bath oils are especially beneficial for psoriasis that is widespread on the body. These over-the-counter (OTC) products have been successful psoriasis treatments for many years.

Bring on the salicylic acid. To remove scales, you may also want to use "sal acid," as salicylic acid preparations are sometimes called. Shampoos, creams, gels, and other topical psoriasis treatments containing salicylic acid are sold without a prescription.

Try OTC cortisone. Nonprescription topical medications containing 1 percent cortisone (Cortaid is one familiar brand) can also relieve the itching and irritation of psoriasis, especially for plaques that arise in skin folds or on the face. Be sure to get your doctor's okay before using one of these medications, though, and follow the package directions carefully; overuse of topical steroids such as cortisone can cause thinning and easy bruising of the skin.

Pass the plastic wrap. Doctors have known for years that covering psoriasis lesions helps them go away. The cover-up strategy also helps to work medications into the skin and to keep moisturizers in place longer. You can use regular kitchen plastic wrap, or you can buy special OTC patches (Actiderm). Apply your prescribed medication (be sure to confirm with your doctor first that the medication you are using can safely be used with an occlusive wrap) or moisturizer, then cover the area with the wrap. Don't keep the wrap on so long that the skin becomes soggy, since it's more susceptible to secondary infection that way; consult your doctor or pharmacist if you need more specific instructions.

Choose soaps carefully. Harsh soaps can dry and irritate the skin and increase itching, so opt for a mild soap instead. Many mild, "superfatted" soaps that contain moisturizers, such as Basis, Alpha Keri, Purpose, Nivea Cream Bar, and Oilatum, are available. You can also choose one of the many soap-free cleansers, such as Lowilla Cake, Aveeno Cleansing Bar, or pHisoDerm Dry Skin Formula, if your skin is already dry and irritated. If you're not sure which product to choose, ask your pharmacist or doctor for recommendations. And no matter what product you choose, be sure to rinse off well and then apply moisturizer immediately to prevent dryness and itching.

Pass the warm olive oil. If psoriasis scale is a problem on your scalp, warm a little olive oil and gently massage it into the scale to help soften and remove it. Then shampoo as usual and rinse thoroughly.

Wipe out the itch with antihistamines. Scratching can damage the skin, something you don't want to do. If the itch from psoriasis is more than you can handle, try an OTC antihistamine;

Kitchen Solutions

Many anti-itch remedies can be made up right in your own kitchen. The National Psoriasis Foundation suggests the following do-it-yourself recipes:

- Dissolve one-and-a-half cups baking soda in three gallons water to use in an anti-itch compress.
- Add a handful of Epsom salts or Dead Sea salts to your bathwater. You can also add a squirt of mineral oil or baby oil to the water with the salts (but use extra caution when getting into and out of the tub, as the oil will make the tub slippery).
- Put three tablespoons boric acid (available in pharmacies) in 16 ounces water, and use in a compress.
- Add two teaspoons olive oil to a large glass of milk for a soothing bath oil (but use extra caution to avoid slipping when getting into and out of the tub).
- Add one cup white vinegar to the bathwater to ease itching.
- Soak in oats. Toss a cup of oats in your bathwater, or add a commercial bath product that contains "colloidal oats."

ask your pharmacist to help you choose a suitable product. (Before you reach for the antihistamine, however, you may want to sample the homemade anti-itch remedies in "Kitchen Solutions," above.)

Try fish oil. Doctors have long known that Greenland Eskimos, who eat large quantities of cold-water fish, rarely suffer from psoriasis, and some experts believe fish oil may be the reason. Research from the University of California at Davis and the University of Michigan at Ann Arbor has suggested that large oral doses of fish-oil supplements may help control psoriasis. Participants in the fish-oil studies had to consume unusually large quantities of the fish-oil supplement to achieve positive results, however, and regularly consuming such high doses of straight fish oil could potentially result in overdoses of vitamins A and D. Also, like any other fat, fish oil is high in calories. If you're considering going the fish-oil-supplement route, talk it over with your physician first.

Substituting cold-water fish for most of the red meat in your diet is generally considered to be a healthy move by most dietary experts, so there's probably no harm in upping your fish-oil intake that way. However, it's not likely to provide you with anywhere near as much fish oil as was used in the study to control psoriasis.

Humidify. Dry indoor air is associated with dry skin, which is bad news for psoriasis sufferers. Use a room humidifier to raise the humidity.

Avoid injuring your skin. Even mild injuries such as sunburn, scratches, and irritation from tight clothing can cause or worsen psoriasis. Dermatologists call this psoriasis trigger "the Koebner phenomenon."

Use skin products carefully. Psoriasis causes the skin to be unusually susceptible to irritating substances, so use products such as hair dyes, perms, or straighteners with caution. Use potential irritants only when your skin is relatively free of lesions, and avoid them altogether if you have open wounds.

Try a little hot pepper. A potential exception to the no-irritant rule may be capsaicin, the ingredient that gives hot peppers their bite. There is some evidence that capsaicin can help ease the itching, scaling, and discomfort of psoriasis. It is found in a variety of OTC topical products used to relieve the pain of arthritis, muscle strains, and the like. It may cause an initial, brief burning sensation when applied to plaques, and it must be kept away from the eyes and mucous membranes because it can produce an intense burning sensation that is certainly irritating. But you may want to try a little capsaicin-containing cream on a small psoriasis lesion to see if it helps.

Treat infections pronto. Systemic infections like strep throat (streptococcal infections) can trigger psoriasis flares in some people. Contact your doctor at the earliest sign of infection (such as sore throat or fever).

Stay trim. For reasons doctors haven't been able to identify, psoriasis tends to be worse and harder to control among people who are obese. While a cause-and-effect connection between weight and psoriasis hasn't been established, it's a good idea to maintain a healthy weight. If you're already overweight, try eating a low-fat, lower-calorie diet and getting regular exercise to help shed some excess pounds.

Be careful with medications. Certain medications, including antimalarials, beta-blockers (such as Inderal), lithium, and others, can worsen psoriasis in some people. Be sure all of the doctors who treat you know about your skin condition, and if a current medication appears to be aggravating your psoriasis, discuss with your doctor the possibility of a reduced dosage or alternative medication.

Relax. Doctors agree that stress can cause psoriasis to flare up. Accept that life will leave your emotions frayed now and then, and find a way to mellow out. One study found that the skin of patients undergoing phototherapy cleared up faster if they listened to meditation-based relaxation tapes. Some other effective relaxation techniques that psoriasis patients use include hypnosis, massage, visualization, tai chi, and yoga.

Restless Legs Syndrome

12 Ways to Squelch the Squiggles

It's bad enough when you can't get to sleep and you just lie there, staring at the ceiling. But people who suffer from restless legs syndrome don't just lie there. They are seized by an uncontrollable urge to move their legs. Their legs actually twitch or jerk, while they experience the sensation of something squirming or wiggling under the skin of their legs. Consequently, restless legs syndrome can lead to problems associated with sleep deprivation, such as anxiety and depression.

Researchers say this is a condition that's still shrouded in much mystery. Although there seem to be connections with other conditions—such as heart, lung, and kidney disorders; circulatory problems; and arthritis—the culprit sometimes appears to be as simple as excessive caffeine consumption or too little exercise.

The following home remedies are designed to help you combat this problem. If you find that your legs are still twitching after you've tried these tips, however, it's time to get a medical evaluation.

Get up and walk. Walking around may be the only thing that helps. A midnight stroll through the house may calm your legs enough to keep them still when you go back to bed.

Check out your caffeine consumption. Coffee, tea, chocolate, sodas, and even over-the-counter (OTC) medications may contain caffeine. Try cutting your consumption of caffeine-containing foods and medications (or substituting varieties without caffeine) to see if your condition improves. Avoid tobacco, which contains the stimulant nicotine, and alcohol, which can have its own detrimental effects on sleep, as well.

Modify your medication. Some OTC medications, such as certain cold medications and allergy pills, contain ingredients that are mildly stimulating and can make you and your legs even more jittery. Ask your pharmacist if any medications you are taking contain stimulants and whether there are any nonstimulating alternatives.

Take a bath. A warm bath or massage before bed relaxes muscles and therefore may be helpful.

Change your temperature. Sometimes, a change from hot to cold, or cold to hot, can do the trick. Try putting a heating pad or hot pack on your legs for a short while. If that doesn't work, drape a cool towel over your legs, or dip your feet in cool water.

Make sure you're eating well. There are some indications that a deficiency in iron, folate, or magnesium may contribute to restless legs syndrome. By eating a wide variety of nutrient-rich foods, you should get the vitamins and minerals you need. However, your doctor may recommend supplements of these specific nutrients.

Make a bedtime habit. Get into a regular routine that will help your mind and body settle down and prepare for sleep.

Stick to a schedule. Getting to bed at about the same time each night and allowing for a full night's sleep may help you avoid the fatigue that could be a contributing factor to restless legs syndrome.

Soothe your stress. Stress may not be the cause of restless legs syndrome, but it can exacerbate it. Try to eliminate some of the stress in your life. Regular exercise and some form of relaxation technique, whether yoga, meditation, visualization, or even an engaging hobby, may help you to "de-stress."

Exercise your legs. Moderate exercise often helps, although excessive exercise can aggravate restless legs symptoms. A daily walk at a moderate pace is an excellent exercise, especially for folks who haven't been very physically active in a while.

Stretch your legs. Try stretching your calves, hamstrings, and gluteal (butt) muscles before bed.

Wear socks to bed. Some experts have found that a lot of people who suffer from restless legs syndrome also seem to have cold feet. Although nobody has studied the connection, it might not hurt to bundle up your tootsies for the night.

Who Ya Gonna Call?

Doctors with some expertise in restless legs syndrome hail from a wide variety of medical specialties. Although neurology seems to be the logical category for this mysterious ailment, which was first identified more than 50 years ago, some of the most informative studies on the syndrome have come from doctors who have chanced upon it while treating conditions that seem to be totally unrelated.

So where do you turn for help when home remedies fail? Ask your doctor for a referral to a sleep-disorders specialist or to one of the hundreds of sleep-disorders clinics in the United States.

Seasonal Affective Disorder (SAD)

9 WAYS TO STAVE OFF THE SADNESS

Few people look forward to the gray days and long, dreary nights of winter. In fact, most people feel better in the summer, when the days are longer, sunnier, and warmer. We get out more, exercise harder, and eat less. But for some people, the transition from summer to winter triggers feelings of depression.

For these individuals, the change in seasons signals a marked change in personality—from happy (or at least okay) and relaxed to depressed and tense. They may have trouble getting out of bed in the morning, concentrating, and moderating their eating

(especially when it comes to carbohydrates, which they crave). They lose interest in the activities that they ordinarily enjoy, and they may feel irritable and down. Then, when spring comes, they feel like themselves again.

Until the 1980s, people suffering from this seasonal change in personality had no idea what was wrong with them. But then Nor-man E. Rosenthal, M.D., who worked at the time at the National Institute of Mental Health, made the connection between the shorter, darker days of winter and the onset of seasonal depression. He and his colleagues began studying this phenomenon and gave it the name seasonal affective disorder (SAD). It has since been added to the primary diagnostic manual for mental health disorders.

Nobody knows what causes SAD. Experts believe that light plays a part and that exposing people with SAD to extra light sometimes improves their mood. The hormone melatonin also appears to be involved. In animals, melatonin regulates hibernation. Melatonin is secreted in the dark, and humans have more of it in their bloodstream during winter than summer. In fact, when scientists administer melatonin to research subjects, their body temperatures decrease and they become drowsy. Scientists further speculate that people with SAD often benefit from light therapy because light shuts off melatonin production.

SAD appears in varying degrees. Some people feel mildly depressed;

others are so depressed they require hospitalization. In others, mood is unaffected, but their energy levels are so low that they aren't able to accomplish the things they would like to or would normally be able to during other seasons.

For most people who have SAD, it takes two or three days of bright sunshine to elicit a reversal of symptoms. Indeed, it serves as a form of confirmation that you are suffering from SAD if you find your symptoms greatly diminish when you travel toward the equator.

SAD strikes men and women, although women are more likely to develop it. Women appear particularly vulnerable during their reproductive years.

So what can you do about SAD, short of taking a warm-weather vacation every few weeks during the winter? The following may help:

Soak up the morning light. Get as much natural light as possible between 6:00 A.M. and 8:00 A.M. Get outside and go for a walk, or at least sit by a window.

Eat foods containing the amino acid tryptophan. The carbohydrate craving common in people with this disorder is thought to be caused by decreased levels of the brain neurotransmitter serotonin. Since tryptophan is a precursor of serotonin, getting

Summer Sadness

While winter depression tends to be the most common type of seasonal affective disorder (SAD), some patients actually have the opposite problem: They experience depression during the warm, summer months. These patients experience depression that begins between March and June and ends between August and October. The symptoms are similar to those found in the winter variety of SAD. In these cases, warm temperatures, rather than lack of light, seem to be the culprit in causing SAD.

Improvement in the symptoms tends to occur when patients take summer vacations in the north, when they bathe in cold lakes in the summer, and when they are exposed to extreme amounts of air-conditioning during the warmer months.

more of this amino acid may increase the body's production of serotonin and help you feel better. Although there is no solid research that supports the benefits of tryptophan-rich foods, you might try eating more of these foods to see if your symptoms improve. Foods rich in tryptophan include turkey, milk, and egg whites.

Avoid self-medication with alcohol or caffeine. Caffeine may give you a brief lift, but it can also cause anxiety, muscle tension, and gastrointestinal problems. Alcohol, on the other hand, is a depressant, which can further exacerbate your low mood.

Engage in regular aerobic exercise. Again, we don't know for sure if exercise helps people with SAD, but some evidence suggests that it does. Aim to exercise outdoors in the early morning hours.

Eat lunch outside. If you can't get out in the morning light, at least get out on

Getting Professional Help

If you're feeling the effects of SAD, see your doctor for a physical examination. Other health problems, such as an underactive thyroid, can cause SAD-like symptoms. If you get a clean bill of health, try the remedies discussed here. If they don't work, seek the help of a professional—a psychologist, psychiatrist, doctor, nurse, or social worker—who has experience treating people with SAD. You can ask your doctor for a referral to a SAD specialist, or you can check the following sources:

- Your local medical school's department of psychiatry. The school may have researchers who focus on SAD.
- The American Psychiatric Association, 1000 Wilson Blvd., Suite 1825, Arlington, VA 22209 or *www.healthyminds.org*.
- The book *The Winter Blues* by Norman E. Rosenthal, M.D. To find out more about his work, go to *www.normanrosenthal.com*.
- The Society for Light Treatment and Biological Rhythms (SLTBR). While this is a nationwide professional society for experts in the field, its membership roster includes health professionals who are qualified to do light therapy. Write to SLTBR, 174 Cook Street, San Francisco, CA 94159, or visit www.sltbr.org.
- The National Organization for Seasonal Affective Disorder at www.nosad.org.

The treatments you would most likely receive from a professional include light-box therapy, dawn-simulator therapy, and/or antidepressant medication.

your lunch break. Even if it's cloudy, the natural light will do you good.

Maintain a regular schedule. Keep your body's clock in sync by rising and retiring at the same time each day, even on weekends or days off from work.

Let the sun shine in. Open the curtains, pull up the shades, and spend time in the sunniest room in the house.

Get yourself a box of light. One of the most effective treatments for SAD is regular (usually daily) exposure to a specially designed light box, one that provides enough intensity of light to

positively affect SAD symptoms (the light needs to be at least ten times the intensity of regular household or office lighting). Two variations on the basic light box are also available: a special light visor (you want the particles of light from a light device to actually enter your eyes) and a "dawn simulator," which is a light box that simulates sunrise by switching on when you awaken and growing brighter and brighter as the morning wears on. The amount of exposure time required each day can be as little as a half hour to as much as several hours, and you are encouraged to go about normal activities such as eating or reading during exposure time. Talk with your doctor about whether you should try one of these devices.

If possible, move to a sunnier climate. Most people can't just get up and relocate. But for those who can, moving to a sunnier area helps SAD symptoms disappear. Indeed, SAD rarely affects people living within about 30 degrees of the equator.

Shin Splints

10 WAYS TO SAY GOODBYE TO PAIN

Perhaps you were in the middle of your morning run or your evening aerobics class and it came on like gangbusters: shooting pain starting at the front of your ankle and continuing up almost to your kneecap. Now, when you touch the area on either side of your shin bone, it feels sore and tender. Could it be shin splints?

Although annoying, shin splints (and, indeed, most shin pain) is not an indication of a serious problem. It is an inflammation of the muscle or other tissue at the front of the lower leg that results from repeated, minor trauma or irritation, and it can be treated or prevented using the tips that follow. However, if shin pain persists or recurs despite your self-treatment, see a doctor. You may be suffering from a stress fracture—a tiny chip or crack in the bone. Stress fractures won't go away on their own and, without treatment, may become serious.

Don't work through the pain. You won't earn points in athlete's heaven for trying to tough out the pain of shin splints. At best, the pain won't lessen and at worst, you'll be setting the stage for a more serious injury. Stay off your feet, or at the very least, decrease your mileage while you're nursing a case of shin splints.

Ice it. Ice is the treatment of choice for reducing the inflammation of any sports injury, and shin splints is no exception. A handy method: Fill a foam or paper cup with water and stick it in the freezer. Once the water is frozen solid, peel back the lip of the cup to expose some ice, and massage the shin area for ten minutes at a time, up to four times a day for a week or two. You can also try icing the area with a bag of frozen vegetables, such as peas or corn kernels.

Tape it. Taping up your shin with an elastic bandage or wearing a neoprene sleeve that fits snugly over the lower leg may provide some comfort by compressing the area, which may help limit inflammation, and by supporting the tissues and permitting less muscle movement. (By the way, while it's wise to take it easy for at least a few days, you don't want to totally immobilize the leg; gentle movement helps bring nourishing blood to the damaged tissue while taking away excess fluid from inflammation.)

Choosing an Athletic Shoe

A good athletic shoe is an important investment for anyone who runs, does aerobics, or engages in other weight-bearing exercises. Wearing shoes with worn-out or poorly cushioned insoles (or outer soles) only paves the way for overuse injuries. When shopping for athletic shoes, look for a good fit (with at least a thumb's-width of room at the toe, and the heel held firmly), good cushioning (especially in the forefoot, for an aerobics shoe), and extra supportive material on the inside heel-edge of the sole.

Runners and walkers should replace their shoes approximately every 500 miles; aerobicizers every four to five months.

Take two aspirin. The over-the-counter analgesics aspirin and ibuprofen are usually quite effective in relieving the pain of shin splints, so you may want to give one of these a try. (Read the warnings in the box on page 21 first, however.) Either of them will also help diminish the associated swelling and inflammation. Acetaminophen, on the other hand, may ease the pain, but it won't help with inflammation.

Tune in to your body. The biggest reason people get overuse injuries is they don't pay attention to the signals their body gives them. If something hurts, rest it, ice it, and, if necessary, talk with your doctor about it to see what you can do to prevent the pain or injury from recurring.

Try an athletic insole. Since shin splints often occurs as a result of the excessive pounding shins take during jogging or other high-impact, weight-bearing activities, a padded insole placed inside the shoe may offer relief. The insole helps soften the blow as your foot lands on hard ground. You can purchase a pair at an athletic-shoe store, sports-supply store, or drugstore. They range in price from about $7 to $20. In addition, check to be sure the shoes you wear during the activity still have plenty of cushioning (see "Choosing an Athletic Shoe," on page 251).

Stay off the cement. Another way to lower the impact of your routine is to be sure you exercise on a forgiving surface such as a running track, crushed gravel, or grass. If you have to run on roads, try to choose streets paved in asphalt rather than concrete. If you do aerobics, you may need to stay away from cement floors, even carpeted ones. Suspended wood floors are best.

Cross-train. One way to rest during an episode of shin splints without cutting out exercise altogether is to switch to another type of activity. If you're a runner, add some swimming, stationary cycling, or other activity that doesn't tax your shins as much as running.

Don't run on hills. Running up and down hills may contribute to or aggravate shin splints.

Prevent the injury from occurring in the first place. Always warm up before exercising to get blood flowing to the tissues. Warm muscles are less likely than cold muscles to be injured. Warm up with a few minutes of easy walking or other gentle movement.

Sinusitis

5 Ways to Head It Off

Like it or not, your nose is an immeasurably valuable part of your anatomy. On the outside, it serves to hold your sunglasses in the vicinity of your eyes. On the inside, it incorporates an intricate system of narrow passages and eight hollow, air-containing spaces—connected to both your eyes and ears—that enable you to inhale air from the environment and process it before it gets to your lungs. While it is easy to understand how a passageway is necessary in this process, what possible function can be carried out by the hollow spaces?

Pairs of these hollow spaces, known as the paranasal sinuses, are located behind the eyebrows, in the cheekbones, behind the nose, and between the eyes. Because they are filled only with air, they act as a sort of "echo chamber," giving resonance to your voice. They also lessen the weight of your skull, cushion it against shocks, and give you better balance. The most important function of your sinuses, however, is as a "conditioner" for inhaled air on its way to your lungs. Normally, the membranes lining the nose and sinuses produce between a

pint and a quart of mucus and secretions a day. This discharge passes through the nose, sweeping and washing the membranes and picking up dust particles, bacteria, and other air pollutants along the way. The mucus is then swept backward into the throat by tiny undulating hairs called cilia. From there, it is swallowed into the stomach, where acids destroy dangerous bacteria. It's all in a day's work for the lining of the sinuses and the nasal cavity.

But when those nasal passages become irritated or inflamed by an allergy attack, air pollution, smoke, or a viral infection such as a cold or the flu, the nasal and sinus membranes secrete more than the normal amount of mucus. They also swell, blocking the

Know Thy Headache

It's a common scenario in doctors' offices: A patient shows up complaining of "sinusitis." But an examination turns up no sign of sinus disease. It could be that consumers have seen so many ads for "sinus headache" products that we're too quick to diagnose ourselves with the problem. Whatever the reason, doctors say that only about 10 percent of people who seek medical attention for sinus trouble actually have anything wrong with their sinuses. The rest may truly be suffering from headaches, but not because their sinuses are inflamed.

Interestingly, those same patients who take preparations marketed for relief of sinus headaches may end up feeling better, at least in the short term, since these products contain an analgesic. However, if you suffer from chronic headaches, see a doctor to investigate the cause and find out how to prevent and treat them.

openings and preventing an easy flow of mucus and air and setting the stage for bacteria to flourish.

Sinus trouble comes in two versions: acute and chronic. The acute attack of sinusitis, which lasts for a week to ten days, produces a headache that can range in intensity from minor to what feels like bone-shattering. Chronic sinusitis—which occurs when a sinus opening is blocked for an extended period—seldom causes head pain, although it does cause unpleasant discharge, chronic coughing, recurrent ear infections, and a roaring case of postnasal drip. But the lack of real pain is misleading; chronic sinusitis can be serious indeed, because bacteria can become so entrenched after repeated infections that no antibiotic can touch them. That's why it's wise to have your sinus problem checked out by a doctor, especially if your sinus drainage is greenish in color or if you have a fever.

If your sinuses make your life miserable, do you have to live with it? Not necessarily, say the experts; there are ways to head off the worst of your symptoms.

Take good care of yourself. Unless you're a hermit, you stand at least some chance of catching a case of the sniffles at some point in the year, whether from a loved one, the sneezing passenger next to you on the airplane, or the cashier at the local supermarket. But maintaining a healthy immune system will bolster your resistance to all sorts of germs, leaving you less likely to catch a cold or come down with the flu and making symptoms more manageable if you do end up getting sick. To shore up your body's defenses, you can start by eating right, staying in good physical shape through regular exercise, and getting plenty of rest.

Live the sanitary life. You don't have to move into a sterile, germ-proof

bubble, or walk around wearing a surgical mask. Just use common sense: If the guy next to you at the bus stop is coughing his brains out, move away. If someone in your family has a cold or the flu, avoid unnecessary contact with his or her germs. For example, don't share eating utensils or drink from the same glass, encourage them to use tissues to catch sneezes and coughs, and wash your hands often.

Hydrate. Keeping yourself well-hydrated helps to ensure that your sinuses are functioning well, which can

ease sinusitis symptoms. So drink plenty of fluids—eight tall glasses of water a day is a good goal. Fill a tall bottle with cool water and keep it at hand so that you can take small sips throughout the day.

Clear the air. Avoid pollutants in the air as much as possible, stay indoors if the air quality is poor, and above all, avoid anyone who is smoking tobacco.

Avoid Rebound

Advertisements touting products that supposedly relieve sinus pressure, congestion, and pain are everywhere. Do they deliver what they promise? Medicated, decongestant nasal sprays and nose drops can clear up a stuffy nose, but chronic use of these medications can lead to trouble. What happens is that each time the medication wears off, there is more swelling, more congestion, and more discomfort, not because of the original infection, but because of withdrawal from the constricting effect of the spray. (Nonmedicated saline, or saltwater, nasal sprays and drops can help ease congestion without causing this rebound effect.)

In addition, some people with asthma have aspirin intolerance, and if they use any of the medications containing aspirin, they may unwittingly intensify their problems, perhaps triggering a stuffy nose or even an asthma attack. These reactions often don't occur until three or four hours after taking aspirin, so many users don't make the cause-and-effect association.

Nose drops and nasal sprays should not be used for more than three days in a row. If your symptoms don't improve within a few days of home treatment, see your doctor.

Obviously, puffing on a cigarette, cigar, or pipe yourself is like writing a prescription for a sinusitis attack.

Control allergies. Since allergies can cause sinusitis, it's important that you work with an allergist to identify all the substances that trigger your allergies (called allergens) and then take whatever steps you can to avoid them. (See ALLERGIES for more information on common causes of allergies as well as loads of specific practical tips on avoiding allergens.) If you find it impossible to escape your allergens, talk to your allergist about desensitization treatments, which are designed to help the body develop an immunity to offending substances.

Slivers

5 WAYS TO REMOVE THEM SAFELY

A sliver (or splinter) is basically a puncture wound with debris in it. You can get slivers of glass, metal, or plastic, but wood slivers are by far the most common.

While a cut is a vertical slice into the skin and a scrape is the horizontal removal of a patch of outer skin, a puncture wound is a stab deep into the tissue. In the case of a sliver, it's the foreign object—the sliver—that causes the puncture and stays in the tissue. Most slivers aren't serious and can be treated at home. Here's how:

Tweeze it. If a sliver is sticking out of the skin, sterilize the tips of a pair of tweezers with alcohol, carefully pinch the sliver as close to the skin as possible, and gently slide it out.

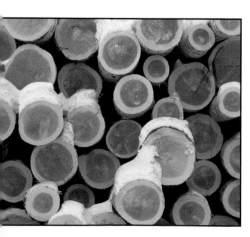

Needle it. If the sliver isn't poking out of the skin, use a needle instead of tweezers. After sterilizing it with alcohol, use the needle's tip to push the sliver from the bottom (the end that entered the skin first) toward the puncture hole in the skin's surface. Be sure to start at the very bottom of the sliver, or you risk breaking it and leaving part of it in the skin.

Slice it. Too often, slivers are in deep and people poke and prod with tweezers, only to end up bruising the tissue around the sliver. In this case, you'll need a new razor blade. After sterilizing the blade with alcohol, make a shallow incision just above and parallel to the sliver. Keep in mind that the top layer of skin is dead tissue, so a small incision is not likely to hurt at all. Once the incision is made, gently part the skin and use a sterile needle to slide the sliver out.

Clean it. No matter which method you use, once you've got the sliver out, clean the wound thoroughly with soap and water to help prevent infection. After cleaning the wound, pour on a drop of hydrogen peroxide to help clear out any remaining debris and speed healing.

Squeeze on antibacterial ointment. If the wound hasn't immediately closed up or if you had to slice the skin, apply an over-the-counter antibacterial ointment (Neosporin, Polysporin, or an equivalent product) and cover it with a bandage.

Snoring

10 Ways to Turn Down the Volume

If you snore, you make a raspy, rattling, snorting sound while you breathe during sleep. Snoring is a fairly common affliction, affecting 40 percent of men and 25 percent of women. Older people are particularly prone to snoring: About one-third of people aged 55 to 84 snore. Despite its frequency, however, snoring is a sleep disorder that can have serious medical and social consequences. The tips that follow may help you—and your sleep partner—sleep more peacefully. Pleasant dreams!

Sleep on your side. You're more likely to snore if you're lying on your back, and sleeping on your stomach is stressful on your neck.

Use tennis balls. Not to shove in your mouth, but to keep you from rolling onto your back during sleep. Sew a long, tight pocket onto the back of your pajama top, and put two or three tennis balls into it. (Don't sew? Put the tennis balls in a sock and then use a diaper pin to both close the sock and attach it to the back of your pajama top.)

Avoid alcohol and tranquilizers. Both alcohol and sleeping pills can depress your central nervous system and relax the muscles of your throat and jaw, making snoring more likely. These substances are also known to contribute to sleep apnea, a dangerous condition often marked by snoring that has been linked with cardiovascular disease (see "When Snoring Becomes Serious" on page 258). And they should never, ever be used together. If you have difficulty sleeping without resorting to sleeping pills (or if you use alcohol to help yourself fall asleep), see INSOMNIA and, if necessary, discuss it with your doctor.

Lose weight. Excess body weight, especially around the neck, puts pressure on the airway, causing it to partially collapse.

When Snoring Becomes Serious

Snoring is a nuisance—it can keep your bed partner awake, and it can prevent you from getting the restful sleep you need for good physical and emotional health. Snoring may also indicate that you have a serious sleep disorder called sleep apnea. The National Sleep Foundation (www.sleepfoundation.org) recommends that you see your doctor if you:

- Wake up during the night choking and gasping for breath.
- Have been told that your snoring is disturbing to others.
- Don't feel refreshed when you wake up after a full night's sleep.
- Are extremely tired during the day.
- Wake with a headache.
- Are gaining weight even though you haven't changed your diet or activity level.
- Have trouble concentrating, remembering, or paying attention.
- Have been told by your bedmate that your breathing stops briefly while you are sleeping.

It's important to have sleep apnea treated, not only because it interferes with your daily functioning, but because it boosts your risk of vascular disease.

Sleep apnea can be treated with lifestyle modification, surgery, oral mouth guards, or a CPAP machine, which blows air into the back of your throat while you sleep.

Get your allergies treated. Chronic respiratory allergies may cause snoring by forcing sufferers to breathe through their mouths while they sleep. Taking an antihistamine just before bedtime

may help. If your nose is stuffed up, try using an over-the-counter saline spray or a humidifier. (See ALLERGIES for more tips.)

Buy a mouth guard. Your dentist or doctor may be able to prescribe an antisnoring mouth guard that holds the teeth together and keeps the lower jaw muscles from becoming too lax.

Stop smoking. Smoke damages the respiratory system.

Keep a regular shut-eye schedule. You're more likely to snore if you're exhausted, so get plenty of sleep. Go to bed and get up at the same time each day to help prevent sleep problems.

See a doctor if you are pregnant and snoring. Sometimes, women who are pregnant will begin to snore. The snoring may begin because of the increased body weight and because the hormonal changes of pregnancy cause muscles to relax. Whatever the cause, snoring during pregnancy may rob your baby of oxygen. Talk with your doctor about it.

Elevate your head. Sleeping with your head raised may take some of the pressure off of the airway, making breathing easier. Raise the head of the bed by putting blocks under the bed posts, or prop up your upper body (not just your head, which will bend your neck and can actually inhibit breathing) with pillows.

Sore Throat

10 STEPS FOR QUICK RELIEF

A sore throat can be a minor, but annoying, ailment, or it can be a symptom of a serious illness. Causes range from a stuffy nose or a cold to strep throat (a bacterial throat infection caused by *Streptococcus pyogenes*). Since untreated strep throat can lead to rheumatic fever and scarlet fever, it's important to get medical help as early as possible. Along with producing severe soreness in your gullet, strep throat may be accompanied by fever, body aches and pains, and malaise. If you have these symptoms, or if you have a sore throat lasting more than two or three days, it makes good sense to see a doctor. For mild sore throats that accompany a cold or allergies, the tips below may help ease your discomfort.

Gargle with warm salt water. If you can gargle without gagging, make a saline solution by adding half a teaspoon salt to a cup of very warm water. Gargling with this fluid can help soothe a sore throat.

Gargle with Listerine. Another good gargling fluid is Listerine mouthwash. If you share the product with anyone else in your household, don't drink straight from the bottle; instead, pour a small amount into a cup (and don't share that, either).

Drink hot liquids. Especially if you're not good at gargling, drink hot fluids, such as coffee, tea, or hot lemonade. Coating the tissue in your throat with hot liquid provides a benefit similar to applying hot packs to infected skin. (And sipping hot tea is more pleasant than trying to swallow a hot pack.)

Take an analgesic. Plain old aspirin, acetaminophen, or ibuprofen can do wonders for sore-throat pain. However, aspirin should not be given to children under the age of 19 because of the risk of Reye syndrome, a potentially fatal condition. Be sure to read the warnings in the box on page 21 before taking one of these painkillers.

Rest and take it easy. Common sense dictates staying in bed or at least

An Old-Fashioned Sore-Throat Tonic

What do good, old-fashioned general practitioners prescribe for a sore throat? Besides the tips on these pages, mixed with a tincture of time, some advise special brews guaranteed to soothe body and soul. The following was extracted from a book of home remedies published more than 130 years ago. Some doctors still swear that it is surprisingly palatable and works wonders. (Do not give it—or any other honey-containing food or beverage—to children under two years of age. Honey can carry a bacterium that can cause a kind of food poisoning called infant botulism and may also cause allergic reactions in very young children.)

1 tablespoon honey, any kind
1 tablespoon vinegar, preferably apple-cider vinegar
8 ounces hot water

Mix all the ingredients together in a mug and sip slowly (but don't let it get cold). Use as often as desired.

resting when a sore throat's got you down. Taking it easy leaves more energy to fight the infection.

Suck on hard candy. Think of a sore throat as an excuse to indulge your sweet tooth, since some doctors say that sugar can help soothe

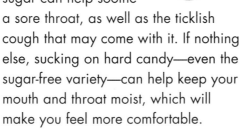

a sore throat, as well as the ticklish cough that may come with it. If nothing else, sucking on hard candy—even the sugar-free variety—can help keep your mouth and throat moist, which will make you feel more comfortable.

Keep your nasal passages clear. Doctors agree that two of the most common causes of sore-throat pain are postnasal drip and a dry throat that results from sleeping with your mouth open when your nasal passages are blocked. Decongestants, especially those containing pseudoephedrine (read package labels), may be helpful in stopping the flow; follow package directions carefully. Using saline nasal spray can help make breathing easier promptly though temporarily, and it's probably worth investing in a humidifier to run in your bedroom at night.

Spray it. Analgesic sprays, such as Chloraseptic, may be effective in temporarily relieving sore-throat pain. The only problem is that the effect doesn't last long. You may have to spray several times an hour. However, the sprays won't harm you if you follow the directions for use and may take the edge off an extremely painful throat.

Steam it out. One traditional remedy for a cold or sore throat is a steam tent—sitting with your face over a bowl of steaming hot water and your head covered with a towel to keep the steam in. While it's easy to dismiss such a simple measure as old-fashioned, several scientific studies have shown steaming can actually shorten the duration of a throat infection.

Keep the fluids coming. Drink as much fluid as possible—at least eight to ten 8-ounce glasses throughout the day. Keeping your throat well lubricated with soothing liquids can prevent it from becoming dry and irritated and may even help banish the infection faster.

Stings

14 Ways to Avoid and Treat Them

You hear the buzz, you see the bee, but before you can react—*Oweee!* You've been stung. Almost all of us have had this experience at least once, and it's no fun. But if you know what to do, you can take the ouch out of being stung or perhaps even prevent the attack from happening in the first place.

Bees, yellow jackets, hornets, wasps, and fire ants all have stingers that inject venom into their unfortunate victims. The most common reaction is redness, pain, itching, and perhaps some swelling around the sting that lasts for a few hours. Some individuals may experience more severe swelling, covering a patch of skin five inches wide or more or causing an entire limb to puff up for a day or two.

For more than two million people in the United States who are allergic to the venom of stinging insects, however, the consequences can be much worse. Symptoms may include hives, wheezing, difficulty breathing, dizziness, and nausea. In the most severe allergic reaction, called *anaphylaxis,* shock, unconsciousness, and cardiac arrest can occur. People suffering from allergic reactions to insect venom require immediate medical treatment. It's estimated that fifty people die every year from anaphylactic shock brought on by insect stings.

For most people, however, a sting is little more than a minor nuisance. And it's one you can do something about.

Easing the Pain

Here are some simple suggestions for minimizing a sting's pain quickly and easily. Be sure to keep an eye out for signs of a more severe reaction so that medical help can be sought immediately if necessary.

Apply meat tenderizer. Simply applying a teaspoon of unseasoned meat tenderizer mixed with a few drops of water to a sting can bring quick relief. An enzyme in the tenderizer, either papain or bromelain, dissolves the toxins the insect has just injected into you. Carry a bottle filled with the solution with you when you

Killer-Bee Update

Killer bees have arrived in the United States and they're here to stay. On October 15, 1990, the first colony of killer bees was discovered near Hidalgo, Texas, after crossing the Mexican border. Since then, swarms and nests of so-called Africanized honeybees have turned up in Alabama, Arizona, Arkansas, California, Nevada, New Mexico, and Oklahoma. About the only good news regarding these tenacious stingers is that experts say they probably won't migrate past the southern third of the country, perhaps no farther north than the Carolinas.

What will stop their advance? Nothing high-tech, just cold temperatures. That's one big difference between killer bees and the European bees we're used to. Africanized bees can't withstand long, cold winters. Another well-known difference is that it appears to take very little provocation for Africanized bees to become aggressive and attack.

So what should you know if you're in killer-bee country? Keep your eyes open, because killer bees nest in a much greater variety of places than European bees do. If you see a hive, don't disturb it, no matter what. Slowly and carefully walk away. If you start getting stung, you need to get away fast. Sting for sting, killer bees are no worse than other honeybees, but they sting in much greater numbers, so don't try to stand your ground and swat them away. Instead, run as fast as you can or seek refuge in a car or building. Although killer bees will chase you, it's possible to outrun them.

know you're going to be outdoors in areas where bees are likely to be present. This remedy only works if used immediately after being stung. If you wait until you return home to apply the solution, it probably won't help much, since the tenderizer can't reach venom proteins once they have penetrated deeply into the skin.

Try a baking-soda paste. Think of this as "plan B" if you don't have any meat tenderizer. Although baking soda can't neutralize insect venom, it will help relieve itching and swelling.

Scrape the stinger out. Bees and some yellow jackets have barbed stingers that anchor in your skin after you're stung. (Other stinging insects have smooth stingers that remain intact on the bug.) You should get the stinger out as soon as possible, because it will continue to release venom into your skin for several minutes after the initial sting. Resist the urge to squeeze, grab, or press the stinger, however. Doing so will just make matters worse by pumping more venom into your skin. Try this, instead: Using a clean knife blade, or even a fingernail, lift the stinger up and gently scrape it away.

Put it on ice. Rub ice over the sting site. This may help reduce some of the inflammation and swelling.

Take an antihistamine. If the itchiness from a sting is really bugging you, you might try an over-the-counter oral antihistamine for relief. Follow the package directions carefully.

Preventing Future Stings

Even better than calming the discomfort of a sting is preventing one from happening in the first place. Here's what you can do to protect yourself:

Keep your cool. If a wasp, yellow jacket, or any stinging insect flies near you, stay calm. Slowly move away from the area and do not flail your arms or try to swat the bug. Getting agitated may incite the insect to sting.

Unsweeten your sweat. Ever notice how two people can be sitting outdoors and insects will hover over one but ignore the other? No one is sure why, but some experts think insects find certain varieties of sweat or body odor more appealing than others. According to one theory, so far unsubstantiated, changing the smell of your sweat may repel insects. Some believers suggest that eating onions and garlic can drive bugs away. The downside? You're likely to repel humans, too.

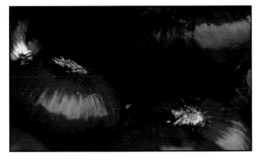

Don't wear bright, flowery clothes or rough fabrics. These seem to attract insects. Stick to smooth fabric and light-colored outfits in tones of white, tan, green, or khaki when you plan to spend time outdoors.

Go fragrance-free. Perfume, cologne, and scented aftershave, hair spray, and soap will attract insects. You may feel a bit bland without your favorite fragrance, but it may be well worth it to avoid painful stings.

Leave bright, shiny jewelry at home. Bright jewelry and other shiny metal objects attract insects.

Keep your shoes on. Walking barefoot through the grass may feel great, but it's not such a wise idea. Bees are attracted to the clover that covers many lawns, and yellow jackets build their homes in the ground, so going shoeless can mean stepping into trouble.

Keep food covered when outside. Picnics are a summer family favorite, but open food attracts stinging insects. Keep covers on food and lids on garbage cans as much as possible. It's best to steer clear of public trash cans that are partially or fully open on top.

Watch what you drink from. If you're downing a cold drink outdoors, use caution. Insects can fly into drink containers, so guzzling a cola could lead to a sting on the tongue or throat. While outdoors, avoid drinking from cans or other lidless, narrow-lipped, opaque containers that might allow bugs to launch a sneak attack when you take your next sip.

Be aware of your surroundings. When gardening or doing yard work or other outdoor chores, be on the lookout for hives. Nests can be found in the eaves and attic of your home and in trees, vines, shrubs, wood piles, and other protected places. Disturbing a nest, even by accident, can irritate the insects. The American Academy of Allergy, Asthma & Immunology suggests using extreme care when operating power lawn mowers, hedge clippers, and tractors, as well.

Stomach Upset

23 Ways to Tame Your Tummy

There are two kinds of stomach problems. Chronic, long-term stomach upset is fairly serious and should be discussed with your doctor. Temporary stomachaches are usually less serious and tend to be caused by something you ate or the stomach flu. If you find yourself with a bellyache, here are some tips that may help:

Try some soda. Soda pop, particularly ginger ale, lemon-lime, and other noncaffeinated varieties, helps settle stomachs.

Take fruit juice for stomach flu. If you have the stomach flu (which is not really a flu, or influenza, at all but generally some type of microbial infection, like food poisoning) and it is accompanied by diarrhea and/or vomiting, fruit juice will help resupply the potassium and other nutrients your body is losing.

Don't count on milk. Milk often hinders rather than helps stomachs because many people can't digest it easily (see LACTOSE INTOLERANCE).

Ease up on coffee, alcohol, and smoking. They irritate the stomach lining. Even decaf coffee bothers some people. And if you smoke, you can add this to the very long list of reasons to quit.

Pass on pepper. Red and black pepper are frequently identified as gastrointestinal irritants, so try skipping these to see if your stomach feels better. As far as spices, limit these only if you are sometimes bothered by them. Some people can eat spicy foods without ever experiencing unpleasant side effects, and if you're one of them, depriving your taste buds probably won't help your stomach and so may be unnecessary.

Opt for less fat. If your stomach has been acting up, reach for foods that are easy to digest, such as whole grains and lean protein. Avoid foods that are fried or high in fat, which can cause or aggravate stomach upset.

Increase fiber gradually. A high-fiber diet is good for your health, but don't go too high too fast. A gradual change of diet, with a slow but continual addition of fiber and extra fluids, will help your system adjust gradually.

Choose veggies carefully. You may love broccoli, but if you're having a problem with gas, cut back. Too much of certain gassy vegetables, namely broccoli, cauliflower, and brussels sprouts, can aggravate stomach woes.

Limit problematic fruits. Some people experience stomach discomfort from eating apples and melon. Pay attention to whether your stomach upset follows eating either of these. If so, you may need to choose other fruits instead to avoid upset.

Eat moderately. Stuffing your stomach can irritate it.

Cook gasless beans. If you throw out the water in which you've soaked the beans overnight, then cook them in fresh water, you'll significantly decrease their gas-causing potential. (See the more-detailed instructions in BELCHING.)

Track your diet. If you have been experiencing temporary stomach upset fairly often, try keeping a food diary for a few weeks to see if you can identify any links. Different foods bother different people. If you can identify the foods that you seem to be sensitive to, you can limit or avoid them—along with the trouble they cause you.

Exercise your body. Even a brief stroll, particularly after meals, may aid digestion and help an overstuffed or crampy stomach feel better.

Drink plenty of water. Aim for eight glasses of water a day to keep your stomach and intestines running smoothly.

No More Bland Diets

Here's some news your stomach will like: Remember the "bland diets" that people with ulcers and other stomach problems were condemned to eat? Just looking at those drab, tasteless foods was enough to make you feel sick to your stomach. Well fortunately, more-recent research has shown that boldly flavored foods usually don't bother the stomach. So you don't have to punish your taste buds to make your tummy feel better. However, high-fat foods *have* been shown to irritate the stomach, so opt for low-fat meals.

Check your calendar. Morning sickness is one possible cause of stomach upset in women who are capable of bearing children, so before you consider reaching for any medication or making any major changes in your diet to ease your stomach woes, you may want to be sure that pregnancy isn't the culprit.

Avoid laxatives. If constipation has your digestive system out of whack, go the more natural route and take bran or a commercial bulking agent such as Metamucil (with plenty of water) to get things moving again.

Lay off the aspirin. Aspirin and other nonsteroidal anti-inflammatory drugs, such as ibuprofen, can irritate the stomach. Choose acetaminophen or enteric-coated aspirin instead. Be sure to check the warnings in the box on page 21 first, though.

Investigate your medications. If you've recently started taking any new medication, whether prescription or over-the-counter, or increased the dose of your regular medication, ask your doctor or pharmacist if it could be causing your stomach upset. Many medications can trigger digestive discomfort, especially during the early days of treatment. A lower dose or different drug may be easier on your stomach, although it's possible that drug-related stomach upset will resolve on its own in a few days as your body adjusts to the drug.

Take an antacid. Antacids are very effective in soothing stomachs, but they can have side effects. For example, magnesium-based antacids can cause diarrhea, while calcium-based antacids can cause constipation. Antacids with aluminum hydroxide can also cause constipation. Be sure to read and follow the directions for use carefully to avoid additional side effects.

Try an antacid in tablet form. The dose in a tablet is lower than in liquid preparations and therefore may be less likely to contribute to secondary problems, such as constipation or diarrhea.

Switch brands. Sometimes, a different brand of antacid may prove more effective than your old favorite.

Don't take an antacid too long. Side effects from antacid use usually don't appear unless a person has taken the medication for several days. But if your stomach problem has persisted that long, it's time to call the doctor.

Relax. Stress can cause or exacerbate gastrointestinal ailments such as indigestion, irritable bowel syndrome, constipation, and diarrhea. Relieve stress by reducing the commitments in your schedule, going on vacation, learning to meditate, exercising, and/or taking up a hobby.

Sty

6 TREATMENT AND PREVENTION TIPS

It's just a tiny red bump at the root of an eyelash, but a sty can be mighty uncomfortable—and mighty unsightly.

A sty occurs when a gland at the root of an eyelash becomes blocked due to an infection. The gland swells and turns red, causing pain and discomfort. It may eventually come to a head as it fills with pus.

Doctors agree that you can take the first steps in treating and preventing sties at home. Here's how:

Use warm compresses. Heat increases circulation, so warming the skin near the gland will bring more infection-fighting white blood cells to the scene. Soak a *clean* washcloth in warm water—as warm as you can tolerate, but not hot enough to burn the sensitive skin in the eye area. Wring it out and place it on the eyelid for five minutes at a time. You may have to run the cloth through warm water several more times to keep it hot enough. Do this at least two or three times a day.

Do *not* squeeze, poke, push, or pick at the sty. You risk spreading the infection. Even if the sty has come to a head, don't try to pop it by squeezing it; let it drain on its own.

Skip eye makeup while the sty is present. Otherwise, you risk contaminating your makeup and applicators with bacteria.

Always practice good lid hygiene. To keep sties from returning, try washing the roots of your lashes each day with diluted baby shampoo or mild soap on a cotton ball or washcloth. An alternative is to use the over-the-counter cleanser Cetaphil, which won't sting or excessively dry the skin.

Remove eye makeup. Once the sty is gone and you start wearing makeup again, be diligent about removing it daily. In other words, don't be tempted to go to bed without washing off makeup first. And wash your eyelids again in the morning before re-applying makeup.

Don't share eye makeup or applicators. You wouldn't share your toothbrush, would you? Using a friend's or family member's eye makeup could pass infection to others, or vice versa.

Hello, Doctor?

Anytime a child has a swollen eyelid for more than 24 hours, it's time to see the doctor. Likewise, if an adult with a sty fails to see any improvement after applying warm compresses for two to three days, it's time to get medical attention.

Furthermore, if you're suffering from recurring sties or you have any sort of bump on the lid that remains for weeks or months, you need to see your doctor.

Sunburn Pain

23 Ways to Soothe or Prevent the Sizzle

The sun. People have worshipped it for thousands of years. But only in the last century have people worshipped the sun by intentionally baking themselves to a golden tan—or, as may be more often the case, an angry red burn—beneath it. But the sun can do much more damage than simply giving you a painful sunburn. Dermatologists (skin doctors) say that prolonged exposure to sunlight causes brown spots; red, scaly spots; drying and wrinkling; and, worst of all, skin cancer.

Although few things can penetrate the skin's outer layer (stratum corneum), the sun's ultraviolet rays easily pass

through this protective envelope and damage the cells and structures beneath. Ultraviolet rays that reach the Earth's surface come in two varieties: ultraviolet A (UVA), the so-called "tanning rays," which do not cause sunburn (except at very high doses), and ultraviolet B (UVB), the "burning rays." UVA rays can pass through window glass in

cars, houses, and offices, while UVB cannot. But both types penetrate the outer layer of the skin, cause damage, and contribute to the development of skin cancer.

Ultraviolet rays that pass through the stratum corneum cause pigment-producing cells called melanocytes to produce brown pigment (melanin). This is the skin's effort to protect itself from the invading rays and prevent further damage to skin structures, and it's how and why a "tan" develops. How much pigment the melanocytes can produce and how quickly they can produce it depends largely on genetics. Dark-skinned people more readily produce melanin, while light-skinned individuals, especially those of Northern European ancestry and Asians, don't produce it well or produce it in blotches that appear as freckles. These people can't tan no matter how hard they try and tend to be "quick fryers," readily burning even with mild sun exposure.

If your skin doesn't produce the protective melanin pigment well or if you're exposed to the sun before enough pigment can be manufactured and dispersed, the ultraviolet rays kill skin cells. Even a mild sunburn that produces only a little redness destroys the top layer of your skin, just as if you had seared it with a hot iron.

Damage to skin cells is more prevalent among fair-skinned people, and the immediate effect is a sunburn. Over time, the effects can be much more serious—blotchy brown spots and even skin cancer.

Ultraviolet light can even damage the dermis, the layer that gives your skin its shape, texture, strength, and elasticity. Sunlight breaks down the thick, strong tissue structure of the dermis, rendering it weak, thin, and less elastic and making it appear wrinkled and saggy. Indeed, you'd probably never expose yourself to a sunburn again if you could see the dramatic damage to your skin under a microscope—cells are shriveled and dead; formerly thick, red bundles of connective tissue have been ground into a gray smudge; thin-walled, superficial blood vessels are dilated and may be leaking fluid; and DNA sequences, the "software" that tells the skin how to repair and replicate itself, are damaged, causing the skin to produce abnormal precancerous cells and, in some cases, cancerous cells.

Easing the Pain

Despite these increasingly well-known dangers of sun exposure, many of us, on occasion, get lazy when it comes to protecting our skin or just can't resist the myth that getting some color from the sun makes us look healthier. If you've overexposed your skin to the sun and end up with a painful sunburn, the home remedies that follow can help make you a bit more comfortable until Mother Nature can heal the burn. Keep in mind, though, that these remedies cannot reverse the very real damage to your skin caused by unprotected exposure to the sun's rays. The best way to keep your skin from both pain and permanent damage is to stay out of the sun.

Apply cool compresses. Soak a washcloth in cool water and apply it directly to the burned areas (do not apply ice or an ice pack to sunburned skin) for several minutes, rewetting the cloth often to keep it cool. Apply the compress multiple times throughout the day as needed to relieve discomfort. You can also add a soothing ingredient, such as baking soda or oatmeal, to the compress water. Simply shake a bit of baking soda into the water before soaking the cloth. Or wrap dry oatmeal in a cheesecloth or a piece of gauze and run water through it. Then toss out the oatmeal and soak the compress in the oatmeal water.

Don't go back out there. Sunburned skin is much more vulnerable to additional burning, so plan on staying out

Hello, Doctor?

While sunburn discomfort can usually be treated at home with the remedies described here, you should call the doctor if:

- You have extensive blistering.
- You have a full-body burn.
- Your blisters break and become infected.
- You develop chills and a fever and feel shaky.
- You feel unwell, as if you have the flu.
- The pain and itching get worse after the first 24 hours.

of the sun for at least a few days to avoid further damage to your skin. Be aware that when you're outdoors during the day, even if you're in the shade, you're being exposed to ultraviolet light. While shade from a tree or an umbrella helps, much of the sunlight your skin is exposed to comes from light reflected off surfaces such as concrete, sand, water, even boat decks. Ultraviolet rays can also penetrate clothing. As much as 50 percent of the sun's damaging rays can get through clothing. So if you're already sunburned, indoors is the best place for you.

In addition to staying out of the sun, it's important to stay cool, too. A burn causes the skin's blood vessels to dilate and literally radiate heat from your skin. You'll be more comfortable if you drop the room temperature and keep it cool inside.

Cool off with a soak. Slipping into a tub of chilly water is a good way to cool the burn and ease the sting, especially if the burn is widespread or on a hard-to-reach area (such as your back). Avoid using soap, which can irritate and dry out the skin. If you feel you must use soap, use a mild one, such as Dove or Aveeno Bar, and rinse it off well. Definitely skip the washcloth, bath sponge, and loofah. Afterward, pat your skin gently with a soft towel.

If you're usually tempted to linger in the tub for hours, skip the bath and take a cool shower instead. Ironically, soaking too long can cause or aggravate dry skin, which can increase itching and peeling.

Toss in some oatmeal. Adding oatmeal or baking soda to bathwater may help soothe skin even more than applying it in a compress or just soaking in plain water. Prepare the oatmeal as you would for an oatmeal compress, holding the bundle under the faucet as the tub fills, or buy Aveeno oatmeal powder at your local pharmacy or health-food store and follow the directions. If you use baking soda, sprinkle it liberally into the water. Soak no longer than 15 to 20 minutes to avoid overdrying the skin.

Moisturize. The sun dries out the skin's surface and causes cells and blood vessels to leak, leading to even greater moisture loss. In addition, while cool baths and compresses can make you feel better, they can also end up robbing moisture from your injured skin. To prevent drying, apply moisturizer immediately after your soak. For cooling relief of pain and dryness, chill the moisturizer in the refrigerator before using.

Bring on the aloe vera. The thick, gel-like juice of the aloe vera plant causes blood vessels to constrict and can help ease the sting and limit redness if it's applied immediately to a new burn. Aloe vera plants are available at nurseries. Simply slit open one of the broad leaves and apply the gel directly to the burn. Apply five to six times per day for several days. (If your sunburn is extensive or you don't have a green thumb, you can purchase a bottle of plain aloe vera gel at many drugstores.)

Take an over-the-counter (OTC) pain reliever. Nonprescription pain relievers such as aspirin and ibuprofen can relieve pain and cut the inflammation of a sunburn. If aspirin and ibuprofen upset your stomach, consider taking OTC acetaminophen, which can help ease pain but won't relieve inflammation. Be sure to read the warnings in the box on page 21 before trying any of these, however.

Drink up. You can easily become dehydrated when you have a bad sunburn. Drink plenty of fluids, especially water, like you would if you had a fever. You can determine whether you're keeping adequately hydrated with a quick check in the bathroom: If your urine is relatively clear, you're doing fine. If it's dark, you need to drink more water.

Try a topical anesthetic. Topical anesthetics such as Solarcaine may offer some temporary relief from pain and itching. Look for products that contain lidocaine, which is less likely than some of the other topical anesthetics to cause an allergic reaction.

Because some people do have allergic reactions to such products, test a small area of skin before using it all over.

Topical anesthetics come in both creams and sprays. The sprays are easier to apply to a sunburn, especially when it is widespread. If you use one, avoid spraying it directly onto the face. Instead, spray some onto gauze and gently dab it on your face.

Get relief with hydrocortisone. OTC hydrocortisone creams or sprays can bring temporary relief from sunburn pain and itching. Look for those containing 0.05 percent or 1 percent hydrocortisone.

Watch for blistering. A serious sunburn can cause the skin to blister. Extensive blistering from a sunburn can be life threatening, so if your skin is covered with these sores, get medical attention immediately. If you have just a few tiny blisters, watch that they don't become infected; don't pop them or remove their protective skin covering.

Take a tincture of time. Ultimately, the one thing that will heal your sunburn is time. No product can speed the process. Even when your sunburn is healed, however, you'll need to be careful in the sun, because it'll take several months for your skin to return to its usual level of sensitivity. If you overdo it in the sun while your skin is still healing, your skin will burn faster and be more damaged than before.

Rising Danger?

For years, we've heard doctors warn us about the drying, wrinkling, burning, and cancer-causing effects of the sun. Many of us ignore those warnings because we think a golden-brown tan makes us look healthier and more attractive. But recently, scientists have found that the danger may be even worse than they thought.

Scientists know that the earth's layer of ozone, a gas that absorbs ultraviolet light and protects us from much of the damaging effects of the sun, is being destroyed at an alarming rate. Originally, scientists believed that the ozone depletion was centered only over the unpopulated South Pole. Australia, near the South Pole, already has the highest rate of deadly skin cancer (melanoma) in the world. Now, new evidence from the National Aeronautics and Space Administration (NASA) seems to suggest that a hole in the ozone layer may form over the northernmost parts of the United States, Canada, Europe, and Russia by about 2015.

Preventing Sunburn and Skin Damage

About one million Americans were diagnosed with some form of skin cancer in 2005. In fact, according to the Skin Cancer Foundation, the disease makes up one in three cancers diagnosed in this country. Fortunately, there is plenty you can do to protect your skin not only from the stinging pain of sunburn but also—and more importantly—from the cancer-causing effects of the sun.

Cover up. The Skin Cancer Foundation says that hats and clothing made of dark, tightly woven materials absorb ultraviolet light better than cotton fabrics in lighter shades. Dry fabrics offer more protection than wet ones.

Spread on sunscreen. The Centers for Disease Control and Prevention recommends wearing sunscreen with a sun protection factor (SPF) of at least 15. Be sure to spread on a thick enough layer: Applying only a thin coat of a sunscreen can reduce the effectiveness of the product by as much as 50 percent. Apply the sunscreen 20 to 30 minutes before exposure to allow the skin to absorb it. And reapply it every two hours—more often if you're sweating or getting wet. If you have fair skin, you might even want to begin preparing for sun exposure the night before by putting on a layer of sunscreen before bed; this will allow it to be thoroughly absorbed into the skin's outer layer. Then apply the usual coat of sunscreen the next day, about a half hour before you go outside.

Protect your ears. Too often, people forget to protect sensitive spots like the tops of the ears, the hairline and the scalp where the hair is parted, the "V" of the chest, the nose, and the hands. The Skin Cancer Foundation says 80 percent of skin cancers occur on the head, neck, and hands. The Foundation therefore recommends that you wear a hat made of a tightly woven fabric such as canvas rather than one of straw and that you wear a sunscreen with SPF 15 on your hands and other exposed skin. Protruding horizontal surfaces like the nose present special sun-protection challenges. Lifeguards often wear zinc oxide paste on their noses, but it only provides an SPF of about seven. Instead, apply a sunscreen with an SPF of at least 15, let it soak in a few minutes, and then, for maximum protection, apply the zinc oxide paste. And if you'll be going shoeless, use the same level of protection on the tops of your feet.

Protect yourself from reflected light. Keep in mind that even umbrellas or shade trees provide only moderate protection from ultraviolet light, and they don't protect you from rays reflected off sand, snow, concrete, and many other surfaces. Ultraviolet light isn't reflected by water, but it can easily penetrate water, so being in the water doesn't protect you, either. Be careful to protect surfaces, such as the under part of the chin, that are especially vulnerable to reflected light.

Be careful between 10:00 A.M. and 4:00 P.M. The sun's rays are most intense during this time of the day, so stay indoors, or if you must be outdoors, cover up and wear sunscreen.

Take care on cool, cloudy days. Ultraviolet light can penetrate cloud cover. Take precautions even when the sun isn't shining brightly.

Don't let the snow fool you. During the winter months, many winter recreationists, such as snow skiers, learn the hard way that high altitudes (which have little atmosphere to filter out the sun's rays), blustery winds, and white snow can be a painful combination. Cover up with appropriate clothing and a sunscreen with an SPF of at least 15. Don't forget to wear sunglasses, too, to avoid "sunburning" your eyes.

Don't leave out your lips. The sun can burn the sensitive skin on the lips just as easily as it fries the rest of your body. At worst, the damage can lead to skin cancer. Use a lip balm with an SPF of at least 15 and reapply often.

Avoid sunbathing. Doctors can't say it enough: There is no such thing as a "healthy tan." But while sunbathing is a no-no for everyone, it's an especially bad idea for fair-skinned people. Many of them can't tan anyway and only risk getting a serious burn.

If you refuse to give up sunbathing, take it slowly and allow your skin to gradually build up melanin to provide some protection. And don't use tanning oils, which enhance the effects of ultraviolet rays and worsen the burn. You may as well be slathering yourself with cooking oil.

Watch for photosensitivity. Some drugs, such as tetracycline and diuretics, can make your skin extra sensitive to sun exposure and increase the risk of sunburn. Some herbal medicines, such as Saint-John's-wort, have a similar effect. Talk to your doctor or pharmacist about this possibility if you are taking any medications.

Stay out of tanning booths. In search of "safe" tanning, many people resort to tanning booths or tanning beds. While tanning companies will tell you their light machines produce only the nonburning UVA type of radiation, those UVA rays are far from safe. In fact, UVA rays penetrate the skin more deeply than UVB rays do. Over time, exposure to UVA rays can make skin dry and wrinkled and increase the risk of skin cancer.

Swimmer's Ear

5 Ways to Avoid It

The water, the sun, plenty of swimming and splashing around—to many people, these are the ingredients for a perfect summer day spent by the pool or at the beach. Add a painful ear infection to the picture, however, and the scenario quickly slides downhill. That's what can happen to you if swimmer's ear strikes, unless you know how to prevent it.

Swimmer's ear is an infection of the outer ear canal caused sometimes by fungus but most commonly by bacteria. The frequent, prolonged exposure to water that occurs when someone swims regularly can wash away the oily, waxy substance that normally lines and protects the ear canal. In addition, even after the swimmer leaves the pool or pond, water can remain in the ear canal, creating a warm, moist environment perfect for breeding bacteria.

Despite the name, however, these external ear infections don't just occur in swimmers or in the summertime. Water can enter and pool in the outer ear canal after showers, too. And sometimes, exposure to water isn't required at all. Inserting anything into the ear, including a cotton swab, key, or fingernail, can scratch the skin in the ear canal and open the door to infection.

No matter its cause, swimmer's ear usually first advertises its presence with an itching or tingling sensation in the ear. Resisting the urge to scratch is essential, however, since rubbing or digging in the ear will only make the problem worse. The next symptom to appear is generally mild to severe pain in the external ear. Indeed, one way to distinguish swimmer's ear from an infection in the middle or inner ear is to gently tug on the earlobe, wiggle it, and move it back and forth. If such manipulation hurts, you likely have an outer-ear infection, or swimmer's ear. In more serious cases, pain is accompanied by discharge from the ear and even some hearing loss due to swelling

of the ear canal. For anything more than a mild, temporary case of swimmer's ear, you should see a doctor right away (see "Hello, Doctor?" on this page).

So that you won't have to suffer through any of this, here's what you can do to prevent swimmer's ear:

Watch where you swim. Avoid jumping into pools, ponds, lakes, oceans, or any other body of water in which the water may not be clean. Dirty water means more bacteria.

Get the water out. A key to preventing swimmer's ear is to not let water sit in the ear. If you feel or hear water swishing around in your ear after a shower or swim, try shaking your head in the direction of the affected ear to dislodge the water.

Add a few drops. Over-the-counter antiseptic eardrops, such as Aqua Ear, Ear Magic, or Swim Ear, used after swimming may help prevent or ease the problem for those who swim a lot and are already familiar with the symptoms of swimmer's ear. According to the Academy of Otolaryngology–Head & Neck Surgery, as long as you have a normal eardrum and your doctor says it's safe for you, you can also use a homemade antiseptic mixture: In a small, clean container or bottle, mix equal amounts rubbing alcohol and white vinegar, then use a clean dropper to instill a couple drops in each ear after swimming or bathing. The white vinegar kills bacteria and fungus. The alcohol absorbs water and may also help kill bacteria and fungi. (You can buy a dropper bottle at a pharmacy.) Along the same lines, some regular swimmers use a couple drops of rubbing alcohol or a mixture of equal parts white vinegar and clean water in each ear after leaving the water to keep the ears dry and free from infection.

Cover your head. While a swim cap may not afford much protection for a competitive swimmer whose head is constantly in the water, it may keep water out of the ears of a casual swimmer or someone doing water exercises. Choose a swim cap that covers the ears tightly.

Stay out of your ears. You can exacerbate a mild case of swimmer's ear or promote infection by poking, swabbing, or scratching inside your ears. The wax produced in the ear is antibacterial and forms a natural protective barrier against moisture and minor irritation. So don't make it your goal in life to rid your ears of wax. And don't put anything in your ear that's smaller than your elbow. (If you're concerned that heavy wax buildup might be hindering your hearing, see an ear doctor, who can tell for sure and, if necessary, remove the extra wax safely.)

Hello, Doctor?

A mild case of swimmer's ear with only minor discomfort may improve if you keep your ears dry (do not swim while you have any type of ear infection) and use antiseptic eardrops for a few days. But if you have persistent pain in your ear that lasts more than an hour, if there's discharge from the ear, or if your hearing is affected, see a physician immediately. The Academy of Otolaryngology–Head & Neck Surgery cautions that if you have ever had a perforated, punctured, ruptured, or otherwise injured eardrum or have had ear surgery, you should consult an ear doctor before you go swimming and before you use any type of eardrops.

Tartar and Plaque

15 TIPS TO CONTROL THEM

Advertising claims have added the terms "tartar" and "plaque" to the vocabulary of the average American, as products promise to rid our mouths of these pesky substances. How true are these claims? And what roles do tartar and plaque play in our oral health?

For starters, let's define the two players. Plaque, which is by far the most villainous, is a soft, sticky, nearly invisible film of bacteria that accumulates on teeth and dental restorations (fillings, crowns, and dentures, for example) and on the gums and the tongue. Some of the bacteria in plaque cause tooth decay, and some are responsible for periodontal, or gum, disease. Plaque is always with us. A newborn baby's mouth is sterile, but only for the first ten hours or so of life.

Tartar is a calcified material that often contains bacterial debris and sometimes plaque. It's a white, chalky substance. Although tartar (also called calculus) can make it easier for plaque to stick around, the stuff is generally considered to be primarily a cosmetic problem.

Plaque is the culprit in cavities and gum disease. The longer plaque hangs

around in your mouth, the more trouble it causes. As certain bacteria in plaque feed off fermentable carbohydrates (which include sugars, even those in fruit and milk, and starchy foods such as breads, pastas, and crackers), they produce an acid that eats away at tooth enamel, causing cavities. Other bacteria infect the gums, producing the first symptoms of gum disease, such as redness, inflammation, and bleeding. If left untreated, gum disease may progress to the point that the infection literally destroys the bone that holds the teeth roots in place. That's why gum disease is the major cause of tooth loss among adults over age 35.

Both plaque and tartar can form above and below the gum line. It takes a dentist or dental hygienist to remove tartar from anywhere in the mouth and to remove plaque from below the gum line. And regular, professional cleanings—as often as your dentist recommends—will help make your dental care at home more effective. It's also important to have the condition of your gums checked through a periodontal probing during your checkups. Make dental checkups and cleanings part of your annual health-care routine, along with blood-pressure readings and cancer screenings.

You can keep plaque under control and prevent it from destroying your smile, but it takes a little time and effort. Since the alternative is painful gum disease and tooth loss, it's worth it. Here's what you can do:

Brush. Focus on quality, not quantity. You may brush after every meal, snack, or sip of soda, but if your technique is lousy, you won't be doing your teeth much good.

The American Dental Association (ADA) recommends the following method:

1. Hold the brush at a 45-degree angle against the gum line. Point the brush upward, or toward your nose, when you're cleaning the upper teeth; downward, or toward your chin, when you're doing the lower teeth. Working the bristles at this angle will ensure that you clean the gum line, which too many brushers miss.

2. Use a short (about the width of half a tooth) back-and-forth motion to clean the outer surfaces of your teeth. Focus on just one or two teeth at a time. And be gentle; you're not scrubbing the floor or the bathtub. Brushing too hard can damage the gums and the teeth.

3. Use this same stroke on the inside surfaces of all the teeth, except the front ones. Remember to keep the

The Foods You Eat

"Grazing" all day long can be cruel to your teeth. Every time you eat, you also feed the plaque in your mouth. Those bacteria like to feast on far more than the simple sugars that we all know can cause cavities. They like all "fermentable carbohydrates"—that includes starches such as bread, crackers, and pasta. Natural sugars, such as honey and molasses, are tasty to the bacteria, too, as are the sugars found in fruits and even milk.

You can't stop eating all of these foods, of course, but you can try to adopt some habits that are kinder and gentler to your teeth. Try the following strategies:

Limit how often you consume sugary foods and drinks. If you would rather lose a limb than give up sweets, relax. At least in terms of your dental health, the amount of sugar you consume is less important than how often you consume it. Having a soda with lunch or a slice of cake after dinner is fine, provided you brush afterward. But sucking on hard candy all day long or always having an open can of soda at your desk creates a constant sugar bath in your mouth, giving bacterial plaque an uninterrupted flow of carbohydrates to feed on.

Be a straw man—or woman. Use a straw when sipping soda and other cold drinks that contain sugar. Try to position the straw in the back of your mouth to limit how much of the beverage swishes around your teeth and gums. Studies suggest that people who sip soda through straws have healthier teeth.

Chew sugarless gum. The gum stimulates the flow of saliva, which helps cleanse the mouth and protect the teeth.

Choose tooth-healthy snacks. Munch on raw vegetables, crunchy fruits like apples (which, though they contain natural sugars, are low on the danger-to-teeth list), plain peanuts, and cheeses. The French have the right idea, apparently, with ending a meal by eating cheese (although some varieties are high in fat and sodium, so you may need to be selective to protect other aspects of your health). Drink plain club soda or unsweetened or artificially sweetened tea, coffee, or soda instead of sugar-containing drinks.

brush angled (at 45 degrees) toward the gum line.

4. Scrub the chewing surfaces of your back teeth with the brush held flat in the same back-and-forth motion.

5. Tilt the brush vertically, and use the front (or top) part of the brush in short up-and-down strokes to clean the inside surfaces of the front teeth, both top and bottom.

6. Don't forget to brush your tongue. It can harbor disease-causing plaque, too.

Use the right tools. The ADA recommends a soft nylon brush that has rounded-end, polished bristles. Hard bristles (as well as brushing too hard) can wear away the enamel that protects your teeth and can form grooves in the teeth. What's more, abrasive bristles can damage tender gums, causing them to recede, or pull away, from the teeth. Get a brush with a head that's small enough to reach all of your teeth, especially those in the back. Some adults may actually prefer using a child-sized brush. Don't be stingy with toothbrushes, either—replace your brush every three months, or sooner if the bristles become frayed, splayed, or worn.

Don't worry about going high-tech. An old-fashioned manual toothbrush can clean teeth just as effectively as any electric product. But if your manual dexterity's limited or you think having a cool gadget will make you brush longer and more often, an electric brush may be worth it.

Use a fluoride toothpaste. Choose a product with the ADA's seal of acceptance. What's so wonderful about fluoride? It combines with the minerals in saliva to "remineralize," or strengthen, the teeth, preventing cavities in both children and adults. You may think you don't get cavities anymore, but as you get older, your gums recede, exposing the roots of teeth, which lack the protective coating of enamel and are prone to a type of decay known as root caries.

Try a tartar-control toothpaste. If you tend to develop a lot of tartar, using such a product can help. While these toothpastes don't eliminate tartar altogether, studies show that they can reduce tartar deposits by 30 to 40 percent. Chemicals such as pyrophosphate in tartar-control pastes interfere with the deposition of calcium salt.

Floss. Too many people think of flossing simply as a way to dislodge the roast beef or popcorn kernels stuck between their teeth. But regular (once a day, at the very least) use of dental floss is essential for cleaning between teeth and under the gums and warding off both cavities and gum disease.

Here's how to floss correctly:

1. Start with 18 to 24 inches of floss, and wind most of it around the middle or index finger on one hand (whichever finger is the most comfortable for you).

2. Wrap the rest of the floss around the same finger on the other hand. Think of this other finger as the take-up spool for the used floss. Don't scrimp. Use a clean section of floss as you work between each pair of teeth. Otherwise, you're just moving bacteria from one tooth to another.

3. Hold the floss tightly with your thumbs and forefingers, leaving about an inch of floss between them. The floss should be taut.

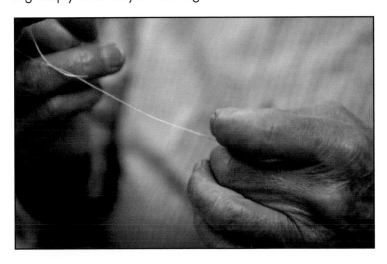

4. Use a gentle "sawing" motion as you pull the floss between the teeth. Be careful not to snap it into the tender gum tissue.

5. When you've reached the gum line, curve the floss into a "C" shape to fit snugly around the tooth, and slide

Plaque Fighters: Can You Toss the Floss?

In recent years, the makers of various toothpastes, rinses, and other oral-care treatments have promoted their products for reducing plaque and even treating gingivitis, the early stage of gum disease. But in 2005, the courts decided that Pfizer, the company that makes Listerine mouthwash, had gone too far.

Advertisements for Listerine had been claiming that the mouthwash removes plaque between teeth and reduces the risk of gingivitis just as well as flossing. Dentists were outraged. So was at least one of Pfizer's competitors, who sued to force the company to quit making its bold claim. Pfizer officials pointed to two studies showing that swishing with Listerine and flossing were equally effective for cleaning out plaque and fighting gingivitis. But a federal judge decided that the studies were flawed, since the flossers were unsupervised—meaning they may have done a poor job or skipped flossing altogether some days. The judge ordered that the bold claims be stricken from Listerine ads.

There is evidence that using a mouth rinse such as Listerine can be a helpful addition to your daily oral-care routine. But the American Dental Association emphasizes that your routine should include brushing at least twice a day and cleaning between teeth with floss or some other interproximal cleaner.

it gently into the space between the gum and tooth.

6. Bring the floss out from the gum and scrape the side of the tooth, following its contour from bottom to top to remove as much plaque as possible. After you pull it out, use a clean section of floss to clean the tooth on the other side of that space.

7. Be sure to clean the back side of the last tooth on each side, both top and bottom.

Relax about wax. Don't worry about choosing between waxed or unwaxed floss. Pick what's comfortable. Flavored flosses are fine, too, especially if you find yourself using them more frequently. If your fingers are too awkward, you suffer from arthritis, or you have a lot of bridgework, floss threaders and/or any of the various floss holders may help; they're available at drugstores.

Know that there's no substitute for flossing. Flossing is the best way to clean between your teeth. No other method works nearly as well. But if you absolutely, positively refuse to floss, ask your dentist or hygienist about alternatives. Some dentists recommend soft interproximal cleaners, like Stim-u-Dents (the rubber tips on some toothbrushes). Interproximal brushes, which look like tiny bottle brushes, work, too, but won't always fit in tight spaces between teeth. Oral irrigators can help hose down the nooks and crannies in your teeth, too, but these products are not a replacement for flossing. A word of caution: Don't use Stim-u-Dents or oral irrigators until after you've brushed your teeth; otherwise, you could end up pushing debris or plaque deeper into a pocket.

Test yourself. Disclosing tablets or solution, available at drugstores, can reveal the plaque that's left after you've brushed and flossed. At first, you may be shocked by how much plaque you've been missing, but don't get discouraged. While it's impossible to remove every bit of this bacterial nuisance, using these tablets can show where you're not cleaning thoroughly and help you improve your brushing and flossing skills.

Wet your whistle. Saliva naturally cleanses the mouth and helps fight bacteria. But dry mouth is a side effect of some 300 to 400 different medications, including antidepressants, antihistamines, and drugs used to treat high blood pressure and Parkinson's disease. A disease called Sjogren's syndrome, which can accompany some rheumatoid conditions, also slows down the flow of saliva (and causes dry eyes, too). If you've had radiation therapy to the head and neck for cancer, your salivary glands may have been damaged. You can fight dry mouth with sugarless gum or candy or with artificial saliva, available without a prescription. It's also wise to take frequent sips of water. And because dry mouth tends to worsen during sleep, try coating your lips, mouth, and tongue with mineral oil (then spitting it out) before getting into bed (but after brushing and flossing).

Don't rely on "miracle" rinses. The commercials on television look so appealing: A swig of this product, a few swishes in the mouth, and, almost like magic, all that nasty plaque is gone. If only it were that simple. You can't rinse away plaque and tartar.

Only two products have the acceptance of the ADA's Council on Dental Therapeutics for reducing plaque: Peridex, available by prescription only, contains 0.12 percent chlorhexidine, a powerful germ-fighter, and over-the-counter Listerine, which relies on a combination of oils, including menthol, eucalyptol, and thymol, along with alcohol. However, even if you add one of these rinses to your daily oral health-care regimen, you still need to brush and floss.

Teething

8 TIPS TO EASE BABY'S DISCOMFORT

Drooling. Gum inflammation. Irritation. Fussiness. Anyone who has cared for a baby knows well the symptoms of teething, the process of the first set of 20 teeth (known as primary, or baby, teeth) erupting through the surface of

the gums. The primary teeth, which form before the baby is born, usually begin surfacing around six or seven months of age with a single lower central incisor. But, like many things in nature, there is a wide range of "normal" when it comes to the timing of tooth eruption. Don't be surprised, then, if a baby starts sprouting choppers at 2 months or doesn't begin teething until he or she is 12 months old.

In general, teeth begin to appear on the following schedule: the central incisors, the teeth right in the middle of the jaw on the top and bottom, come in at 6 to 12 months; lateral incisors at 9 to 13 months; canine (cuspids) at 16 to 22 months;

the first molars at 13 to 19 months; and the second molars at 25 to 33 months. Most children have all of their primary teeth by age three.

The process of teething, or "cutting" all of these baby teeth, can be painful for both the baby and the caregivers. When a tooth pushes through the sensitive gum mucosa, it hurts, and the baby is likely to become cranky and fussy. But no two babies respond to teething in the same way. Some infants seem to sail through the process of cutting new teeth without so much as a whimper; others struggle through each and every eruption. How long teething lasts varies widely, too. Some baby teeth burst through the gums in just a few hours. In other cases, the tiny teeth may take days to emerge.

Teething symptoms often include crankiness, drooling, chewing, crying, gum redness, decreased appetite, and difficulty sleeping. In addition, some babies spit up and have mild diarrhea due to gastrointestinal reactions to changes in the character and amount of their own saliva. Other babies develop a red and slightly swollen rash on the cheeks, chin, neck, and chest from the saliva's contact with the skin. Sometimes, teething causes babies to develop a mild fever, congestion, and ear pulling that often mimics middle-ear infection. All of these symptoms are normal. (But of course, if you are worried, you can always call your pediatrician's office just to put your mind at ease.)

Knowing that your baby's suffering is normal, however, doesn't necessarily make it any easier for you to witness. So try the hints that follow to help ease your baby's discomfort during teething.

Massage those gums. Gentle pressure can help relieve teething pain. Softly rub the baby's gums with a clean finger.

Cool it. Giving the baby something cold to chew on not only helps soothe inflamed gums, but it can distract the child. A washcloth soaked in water and then frozen or a chilled pacifier will work, though something tasty—such as a frozen banana or cold carrot wrapped in a thin washcloth or cheese cloth—might keep the baby preoccupied longer. You'll need to hold the washcloth for the child, however, to guard against choking. You can also let the child suck on an ice cube, but only if it's wrapped in a washcloth, too, because chewing directly on ice could damage the child's gums. The washcloth also allows you to comfortably hold the ice

cube for the child and prevent it from slipping into the child's throat.

Baby-bottle it. Try this trick: Fill a baby bottle with water or juice, tip it upside down so the liquid flows into the nipple, and place it in the freezer in that position until frozen. The baby can then happily gum the bottle's frozen nipple. Just be sure to check the nipple from time to time to be sure it's still all in one piece.

Let 'em chew. Chewing can help teeth work their way through the gums, so keep your baby's jaws moving. Any object is fair game as long as it's clean, nontoxic, chewable, and either too large or too small to block the child's airway should it get swallowed. You might try giving the baby an apple wedge wrapped in a washcloth that you hold. Commercial teething biscuits are a good choice, too (although they

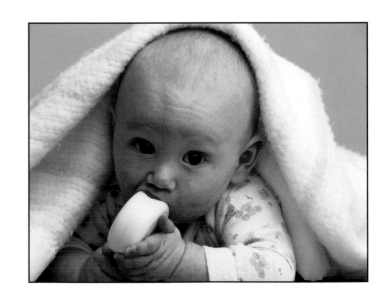

Hello, Doctor?

Sometimes, teething symptoms can mimic other, more serious health problems. Call the doctor if the baby develops:

• A very severe rash that covers the back, arms, and legs. This may indicate a bacterial or viral infection.
• A sustained fever or pus in the eyes. The baby may have a respiratory infection.
• Fever, fussiness, vomiting/diarrhea, and pulling on or gesturing to the ear. The baby may have an ear infection.

can be messy), and slightly stale bagels make excellent baby chewies. Of course there's also a seemingly endless variety of commercial teethers available, too.

Distract them. The best solution may be to keep your baby's mind off his or her sore gums. Try playing together with a favorite toy or rocking or dancing around with the child in your arms. Sometimes, a rousing game of peekaboo is all that's needed to distract baby from the discomfort.

Try pain relievers. An over-the-counter pain reliever that's designed specifically for children, such as children's-strength liquid acetaminophen (Children's Liquid Tylenol is one brand), can offer relief for up to four hours. (Contact your pediatrician if you have any questions about what or how much pain reliever you can safely give to your teething child.) You can't give children pain relievers around the clock, however, so save them for when they are most needed—such as bed-

time or when nothing else is helping. Be sure to follow the package directions carefully, and don't give the medicine more often than three times in 24 hours.

Numb those gums. Commercial oral anesthetic teething gels (for example, Orajel and Anbesol) give temporary relief (30 to 40 minutes worth) and can often get baby through a difficult time.

Keep a towel handy. Teething often causes plenty of drooling, and the saliva can cause skin irritation that will only make baby feel more uncomfortable. Keep a soft towel handy to wipe off the baby's mouth and chin area. If that isn't enough, protect the skin with petroleum jelly or zinc oxide ointment.

Temporomandibular Joint (TMJ) Problems

6 STRATEGIES TO EASE THE ACHE

If you experience frequent headaches, bothersome clicking and popping in the jaw, or pain in the face, neck, or shoulders, the problem may literally be all in your head. You may be suffering from a misalignment of the temporomandibular joint (TMJ), the joint that allows your jaw to open, close, and move sideways. The American Dental Association estimates that as many as ten million Americans may have what's known in dental circles as TMJ Disorder or Dysfunction (TMJD) or TMJ Syndrome (TMJS). Unfortunately, it's a condition that often goes undiagnosed or misdiagnosed and untreated.

Five pairs of muscles and the temporomandibular joints that connect the upper and lower jawbones allow you to open and close your mouth and control the forward, backward, and side-to-side movements of the lower jawbone. Any problem that prevents this complex system of muscles, ligaments, bones, and joints from working together may result in the pain and other problems known as TMJD.

The jaw joints can become misaligned from a variety of causes—teeth that don't fit together properly due to genetics, orthodontia, or grinding (bruxism); habits such as cradling the phone between the ear and shoulder; or injuries such as whiplash or a blow to the jaw. Stress plays a major role, too, and people often experience their first TMJ discomfort during stressful times.

Not everyone who has misaligned jaw joints experiences severe symptoms. In some cases, conservative home care can alleviate pain and discomfort. In others, professional help is important.

The following are some tips for coping with your TMJ problem. If the conservative treatments described here don't give you relief, seek help from a dentist, preferably one who is a TMJ specialist.

Is It TMJ Disorder?

One unfortunate aspect of TMJD is that it's difficult to diagnose. If you answer yes to more than two of the following questions, you may indeed want to further pursue the possibility that TMJD is the cause of your symptoms by consulting a TMJ specialist (see "Find a TMJ Pro" on page 287):

- Do you have frequent headaches, especially in the morning?
- Do you clench or grind your teeth?
- Have you noticed any of your teeth, especially the eye teeth, wearing down?
- Do your jaw muscles feel tender?
- Does your jaw sometimes (or always) make popping or clicking sounds when you open your mouth?
- Do you have difficulty opening your mouth?
- Do you have facial pain? Neck pain? Pain in more than one tooth? Shoulder pain?
- Is it painful to chew, yawn, or open your mouth widely?
- Does your jaw ever get stuck open or closed?
- Do you have pain in or around the ear?
- Do your ears feel stuffy or itchy?
- Do you suffer from earaches without ear infections?
- Do you have ringing, roaring, hissing, or buzzing in the ears?
- Do you often feel dizzy?

Massage those jaws. Pain can come from muscle spasms. Massaging the jaw joints, which lie just in front of the ears, will help relax tight muscles.

Heat them up. Heat is an excellent muscle relaxant. Use a heating pad or hot-water bottle to ease aching jaw, neck, and shoulder muscles. Be careful to keep the heat low enough not to cause burns to the skin in these sensitive areas, though.

Cool it down. Ice packs placed on the jaw joints are excellent for relieving pain. To combat both muscle tightness and pain, you might also try alternating heat and cold treatments; apply

heat for about 20 minutes, followed by cold for about five or ten minutes, switching between the two until you achieve relief.

Take an over-the-counter (OTC) pain reliever. OTC aspirin, acetaminophen, or ibuprofen can relieve pain in the muscles. Aspirin or ibuprofen can also help bring down any inflammation that may be present. Be sure to review the analgesic warnings in the box on page 21 before taking any of these, however.

Teach an old dog new tricks. Become aware of and eliminate habits—such as resting your chin in your hand, cradling the phone between your shoulder and cheek, or clenching your teeth—that tend to stress the jaw joint. If you work at a desk, sit up straight in a supportive chair and raise your work surface if necessary to prevent yourself from hunching over with your chin propped on your hand. If you need to use both hands while talking on the phone, invest in a headset or use the speaker setting if available. And, if you often catch yourself unconsciously clenching your teeth while reading or working, try holding a cork gently between your front teeth to keep your jaws separated and relaxed.

Relax. Stress is a major contributor to TMJ problems. Relaxation techniques such as deep breathing, yoga, or progressive relaxation (in which you consciously tense and relax muscles starting with the head and working down the body to the feet) can help relieve stress, as can an enjoyable hobby or regular exercise.

You might also try visualization exercises to let go of stress. Find a quiet, comfortable place where you won't be disturbed. Close your eyes and take a couple of slow, deep breaths. Now, imagine yourself in one of your favorite places—a beach, a mountain meadow, a country lane. Imagine what you would feel, see, hear, and smell if you were really there. Feel yourself relaxing in this special place. Tell yourself there's nothing you have to do, nowhere else you have to go. After several minutes of enjoying this visualization, take another couple of slow, deep breaths and slowly open your eyes. You may find that you feel amazingly relaxed and refreshed from this "mental vacation."

Find a TMJ Pro

If you suspect or have been told that you have TMJD, and self-care hasn't relieved your symptoms, you need professional help. A dentist may need to create a special mouthpiece, or "splint," to help the muscles relax, especially at night. The jaw may need to be permanently realigned through subtle shaping of the tooth surface (equilibration), moving teeth (orthodontics), or moving bony structures (orthopedics). In a few cases, surgery is even required.

That's why it's best to find a dentist who has extensive training and/or experience in the treatment of TMJ problems. Successful treatment may also require the services of an orthopedist; a neurologist; an ear, nose, and throat specialist; and a physical therapist or chiropractor. And if you're struggling with reducing or coping better with stress, you might benefit from a visit with a mental-health professional. Look for professionals with whom you feel comfortable and who will take the time to explain things to you.

You can ask for a referral from your regular dentist, contact your local dental association, or check the yellow pages to locate a TMJ specialist. Then use the following questions to help evaluate candidates and ensure that you get the expert care you need:
- What is your experience in treating TMJD?
- What special training have you received in treating TMJD?
- How many TMJD patients have you treated? What is your success rate in relieving TMJ problems?
- How long does treatment usually last? How much does it cost?
- How do you feel about a team treatment approach? What specialists do you typically use?

You simply need to find something that helps you relax, then incorporate it into your daily life.

Tendinitis

17 Ways to Take Care of Your Tendons

Sometimes, it's hard to tell what hurts more: The constant throbbing of the tendinitis itself or the fact that you can't do all the activities you were doing before you got sidelined by the pain. Tendons are sinewy connective-tissue fibers that attach muscle to bone. Tendinitis is a warning flare sent up by a tendon that has become inflamed, usually as a result of your doing too much of what you thought was a good thing. Tendinitis also lets you know, in no uncertain terms, when you're working at too quick a pace—on a keyboard or at the track—without the proper training or warm-up. (Tendinitis in the arm is sometimes confused with another repetitive-movement disorder, CARPAL TUNNEL SYNDROME, which affects a tendon that runs through the wrist.)

As you're swearing to yourself that you'll take it easier and warm up properly next time, here are some tips you can try to help you through today's pain and get back in the game:

Ice the area. When a tendon flares up, cold can reduce the inflammation. Pick up a reusable cold pack or wrap a thin towel around a plastic bag filled with ice, an unopened bag of frozen peas, or a resealable bag filled with frozen popcorn kernels, and apply it to the tender tendon. Ice the area for five to ten minutes, three or four times a day, until the symptoms subside.

Cup the pain. Create a nifty ice massager by filling a paper or foam cup with cold water and putting it in the freezer. Once the water has frozen, tear off the lip of the cup to expose a layer of ice. Place a thin, wet towel on the affected area, and rub the ice over it. As the ice melts, tear off more of the cup. Put your homemade ice massager back in the freezer between uses.

Get help from aspirin. Aspirin and ibuprofen are two over-the-counter anti-inflammatory medications that can help alleviate pain and stiffness. (Aceta-minophen can help reduce pain, but it does not reduce inflammation or speed the healing process.) Before taking either one, though, check out the warn-ings in the box on page 21.

Elevate the area. If possible, keep the affected tendon propped up above the level of the heart to help control swelling.

Tape it. An elastic bandage wrapped around the affected knee, ankle, or elbow may help support the joint and keep swelling to a minimum. However, the bandage will be of no use if it is not wrapped properly and securely (but never too tightly). Read package instructions or consult a health-care practitioner, and check the fingers or toes beyond the bandage often for signs (such as cold or pale skin) that it is wrapped too tightly.

Splint it. Some experts recommend a splint instead of tape because it's stiffer and can be used to keep the affected area in a neutral position.

Consider cross-training. Since tendinitis is often brought on by a constant, repetitive motion, you may want to alternate your favorite exercise with other ones. It will minimize the chance that you'll overwork one set of muscles, which can leave the tendons prone to tendinitis. For instance, swimming doesn't pound the legs the way running does, so it's a good alternate exercise for regular joggers. Cross-

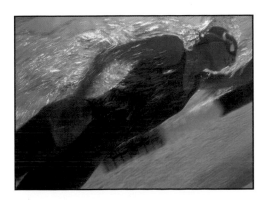

training can be as simple as alternating days of swimming with days of jogging. Such cross-training also allows you to exercise different muscle groups on different days, increasing your overall fitness.

Build up your body. Before undertaking an exercise routine, such as running or swimming, condition the muscles you'll be depending on to get you through. Weight training is the best way to firm up specific muscle groups. Do arm or leg curls, for instance, with free weights or on a weight-training machine.

Warm up before you warm up. For the physically active, stretching is synonymous with warming up. But there's more to it than a few tugs and pulls. Before doing any stretches, you should do some form of mild, body-warming aerobic exercise for a few minutes, since stretching cold muscles can lead to tendinitis. A pre-warm-up warm-up

can take the form of jogging in place, jumping rope, taking a brief and leisurely ride on a stationary bike, or even walking. (If walking is the activity

Check Your Shoes' Warning Signs

Wearing the right shoes when you're working out is important, but so is wearing those shoes correctly. Once the shoes are laced up, your feet should be able to wiggle a bit but not slip around. If your shoes are too loose, your body must work harder to keep your feet in the proper position. And if your shoes are too tight, you won't be giving your feet and legs the natural maneuverability they need to perform properly.

In addition, look at the sole below each heel. Has either sole worn unevenly? If so, you may need more than new shoes—you may also need orthotics. These specially made shoe inserts help correct for structural discrepancies, such as pronation (your feet tend to roll inward as they land) or supination (your feet rotate outward). By setting the foot right, your whole body will work right when you're active, and it's less likely tendinitis will stop you. If you suspect your tendinitis is due to excessive pronation or supination, see a podiatrist or sports-medicine physician to get proper orthotics.

you'll be engaging in as exercise, you can warm up simply by walking at a slower pace than you'll be using in your workout; the same holds for running and swimming.)

Stretch painlessly. Stretch until you feel resistance in the muscle, but no farther. If it hurts, you're going too far. Also, perform each stretch gently and slowly, without bouncing or jerking.

Take it slow. If you're starting a new exercise activity or getting back into an old one after a bout of tendinitis, start off with an abbreviated, not-too-taxing routine.

Run one or two miles instead of four or five; cycle on a flat course, not on hilly terrain; walk at a moderate pace rather than at top speed.

Wear the right shoes. These days, you can find athletic footwear specially designed for virtually every type of activity, and it behooves you to take advantage of that variety whenever possible. If you think your tennis shoes will give you the support and cushioning you need for running, you could be—quite literally—sorely mistaken. When buying a new pair of shoes for a specific activity, think about the kinds of stress the activity places on your feet and legs, and choose shoes with features that can help lessen those stresses. For a sport with lots of pounding or jumping, for example, look for shoes with air chambers in them; these will provide the extra cushioning you need to absorb some of the shock that would otherwise travel up from your

feet into your ankles and knees. You should also pay attention to how you wear your shoes (see "Check Your Shoes' Warning Signs" on page 290).

Vary your terrain. Runners often follow the same route, running in the same direction, on the same surface, day after day. This repetitive routine can lead to tendinitis. Whether you realize it or not, most roads, paved streets, paths, and even running tracks have a slight slant to them, usually to facilitate drainage. Running on a surface that is even slightly tilted puts greater strain on one side of your body than the other, and if you take the same path in the same direction each time, the side that bears the strain never gets a break and becomes ripe for tendinitis. So make a point of varying your route to prevent either side of your body from taking a pounding every time. If your options are limited, changing the direction you run on a track or path will help. But if you can, try to vary the surfaces you walk or jog on, as well; switch amongst asphalt, clay, grass, and crushed stone (but try to avoid surfaces that are exceptionally hard or soft). Variety can not only help prevent tendinitis, it can also help prevent burnout by keeping your exercise routine interesting.

Bag the sand. While running or walking briskly on a beach may sound like a lovely way to exercise, sand is not a great workout surface for such activities. The sand causes knees and ankles to twist, which can lead to a strain, sprain, or tendinitis. The same is true of snow.

Cool down after a workout. Spend the last few minutes of your exercise time in less intense activity, so your body can cool down gradually, then gently stretch your fatigued muscles. And if you're prone to tendinitis or are still healing from a bout of it, ice the area to help prevent a flare-up.

Use caution with cleats. Football, baseball, and soccer players listen up: A tendon is more likely to take the full force of a hit or a slip when you're wearing this type of athletic shoe, which anchors the foot to the ground.

Wear knee and/or elbow pads. They help cushion impact and protect these vulnerable joint areas during such sports as volleyball, hockey, and football.

Toothache

9 WAYS TO EASE THE PAIN

"For there was never yet philosopher that could endure the toothache patiently." Shakespeare was right. The toothache isn't easy to endure. The good news: With improved dental care and regular checkups, the excruciating pain of a toothache is not as common as it once was. But when pain does occur in the mouth, it's an important signal that you should not ignore—even if it goes away on its own.

Tooth pain is varied. Perhaps most common is the minor pain caused by sensitive teeth. You eat or drink something hot, cold, or sweet and feel a momentary twinge. Some people suffer achy teeth because of sinus problems; that's probably the case if the pain is limited to your upper teeth and several teeth are affected at one time. Bruxism (teeth grinding) or a problem with your temporomandibular, or jaw, joint

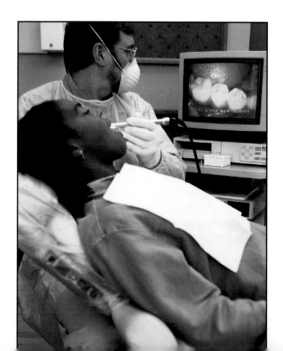

can also cause aching or sensitivity in multiple teeth (see TEMPOROMANDIBULAR JOINT (TMJ) PROBLEMS). And, recent dental work can cause a tooth to be sensitive to temperature changes for a few weeks.

Some types of pain deserve immediate attention from your dentist, however. If you feel a sharp pain when you bite down, for instance, you may have a cavity, a loose filling, a cracked tooth, or damaged pulp (that's the inner core of the tooth that contains the blood vessels and nerves). Pain that sticks around for more than 30 minutes after eating hot or cold foods can also indicate pulp damage, either from a deep cavity or a blow to the tooth. And the stereotypical toothache with constant and severe pain, swelling, and sensitivity is definitely a sign of trouble. As a rule of thumb, if a tooth hurts enough to wake you up at night or interferes with your ability to function normally during the day, it's time to dial up the dentist. You could have an abscessed tooth; that means the pulp of the tooth has died, resulting in an infection that can spread to the gum and even to the bone.

Pain associated with the pulp of the tooth is kind of tricky. It can let you know that damage has occurred. But nerves in the pulp can die rapidly—in as little as 12 hours, after which the pain fades. However, soon the tooth hurts again as the dead tissue becomes infected, or abscessed.

That's why putting off dental attention for a toothache can mean bad news. But if it's 3:00 in the morning or the middle of Sunday afternoon, you can take some temporary measures to deal with the pain until you can get to the dentist's office:

Take aspirin... or acetaminophen or ibuprofen—the same over-the-counter pills you take for everyday aches and pains. Ibuprofen may be the best choice, since it relieves the inflammation that may accompany a toothache. But see the warnings in the box on page 21 before using any of these.

Apply oil of cloves. You can pick this up at the pharmacy. Follow the directions for use carefully (too much can lead to poisoning), and put it only on the tooth and NOT on the gum. Otherwise, your burning gums may distract you from your toothache. And remember, oil of cloves won't cure the toothache; it just temporarily numbs the nerve.

Cool the swelling. Put a cold compress on the outside of your cheek if you've got swelling from the toothache.

Chill the pain. Holding an ice cube or cold water in the mouth may relieve the pain. But if you find that it simply aggravates your sensitive tooth, skip it.

Keep your head up. Elevating your head can decrease the pressure in the area and may lessen throbbing pain.

Rinse. You can't really rinse away the pain (although it's a pleasant thought), but you can rinse with warm water to remove any food debris that may be causing or aggravating the pain. A piece of food that gets stuck in the gum can hurt as much as damaged tooth pulp. Stir one teaspoon salt in a glass of warm water, swish it around in your mouth, then spit it out.

Floss. No, it's not a cure, but flossing is another way to remove any food debris that could be trapped. The rubber tip on your toothbrush or a toothpick (if used with caution) can help dislodge stuck food, too.

Be careful with the hot, the cold, and the sweet. These foods and beverages may aggravate an already sore and sensitive situation.

Plug it with gauze or gum. If the tooth feels sensitive to air, cover it with a piece of gauze, a small piece of dental wax (available at many pharmacies), or a bit of chewed sugarless chewing gum (use the teeth on the opposite side of the mouth to chew the gum) until you can get to the dentist.

When Good Pulp Goes Bad

Most of us don't think of our teeth as being alive, but they are. Each tooth contains what's called the pulp, composed of nourishing blood vessels and nerves.

If that pulp is damaged or exposed, the nerves can die, and the tooth can become infected, or abscessed. What can cause this? A deep cavity, a cracked tooth, or a hard blow to the tooth (from biting down on a popcorn kernel, for example). Your body cannot repair damaged or exposed pulp, so if you experience pain in your mouth, even if it goes away on its own, see a dentist.

Traveler's Diarrhea

20 WAYS TO BATTLE IT

Montezuma's revenge, Delhi belly, Turkey trot, and Casablanca crud. Such colorful names give you a good idea of the misery to expect from traveler's diarrhea, a disease that can spoil an expensive and eagerly anticipated vacation.

It was once believed to be caused by a change in water, indulgence in spicy foods, or too much sun. Not so anymore. Researchers have found specific bacteria to blame. These bugs take up residence in the upper intestine and produce toxins that cause fluids and electrolytes (minerals like sodium and potassium that help regulate many body functions) to be secreted in a watery stool.

If you visit nearly any developing country in Latin America, Africa, or Asia, you've got a 30 to 50 percent chance of spending a few days in close contact with a toilet. Less risky are places such as southern Spain and Italy, Greece, Turkey, and Israel, where some 10 to 20 percent of tourists come down with traveler's diarrhea. Posing the lowest risk are Canada and northern Europe.

Your actions, however, can help influence that risk. If you really want to try food from the local street vendor or insist on drinking tap water, you're increasing your chances of coming down with traveler's diarrhea.

If you do get sick, it will probably last for two to four days, although some 10 percent of cases can last for more than a week. And you may also experience—as if the diarrhea weren't enough—abdominal pain, cramps, gas, nausea, fatigue, loss of appetite, headache, vomiting, fever, and bloody stools.

Most common is watery diarrhea, sometimes accompanied by vomiting and a fever under 101 degrees Fahrenheit. If you actually get bacillary dysentery (caused by Shigella bacteria), you'll have a fever over 101 degrees Fahrenheit, much more abdominal pain and cramping, and, often, blood in your stools.

The following are prevention and treatment options that can help save your trip:

Prevention Strategies

Here's what you can do to try to prevent traveler's diarrhea:

Give up ice cubes for the duration. They're made with tap water, and despite some people's beliefs, freezing will not kill the bacteria. Neither will floating those cubes in an alcoholic drink; the alcohol isn't strong enough to kill bacteria.

Drink bottled water. Don't drink water delivered to your table in a glass and don't drink water straight from a tap. And if you don't like the looks of the water in the bottle, don't drink it.

Open your own bottles. Whether it's water, a soft drink, or beer, ask to open the bottle yourself. That way you'll be sure that nothing has been added to it, or that the mouth of the bottle hasn't been touched by dirty hands.

Use caution with other beverages. Fresh lemonade may sound appealing, but you don't know the source of the water. Tea and coffee are more likely to be safe since they're made with boiled water, but only if the water has been boiled thoroughly.

Know your dairy products. Don't consume unpasteurized milk and dairy products.

Stick to cooked foods. This is not the time to indulge in raw oysters. You'll have to pass on that green salad, too. Avoiding raw vegetables is one of the most important things you can do.

Eat your cooked foods while they're hot. If they have time to sit around and cool off, bacteria-carrying flies have time to visit your food before you eat it.

Eat only fruits you peel yourself. The same advice goes for hard-boiled eggs. Sometimes bacteria aren't *in* the food, they're *on* the food, inadvertently placed there by the unwashed hands that so graciously peeled the orange for you.

Take your own care package. Pack granola bars, cereal, and other sturdy food. You can make your own tea, for example, if you boil the local tap water *thoroughly*.

Coping Tips

If, despite all your precautions, you still get sick, don't despair. Simply follow the same instructions for diarrhea that you would at home:

Beware of becoming dehydrated. The danger in diarrhea is in losing both fluids and electrolytes. So once diarrhea has begun, you should start replacing them; don't wait until you are dehydrated.

Try oral rehydration therapy. Most drugstores in foreign countries sell

What If There Is No Bottled Water?

If you're roughing it in the wilds of some developing nation, bottled or even boiled water may not be a practical option. You've got two alternatives:

- Purify the water by adding iodine drops or chlorine tablets, which can be purchased at a camping-supply store in the United States before your departure.
- Pack a water purifier. The type with both a filter and iodine resin has been tested and shown to remove bacteria, viruses, and parasites.

Antibiotics as Prevention?

It's generally not recommended for most people, but taking an antibiotic every day during your trip as a preventive measure may be appropriate if:

- You're over 65 or have a history of heart disease or stroke. Diarrhea in such circumstances can quickly become life threatening.
- If you're on a tightly scheduled business trip.
- If you're on your honeymoon.

Talk to your doctor before your trip to see if your specific circumstances warrant preventive antibiotic therapy.

packets of powder that you mix with water and drink for oral rehydration therapy (ORT). Use the best water available. It's important to get fluids.

Make your own ORT solution. If you can't get to a drugstore, you can use common kitchen ingredients to make your own ORT drink. Mix four tablespoons sugar, ½ teaspoon salt, and ½ teaspoon baking soda in one liter water.

Drink a combination of fluids. Remember, the biggest danger in diarrhea is becoming dehydrated. You're also losing electrolytes, so drink a combination of liquids in addition to water, such as weak tea with sugar; clear broth; moderate amounts of fruit juices (be careful—some have a laxative effect); regular (nondiet), caffeine-free soda that has been allowed to go flat; or, if you can find any, a sports drink, such as Gatorade.

Sip, don't guzzle. Try to take frequent small drinks, which is less irritating to your gut than gulping down a lot of fluid all at once.

Eat a bland diet. Forget the enchiladas and salsa or anything else that might irritate your digestive tract. This is the time for toast, rice, noodles, bananas, gelatin, soups, boiled potatoes, cooked carrots, and soda crackers.

Pack the pink stuff. Pepto-Bismol—or its generic equivalent—is definitely the

first choice when it comes to treating traveler's diarrhea.

Don't rely on over-the-counter medicines that decrease motility. Avoid drugs such as Imodium and Kaopectate that decrease motility (slow the movement) of the bowel, which can have serious repercussions, especially if you have dysentery. Keep in mind: You have diarrhea because your body is trying to flush out a harmful bug, so taking a drug to counter that natural cleansing response is simply aiding and abetting the bad guy. (If your diarrhea is so extreme that you can't stay hydrated no matter how much liquid you drink, you need immediate, professional medical care.)

Bring along an antibiotic—just in case. Consider visiting your doctor *before* you leave on vacation and getting a prescription antibiotic, such as doxycycline, sulfamethoxazole, or a quinolone, that you can start taking at the first sign of traveler's diarrhea. Beginning treatment as soon as symptoms appear may shorten the course of the illness from four or five days to one or two. You and your doctor may choose this route especially if you will be traveling to a remote area where safe, reliable medical treatment is unavailable.

Ulcer

7 CARE TACTICS

Not long ago, the stereotype of a person with ulcers was that of an aggressive, stressed-out businessman who worked long hours, surviving on three-martini lunches and too much spicy food. Many sufferers took a strange pride in that pain in the gut, considering it evidence of their ambition and selflessness.

What a letdown: Scientists proved in the 1980s that most ulcers are caused not by too much sweat and toil but...by bacteria. What's more, while males were once thought to be the most common victims of this gastrointestinal menace, doctors now diagnose ulcers in women just as often as in men.

That doesn't mean that stress, spicy foods, and alcohol don't matter, since these and other lifestyle factors seem to irritate peptic ulcers, which can form in the lining of the stomach or, far more commonly, in the duodenum (first part of the small intestine). But the problem begins, in most cases, with a spiral-shaped germ that seems to live for one purpose—digging holes in our stomachs. This bacterium, known as *Helicobacter pylori (H. pylori* for short), is very common: It's found in about half of all people under 60 in the United States. *H. pylori* never causes problems in most people, but in an unlucky minority, the bug burrows through the stomach's protective mucous coating. The bacteria and stomach acid then irritate the sensitive lining beneath, causing ulcers to form.

About five million Americans have peptic ulcers. In some cases, *H. pylori* isn't the villain, however. People who use nonsteroidal anti-inflammatory drugs (NSAIDs) regularly for pain relief over long periods can develop ulcers, too. Less often, stomach and pancreatic cancers cause these sores to form. And ulcers can be quite sore; patients describe a burning pain or dull, gnawing ache in the gut that usually sets in two to three hours after eating or in the middle of the night, when the stomach is empty.

The good news: Most ulcers caused by *H. pylori* can be cured with a combination of antibiotics and acid-blocking drugs or bismuth subsalicylate (better known as Pepto-Bismol).

Unfortunately, even though this information has been widely disseminated in medical journals, some doctors still send ulcer patients home with little more than orders to take it easy, knock off the booze, and eat a bland diet. If you have ulcer-like symptoms, ask your doctor to perform tests that can determine whether you have the *H. pylori* bug, so that if prescription medications are appropriate for your condition, you get them. At the same time, there are some steps you should be taking at home to care for your digestive tract. Here are the most recent recommendations for those who have been diagnosed with a peptic ulcer:

Go by gut reactions. Highly spiced and fried foods, long thought to be prime culprits in instigating ulcers, are now considered to have little bearing on either the development or course of an ulcer. However, they do bother some people who already have ulcers. If you find that spicy meals, for example, are always followed by a severe gnawing pain, take the hint and pass on them in the future. The same goes for any other food that seems to cause you discomfort.

Eat wisely. The real key to keeping gastric juices from attacking the lining of the digestive tract is to keep some food present as much of the time as possible. Try eating smaller meals more frequently. Don't overeat, though—too much food causes formation of more gastric juices and contributes to weight gain. Simply spread your normal amount of calories over more and smaller meals.

Skip the milk solution. One of the earliest treatments for ulcer flare-ups was milk, which was believed to neutralize stomach acid. However, scientists now know that foods high in calcium increase stomach acid. So while the protein part of the milk may soothe, the calcium may make matters worse.

Rechannel stress. Remember, stress doesn't cause ulcers, as once believed, but it can make you feel worse. The idea that one has to eliminate stress is unrealistic, since stress is very much a part of everyday life. However, you can change how you react to and cope

with stress. Work on ways to deal with stress more effectively. Take a stress management class, find an enjoyable hobby, learn to meditate, start an aerobic exercise program, or do whatever helps you blow off some steam and manage stress more effectively.

Give up the smoke screen. Although the results of research into the link between cigarette smoking and ulcers have been mixed, most medical authorities generally agree that there is a relationship between the two. Smoking increases stomach-acid secretion and inhibits the secretion of prostaglandins and sodium bicarbonate, substances naturally produced by the body that normally help protect the stomach lining (nonsteroidal anti-inflammatory drugs also interfere with the secretion of prostaglandins). Smoking also decreases blood circulation to the stomach lining (as well as to the rest of the body), which may negatively affect the lining's ability to heal.

Drink only lightly. The question of alcohol's impact on ulcer formation remains unanswered. Many medical experts believe that people who drink heavily are at higher risk of developing ulcers than those who drink lightly or not at all.

Self-medicate with care. Ulcer sufferers are never far away from their antacids. But if you use these medications, do so with care. Without a doc-

How to Reach for Relief

Before doctors knew that most peptic ulcers can be cured with antibiotics, the standard treatment for this condition was prescription medication that blocked acid production in the stomach, protecting the lining from irritation. Physicians still recommend acid-blocking drugs to ulcer patients to ensure that the eroded areas of their stomachs heal. Many of these so-called H2 blockers, as well as a related medication called a proton pump inhibitor, are available over-the-counter today. While these drugs, along with antacid pills and liquids, are found in the medicine chests of many ulcer patients, it's important to keep in mind that these products need to be used properly to be both safe and effective. What's more, even though they are available without a prescription, these medications are not without risk and should be used with caution in certain situations:

- Side effects are not common with H2 blockers, such as cimetidine (Tagamet) and ranitidine (Zantac), but these drugs may cause a long list of problems, from stomach pain to insomnia.
- The same goes for the proton pump inhibitor (omeprazole, or Prilosec), which can cause gastrointestinal problems or a rash.
- Aluminum-based antacids frequently cause constipation and may also interfere with absorption of phosphorus from the diet, resulting in weakness and bone damage if used over a long period.
- Magnesium-based antacids can cause diarrhea. And in individuals with impaired kidney function, blood levels of magnesium may increase, causing weakness and fatigue.
- Prolonged use and then sudden stoppage of these medications can lead to an increase in stomach acid.
- All such products interfere with absorption and metabolism of other drugs. Check with your pharmacist about possible interactions with your prescription and over-the-counter medications.
- Consistent use of antacids may mask the symptoms of a more serious disorder.
- Consult your doctor before taking antacids for an extended period of time. If you find yourself needing to take more and more of an antacid to get relief, contact your doctor.

tor's supervision, you may under- or overmedicate. Not to mention overspending—you may end up paying as much as you would for prescription drugs (see "How to Reach for Relief," above).

Varicose Veins

20 COPING TECHNIQUES

The circulatory system could be compared to a big city's freeways, where the streaming cars, in this case the frenetic blood cells, deliver oxygen and nutrients to every part of the body. The pumping heart maintains the pulse of the "traffic" by pushing the blood cells through the arteries to their organ and cell destinations.

On the cells' return trip to the heart and lungs, the flow of traffic is not always quite so smooth, and congestion can take a toll on the roadway of veins. For one thing, the pressure, caused by the pumping heart, that keeps the blood moving is decreased. For another, the veins below the heart, in the legs and torso, must work against gravity, as the blood makes its way up from the feet. So these vessels depend more on the leg muscles to help pump the blood back to the heart. The veins also contain special one-way valves that aid the return of blood to the heart and lungs. The valves work like locks in a canal. As blood flows through a valve, its "doors" slam shut so the blood can't flow backward.

When any one of these valves fails, blood can seep back down and begin to pool, often in the lower legs. The extra pressure from the increased volume of pooling blood can, over time, cause additional valves to fail. Eventually, the pressure from the pooling blood can cause the vein's walls to bulge and become misshapen. At this point, the vein may show through the skin's surface, looking knotty, bumpy, and gnarled and taking on a dark blue or purple hue. The swollen and twisted—or *varicose*—veins can be more than a cosmetic problem, however. They may also cause aching, throbbing, or burning pain; a feeling of heaviness in the lower legs; swelling around the ankles; and even itchiness, all of which tend to be more pronounced after prolonged sitting or standing. In some cases, varicose veins may signal a more serious underlying problem with circulation or be associated with potentially serious blood clots (see "Clots: Be Careful!" on page 301). And if varicose veins are accompanied by skin ulcers near the ankle or sudden swelling of the leg, they require immediate medical attention.

It's estimated that 25 percent of all women and 10 percent of all men are affected by varicose veins. There are medical and surgical treatments available to deflate or remove them. But there are also ways to prevent or, at the very least, postpone their development; decrease their severity; and ease some of the discomfort they can cause. Here's how:

Check your family tree. Varicose veins run in families, although the reason is unknown. Some experts believe there is a weakness in the gene that governs the development of the veins. This may lead to defects in the structure of valves and veins or, in some people, a decrease in the number of valves in the veins, causing the few that are there to get overloaded. If varicose veins run in your family, the sooner you follow preventive measures, the better.

Get moving. While exercise may not prevent varicose veins, doctors agree it can lessen the symptoms by improving circulation, which prevents blood from pooling. As working muscles in the lower limbs contract, they push blood through the veins, back to the heart. To get your legs moving, almost any exercise that involves them will do, from aerobics to strengthening to spot-toning activities, say the experts. Ride a bike, take an aerobics class, go for a walk or a run, use the stair machine in the gym, or climb the stairs at work during your lunch hour. Spot-toning exercises, such as leg raises, that specifically build the muscles in the buttocks, thighs, and lower legs are also recommended.

Lose weight. Not only does obesity tax just about every system in the body, but carrying around extra baggage makes most people less active, which means their leg muscles do less work. As a result, overweight people usually can't pump blood from their lower limbs back to the heart efficiently. In addition, an overweight person's blood vessels carry more blood than a thinner person's, so the strain is greater on the vessels themselves.

Eat a balanced diet. Besides helping you maintain a healthy weight, a balanced diet can give you nutrients that may actually help prevent varicose veins. For example, protein and vita-

Clots: Be Careful!

Though thankfully rare, clots can form within varicose veins. Thrombophlebitis, the inflammation of a vein caused by a clot, can be potentially dangerous if the clot begins to travel through the veins. The traveling clot, then called an embolism, can end up blocking part of the blood flow in the heart or lungs.

If the clot forms in what's called the superficial venous system, you may feel pain and tenderness, and the skin on your leg may turn red. If the clot forms in what's known as the deep venous system, you won't be able to see the clot, but you may have swelling and tenderness in all or part of either leg. If you experience any of these symptoms, see your doctor.

Some of the best measures to help prevent clotting: Keep active; maintain a desirable weight; and take breaks from sitting, especially on long car and plane rides and during long hours of sitting at home or at work.

min C are both components of collagen, part of the tissue in the veins and valves. If the collagen is in good shape, the tissues are likely to be more resilient. A balanced diet that includes a wide variety of foods, including fresh fruits and vegetables, whole grains, and lean sources of protein, is the best way to get the right amounts of valuable nutrients. However, while a healthy diet can strengthen your vascular system, it can't cure varicose veins.

Take a break from standing. When you're standing in one place, the blood in your leg veins must not only make a long uphill journey against the force of gravity, it has to do so without the pumping assistance that expanding-and-contracting leg muscles can provide. (It's a little like trying to get up a creek without a paddle!) As a result, the blood tends to pool in the lower legs, leading to the development of varicose veins. If possible, take frequent breaks to walk around or, preferably, to sit with your feet up. And while you're standing in one spot, shift your weight from one leg to the other and/or occasionally get up on tiptoes; it will engage your leg muscles in the task of pushing blood up toward your heart.

Prop up your legs. Putting your feet up is good, but elevating them above the level of your heart is even better. It's a way to use gravity to *help* the blood move from your feet and ankles back to your heart. So lie down on a couch and prop your feet on the arm or put three or four pillows under them (or lie on the floor and rest your feet on the seat of a chair). Can't lie down? Sit on one chair and prop your feet on the back of another chair. When possible, try to elevate your legs for ten minutes once an hour.

But don't sit too long, either. Some experts theorize that even sitting for extended periods can contribute to varicose veins. Bent knees and hips, the thinking goes, complicate and slow the return of blood to your heart. So it's very important that on a long car or plane ride or during a day of sitting at the office (or at home, for that matter) you get up and stretch your legs once in a while. When you need a break, try this rejuvenator: Stand on your toes and raise your heels up and down ten times.

Don't be crossed. Sitting with your legs crossed can slow circulation to and from your lower legs.

Check your seat. The same can happen if you sit in a chair with a seat that is too deep for your leg length: The front edge of the chair digs into the back of your knees, compressing blood vessels and restricting blood flow. Get a chair that fits your body better, or, if that's not possible, scoot your backside away from the chair's back until the pressure on your legs is relieved.

Flex your feet. Contracting the muscles in your feet may help force blood upward and out of the veins. While seated—and even while your legs are elevated—try these three exercises to really get the blood pumping out of your feet and back to your heart:

- **The Ankle Pump:** Flex your foot up and down as you would when you pump a piano pedal or when you press and release your car's gas pedal. Repeat with the other foot.
- **Ankle Circles:** Rotate your feet clockwise and counterclockwise.
- **Heel Slips:** With your knees bent, slide your heels back and forth.

Sleep with elevated feet. If you have chronic swelling in the lower legs, sleep on your back with a few pillows under your feet.

Lower your heels. Shoes with lower heels require your calf muscles to do more work than high-heeled shoes—a plus for better circulation.

Wear tennis shoes. If your feet habitually swell, it may be worthwhile to wear tennis shoes or other lace-up shoes that can be opened up or loosened to alleviate the pressure and allow for freer circulation.

Loosen up. Your clothing, that is. Stay away from pants or other clothing that are tight at the waist or groin; they can act almost as tourniquets that restrict blood flow at these important circulation points.

Consider "stocking" up on support. Ask your pharmacist or doctor about special compression stockings designed to improve circulation in the legs. How do they work? They apply more pressure to the lower legs than to the thigh area. Since more pressure is exerted on the lower legs, blood is more readily pushed up toward the heart. The stockings' compression on the legs is measured in millimeters of mercury (mm Hg) and ranges from 20 mm Hg for weaker support to 60 mm Hg for strong support. (In comparison, the support hose you can buy at any department store provide pressure of 14 to 17 mm Hg.) The stronger versions require a doctor's prescription. The lower-strength stockings are sometimes recommended for pregnant women (see "Advice for Moms-to-Be" on page 304).

These days, compression stockings come in a variety of styles—below the knee, midthigh, full thigh, and waist high—and an increasing variety of colors as well as different strengths. A possible downside: The stronger stockings have a tendency to feel hot. They can also be relatively expensive, although you should check with your insurer to see if any or all of their cost is covered. The stockings are available

Spider Veins: "Cousins" to Varicose Veins

Eighty percent of varicose-vein sufferers will also develop spider veins. And half of all spider-vein sufferers also have varicose veins. But unlike knotty and often uncomfortable varicose veins, spider veins are thin, dilated blood vessels that form a weblike pattern (hence the name) on the skin, most commonly on the legs, neck, and face. They are no thicker than a thread or hair and do not bulge out. Except for their link to pregnancy and hormones (see "Advice for Moms-to-Be" on page 304), no one knows for sure why they crop up. Because the cause hasn't been pinpointed, the veins can't be prevented. But on the plus side, they rarely cause problems—perhaps only a little itching now and again.

Advice for Moms-to-Be

Pregnancy can lead to the development of varicose veins and spider veins. Surging hormones weaken collagen and connective tissues in the pelvis in preparation for giving birth. Unfortunately, as a side effect, the hormones may also weaken the collagen found in the veins and valves of the body. These weakened tissues have a more difficult time standing up to the increased blood volume that comes with carrying a baby. In addition, the weight of the fetus itself may play a role in the development of varicose veins in the legs by compressing the veins between the legs and heart. Elevating the legs whenever possible can be helpful, and compression stockings in the 20 to 30 mm Hg range may be prescribed by your doctor. The good news is that for many women, the swollen veins subside within a few months after the baby is born.

the beach because you're embarrassed by your varicose veins, make them "disappear." There are products specially made to cover the blue vein lines. Available in a variety of shades to match your skin, the cream is applied by hand and blended. Leg Magic by Covermark Cosmetics is waterproof and even has a sun protection factor (SPF) of 16 to protect your legs from the sun's harmful rays. Wearing stockings over the cream won't make it fade or rub off, and you can even go for a swim without washing away all your cover. While these types of products obviously won't fix the veins or relieve physical discomfort, they can make you feel better about the way your legs look.

Consider the effects of estrogen. The hormone is generally believed to have a detrimental effect on the collagen and connective tissue of the veins. If you have varicose veins or have a strong family history of them and you are considering an oral contraceptive or hormone replacement therapy, you may want to specifically ask about this potential side effect when you discuss the pros and cons of such therapy with your doctor. While estrogen probably doesn't have a direct effect on varicose veins, the hormone can increase the risk of embolisms, or blood clots, which interfere with blood circulation (see "Clots: Be Careful!" on page 301).

in most pharmacy and medical-supply stores as well as through mail order and Web sites. It's important that the stockings fit properly, however, so you may want to ask your pharmacist for assistance with measuring.

Slip into spandex pants. Like nonprescription, store-bought support hose, pants made from this elastic material apply slight pressure to the legs and may help somewhat. Be sure, however, that they aren't so tight in the groin or waist that they cut into your skin and limit circulation.

Cover up the blues. If you've stopped wearing shorts or going to

Warts

10 Ways to Wipe Them Out

Most of us have had one of these ghastly bumps at one point or another. Warts are caused by the human papilloma virus (HPV) and are contagious. That's why an initial wart can create a host of other ones. Common warts are the rough-looking lesions most often found on the hands and fingers. The much smaller, smoother flat warts can also be found on the hand but may show up on the face, too. Warts that occur on the soles of the feet are called plantar warts and can sometimes be as large as a quarter. Genital warts, which have become a growing problem, develop in the genital and anal area (see "Caution: Genital Warts" on page 306). If you suspect that you have a genital wart, see your doctor; do not try the remedies suggested here.

No one knows why warts occur and disappear and later recur in what appears to be a spontaneous fashion. For example, some women say they develop warts when they become pregnant, but the gnarly lumps disappear soon after they have their babies. And researchers have yet to find a way to get rid of warts for good. The solution may lie in a wart vaccine, but a safe vaccine has yet to be approved. That leaves the wart sufferer with two options: Having a dermatologist treat the warts or trying a few self-help methods. As for home remedies, some people swear by certain tactics, while

Can You Wish Warts Away?

Some dermatologists agree that the power of suggestion, especially when used on children, can be very effective in making warts disappear. It may be that the warts were about to vanish anyway (children's warts usually disappear more quickly than warts in adults), or perhaps positive thoughts boost the immune system. No one knows for sure.

Taking the power of suggestion one step further, there have been studies of the use of hypnosis in the treatment of warts. For many people, the very word hypnosis conjures up images of a Houdini-type magician gently swinging a crystal bauble in the face of an unsuspecting rube who is about to unwillingly reveal some embarrassing secret—or flap his arms and cluck like a chicken. Contrary to what many people believe, hypnosis can't make you do something you don't want to do. Today, it's an acceptable tool for helping people quit smoking and can be used as an adjunct to diet and exercise in weight-loss programs.

In one study, 17 people with warts were treated with hypnosis once a week for five weeks. Seven other patients were not treated with hypnosis. Both groups were asked to abstain from any wart treatment, including home remedies. The patients who underwent hypnosis were told that they would experience a tingling sensation in the warts on one side of their body and only those warts would disappear. Nine of the hypnotized patients lost more than three quarters of all their warts, and four of them lost all their warts. Meanwhile, the untreated group showed no improvement. It's not clear why the patients who underwent hypnosis had better luck getting rid of warts, but it's possible that the power of suggestion strengthened their immune systems, which defend against viruses.

Caution: Genital Warts

The number of cases of genital warts is growing at a phenomenal rate, says the American Academy of Dermatology. The reason: Genital warts are extremely contagious. The usual mode of transmission is through sexual contact. It's also possible for an infected woman to pass on the virus to her fetus during pregnancy or birth.

The use of condoms can help protect against sexually transmitted diseases, including genital warts. Yet, many people still choose not to protect themselves, possibly because the threat seems remote—they simply can't believe they are truly at risk. If you need additional incentive for using condoms, consider that certain strains of HPV have now been linked to cancer.

others never have any success with them. And it seems that in some cases, prevention may be the best medicine. Here are some tips to help you be wart-free:

Make sure it's a wart. First and foremost, before you try any type of treatment, know whether your skin eruption is a wart or another condition. Warts (except the small, smooth flat wart) commonly have a broken surface filled with tiny red dots. (Some people mistakenly call these dots seeds, when in reality they are the blood vessels that are supplying the wart.) Moles, on the other hand, are usually smooth, regularly shaped bumps that are not flesh-colored (as flat warts can be). A rough and tough patch that has the lines of the skin running through it may be a corn or a callus. There is also a chance that the lesion could be skin cancer. You may be able to recognize skin cancer by its irregular borders and colors. When in doubt, see your doctor. In addition, if you have diabetes, circulation problems, or impaired immunity, do not try any home therapy for wart removal; see your doctor.

Don't touch. The wart virus can spread from you to others, and you can also keep reinfecting yourself. The virus develops into a wart by first finding its way into a scratch in the skin's surface—a cut or a hangnail, for instance. Even the everyday task of

shaving can spread the flat warts on a man's face. Inadvertently cutting a wart as you trim your cuticles can cause an infection. So keep viral travels to a minimum by not touching your warts at all, if possible. If you do come in contact with the lesions, wash your hands thoroughly with soap and hot water. Children should also be told that picking or chewing their warts can cause them to spread.

Stick to it. Doctors have known for years that adhesive tape is an effective treatment for warts that's cheap and doesn't leave scars. In fact, a 2002 study found that tape therapy eliminated warts about 85 percent of the time, compared to a standard medical treatment using liquid nitrogen, which was only successful on 60 percent of warts. Researchers in this study used duct tape, but plain old adhesive tape seems to work, too. Try this: Wrap the wart completely with four layers of tape. Be sure the wrap is snug but not too tight. Leave the tape on for six and a half days. Then remove the tape for half a day. You may need to repeat the procedure for about three to four weeks before the wart disappears. You can try the procedure on a plantar wart, but be sure to use strips of tape that are long enough to be properly secured.

Try castor oil. The acid in castor oil probably does the trick by irritating the wart. It works best on small, flat warts on the face and on the back of the hands. Apply castor oil to the wart with a cotton swab twice a day.

"C" what you can do. Vitamin C is mildly acidic, so it may irritate the wart enough to make it go away. Apply a paste made of crushed vitamin C tablets and water. Apply the paste only to the wart, not the surrounding skin. Then cover the paste with gauze and tape.

Heat it up. One study found that having patients soak their plantar warts in very hot water was helpful because it softens the wart and may kill the virus. Make sure the water is not hot enough to cause burns, however.

Take precautions with over-the-counter (OTC) preparations. The Food and Drug Administration (FDA) has approved wart-removal medications made with 60 percent salicylic acid, but most common OTC remedies contain 17 percent. While the stronger formulas may work well for adults (except for those who have sensitive skin), they are not recommended for children. Salicylic acid works because it's an irritant, so no matter which strength of solution you use, try to keep it from irritating the surrounding skin. If you're using a liquid medication, do this by smearing a ring of petroleum jelly around the wart before using the medication. If you're applying a medicated wart pad or patch, cut it to the exact size and shape of the wart. Apply OTC medications before bed and leave the area uncovered.

Don't go barefoot. Warts shed viral particles by the millions, so going shoeless puts you at risk for acquiring a plantar wart. The best protection: footwear. Locker rooms, pools, public or shared showers, even the carpets in hotel rooms harbor a host of germs—not just wart viruses. You can catch any of a number of infections, from scabies to herpes simplex. Never go barefoot; at the very least, wear a pair of flip-flops, or thongs.

Keep dry. Warts tend to flourish more readily in an environment that's damp, especially in the case of plantar warts. That's why people who walk or exercise extensively may be more prone to foot warts, says the American Academy of Dermatology. So change your socks any time your feet get sweaty, and use a medicated foot powder to help keep them dry.

Cover your cuts and scrapes. The wart virus loves finding a good scratch so it can make its way under your skin. By keeping your cuts and scrapes covered, you'll help keep the wart virus out.

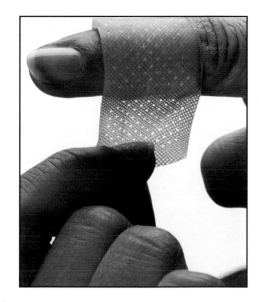

Yeast Infections

12 Strategies to Beat Them

Most women are bothered at one time or another by vaginitis—the itching, burning, pain, and discharge that comes with a vaginal yeast infection. Yeast infections can be caused by a number of organisms, many of which inhabit the healthy vagina. One of the most common causes of vaginitis is the fungus *Candida albicans.* The annoying symptoms can include itching, discharge that has a "baked bread" odor, and reddening of the labia and, in some cases, the upper thigh.

Yeast infections, especially recurrent ones, are a signal that your body is out of balance. *Candida* normally

grows in a healthy vagina, where the slightly acid pH environment keeps *Candida* and other microorganisms from multiplying rapidly enough to cause infection. However, if the normal vaginal pH is altered, one or more microorganisms can begin to grow there unchecked. The itching, burning, pain, and discharge are caused by the waste products of rapidly multiplying *Candida* (or other) organisms.

There are a variety of factors that can throw your vaginal environment out of balance, including:

- **Pregnancy.** The hormonal changes associated with pregnancy alter the vaginal pH and increase the production of blood sugar, which provides food for infectious organisms, including yeast.

- **Menstruation.** Some women report more yeast flare-ups in the days immediately before or just after their menstrual periods.

- **Antibiotics.** *Candida* live in the healthy vagina in balance with other microorganisms, especially lactobacillus. Tetracycline, ampicillin, or another antibiotic, taken for an unrelated infection, often kills the vagina's lactobacillus, which in turn allows *Candida* to multiply out of control. Some antibiotics, especially tetracycline, also appear to stimulate the growth of yeast organisms.

- **Poorly controlled diabetes.** When diabetes is poorly controlled or uncontrolled, the level of sugar in the urine and vagina, as well as in the blood, increases, providing food that can fuel increased yeast growth. Indeed, repeated yeast infections in the vagina or mouth are often the clue that prompts doctors to test patients for the presence of previously undiagnosed diabetes.

- **Illnesses or drugs that impair immune function.** Illnesses and diseases such as AIDS as well as corticosteroids and other medications that suppress the body's immune system can also affect the balance of microorganisms in the vagina and, thus, the body's ability to keep yeast organisms in check.
- **Stressful times.** Doctors don't fully understand the stress/yeast connection, but many women report an increase in yeast infections during times of high stress. It is possible that part of the explanation lies in the effects chronic or uncontrolled stress have on the body's immune function.

While yeast infections can often be treated successfully at home, it's important to be sure that yeast is really the culprit. Infection with other types of organisms, which may require treatment with prescription medication, can often cause symptoms similar to those of a yeast infection. If the discharge is foul-smelling, yellowish, and frothy, you may be infected by a one-celled proto-

zoan called trichomonas, or "tric." If you have a heavy discharge without much irritation and notice a fishy odor, particularly after intercourse, your symptoms may be due to a bacterial infection that doctors call "bacterial vaginosis." Indeed, bacterial infections are the most common cause of vaginitis. Both of these infections require treatment with prescription medication. In addition, symptoms similar to those of vaginitis may be caused by sexually transmitted diseases such as gonorrhea or chlamydia. *Therefore, it's important to have your vaginal symptoms evaluated by a physician to ensure proper treatment, especially if you have any symptoms that you have never experienced before.*

Many women who suffer from recurrent yeast infections have had their symptoms diagnosed by a doctor and know all too well the signs and symptoms of a yeast flare-up. If you're sure your vaginitis is caused by a yeast infection, you may want to try these home remedies:

Use a vinegar douche. At the first sign of infection, try douching with a mild vinegar or yogurt douche. For a vinegar douche, use one to three tablespoons white vinegar in one quart warm water; for a yogurt douche, make a dilute mixture of plain yogurt and warm water (see "Self-Care Douche" on page 312).

(see "Self-Care Douche" on page 312).

Hello, Doctor?

While mild cases of yeast infection can be effectively treated at home, it's important to see a physician if:

- You have abdominal pain.
- You have recurrent or significant amounts of bloody discharge between periods.
- Your vaginal discharge gets worse or persists for two weeks or more despite treatment.
- You may have been exposed to a sexually transmitted disease.
- You have recurrent yeast infections. Your doctor should rule out diabetes or a prediabetic condition as a factor in your frequent infections.
- Your discharge is thin, foamy, and grey or yellowish green in color.

Douche Danger

The advertisements for douching preparations admonish women to "feel fresh." And some women erroneously believe that douching after intercourse will prevent pregnancy (it doesn't). But evidence shows that routine douching may actually do more harm than good.

For instance, routine douching has been linked to an increased risk of pelvic inflammatory disease, or PID, an infection of the uterus, fallopian tubes, or ovaries. PID can cause scarring of the fallopian tubes and result in infertility. If the infection spreads to the circulatory system, it can be fatal.

A 1990 study showed that women who douched three or more times per month were three-and-a-half times more likely to have PID than women who douched less than once a month.

The symptoms of PID include fever, chills, lower abdominal pain or tenderness, back pain, spotting, pain during or after intercourse, and puslike vaginal discharge. In most cases, a woman does not show all of the symptoms listed. *If you have any PID symptoms, consult a physician immediately.*

Not only has routine douching been associated with an increased risk of PID, some researchers believe it may increase a woman's risk of developing cervical cancer. A study that appeared in *The American Journal of Epidemiology* showed that women who douched more than once a week were nearly five times as likely to develop cervical cancer as women who douched less often. The researchers suspect that vaginal secretions and normal vaginal bacteria may somehow protect the pelvic area and that routine douching may invite microbes that trigger cancer.

The message is clear: While an occasional douche during an infection might be helpful, don't make a habit of douching.

Bring on the boric. Several studies have shown boric acid to be a safe, inexpensive, and effective yeast remedy. If your doctor approves of the idea, try using a boric-acid capsule as a suppository the next time you have a flare-up. To make your own suppositories, fill size "O" gelatin capsules with boric acid. Insert one capsule vaginally once a day for a week. (Check with your pharmacist for the gelatin capsules and boric acid.)

Skip this remedy if you are or may be pregnant, however, since boric acid hasn't been studied among pregnant women. Instead, talk with your physician about other treatment options.

Use an over-the-counter fungal cream. Both miconazole (Monistat) and clotrimazole (Gyne-Lotrimin) are effective in treating yeast infections. These products, which used to be available only by prescription, are available over-the-counter in pharmacies and many variety stores. Apply the medication as directed by the package insert. Complete the full course of treatment recommended by the manufacturer; do not stop using the medication early, even if your symptoms subside. If you find that you frequently get a yeast infection around the time of your menstrual period, try using one of these antifungal creams a few days before and/or after your menstrual period as a preventative.

Try yogurt tabs. Another alternative is to use lactobacillus tablets vaginally once or twice a day and douche with vinegar twice a day for two days. Check the natural-supplement aisle of your local pharmacy or a health-food store for the lactobacillus tablets.

Wash out the secretions. The organisms that cause yeast infection produce secretions that are irritating to the genital tissues. The nerve endings that sense the presence of the yeast are located at the vaginal opening. Although you may have an infection inside the vagina, you can often get symptomatic relief simply by frequently washing away the secretions with water until your chosen treatment knocks out the infection.

Stay dry and loose. Yeast organisms like warm, moist conditions, with little or no oxygen. In order to deny them the perfect growing medium, dry your vaginal area thoroughly after bathing or showering. Avoid wearing panties, pants, or hose that fit tightly in the vaginal area. Opt for "breathable" cotton underwear and loose pants, and, if you must wear nylons, choose those that have a built-in cotton-lined panty. Also, avoid lounging around in a wet swimsuit; change into dry clothing as soon as you're done swimming.

Avoid harsh soaps, "feminine hygiene" sprays, and perfumed products. Not only can the alcohol and other chemicals in these products cause irritation, but they may alter the pH balance of the vagina, allowing yeast to flourish. Keep in mind that the vagina is a self-cleaning organ; you don't need to wash it out or "freshen" it with chemicals or soap of any kind.

Rethink your contraception. Women who take birth control pills or use contraceptive sponges appear to be at increased risk of developing yeast infections. While researchers haven't established a cause-and-effect relationship between the Pill and yeast, some studies have shown that oral contraceptives increase the glycogen (the body's storage form of sugar) in the vagina, providing more food for yeast reproduction.

Contraceptive sponges seem to be a yeast culprit, too, although no one is sure why. If recurrent yeast infections are a problem for you, consider an alternative birth control method such as condoms, a diaphragm, a cervical cap, or an intrauterine device (IUD); discuss this with your doctor.

Have both partners treated. Sexual partners can play "hot potato" with yeast infections, passing them back and forth, even if one of them has gotten treatment. Often, men harbor

Self-Care Douche

Routine douching isn't a good idea if you don't have vaginal symptoms. However, for women with yeast-infection symptoms, a mild vinegar douche can help restore the vagina's normal pH (which is about 4.5). Douching with yogurt that contains live lactobacillus or acidophilus bacteria may help restore the friendly microorganisms lost during infection or as a result of antibiotic use. For the best douche results, follow these easy steps:

1. Prepare the douche solution as outlined on page 309.
2. Make sure the container, tube, and irrigation nozzle are very clean. If not, clean them with a good antiseptic solution.
3. Lie in the tub with a folded towel under your buttocks and with your legs parted.
4. Suspend the container 12 to 18 inches above your hips.
5. Insert the nozzle into your vagina with a gentle rotating motion until it encounters resistance (two to four inches).
6. Allow the solution to flow in *slowly*. Use your fingers to close the vaginal lips until a little pressure builds up inside. This allows the solution to reach the entire internal surface. An effective douche should take ten minutes or so.

yeast organisms, especially in the foreskin of an uncircumcised penis, but show no symptoms. So when one partner is treated for a yeast infection, the other should be treated at the same time to avoid reinfection.

Wash up, and use condoms. If you have a yeast infection, you should

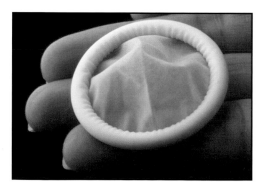

wash up extra carefully before lovemaking and should ask your sexual partner to do the same. Couples who make love before a yeast infection has been completely cured should also use condoms during intercourse (even if another form of contraception, such as the Pill or an IUD, is being used) to act as a barrier and prevent passing the infection.

Avoid routine douching. Women who douche frequently in the belief that it's a healthy practice may actually increase their risk of yeast infections by altering the vagina's pH balance. Routine douching is simply not necessary, because the vagina is able to clean itself. (See "Douche Danger" on page 310.)

Practice good hygiene. While yeast is usually passed between sexual partners, it can also be passed to others, including children, through activities such as shared baths. To ensure you're not passing yeast, avoid bathing or sharing towels or bathwater with your children; wash your hands frequently—and always after using the bathroom—with soap and water; and wash your clothing in hot water. The high water temperature in your washing machine should destroy any yeast organisms on your clothes. But if you want to be sure they're all gone, add a cup of white vinegar during the rinse cycle.

Index